EDUCATION: THE CAPTIVE PROFESSION

*In honor of Matthew, Meghan, Reilly,
and those who follow*

Education: The Captive Profession

Theory, Practice and Prospects for Achieving Improvements in Educational Outcomes

DAVID H. REILLY
The Citadel
Charleston, SC 29409

Avebury

Aldershot • Brookfield USA • Hong Kong • Singapore • Sydney

© D.H. Reilly 1996

Published by
Avebury
Ashgate Publishing Limited
Gower House
Croft Road
Aldershot
Hants GU11 3HR
England

Ashgate Publishing Company
Old Post Road
Brookfield
Vermont 05036
USA

ISBN 1 85972 376 4

Library of Congress Catalog Card Number: 96-84889

A CIP catalogue record for this book is available from the British Library

Printed in Great Britain by The Ipswich Book Company, Suffolk

Contents

Tables

Acknowledgements

This book had its origins while I served as dean of a school of education for over a decade at a major university. During these years I observed many fine, talented and competent faculty members and teacher education students who had the best interests of children at heart. They truly wanted to do what was best for children, for education, and for improving students' learning. Surely, this type of dedicatedand able professional is duplicated at thousands of other teacher preparation programs around the world. If this is the case than why is education perceived as being ineffective? This book was formed from seeking an answer to this question.

During the same years I saw these many fine, committed, and concerned professionals I also observed many faculty members, both within and external to a school of education, who were more concerned about their own egos and/or disciplines than they were about helping students learn. I also observed many individuals in positions of political power, as well as university administrators and school system personnel who were less concerned with changing and improving the educational system than they were with maintaining their own positions of power and authority.

I became convinced that it was persons in these latter groups who were responsible for keeping the profession of education in a captive status. They were not able or willing to make the decisions necessary to improve learning outcomes of students. They did not understand how learning occurred or what was necessary to improve it, and many of their decisions were designed primarily to enhance their political status.

This book is dedicated to the thousands of teachers who toil everyday under captive status to teach and help their students learn. Instead of constantly criticizing their efforts we must find ways to liberate them, to support their efforts, and thank them for working under the constraints they have had imposed on them. It is because of their efforts under very difficult circumstances that education has achieved as much as it has. By freeing these professionals they will be able to achieve even more and our children will be the beneficiaries.

I gratefully acknowledge my family, Jean, Scott, Chris, and Sandra, who did not always know what I was doing but who were always supportive. A special thanks goes to Kim Brock, who as always, somehow found a way to format my work into readable form.

David H. Reilly
Charleston, SC

1 Introduction and overview

Education is in a state of crisis. This is not a new statement; many authors have said it before. This crisis is not only apparent in America; it is a catastrophe of world wide proportions. It is not, however, a crisis formed by educators. It is an emergency born of the political, economic and social conditions of the world, particularly by the economic drive for profit. This drive insists that all educational development be focused on the production of a well-trained working force, to the exclusion of more social, moral, personal and cultural goals. The economic condition, particularly, has created a pressure on education that few schools can satisfy (Plank and Adams, 1989).

This issue was the major topic at a 1967 conference of educators and economists from all over the world. The conclusion of this conference was that the crisis of education went well beyond the common kind that has been a part of educational systems since their inception. The world crisis of education was expressed in the interrelations among three words — change, adaptation and disparity (Coombs, 1985). The essence of the conclusions developed from this conference was that since 1945 all countries had experienced extreme changes. These changes were caused by rapid developments in science and technology, in the economic and political arenas, in social structures and in demographic shifts.

Educational systems, however, had not kept pace with these environmental changes. Education had not changed or adapted sufficiently to the sweeping alterations of societal developments. Thus, the disparity between the educational system and their environments had increased. Coombs (1985) noted four reasons for this disparity. First, the public began questioning the benefits of education. Second, there was a general shortage of resources, but particularly as allocated to education. Third, there was an inherent inertia in educational systems' capacities to respond to environmental changes. Fourth, the inertia of societies blocked them from

1

making optimal use of education's capacities (Coombs, 1985). These causes focus the reasons for the disparity on both society and education (educators). The need for mutual adaptation by both society and education was evident.

In 1985, Phillip Coombs, the author of the 1968 book *The World Education Crisis: A Systems Analysis*, detailing the findings and recommendations of the 1967 conference, revisited the report of the conference. He sought to determine whether there had been significant changes in the situation since the original publication. He concluded that the crisis had intensified, evidenced by a growing disparity between educational systems and their environments and by new dimensions of concern about education (Coombs, 1985).

Thus, considering the attention and reform efforts imposed on education in America over the years, the major question is "Why hasn't the condition of education improved?" Other questions are: "Why is there a disparity, perceived or real, between the accomplishments of education and its greater environment of systems? Why hasn't education been able to deliver on the expectations of the public? Why hasn't education been able to allow individuals to achieve their aspirations? More importantly, much more importantly, what must be done to improve education so that it *does* deliver what it promises?"

This book addresses these questions, but it is much more concerned with the latter question. It proposes that the causes of education's failures are rooted in the captive status of education, a status in which education is bound by shackles imposed by political, economic and special interest groups. These shackles are so tight that every move of education to improve is thwarted by outside groups causing education to stumble over itself as it seeks to please its many masters.

This book also proposes that the key to educational improvement lies in a re-formulation of the methods utilized previously to reform it. The structure of control of education must be modified so that educators have a shared authority and responsibility for developing policies, for allocating resources and for determining the mission priorities, outcomes and practices of education. Unless such shared authority is developed, education will remain captive to the many forces surrounding it, and the disparity between its achievements and potential will continue to grow wider.

This book is primarily about improving education — so that children's learning and personal-social development and competence are enhanced. Many readers may think this book presumptuous. If America is to provide its children with the best education possible, then it is far too important to both their future and society's future to continue leaving education

2

dominated and controlled solely by the whims, fads, and politics of lay persons and political leaders. We can no longer afford to exclude professional educators from sharing the responsibility and authority for educational policy development and professional practices.

It is to be hoped that this book successfully challenges basic assumptions about current purposes and objectives of education as well as raising issues concerning the control of educational objectives and learning activities. It questions the validity of current teacher preparation and administrator training programs. It questions the wisdom and usefulness of current structures of local and increasing state control of education. In short, this book attempts to improve educational policy development and the delivery of educational services to children by questioning educational structures and governance. It challenges sacred cows, and proposes positive alternatives to many of our most accepted assumptions about education. The proposals offered in this book will raise the ire of some professional organizations as well as that of many current political and business leaders who consider themselves educational experts.

The history of American education is one of reform and a search for continuing improvement. This history is one of repeated failures. Four major reasons for these failures are identified. (1) Educational reformers have not understood or used effective educational change concepts or mechanisms. (2) The education profession has been held captive to the dictates of external decision-makers. (3) Educational reformers have not taken into account the inter-dependent nature of the components of the educational system. (4) With each wave of reform, the mission and goals of the schools have repeatedly shifted until they are diffused, ambiguous and unclear. Cohen (1982), among more recent writers (Fuhrman, Clune, & Elmore, 1988; Elmore and McLaughlin, 1988) has described how schools are expected to resolve the different requirements imposed by successive waves of educational reform.

These repeated efforts at educational reform have represented a search for a magic formula to improve educational outcomes. The searches have been looking in the wrong directions. Instead, a new search format, one that encourages new structures of educational decision-making and practice, and a search program that uses new perspectives for implementing problem-solving is needed.

The numerous reports decrying the quality of American education in the past few years are examples of reformers barking up the wrong tree. The voluminous sets of recommendations that accompanied and followed these evaluative reports, which were intended to cure the many imagined ills of education, have an urgent and almost panicked quality to them. More than 1,000 state statutes affecting education were enacted between 1983 and

3

1988 (Darling-Hammond and Berry, 1988; Timan and Kirp, 1989). These represent more rules and regulations relating to education then were generated during the previous 20 years.

According to these reports, the lack of quality in American public education has brought America to the brink of intellectual bankruptcy and moral decline. Most importantly, a downward slide in our position in the international marketplace was the fault of inadequate schools. The latter concern appears to be the motor driving the current quest for educational reform. And it may well be a valid concern. David Kearns (1988), CEO of Xerox stated, " Public education has put this country at a terrible competitive disadvantage" (p. 566). Others have reflected this concern more strongly. Cuban (1988) stated the feelings of corporate executives who have been key figures in the educational reform movement, "If this nation wants a strong economy that can compete in the world marketplace, it needs schools that can give young people the attitudes, skills, and flexibility to fit into a changing job market" (p. 571). McCall (1988) has stated, "Educational reform is starting in the marketplace and moving onto school property" (p. 8). Fowler, Boyd, and Plank (1993) have commented that market-oriented reforms are spreading across the world and that these reforms in education are justified by the perception that a more highly educated workforce will lead to an economic advantage.

Coombs (1985) describes the recent subservient relationship between education and economic development. He attributes this relationship to a new definition of national development, which began after World War II. New forms of economic planning in Western Europe and Japan were used to put these countries back on their feet. A few years later, these ideas were applied to developing countries. As a result of these ideas and their associated programs, national development became defined as "economic growth," measured by the GNP of a nation. This measure excludes the use of cultural pursuits, the arts, moral and social development, and other non-economic indices as indicators of national development.

Educational reform followed the dictates of the new definition of national development. Economists generally agreed that a rapid expansion of a nation's economic development would require an adequate supply of trained, if not educated, workers. The need to develop education was perceived as a rational and necessary investment of capital that would pay off in economic returns. Political and educational leaders generally welcomed this alliance between economic and educational development. However, this alliance and the concepts underlying its formation did not produce the outcomes desired.

The first sign of disparity between economic investment and educational pay-off in America occurred after Sputnik. When America woke to find

4

itself falling behind the Soviet Union in space exploration and other scientific endeavors, it suddenly realized that American education was not producing the level of quality it expected and needed. Other signs followed. The 1983 publication of *A Nation at Risk* and its companion reports made clear the relationship between the economy and education. According to these reports, education was a tool of economic development for the nation. Little was ittle said in these reports about other purposes of education. Apparently the authors of these reports never realized that the nature of the relationship they perceived between economic investment and education was flawed from its inception and by the programs this relationship spawned. Secondly, it was not realized that the quality of life in a society, including its economic status, is determined more by the personal-social competence of its members than by the expansion of its material possessions.

This relationship between economic conditions and educational quality has had a significant impact at the state and local levels of education. Kirst (1988) believes that the many reports describing the declining quality of education indicate a loss of confidence in the ability of local officials to provide quality education. States are rightfully concerned about their economic condition. Many have developed major economic development strategies and see education as critical to economic growth and competing successfully in the international marketplace. Consequently, state legislatures have felt it appropriate to step in and usurp local decision-making authority, as in New Jersey. Many, if not most, state actions have displaced local control of instructional activities in an effort to improve the qualifications of the U.S. working force (Kirst, 1988). More recently, congress itself has demonstrated a continuing lack of faith in educators and is turning to highly prescriptive mandates (Penning, 1992).

This book does not assume, or accept, as have so many of the recent reports do, that the quality of American education is, at best, mediocre. It does assert that education has performed well those tasks assigned it during the past 30 years. These tasks included a wide variety of responsibilities which educators were not prepared to assume. The educational system was not the social institution best equipped to carry out these responsibilities. This book does not exclude educators from responsibility for education's current condition. It does assert that the problems of education are due more to political and economic considerations and the faulty educational reform efforts these forces have imposed on education than due to anything educators have done.

There have been many attempts to reform education. Elmore and McLaughlin (1988) identify eight. Each of these attempts has had its own unique emphasis and rationale for its purpose. Each successive reform

5

effort has attempted to ignore and/or discard the contributions of the one preceding it, while attempting to instill its own set of values and operations. American education continues to bear the mark and influence of each of these attempts. "New math" is a prime example.

Elmore and McLaughlin (1988) also conclude that previous reform efforts have had little effect on actual teaching and learning in the classroom. Educational reform has had an effect on the size of the institution of education. This is evidenced by its accommodation of the large numbers of students who needed education in order to enter the work force of an industrialized economy.

One result of this institution-building effort was the emergence of educational bureaucracies. These bureaucracies produced standardized curricular topics and teachers to produce standardized graduates. These graduates are then allocated to places in the economic and stratification system. This institution-building had little to do with teaching and learning, and much to do with sanctioning inequality.

Elmore and McLaughlin (1988) suggest that, in the past, educational reform efforts that dealt with teaching and learning have had weak, transitory, and ephemeral effects. Those reform efforts dealing with expanding, solidifying, and entrenching school bureaucracies seem to have strong,and concrete effects. As a result, the promise of educational reform that improves teaching and learning has yet to be realized.

According to Elmore and McLaughlin, educational reform operates on three loosely connected levels: policy, administration, and practice. Each level has its own rewards and incentives and special set of problems Personnel in each level have their own ideas about how the educational system should work.

Policy consists of authoritative decisions on the purposes of education. These include the responsibilities of individuals and institutions, the money required to run the system, and the rules required to make it operate effectively and fairly. The rewards and incentives for engaging in policymaking (and the conditions for awarding rewards) are primarily determined at a political level. Public control of education means political control. The educational system works by responding to public demands filtered through elected officials. Successful performance, however else it is defined in managerial or professional terms, is chiefly a matter of electoral politics and the production of quantifiable results acceptable to the body politic.

Educational practice consists of the instructional decisions necessary to teach a topic, manage a classroom, diagnosis and treat individual learning problems, and evaluate one's own performance and the performance of one's students. The world of educational practice is normally the world of

6

the classroom teacher. Because of the inherent uncertainty and range of student learning rates, patterns, and needs, successful teaching depends upon knowing how learning occurs. This means recognizing the needs of individual students, and successfully applying learning techniques to those needs of the individual students.

Between the teachers on the front line and the policymakers in the public eye exist thousands of administrators at every level. The skills, knowledge levels, competence levels and ambitions of these administrators produce a bewildering array of interpretations and attempts to implement policy decisions made on the school level, the school system level, the state level, and, to some extent, the national level. For these administrators, the incentives and rewards are partly professional, partly bureaucratic, and partly political, in proportions that vary widely from job to job and from level to level. The feature that distinguishes administrators from policymakers and teachers is the administrators' preoccupation with the maintenance of the organization itself.

Elmore and McLaughlin maintain that conflicts among policy, administration, and practice are endemic to educational reform. The use of policy as an instrument of reform intensifies differences among policymakers, administrators, and practitioners. There are differences in roles and incentives that are another part of the problem of educational reform. The differences in need, interpretation and rewards that exist among policy, administration, and practice are another contributing source to the lack of successful educational reform attempts.

The present debate on the relationship between policy and practice grows out of research on recent federal attempts to reform the schools. Current proponents of reform are eager to disassociate themselves from the mistakes of federal reform efforts since 1960. They are likely, however, to repeat these mistakes absent a clear understanding of that experience. The emphasis may have shifted from federal to state and local policy, but the issues are much the same (Elmore and McLaughlin, 1988).

Elmore and McLaughlin glean several general conclusions from an examination of federal reform efforts.

- Federal policy has extended its reach to all activities of schooling.
- There has been a tendency to substitute external authority for the authority and expertise of educational practitioners. Federal policy has communicated, at worst, a fundamental hostility, and at best, an indifference to the authority and expertise of educators.
- Variability is the rule and uniformity is the exception in the relationship among policy, administration, and practice. Reform

7

efforts will succeed, to a significant extent, if they can adapt to and capitalize upon variability.

- Adaptation is not simply a matter of policymakers acquiescing to local and regional differences in tastes and competencies; it is, more fundamentally, active problem-solving.
- Lags in implementation and performance are a central fact of reform.

It must be recognized that reform policies will affect educational practice indirectly and imperfectly. Local response to reform initiatives depends on local incentives, goals, and norms. It also depends on the fiscal, human, and material resources available to support local implementation efforts. The variables characterizing local response to educational reform policies present both problems and opportunities for policymakers. Policies that aim to reduce variables by reducing teacher discretion not only preclude learning from situational adaptation to policy goals, but they can also impede effective teaching. (This important factor will be discussed in the recommendations for change made in the third section.) However, the decision-making authority of teachers must not be restricted to the classroom, but extended to the highest levels of policy development and decision-making.

Reform efforts in education have generally not been characterized by a systematic and coordinated approach to problem-solving. Generally, recommendations for reform in education consider only one, or at most, two areas of concern to education. These are usually change of teacher preparation programs, neglecting administrator programs, and/or improvement of teachers' working conditions. Most often, the more crucial factors in education — the need for a conceptual framework for education, the re-structuring of the control of educational policy and practice (including the organization and administration of schools), and the basis on which resources are allocated to schools — are never considered. As Kelly (1985) has stated, the current reports for reform provide little consensus about what is needed to improve the schools. There is little consistency among the proposals for change. Peterson (1983) pointed out that several of the national reports were flawed in their recommendations for reform and concluded that these commission reports had limited value. Passow (1984) concluded that many, if not most, of the recommendations accompanying the reform reports are simplistic, conservative, and unrealistic. Further, Dodd (1984) concluded that the current reform recommendations were patchwork and unlikely to bring about fundamental educational reform.

In Section One, this book proposes that a major reason these calls for educational reform have flaws is that non-educators are charged with the responsibility of determining educational policy and practice. Professional educators have too long been given the responsibility to educate our children without the requisite authority to develop, change and adapt policies and procedures to the needs of their students. In other words, those making the policies had (and have) little knowledge of the changing needs of the students.

Obviously, each wave of reform arises from needs as perceived at the time. However, the rationale and need for maintaining a particular practice for many of these reforms has long since past and been forgotten. However, the practice remains, serving no useful purpose except maintaining a tradition. One such example is continuing the traditional methods class in teacher preparation programs.

The fact is that American education is rooted in a hodgepodge of assumptions, often masquerading as self-evident truths. Customs and practices abound without supporting research data. Professional turf issues and political compromises continue to weaken educational improvement efforts. As a result, American education has not been able to establish a professional agenda, exert control over its own destiny, or even be allowed a significant voice in deciding what is in the best interest of children. No educational reform efforts have addressed these areas of much-needed change.

Section Two of this book presents a systems-oriented view of the operations of education. This section provides the framework necessary for understanding the components of the educational change process and discusses two types of change and their usefulness for generating needed educational improvements.

The American education system is incorrectly thought by many to be an open social system. Although it does display some of the characteristics of an open social system, it also exhibits some patterns not found in other open social systems. These unique elements must be understood if attempts to improve student learning and development are to be achieved. These elements form the basis for understanding why education systems have withstood attempts to significantly alter their structure despite the many attempts to reform the educational system. These unique elements also provide the basis for developing the educational changes necessary to bring about significant and sustained educational improvement.

The processes for achieving effective educational change must also be understood. These processes must be perceived within the context of the system characteristics if the type of changes necessary for bringing about program quality improvements are to be accomplished. The process of educational change is subject to study and understanding independent of the content associated with any particular change. It is this understanding that has been so lacking in recent educational reform efforts. The

9

recommendations for educational reform have misdiagnosed the critical problem areas of education, mistaking *symptoms* for the *cause* of education's difficulties. These efforts have targeted the schools for change. This is needed, but the mechanisms utilized for such change must be altered first.

Section Three of the book presents a series of second- and third-order changes that address the major problems of education outlined in the first section. These changes are premised on theories of educational change and a framework for continued educational development process described in the second section.

The changes recommended go well beyond the recent reform proposals. As will be discussed more completely in Chapter 7, the changes recommended in most of the national and state reports are considered to be first-order change efforts (Watzlawick, Weakland, and Fisch, 1974). These recommendations do not provide for substantive structural changes that are necessary to improve education in a significant manner, that is, provide for second- and third-order changes.

The first type of change proposed is of third-order magnitude. This is change at the state level that is designed to enable and sustain changes of second-order consequence at the local district level and in teacher preparation. The third-order changes proposed are concerned with providing a structure at the state level that coordinates quality improvement efforts of public and teacher education programs.

The third-order changes propose that coordination at the state level should be under the control of parents, state political leaders and elected teachers. This change proposal suggests that a shared jurisdiction among these parties, with clear lines of authority and responsibility for state and local school systems, is necessary to achieve continuing improvement of student learning outcomes. The critical issue with regard to state-level control is to assure that the coordination mechanisms, developed to synchronize efforts, do not exert control over local change and experimentation efforts designed to improve program offerings and student learning outcomes. The issue of centralized versus decentralized control of education will emerge throughout this book. It is critical that schools identify the mission that educational personnel have been prepared to fulfill.

Fundamental to quality improvement efforts are the control and coordination of education's mission, organization and administrative practices, resource allocation procedures, and education personnel preparation. These factors have traditionally been controlled by lay persons and/or political leaders. Control by these people, instead of by educators, may be a major reason why many perceive education as declining. It may also explain why there are constant attempts to reform it.

The second-order changes proposed address the aforementioned issues. All but personnel preparation occur at the local school system level. The second-order changes proposed are designed to provide a coordinated set of changes that address each of these issues. However, the primary issue is the mission of the schools. This issue determines practically all other elements of school operation.

Currently, schools are expected to fulfill a broad array of missions, from preparing students to excel in college to teaching them how to drive safely. The individual missions arise from a variety of sources, often with separate resource support, which dilutes the allegiance to and authority of local control (Kirst, 1988). In addition to this wide range of missions, which has evolved over the past few decades, the emphasis of the reform agenda of the 1980s has been the development of workers' skills. The local school districts have been subjected to a host of mission mandates which have not, until the recent emphasis on work skills, carried with them mission priorities. Local school districts have not had the freedom or authority to accept, reject, or modify these mission requirements. To complicate this situation, rarely is the individual school or the system examined to determine if it has the fiscal, human or programmatic resources necessary to carry out all mission mandates — either individually or simultaneously.

Chapter 11 proposes two primary missions of schools: (1) to teach students how and what to learn and (2) to enhance the students' personal and social development. The effectiveness of education should be measured by the development of competent cognitive processes and acceptable behavior, rather than by test results. The first two of these are not new purposes for the schools. Many other educators (Fullan, 1982; Sarason, 1982) have identified them previously. Equally, these authors have noted that, in practice, these are not the prime missions of the schools. Even between them there is an over-emphasis on the academic and a neglect of the personal-social (Sarason, 1982). The outcome criteria noted are new ones for the schools. Currently, educational outcomes are measured by the results of extensive testing programs. These test results are products, but little attention is accorded the cognitive processes by which these test results are produced by students. By far, the ultimate criteria of educational success should be the students' effective cognitive processing of various types of information and their capacity to demonstrate acceptable social behavior.

These primary mission priorities require a conceptual and programmatic framework that would allow the mission goals to be achieved. Such a framework should include: (1) a generic knowledge base for all professional educators, based on a sound understanding of how children and adolescents learn and develop, (2) the content of academic programs, and (3) a program design to achieve education's objectives.

11

The knowledge base proposed for the improving the learning of students is the cognitive sciences. This follows from the proposition that public schools in America exist to teach children first of all, how to learn, and secondly, what to learn. Schools do not exist primarily to deliver mental health services, serve as a social service agency, or to meet, as has been demanded in the past, a host of social reform and economic development responsibilities. The first common denominator to all education is learning. The core knowledge base of all teachers should be how children learn to learn, at what developmental stages, and under what conditions. The organization and administrative practices of schools and their resource allocations should be premised on these factors. Preparation programs for teachers and administrators must follow from this mission and conceptual framework.

The development of students' personal and social conduct and attitudes is quite different from enhancing their learning capacities and skills. In order for the schools to be effective in developing appropriate personal and social behaviors, two critical changes would have to take place among the public and among teachers. These are first, both the public and teachers must accept that is one of the schools' major responsibilities to teach and develop these behaviors. Second, teachers must develop the capacities, knowledge and skills to teach them. The public would need to approve, or at least be informed of, the methods and specific attributes to be fostered in each student. The third primary mission of the schools will require an attitudinal shift and acceptance that the "product" of successful school is a process of effective learning, not the mere production of test scores.

Organization of book

Section One consists of Chapters 2-5. Chapters 2 and 3 examine the problems of education at the system and elementary and secondary school levels. Chapter 4 describes the problems inherent in teacher preparation programs. Chapter 5 examines the flaws of recent reform recommendations. One of its conclusions is that the probability for achieving substantive change in educational policy and practice that reformers hoped to accomplish is quite low.

The problems of education specific to the particular issue being discussed are described in these chapters. However, no solutions to these problems are presented in these chapters. The problems of education must be resolved by understanding their gestalt and interdependencies, and their relationships to other aspects of the educational system, as well as to the social, political and economic forces affecting them. Therefore, presenting a solution to each problem as it is described will lead to a fragmented interpretation of the resolutions necessary. Such a method does not enhance the development of a comprehensive depiction of education's mutually dependent parts and processes. Such a view is necessary if a comprehensive process of educational improvement is to occur. At the same time it is necessary to be able to connect problems with proposed solutions. Therefore, each problem presented in Chapters 2-5 will be referenced by one or more second- or third-order changes appropriate to its resolution. These second- and third-order changes will be in *italic* type and include the chapter reference where each is discussed.

Section Two consists of five chapters. They are concerned with a conceptual framework for understanding education as a system and how to bring about successful within the system of American education. Chapter 6 discusses education from a systems theory orientation. It presents an introduction to systems theory and contrasts the educational system with those characteristics that would be expected if schools operated as open social systems. Chapter 7 provides an introduction to change, examining both some principles from educational change theory, as well as some principles of change that are not ordinarily found in educational change source material. These are first- and second-order change, two types of change which can be used for developing appropriate alterations of current educational operations. Chapter 8 discusses educational change processes and findings from a variety of educational change perspectives. Chapter 9 provides a description of a process for continued educational development and improvement.

Section Three consists of Chapters 10-16. These chapters provide the proposed third- and second-order changes necessary to bring about the changes essential for achieving significant improvement of student learning outcomes and personal-social development. Chapter 10 provides the third-order changes. Chapter 11 discusses the second-order changes required in mission and knowledge base for educators to support the mission. Changes of organization, administrative practices, and resource allocation mechanisms that must occur at the local system and school level are discussed in Chapter 12. Chapters 13 and 14 present the coordinated second-order changes that must occur in teacher education and educational administrator preparation programs respectively. Chapter 15 outlines necessary changes in the practice and preparation of support service personnel. Chapter 16 discusses the prospects and processes of educational change that must be considered for designing, managing and achieving second- and third-order changes.

Section One

PROBLEM IDENTIFICATION
AND THE FLAWS
OF EDUCATIONAL REFORM

Serious problems with education in America do exist. However, problems identified in recent reform reports or targeted for change by reform recommendations tend to be the *symptoms* of the problems, not the *causes*. Because the source of the problem was not identified and remedied, the recommendations and efforts to resolve the problems have a low probability of success . For example, many national and state reports identified the working conditions of teachers as a problem area that deserved and needed improvement. This was a valid observation, and many states have moved to improve the conditions of teacher employment. However, the working conditions of teachers result from the professional status and activities of education being controlled by political and economic leaders, rather than by those in the education profession. As long as non-educators control the working conditions in education, no reasonable measure of stability or security for teachers can arise. If educational reformers had properly identified the cause of the problem, they would more likely have resolved the problem.

The problems that infest education at the school system and individual school level result from a lack of prioritized missions and an organizational structure not designed to maximize learning on the part of students. To achieve significant improvements in students' learning outcomes, these problems within the schools must change. However, these very problems are likely to be the most resistant to change. Two prerequisites for improving the outcomes of schooling are (1) the identification and synergy of the schools' missions, and (2) an organizational structure derived from that mission and designed to enhance its accomplishment.

The reform reports did not deal with the schools' mission. Most did not deal with restructuring the schools. An exception is *A Nation Prepared* (1986), which did address the question of school organization. However, the report did not address the mechanism by which any restructuring could occur.

17

Most reform reports addressed very few of the elements vital for achieving comprehensive change in education. For example, some of the reports dealt with change of some elements of public schools, but did not address necessary corresponding changes in teacher education programs. Some addressed the teacher preparation issue but failed to address public school concerns. This omission in reform reports suggests that the authors lack an understanding of the comprehensive, inter-related nature of education and an insufficient knowledge of educational change process itself.

As the following three chapters point out, a number of other serious deficiencies exist, both in public and teacher education, and in the efforts to improve the situation. However, the failure to identify and address the underlying causes of education's problems and the inadequacies and lack of synergy on the part of reform reports are the most serious. These deficiencies suggest that the probability of achieving reform goals (however they might be described) is not high.

2 Identification of education's problems: system-level

The three chapters contained in this section identify the problems at the school system, secondary and elementary school levels and discuss the failure of educational reform efforts to address these issues. This chapter addresses problems of public education at the system level. The next chapter addresses problems at the elementary and secondary school levels. Chapter 4 examines the efforts and failures of educational reform and the attempts to identify and resolve the subsequent problems.

Two interrelated problem areas diminish the ability of the public schools at the system level to improve student learning. These areas are:

1. The mission of the schools *(Chapter 1, Second-Order Changes 1, 2; Chapter 13, Second-Order Changes 21, 22, 26, 30, 32, 33; Chapter 14, Second-Order Change 34; Chapter 15, Second-Order Change 38)* and,

2. The organization of the schools at the system, elementary and secondary levels to achieve their missions *(Chapter 12, Second-Order Changes 3, 4, 6, 7, 9, 10, 11, 12, 13, 15; Chapter 14, Second-Order Changes 34; Chapter 15, Second-Order Change 37).*

The problems associated with each of these areas present significant barriers to improving students' learning and educational outcomes. Combined, these problems and barriers constitute major obstacles to achieving significant, long-term educational change and improving program quality and student performance.

The educational mission

A primary mission for the schools, as determined and agreed to by both the community and professional educators, is critical for educational

19

improvement. The history of American education is replete with new missions as succeeding waves of reform have constantly swept over the schools (Elmore and McLaughlin, 1988). Fantini (1970), almost two decades ago, said that schools simply do not have the capacity to deal with diversity and have been given too many missions for which they are unprepared. Fantini's observations are still valid over 20 years later.

The Task Force on Higher Education and the Schools (Southern Regional Educational Board, 1981) reported that the primary objectives of the schools are to educate our youth. The report also recommended schools limit and/or resist the dumping of additional functions upon the schools by special interest groups. Lapointe (1984) concluded that America does not agree on what are important school objectives. Wassermann (1984) concluded that when it comes to schools, there is a concentration on academics, but that America also wants its schools to have social, vocational, civic, and personal goals. Basically, the schools have too many missions and too many masters to achieve all the tasks imposed on them from external sources. Broudy (1975) described this situation more than a decade ago when he claimed that, as institutions act to protect their functions and functionaries, they respond with confusion, hesitation, and ad hoc improvisations. Broudy further described education's adaptations as transitory and superficial.

The unlimited missions of the schools have accumulated over a period of decades. The earliest days of American education emphasized religious and career training for a select population. New missions or tasks have increased dramatically since those days. These tasks have included career and vocational training, as well as a pre-college curriculum for all who desired such programs. Schools were also expected to serve the goals of social reform by providing equal educational and vocational opportunity. Schools are also expected to produce responsible citizens, solve the drug problem, fuel the industrial and economic needs of the nation, and teach students to read better, communicate more effectively, and compute mathematical problems at higher levels of skill. These are only a few of the missions that schools have been expected to carry with excellence. There is a host of others.

The missions fall into three general areas: (1) learning and academic, (2) social, and (3) economic. Different groups perceive each area in varying degrees of importance. During the decades of the 1950's, 60's and early 70's, the primary focus was for the schools to serve as the nation's social reform leaders. Bruner (1983) has described reforms of the middle and late 1960s as outgrowths of the civil rights movement, which targeted the poor, minorities and the underprivileged. The instruments of this movement were the politics of affirmative action. As the economic crises of the 70's became more apparent, the schools were seen as both the cause and the solution of the problems. With the 1983 publication of *A Nation at Risk*, the emphasis shifted from social reform to educational reform to improve the nation's economic posture. A related emphasis was on accountability for funds expended and results obtained (*A Nation at Risk*, 1983).

The third mission area of the schools, an emphasis on learning and academics and on development of personal-social skills, has been neglected as these other mission areas have predominated. Yet, the primary reason for schools to exist is, and always has been, to teach students. However, unless this mission becomes the first priority of the schools, with all other missions subordinate, schools will not be able to organize their structure and programs to effectively improve student learning.

The current mission

American public education today still has no primary mission. However, educational improvement for economic development is one that appears to be emerging. In order to understand the development of education's current emphasis on economic development, it is necessary to return to 1953, the time of Brown v. Board of Education of Topeka (1953). This Supreme Court case ushered in the desegregation of the schools, which fostered the concept of schools as the primary vehicle for achieving social reform. Four years later, the orbiting of Sputnik in 1957 sparked beliefs that changed forever the educational system of America and the public's attitude toward education.

Other events contributed to changes in education: the turmoil caused by Vietnam, the rejection of authority, the specter of the President and Vice President of the United States resigning in disgrace, Watergate, and a social upheaval previously unseen in America. As Cornbleth (1986) indicated, schools are looked to for alleviation of social, economic, and political problems ranging from racial integration through U.S. competitiveness in world markets to national security.

The effects of these social changes on the schools were significant. Huge sums of money were made available to schools to implement an incredible number of new academic and social programs. Fullan (1982) reports that in New York City, 781 innovative programs were piloted between 1979 and 1981. Fullan indicates the total number of innovative programs is impossible to estimate. In an effort to meet the demands of social reform, government implemented a vast array of programs, and a burgeoning bureaucracy developed. New initiatives included special education programs. Vast numbers of teaching machines and audio-visual tools and equipment accompanied a rejection of academic standards and required courses (*A Nation at Risk*, 1983). The more funds that were appropriated for the schools, the more demands for "relevant" courses were made. The more the emphasis on social programs, seemingly, the less academic rigor was expected of students. Cremin, (1990), wrote that it was not the perceived "mediocrity" and "decline" of the schools that was the problem with American education. Rather, it was attempting to deal with the tremendous variety of demands that have been placed on American schools.

From 1953 to 1983 schools became the world's largest social service and welfare agency. Milstein and Golaszewski (1985) assert from their studies that teachers were asked to solve a wide array of social problems and as a result, the missions, purposes, and objectives of the schools became blurred. Educators in America were unsure if they were to educate the mind or spoil the child. Should they excuse or discipline students for lack of effort? Should they enforce grading standards or fail students and possibly send a 17-year-old to an unpopular war? Should they teach *Macbeth*, sex education, or both?

Even regular classroom teachers were unsure of their roles. They knew they were there to "educate" children, but educate them for what? Should they focus on math, social studies, history, or how to avoid being beaten by a drunken father, how to learn to read in the sixth grade? What was their task? What would it be tomorrow?

As a result of these factors, the focus and purpose of education in America became very diffused. In reality, however, the emphasis was on social factors, not educational attainment or intellectual development. Dodd (1984) concluded that the law requires schools to address all manners of social problems. It was within this context of a shifting, unsettled, conflict-ridden society that the schools attempted to respond to the social needs of America. This emphasis on social factors and social reform goals continued until May 1983. this was when the report of the National Commission on Excellence in Education issued its report, *A Nation at Risk: The Imperative for Educational Reform*.

Between the publication of that report and the summer of 1986, when the Carnegie Foundation published *A Nation Prepared: Teachers for the 21st Century*, 30 national reports calling for changes in elementary and secondary schools were released. At the state level, 200 blue ribbon commissions (an average of 4 per state) were formed and proposed numerous recommendations for change in education. Between 1984 and 1986, state legislatures enacted more than 700 state statutes affecting education (Timan and Kirp, 1989) and between 1983-1988 more then 1,000 pieces of legislation affecting teacher policy were enacted (Darling-Hammond and Berry, 1988). These represent more rules and regulations relating to education then were generated during the previous 20 years. In addition, state legislatures appropriated huge sums of money to implement these recommendations. States, through legislation, were and still are affecting education to an extent never before attempted.

The educational system of America is changing — from a socially-oriented one to one clearly focused on industrial development as the prime educational objective (*A Nation at Risk*, 1983). This focus will probably last for at least the next decade, when once again, unless appropriate changes are instituted, the focus of the schools will shift.

Three questions arise from these changes. (1) What forces were at work to drive this tremendous thrust for educational reform all across the nation? (2) What are the changes being recommended for education? (3) What is the probability that these changes will achieve the desired results?

The forces motivating reform of American education were primarily economic in nature. The 1972-73 oil crisis (Coombs, 1985; Fowler, Boyd, and Plank, 1993) started the latest reforms, initiating two waves of change that had a profound effect on the public's view of and attitude toward education. Americans learned from this crisis that they were no longer in control of the world's economic marketplace. They were extremely dependent on other countries — countries whose language, traditions, and business customs they did not understand. Shocked, and facing a declining leadership role and profit margin, most Americans, and particularly the business leaders, were forced to analyze their own concepts, beliefs, assumptions, and business customs because of these declines. Many began to change. Others who did not change failed to survive. Many asked the question, "How did the decline of American enterprise and business come about and who was to blame?" Rightly or wrongly, they blamed the schools for failing to provide the education necessary to maintain America's economic competitive advantage in the world. *A Nation At Risk* said it clearly, "Our nation is at risk. Our once unchallenged preeminence in commerce, industry, science, and technological innovation is being overtaken by competitors throughout the world" (page 4).

This attitude was reinforced by the second wave of change precipitated by the oil crisis. America entered a deep and long-lasting period of high inflation and recession. Money was scarce. Expenditures were scrutinized. Many social programs were cut back significantly or cut out altogether. Thousands of jobs were lost; early retirements were forced upon thousands of others. America had to tighten its belt. These events, coming as they did after Vietnam and Watergate, both of which left serious wounds on the American psyche, caused the nation as a whole to enter a time of emotional depression. Self-confidence and national pride were shaken as never before. Again, the schools were blamed. The schools were considered too lax with

23

students, who as a result, had not learned to study hard enough, had not learned enough, and had abandoned the traditional American work ethic.

The fact that schools mirror the social climate and context of the times was ignored, as was the fact that nearly all social institutions suffered a similar decline of public trust. Paradoxically, the American public blamed the schools for the ills of society and expected the schools to resolve the problems.

The seriousness of the situation is reflected in the publication of 30 national reports on education in the three years following publication of *A Nation at Risk*. The seriousness of the problems is also indicated by the caliber of the leadership of those who developed these reports. Serving on the committees and task forces shaping these reports were leaders of business and industry, national and state governments, and educational institutions. A special task force of the State Governors Association issued its own report. The leaders of America took their charge to reform education in America very seriously. Uniformly, their reports condemned the quality of American public education.

The state of the American economy was linked directly to the quality of its schools. At least four national reports referenced education and the economy in the title of their reports. In *A Nation Prepared* (1986), issued from the Carnegie Forum on Education and the Economy, the first words leave no doubt of the connection perceived between education and the economy:

> The 1980's will be remembered for two developments: the beginning of a sweeping reassessment of the nation's economic strength and an outpouring of concern for the quality of American education. The connection between these two streams of thought is strong and growing. (p. 11)

Further, the report states,

> Three years ago, the country was in the grip of the most severe recession since the great depression. While most Americans were deeply concerned about our economic prospects, and were persuaded that the economy could not prosper as long as the quality of education continued to decline, few perceived that the world economy was in the midst of a profound transformation, one that demands a new understanding of the educational standards necessary to create the kind of high-wage work force that can compete in a global economy. (p. 11)

This national perception linking economic vitality and educational quality was paralleled at the state level. Governor Lamar Alexander of

24

Tennessee perhaps stated it most clearly. He said, "Better schools is perhaps the major domestic issue today. It's at the center of whether we can become competitive in the world market. That shoots it to the top of the state's list of priorities" (*A Nation Prepared*, 1986, p. 10). Governor Alexander's remarks are typical of those issued in almost every state in America. Everyone believed better educated students would improve economic benefits.

This economic mission of the schools is the most contemporary of the mission changes that have accompanied each period of educational reform in America (Elmore and McLaughlin, 1988). Each period of reform has carried with it a new educational mission emphasis. As a result, American education today suffers from a surfeit of missions with no priorities attached to them *(Chapter 11, Second-Order Change 1; Chapter 12, Second-Order Change 4; Chapter 13, Second-Order Changes 21 & 22).*

The reasons for a diffuse mission profile

Educational operations in America operate from three loosely connected processes: policy, administration, and practice (Elmore and McLaughlin, 1988). These processes operate from the federal, state, and local levels with little effort to integrate initiatives or coordinate and cooperate on issues. The lines of authority of these three levels overlap and often conflict. Policies can be set anywhere from the federal government to the local school principal. Because the administration of these policies often differs from state to state, system to system, and school to school, the objectives of American public education have become blurred and its classroom practices weakened.

Kirst (1988) has indicated that local school officials have been slowly losing their decision-making authority to state officials. One reason is the increasing lack of confidence in the ability of local authorities to maintain and improve academic standards. According to Kirst, this shift of control in education threatens a sharp conflict between state control and local flexibility. He cites the following as recent examples of this shift:

- Tougher high school graduation requirements have been approved in 48 states.
- Textbooks, tests and curricula have been revised and aligned through state policy.
- Teacher policies have been revamped to upgrade qualifications.
- States increased school aid between 1985-88 by over 25% (above built-in increases for inflation) with much of this funding from state omnibus bills with up to 80 separate reforms.

25

The recent flurry of state legislation followed a growth of state control of education throughout the 1970s, when states became involved in such things as accountability, school finance reform, civil rights regulations, and other issues. Actually, the loss of confidence in local authorities began in the mid-1960s. Then, federal and state authorities were not accountable, even though over 100,000 individuals served on local school boards across the nation. During the 1960s and 70s, state and federal officials initiated programs specifying funds for target groups that were either neglected or under-represented at the local level.

In the 1970s increased concern over local academic standards led states to prescribe stricter, but more uniform, standards for both teachers and students. As a result, minimum competency test results rose significantly between 1980-82. In general, state governments did not believe that local authorities were paying sufficient attention to the quality of curricula, teacher preparation or academic standards.

[It should be noted that this shift of decision-making authority to the state level is in direct conflict with research about effective schools. This research strongly indicates that the most important changes in schools take place when those responsible for each school are given more responsibility for decision-making, not less (Kirst, 1988).]

Along with the increasing state control of education, there was also a rapid growth in the specialized functions of the school. Such programs as vocational education, driver education, nutrition, and many others were added to the responsibilities of the schools. Because they were supported by state and federal grants, these programs tended to dilute further the influence and decision-making authority of the local superintendent and school board (Kirst, 1988).

Besides these federal and state initiatives which reduced the control of local authorities, there was also a significant growth in special interest groups at the local, state and federal levels. These interest groups often reflected nationwide social movements such as civil rights, women's roles, ethnic self-determination, and the improvement of conditions for the handicapped. Unlike the 19th century social movements, which created and supported social institutions like the schools, the social movements of the 1960-80s questioned the quality of these institutions and strove to make them more responsive to forces outside the local decision-making authority (Kirst, 1988).

Kirst points out that this changing governance structure does not result in "centralization" of control. There is, in fact, no single control center. Rather there are a number of authority dimensions, including higher authorities, such as federal and state agencies and the courts; outside agencies, such as the Educational Testing Service and the Council for

26

Exceptional Children; local internal interest, such as vocational education program coordinators; and other local agencies such as the police department and the department of health. These influences on education policy development result in a constant shifting of purpose, mission, priorities, programs, incentives, standards and practices. It is no wonder that schools attempt to provide some stability in the face of a continuing siege of change efforts. The question becomes: "How much change and excitement can an institution absorb and still be able to respond to its primary mission and local constituents?"

The extent of this increasing state control was revealed in a study conducted by Goertz (1986). She developed a matrix of instruments which states may use to influence local academic standards and overcome local resistance to state-imposed curricula. She distinguished among:

- *Performance* standards that measured an individual's performance through tested achievement and observations.
- *Program* standards that included curriculum requirements, program specifications and other state requirements affecting time in school, class size and staffing.
- *Behavior* standards that included attendance requirements and disciplinary codes.

Goertz surveyed all 50 states. She noted a trend toward increased influence in all three standards, beginning in 1970 and rising sharply in 1983-86.

There are two major reasons why the schools have had a continuous set of mission, policy, and administrative changes imposed on them. The first is the lack of a single governance structure and mechanism for directing, maintaining and coordinating the mission of the schools. The lack of such a coordinating agency also prevents educators from effectively resisting the continuous changes to its mission. The disorganized and overlapping lines of authority detract seriously from the schools' abilities to establish and maintain a clearly focused set of program activities designed to carry out a single, prime mission.

The second reason why schools have been so vulnerable to external control is the decentralized nature of the educational enterprise in America. As Cornbleth (1986) has indicated, there is no formal integration across organizational levels in American schools and there is no operational central authority. The important question is "Who, or what agencies, control the mechanisms for determining the mission and changes within the huge enterprise of American education?"

27

The answer to who is in control is complicated. Several sources exert control, each in varying amounts, depending on the time, the amount of money to be expended, the issue under consideration, and the political, economic, and social context of the period. All these elements interact to produce a shifting, ebbing, uncertain sharing of power and control over the purposes and objectives of America's schools. This exercise of power and control is shared by public agencies (including local and state boards of education, state departments of public instruction, state legislatures and their study groups and the national government) and private groups (professional educational organizations, teachers' unions, faculty of higher education institutions, parents' special interest groups, and business and civic leaders). Each of these groups exercises power and control through formal and informal means, trade-offs, and often short-lived alliances to achieve short-term objectives.

The legal right to exercise control over educational matters is reserved to state legislatures by state constitutions. State legislatures have delegated their authority to state boards of education. These boards have historically delegated many of their powers to state education agencies — either by formal action on certain issues, or by allowing such departments to gradually assume power unchecked over time.

Local boards of education derive their powers from those delegated by state boards of education. Local control of education began with small towns and villages exercising control over personnel, curricula, teaching methods, and finances. Most states developed their constitutions during the latter half of the 1700's and the 1800's. These constitutions, recognizing the importance of education to the state, gave the state legislature the power to regulate educational matters. As a matter of practice, however, most states did little initially to exercise this power. Control of most educational matters was left to the local community. It was not until the late 1950's that state boards of education began to exercise increased control over educational matters. Many of these increases were due to the burgeoning bureaucracies necessary to monitor the expenditure of funds from the federal government for the many support programs it funded during the 1960's and thereafter (Chapter 11, Third-Order Changes 1, 2; Chapter 12, Second-Order Change 4).

Another, more serious reason why the schools have a continuous set of mission changes imposed on them deals with who is responsible for carrying out the programs. Who bears the responsibility for accomplishing the objectives of the system, however they may be defined? Is it the school superintendent, the principals, the teachers, or support staff? All of these? What about the local school board, those appointed or elected non-professionals charged with oversight and development of system policy (but who lately have shown more and more inclination to meddle in day to day operations of the schools)? Who is responsible for ensuring that the schools achieve their objectives? Normally, the school board holds the superintendent responsible. The superintendent holds the central office personnel and principals accountable. The principals hold the teachers responsible. They, in turn, hold the students and parents responsible. Parents hold all the above responsible, except perhaps themselves.

An interesting example of this "blame the other guy" was reported on the editorial page of the *Washington Post*, May 7, 1990 in which 1988 SAT and ACT scores were reported lower for the third year in a row. In addition, the percentage of students completing high school dropped from 71.7% in 1977 to 71.1% in 1988. Other indicators demonstrated similar declines, such as the number of students passing advanced placement tests. The editorial went on to indicate that Education Secretary Lauro Eavayos blamed insufficient reform efforts and called for drastic re-structuring. The targets of his criticism, from teachers' unions to administrators, responded by discounting the evaluation measures as inaccurate reflections of the job they were doing.

If the chain of responsibility is to work effectively, each higher level must have the authority to ensure compliance by personnel in the levels below. This is not the case in education. For such a process to work effectively, there are certain requisites that must exist. The most important of these is an effective organizational structure and a control mechanism that are designed to carry out the mission and achieve the objectives of the schools in a prioritized manner. Currently, education is poorly organized to do so *(Chapter 11, Third-Order Changes 1, 2, 3 &4; Chapter 12, Second-Order Changes 3, 6, 7, 11,12, 13 & 17; Chapter 13, Second-Order Change 23; Chapter 13, Second-Order Change 30; Chapter 14, Second-Order Changes 34 and 36; Chapter 15, Second-Order Change 37).*

Organization of education to achieve its mission

The failure to achieve significant change in the structural and decision-making elements of the educational system can be attributed to (1) the school systems' decentralized nature and (2) its reactive nature. (Education reacts to pressure from external forces but returns to its previous state when the pressure subsides.) Cornbleth (1986) concluded that major problems of educational reform movements included the lack of an operational central authority and the failure of reform authors to gain wide public support. Almost 16,000 school systems operate in America under several layers of decision-making authority with individual schools and individual classrooms at the lowest level. Despite demands to improve learning outcomes, educational systems have not modified the structure of control or organization. In fact, educational systems have been unable to do so. Thus, the basic framework of education has remained unchanged for many decades (Boyer, 1983).

Over the years, new programs, services and emphases have been attached to the central structure of educational systems. However, the basic governance, organizational and administrative networks of educational systems have remained unchanged as these new programs and functions have been added to schools' responsibilities. Social service and mental health programs, breakfast and lunch programs, and free counseling services for students and their families are only a few of these expensive, time consuming responsibilities that detract from learning time.

These programs and services have been attached in an almost random pattern to the school structure, rarely communicating, or cooperating with each other. Each seems to have a life of its own. Each must defend its territory against others. Each maintains a posture that its services are the most critical in the lives of the children it serves; and each serves only a portion of the total school community. Thus, these add-on programs often detract from, rather than supplement, the prime mission of the schools. They exist on the periphery of the central structure of the schools. They are unable to affect the overall administrative structure of the schools and are destined for an existence for only so long as the objectives and/or funds that established them exist. Dodd (1984) concluded that public schools do not need more special programs, one on top of the other, each adding its own bureaucratic weight to the total.

Within the current central structure of a school system, there are only three categories of personnel necessary to maintain the system: the central office personnel, the principals, and the regular classroom teachers. All other professional personnel, such as guidance personnel, psychologists, media personnel, school social workers, even special education personnel, exist in a twilight zone between the three central categories above and those personnel hired to provide the special add-on programs and services. Each category of personnel has its perception of its role and mission regarding meeting students' needs. Their objectives are determined by their professional organizations, where they received their training, and the source of funds for their particular position. Thus, it happens that a school psychologist, hired by special education funds, cannot assist children or the teachers of children who have not been certified as needing special education services. Guidance personnel often find themselves doing class schedules, filling in for absent teachers and a myriad of activities unrelated to their professional orientation and/or training.

30

Principals are unsure whether they are managers, instructional leaders, supervisors, all of the above or none of the above. Instructional supervisors, working from the central office staff, spend more time talking to other supervisors than they do supervising. In fact, they do very little supervising in the schools (Theis-Sprinthall, 1982).

The list could continue. The point is that school systems are too poorly organized and coordinated to achieve the missions each of these programs perceived as essential for students. Under current conditions, the federal and state programs detract from the schools' primary mission by adding additional responsibilities for teachers and other personnel, responsibilities for which teachers are generally inadequately trained. These programs also divert resources from the schools' primary mission. These programs must be prioritized under the prime mission of schools. Available resources can then be provided on the basis of these priorities. Only then will schools be able to include these programs effectively within the educational structure and administrative framework. Political leaders have resisted efforts to modify the structural components of the educational system to achieve these goals (Cornbleth, 1986). In fact, according to Cornbleth, current reform efforts can be classified as ineffective because, although much activity toward reform is evident, little results are produced. Further, there remains the question of whether the schools should include these programs as part of their mission *(Chapter 12, Second-Order Changes 4, 9, 10, 11, 12, 13)*.

Besides these organizational and structural problems, another element of educational organization prevents the schools from excelling in their mission. The wrong personnel are in charge. Currently, the personnel in charge are the administrators, primarily the principals. These individuals are supposed to develop and maintain effective schools. However, in reality it is the teachers who exert prime and final responsibility for determining the effectiveness of instructional programs. Yet, the teachers are allowed little voice in the policy-making or in the operation of the schools. Principals spend very little time with instructional matters. They spend most of their time with paper work, troublesome students, and other non-classroom activities (Elmore and McLaughlin, 1988). They are, in effect, disconnected from the learning of students. On the other hand, teachers, who are most involved with the instructional programs and the learning of students, have no authority in determining policies and administrative practices at the school or system level. they have no way to improve the conditions that would increase student learning. This lack of organizational authority on the part of teachers is a serious and fundamental flaw that adversely affects the development of mission relevance, organizational structure and effectiveness, and administrative policies. As a result, less-

31

than-effective classroom instructional practices are being utilized because teachers are several steps removed from being able to develop policies and assert administrative practices that will impact classroom needs and student learning *(Chapter 12, Second-Order Changes 3, 5, 6, 7 & 17; Chapter 14, Second-Order Changes 34 and 36; Chapter 15, Second-Order Change 37).*

Summary

School systems in America do have problems. The most serious ones, however, are not those typically thought to be problems of education. Instead, it is the lack of clearly defined, acknowledged, and accepted primary and secondary missions that are the most serious. In addition, the decentralized conglomerate nature of American school systems and the organizational structure of education has caused education and school systems to respond to organizational and control issues with ineffective policies. These responses have foiled the most serious attempts to reform education. Indeed, these attempts at reform have usually been seriously flawed themselves.

The current excess of missions of American schools is the result of many periods of reform, each of which has left its emphasis as part of the diffuse mission of today's schools. The current wave of reform sees improvements in education as a means of promoting workers' skils and increasing industrial capabilities. The lack of a prioritized mission and a clearly specified lines of authority for establishing and coordinating educational policies among public agencies have prevented education from obtaining the student outcomes desired. The organizational and administrative structure of schools has further prevented schools from developing policies that are relevant to classroom practice. The organization and administration of schools do not encourage teacher input in implementing policies and practices — even though their ideas would most likely achieve the purposes of education.

Education does have problems, and they are serious. As the next three chapters illustrate, the general problems of education are made worse by the problems existing at the secondary and elementary school levels. In addition, the efforts at reform have been so seriously flawed in design and implementation that they have had little chance of working. The solutions require a new perspective on the problems and improved procedures. An understanding of how the system works is necessary to coordinate changes in structure that will improve educational outcomes. The perspective, framework and procedures recommended are presented in the third section of this book.

3 Problem identification in elementary and secondary schools: mission, organization, administration and personnel

The problem areas of mission, organization and administration (MOAP) at the elementary and secondary school levels are inextricably related to the same problem areas at the system level. In addition, personnel preparation is a problem found in both elementary and secondary schools. This chapter addresses each of these problem areas separately.

Elementary school mission

Elementary schools serve as children's first introduction to the formal world of education, a world that will dominate and shape their lives for the next 12 or 13 years. A child's economic and social success is, to a significant extent, determined by how well he or she performs in school during these first critical years. The evaluation and prediction of a child's future, based on his performance, occur through both formal and informal educational efforts. Clearly, elementary schools shape, direct and evaluate a child's success in comprehending and coping effectively with modern society and an increasingly technological and interdependent world. Every child's future is shaped by how well she or he masters the initial basic developmental tasks set by elementary schools: reading comprehension, mathematical understanding and skill, and the ability to communicate effectively. These basics have not changed in the past 200 years, even though the environment has changed considerably. There is no doubt that these three tasks are basic to learning to cope effectively, if minimally, with today's modern society. These three areas of mastery also serve to shape the assumed basic mission of elementary schools. However, there are few elementary schools that have a specific statement of mission which shapes and prioritizes the activities of the school.

Both educators and the public must acknowledge that conditions, expectations and needs for successfully coping with the world have changed dramatically in the past 100 years. Yet, the mission and organization of elementary schools have changed little, if at all, during this time. Equally, the skills that children are expected to have mastered by the end of elementary school have changed only slightly. The only expectation that has changed is the degree of skill and the amount of knowledge that elementary school students are expected to demonstrate.

Is this increase in the amount of knowledge and the degree of skill that is expected to be mastered sufficient preparation for entering secondary schools or adequate preparation for learning how to learn for today's and tomorrow's world? If not, two possible changes are necessary: (1) Students in elementary schools could be required to learn more specifics in the subject areas taught in elementary schools. However, this is a self-limiting proposition. At some point soon, elementary school students will reach a limit in the amount of information they can learn. (2) Elementary schools could set a new mission and related objectives, establishing new goals in the type of learning expected and teaching used in elementary schools. The amount of information that a student in elementary school can learn and effectively use is finite. Today's increasingly complex and technologically sophisticated world demands a new mission concept and means for teaching children to adequately learn to cope with such a world.

Clearly, the information and knowledge explosions that have occurred in recent decades has far exceeded the capability of any one individual to learn more than a minute fraction of the information available. Yet, many of these new understandings are increasingly interdependent. A serious dilemma exists as a result. Should schools try to teach generalists or specialists? Is there a way to teach both? A generalist skims the surface of many disciplines. A specialist devotes much time to one discipline and ignores others. The goal should be the acquisition and integration of knowledge from varied sources. A new process of teaching knowledge integration must be developed and implemented in the schools. The observations of Bertalanffy (1968), discussed in Chapter 6, about integrative education should be noted here. The obvious mission change for elementary schools is to focus on teaching students new patterns of knowledge acquisition, relationships and integration *(Chapter 11, Second-Order Changes 1 & 2; Chapter 13, Second-Order Changes 21, 22, 23, 27, 28, 29 & 30)*.

Regarding the mission of elementary schools, the "what" of the question includes three elements: (1) Elementary schools must have a specific mission that provides a sense of direction and prioritized activities that develop goals and improve learning activities and quality program through change and innovative efforts. These do not currently exist. (2) Current concepts, methods and activities used in elementary schools must be consistent with a specific mission focused on the learning and academic goals for elementary school students. The existing absence of a defined and accepted mission for elementary schools permits an ambiguous learning context and non-coordinated set of isolated learning activities exist. (3) Elementary schools should be organized and administered on the basis of the mission and goals established for elementary schools. There is room for much improvement in our elementary schools.

Although they do a relatively better job than do our secondary schools, elementary schools have changed little in the past 100 years in their structure, function, objectives, or methods. Dalin (1978) and Boyer (1985) both address this issue when they describe the goal confusion of American schools and the lack of an overall sense of mission. Only those "innovative" efforts required by law have become permanent fixtures of elementary schools. This is a consequence of the law of second-order change, which is defined and discussed in Chapter 7. Second-order change of schools can only be imposed by forces external to the system. A noteworthy example of such change is the implementation of PL 94-142, the public law requiring equal educational opportunity for all children regardless of handicap. Without such a law it is unlikely that schools would have modified their mission or functions to meet the needs of these children.

Education's priority mission

What should be the chief mission of elementary schools? The answer consists of three interrelated elements. The primary mission should be to teach students how to learn effectively — without worrying initially about how much they learn. Learning is a complex affair, and teaching children how to master this difficult process is not something that can be accomplished in a few weeks. Only after children have mastered the process of learning itself will they be ready to master the content. The learning tasks currently consuming so much of an elementary school student's life in the early years (reading, spelling and mathematics) could be learned much easier and faster once students have learned how to learn.

The second mission of elementary schools should be to teach students how to apply the learning process to various subjects and problem-solving situations. Elementary schools must focus on teaching children how to learn, how to recognize patterns and relationships among similar and seemingly disparate types of information. Students must also learn how to store, relate, and retrieve information, and how to generalize appropriately from one source of information to another. In a major sense, the objective

35

of the elementary school is to teach cognitive development in a way that has not been attempted previously, by using advances and understandings made in recent years in the cognitive sciences. This will not be an easy task. Wassermann (1984) reports a teacher who indicated she approved of teaching thinking, but she could not because she had so much curriculum to cover. Unfortunately, this teacher's attitude of represents the norm rather then the exception. It is the inappropriate organization and administrative practices in the elementary schools that contribute to this attitude. A major factor generating this attitude is that teachers are not prepared or trained to deal effectively with teaching students how to learn.

The third mission element of elementary schools should be the implementation of the principle of equifinality. Individual elementary schools (and secondary schools) must be free to analyze their students' developmental and learning needs of and to design and implement their approaches to meeting these needs. This recommendation is directly opposed to the current trend that requires standardized state curricula and grade-level learning objectives.

Such mission elements as those recommended above provide several advantages for children of elementary schools. Foremost, these schools would concentrate on the primary cognitive skills that their students will need to cope with the world of today and tomorrow. Such skills will depend on an individual's ability to recognize patterns, integrate information and arrive at sound decisions based on such processes. The emphasis will be on teaching fundamental processes that are applicable to a variety of disciplines, fields of study and situations. The advantage in teaching such skills in formative years, rather than later when children have developed some of these skills by trial and error (many of which may be faulty and/or in error), should be obvious.

In addition, with an emphasis on teaching such processes, it will be easier to assess a child's cognitive functioning and to rectify faulty procedures. This emphasis contrasts directly with teachers' and parents' current emphasis on early mastery of content. Further, teaching such cognitive processes should enable children to learn more quickly and easily those subjects traditionally taught in the first years of elementary schools. Still further, because the early emphasis would be on process, not product, young children's failure and frustration with academic subjects should be substantially reduced. However, to carry out these three mission elements effectively, the organization and administration of elementary schools must be significantly altered.

Organization of elementary schools

Today's elementary schools are organized essentially the same as they were in 1900, when the structured school system began in America. Then, a headmaster or head teacher (today's principal) was appointed to oversee the work of the teachers in the school. Children and teachers were assigned to grade levels, and units of instruction were developed for each grade level. Three critical elements of this elementary school organization have persisted over the past nine decades: (1) organization of schools by grade level, (2) organization of grade level by year, and (3) the assignment of teacher responsibility to one grade level each year.

Current patterns of elementary school organization vary greatly. Some schools are organized so that grades' 1-3 are in one school, grades 4-6 in another, etc. Some schools have only one grade level, others as many as six. The only common denominator is that none are based on developmental stages of children. They are based on the number of children in certain age ranges in particular attendance zones, the availability of school buildings within these zones, the cost of bus transportation, and other such factors. Each of these factors is a valid consideration for grouping certain grades within one elementary school. However, these factors should not be the primary basis for organizational decisions. Unfortunately, each of these factors often are the basis of educational decisions and, as a result, the grouping of children according to developmental stages is usually relegated to a second level of priority or neglected altogether.

The second element of elementary school organization relates to the single-year grade level pattern. The curriculum objectives for each grade level have become increasingly specific for each year of instruction. Children are expected to pass uniformly, one year at a time, through these units, progressing from one stage to the next. Those children who cannot keep up are shunted aside to special classes, held back to repeat the same unit of instruction (grade), and/or "socially" promoted. This expectation and process of annual grades does harm to children and does not allow teacher expertise to be used most effectively. *(Chapter 12, Second-Order Changes 9 &10).*

Although they are certified to teach a range of grades, elementary school teachers are generally assigned to one grade level per year (for example, grades' 1-3, 1-4, 4-6). Teachers so certified may be assigned to teach grade 1 one year, grade 3 the next, and so on, depending on the needs of the school and the number of students enrolled. A more functional organizational pattern of elementary schools would be based on knowledge of child development and the related mission of these schools. These two elements should frame the administrative and instructional priorities and activities of the schools.

The problems generated by these situations involve two "what" questions. First, is the current organization of elementary schools derived from the mission of these schools and does it serve to maximize learning on the part of children? If not, would a more appropriate organizational structure for elementary schools better meet the learning needs of students?

The current organization of elementary schools does not meet the criteria of the first question. The pattern of school organization varies greatly. Children are assigned to grade levels by age, and each year they are expected to pass from one grade to the next. They are exposed each year to a different teacher who holds the same certification level as the preceding year's teacher but whose style of teaching, strengths, weaknesses, and personality are different from the students' prior teachers.

Most importantly, each year each teacher must spend one to two months learning the needs, aptitudes, strengths and weaknesses of his students. If the average teacher takes six weeks to learn these factors about each child in his/her class, 17% of the school year is occupied with initial assessment (based on a 36 week school year). Additional time must also be spent in some cases developing instructional strategies and techniques to meet these needs. It is not at all unusual for an elementary teacher to spend the first nine weeks of the school year learning the needs of the students and planning to meet these needs.

The assignment of students to teachers at the elementary level is an annual rite. This assignment is done by the principal, generally over the summer, without consulting the teacher. One of the unfortunate sights in American education is watching teachers and parents swarm about the newly posted class lists to find out which teacher has whose children. Then the scrambling by parents intensifies as they seek to persuade the principal to move their respective children from teacher X to teacher Y. Does the principal dare risk the ire of the parents of the strong students who know exactly what he/she is doing by such assignment decisions? Should he/she place weak students with weak teachers, the strong with the strong, and concentrate on supervising the weakest? Should he/she just assign students randomly and keep all fingers crossed? The problem arises from the lack of control many principals have over the teaching faculty of the school.

A principal does not have the authority to determine which personnel will teach in his/her school. A teacher has no authority to reject students he/she knows he or she cannot teach, or to choose the materials he/she believes are needed to meet their needs, or have the resources to obtain the materials necessary to supplement the required ones.

This situation is made worse by the conditions under which an elementary teacher works. The elementary teacher has no bathroom breaks, or lunch time of his/her own. He must come in early to supervise the buses, collect lunch money, and do other administrative activities. He must do all planning at night. A recent study by the Public School Forum of North Carolina (Pechman, 1987) found hardly believable, but unfortunately true, situations which teachers endure on a daily basis. This study was composed of three parts: a time use analysis study, a working conditions study, and an applications transfer study. The findings from this study are astounding. Teachers spent 48.2% of their work week in direct instruction. Work delays accounted for 3.3% of their time, and 3% of each week was reported for lunch and personal business. There are no teacher's offices, and no private phones to conduct confidential business with parents or others.

A survey conducted by Harris (1988) for Metropolitan Life supported this dismal view of the amount of time teachers actually spend teaching. According to the results of this survey, only 60% of the respondents said they were able to spend more than 75% of their time teaching. About 40% said they teach less than 75% of the time they are in class teaching, and 13% said they spend 50% or less time teaching.

In a related study, Foreman (1985) reported the three factors perceived as the most significant barriers to achieving educational excellence. These were (1) too much paperwork unrelated to educational assignment, (2) too much time spent on non-teaching/non-administrative duties, and (3) lack of commitment or motivation for educational excellence among the student population.

Is there an organizational structure for elementary schools that would better allow their mission to be implemented and their goals achieved? Yes. However, this solution must be perceived in relation to a series of coordinated second-order changes affecting elementary schools *(Chapter 12, Second-Order Changes 4, 9, 10 & 17; Chapter 13, Second-Order Changes 23, 26, 27, 28 & 29).*

Elementary school administration

The administration of elementary schools is usually conducted by one principal and one secretary. Many times the most important administrator in the school seems to be the secretary. Principals spend very little time on instructional matters. They spend most of their time with crisis management, dealing with troublesome students and unhappy parents, managing paper, and similar activities (Blumberg and Greenfield, 1980). A recent study by the Public School Forum of North Carolina (Pecham, 1987) found that principals spent 10.4% of their time managing instruction, 9.5 hours a week supervising, training, assisting, and evaluating all teachers of the school. Their span of management control was deemed too broad, accountability goals were unclear and, they spent large portions of their time on ancillary management functions. Goodlad (1983) suggested that principals' detachment from instructional matters was a result of their not being prepared for instructional leadership. Fullan (1982) noted that the principals' responsibilities had increased significantly in recent decades and were generally unrelated to instructional leadership.

The operation and management of an elementary school are time-consuming, and a complex business. Operating a physical plant that must shelter, feed, care for and instruct several hundred children is a complicated task. When the bureaucratic activities and paper work are added, a principal has little time to supervise instruction. It does not make sense to insist that the principal be the instructional leader of the schools. He/she is too busy with other matters to be an effective instructional leader.

What is more important, the principal is not the right person to be the instructional leader. It makes far more sense for the teachers to be the instructional leaders of the schools. Educational administrators, including principals, tend to measure their performance based on things they can control, such as the processing of reports and papers (Elmore and McLaughlin, 1988). It is no wonder then that principals identify success with the health of those administrative practices they can control, rather than the performance of individual students (Elmore and McLaughlin, 1988). Principals, largely removed and disconnected from the daily instructional activities of the classroom, find it difficult to connect their administrative actions with student learning performance.

Teachers, on the other hand, are intimately connected with the performance of their students' performance. They are professional, and often their personal success is measured on the basis of how well their students perform. Teachers seldom indicate that principals have an influence on their curricular decisions (Leithwood and MacDonald, 1981). Studies do indicate that, when teachers interacted around instructional practices, instructional effectiveness improved (Little, 1981). Since teachers are responsible for the learning and academic success of their students, they should also have the authority to direct the school's administrative practices to support the learning needs and instructional activities of the school's students.

Such authority would require a new definition of teacher and administrator functioning and a second-order change of organizational responsibility. These changes must be related to, and coordinated with, other second-order changes of the elementary schools *(Chapter 12, Second-Order Changes 3, 5, 6, 7, & 17)*.

Personnel preparation

The manner in which the administrators and teachers of these schools are prepared presents a major problem for elementary schools. It prevents

40

serious changes from being made in the mission, organization, administration, and instructional practices of these schools. The solution to this situation involves two considerations, one of which was described earlier. The first consideration entails changing the mission, organization and administration of elementary schools to achieve long-term program quality improvement. The second, and interdependent, consideration is that, to accomplish this type of change, the preparation programs of principals and teachers must be altered significantly.

Administrators

The majority of principals are former teachers (Elmore and McLaughlin, 1988). The only way to advance in education is to become an administrator. Therefore, there is no lack of applicants for administration training programs. The professional areas of these applicants include all those in the profession from elementary and secondary schools, counseling, and other support services. Administration training programs exist only at the graduate level. One can enter after only receiving a baccalaureate degree, and completing some years as a teacher, or another role in education.

Administrator training programs are primarily generic in nature. They generally do not prepare administrators for specific roles such as superintendent, principal, assistant superintendent, etc. Further, they do not prepare a candidate specifically as an elementary principal or secondary principal, but as a generic administrator. Still further, a secondary teacher, trained as an educational administrator, can be hired as an elementary principal. This may not necessarily be bad, but is it the best? Probably not, particularly when the conceptual framework and theories of administration most of these programs use are examined.

Training programs in educational administration are based on theories of administration that have evolved over time. These theories, which are primarily focused on governance issues, bureaucratic procedures, and rules and regulations, frame the organizational and administrative policies and practices of the schools (Hoyle, 1989). Cooper and Boyd (1987) concluded that the educational administrator preparation programs are weak and require little commitment on the part of the candidates. Candidates take courses with minimal disruption to their careers and are certified quickly and easily. It is no wonder that this preparation pattern affected the manner in which schools are organized.

The way schools are organized and administered force children to accommodate to the policies and practices learned during administrator preparation, whether or not they are appropriate.

Most training programs for educational administrators require only one course in child growth and development. Many require none at all, so the

41

only background in child or adolescent development a principal is likely to have had was taken during undergraduate study. Thus, it is entirely possible that an elementary school principal, who was initially prepared as a secondary school or physical education teacher, may have had only one course in child and adolescent development.

Educational administration programs also require very little work in curriculum theory and development, and practically none in evaluation of educational programs or learning outcomes. Yet, these two factors, patterns of child development and curriculum development and evaluation should be a prime focus and concern of the principal. The elementary school principal's knowledge base should include: (1) an understanding of child development; (2) an comprehension of the desired learning outcomes for elementary schools; and (3) methods of developing and evaluating a curriculum that is based on these patterns of development and geared to achieving the desired learning outcomes. The final aspect of an administrator's preparation should be the study of the organizational structure of schools and their administrative policies and procedures.

This curriculum approach should be used for the preparation of both elementary and secondary principals because the knowledge base of developmental patterns, desired learning outcomes, and curriculum development and evaluation are significantly different at these levels. Should theories of administration drive the organization and administration of schools or should the three factors mentioned above shape the organization and administration of schools? Implementing the three factors above as the base for educational administrator preparation would promote a higher probability of producing the desired learning outcomes.

One other aspect of educational administration deserves mention. In recent years there has been a recommendation that the schools adopt more practices of American businesses. This is a surprising recommendation in view of American businesses' dismal record in administration and management. It is surprising because these businesses have had to search internationally for more successful management theories and practices to emulate. Many American companies have begun to copy the management practices of Japanese businesses that have been demonstrated so successful recently. In his book *Made in Japan* (1986), Mr. Akio Morita, chairman of Sony, suggested that the cause of America's fading industrial leadership is "failed management." Mr. Morita warns that American corporate managers have lost sight of their basic responsibility to employees and customers. Instead of pursuing actions that lead to and sustain long-term development, American managers have been guilty of pursuing actions that are short-sighted and geared to a quick return on investments. Mr. Morita further suggests that a manager's prime responsibility is to motivate workers and that American managers have failed to do that.

Mr. Morita does not stand alone in blaming management for many of America's economic problems. Bruce Nussbaum, writing in the October 20, 1986, issue of *Business Week,* makes much the same point. He attributes America's decline in the world marketplace to the failure to save and invest for the future, and the corporate obsession with short-term profits rather than long-term growth. David Halberstam, in his book *The Reckoning* (1986), charges that financial persons and accountants, interested in short-term profits, have been in control at General Motors and Ford, rather than engineers.

It is absurd to propose that schools adopt the practices of a failed endeavor, particularly if the reason for the failure of American business management is the desire for quick investment return. The educational system is a developmental process. It takes years to develop the mind and thinking skills of children. It cannot happen overnight. Practices that attempt to short-circuit this process are not only doomed to failure, but they may actually prevent the very outcomes desired.

Further, the objectives of business and education are entirely different. Therefore, the organization, management, and administrative policies and practices must be different. Teaching a child to learn should not be equated with making a profit. Hence, in business and education, the objectives are too different to allow similar organizational management, administrative policies and practices *(Chapter 12, Second-Order Changes 3, 6 & 7; Chapter 14, Second-Order Changes 34-36).*

In summary, educational administrator training programs are too poorly conceptualized and planned to achieve the primary goal of elementary schools. A different approach to developing leaders for these schools is necessary. Such an approach should proceed from a knowledge base of children are from which the organizational, administrative, and instructional functions of the elementary school can be derived.

Teachers

Teachers are the most important personnel in elementary schools. It is the teachers who are responsible for socializing the youngest students to the world of education — teaching them how to learn and providing them the self-confidence they need to continue to learn effectively. Teacher preparation programs teach methods to accomplish these tasks. The educational objectives are carefully detailed in state and local curriculum guides. In theory, all elementary teachers have to do is apply the techniques they have been taught to their students to achieve the objectives desired.

Teachers at the elementary school level are fairly well prepared to carry out and achieve the objectives of the schools as currently defined. Some elementary preparation programs do a better job of producing capable teachers than others, primarily because of university and program recruitment and admission policies and standards.

However, within the current organizational framework of an elementary school and its grade level subject-determined objectives, elementary school teachers do an acceptable job. This was pointed out by the report of the Committee appointed by William Bennett, then Secretary of Education (1986). In an interview concerning this report, Secretary Bennett indicated that elementary schools do a responsible job, they know what they are about, and they have solid goals.

Nevertheless, questions concerning the desired outcomes of elementary schools and the means of achieving these goals must be raised. These questions revolve around the desired learning outcomes for elementary schools, the organizational framework of these schools, and the curriculum of these schools. The issue that these questions consider is whether elementary schools, as they currently operate, provide the most appropriate climate, goals, curriculum, and outcomes for students. This issue is at the core of needed changes in elementary schools.

By and large, elementary teacher education programs do not provide their students with the conceptual and knowledge base necessary to instruct public school students in the most appropriate learning processes. The organizational and administrative practices of elementary schools further limit the most effective learning climate and procedures from being implemented. It is a combination of conditions that revolve around the individual classroom practices. The ultimate purpose of educational reform is to provide changes that will allow significant improvements in classroom outcomes. To achieve this purpose, significant and fundamental changes must be made in elementary school climate, organization and administrative practices. In addition, elementary school teachers will need to think differently about children and about teaching. They will have to learn new concepts about how children learn and what innovative means would be necessary for educating them. This means that their preparation programs will have to change dramatically *(Chapter 11, Second-Order Change 2; Chapter 12, Second-Order Changes 6, 7, 9, 10 & 17; Chapter 13, Second-Order Changes 21, 22, 23, 24, 26, 29, 27, 28, 30 & 32).*

Summary of elementary school performance

Elementary schools, on the whole, do a satisfactory job of educating their students, given the current expectations for educational outcomes at this level. Elementary schools do suffer from problems of mission, organization and administration, as well as the problems imposed upon them by preparation programs for teachers and administrators. These are problems of the structural elements of elementary education. The basic structure of elementary education has not changed in almost 100 years, despite obvious changes in the environment that have created the need for a new perception of students' learning needs and approaches to meeting these needs. It is education's inability to modify its mission, organization and administrative practices, as well as the mutually supporting problems inherent in teacher preparation programs, that has prevented elementary schools from developing the capabilities to meet these changing needs.

Secondary schools

Things are worse, often very much worse, in secondary schools than in elementary schools. The mission and objectives of secondary schools are unclear. Whom should they serve and for what purpose? The organization of secondary schools is rigid and more geared to maintaining order than increasing student learning. Students are punished but not rewarded. The mission, organization and administration of secondary schools do not proceed from an understanding of adolescence or the mission of such schools. The preparation of secondary school teachers is weak because these programs emphasize content and pay little attention to how students learn. Boyer (1983) noted that it was difficult to find a coherent purpose in today's secondary schools. He attributed this to the fact that these schools are called upon to provide the services of a variety of social institutions. The variety of demands placed upon secondary schools and their teachers are not only confusing but they detract significantly from these teachers' concentration on their primary task — enhancing learning on the part of students.

Mission

The mission of secondary schools is poorly defined, ambiguous and non-prioritized. This lack of mission priority results from several factors. These include a failure to focus on the nature of the student population and goals that are poorly defined and confusing *(Chapter 12, Second-Order Changes 11, 12, 13, 14, 15, & 17)*.

Student population

The student population of secondary schools is composed of people with both adult and child like characteristics. The period of adolescence is

45

marked by a difficult search for identity and independence. Some students wish to prepare for a post-secondary education, some for the world of work, some for marriage. Some only want to be left alone. Some are intellectually mature, but others lack the experiences and maturity to make sound decisions in matters of career, emotional and social matters. The need to meet these complex and far ranging conditions poses a complex problem.

One might think that the mission of secondary schools would include a recognition of the character and problems of adolescence and that it would incorporate it into a mission statement focused on preparing the adolescents for the world of adulthood. This is generally not the case. Secondary schools rarely have mission statements at all. Rather, they have student handbooks which state clearly what students may not, should not, cannot do. If there is a general mission for secondary schools currently, it is to control the behavior of adolescents within acceptable limits. Learning gains are almost a by-product of these schools, unless learning is gained by college preparation students.

By the time students have reached the secondary school, the poorest learners have generally been identified and relegated to special classrooms, where they follow their peripheral educational path, hopefully to the world of vocational employment. Thus, regular classroom teachers in secondary schools usually do not have to be concerned with learning problems resulting from causes like mental retardation. The learning problems these teachers encounter emerge from far more subtle causes: students who cannot read but have been socially promoted, adolescents suffering from disillusionment or identity crises, teens who are rejecting parental authority or identifying with a peer group, students who prefer working to have a car over doing homework, young people who fear becoming adults and having to take on adult responsibilities. In short, the learning problems at this age are caused more by social factors, lapses in decision-making knowledge, and judgmental standards than by learning deficits.

When secondary schools fail to consider the nature of adolescence and to use it to establish an appropriate mission, teacher preparation programs, and instruction methods, serious flaws in secondary school operations result. Failing to establish clearly defined goals is another crucial fault.

What should be the mission of secondary schools? The primary a mission should be to promote learning on the part of all students. Such a mission should take into account the nature of adolescents and provide a climate within which each student has the freedom and opportunity to explore the world of learning and knowledge, the world of work, and the world of decision-making.

Secondary school goals

What are the goals of secondary education? It is difficult to say. The Coalition of Essential Schools, an extension of *A Study of High Schools*, conducted by the National Association of Secondary School principals and the National Association of Independent Schools during 1981-1984, identified five "imperatives" for better secondary schools. These included (1) providing teachers and students more room to work and learn in their own ways, (2) emphasizing student demonstration of mastery, (3) establishing the right incentives for teachers and students, (4) focusing the students' work on the use of their minds, and (5) keeping the structure simple and flexible (Coalition of Essential Schools, 1988). However, these "imperatives" do not appear to be operational in many high schools where the number one goal seems to be maintaining the behavior of students *(Chapter 12, Second-Order Change 14)*. At least, secondary schools' student handbooks give this impression. In almost every school handbook is a list of rules and regulations — do not do this, you can not do that, etc. The book consists almost entirely of "don'ts" accompanied by punishments for violations.

Secondary schools are negative environments. They consider themselves successful if their students do not get into trouble. The school administration focuses on enforcing the strict rules and regulations and getting rid of troublemakers. Is it any wonder that the drop-out rate is so high? The message conveyed to students by such an emphasis on negative sanctions is that they are expected to be "bad," to get into trouble, that they cannot be trusted, and that they are not yet mature enough to assume responsibility for their behavior. Where is the list of positive sanctions that conveys an attitude of optimism about students, that conveys an expectation of positive behavior on the part of students, that emphasizes the importance of learning? There are a few positive handbooks. It would be interesting to compare the learning and social outcomes of students from schools that have positive handbooks with students whose schools operate by negative sanctions.

Many people, including school personnel, have a negative view of adolescents. They expect them to get into trouble and think that most of today's teenagers are much more troublesome and violent then in previous years and decades. Astroth (1994) has coined a word for this attitude, "ephebiphobia" -a fear and loathing of adolescence. Astroth points out several important characteristics of today's teens. They are healthier, better educated, and more responsible than teens in the past. He reports, for example, that 90-95% of teens in Los Angeles do not belong to gangs, yet we tend to think of all teens there as gang members. This over generalization of negative behavior to all teens has colored the perceptiosn of many individuals. Teenagers, at least the vast majority, are really nice people.

Administrators of secondary schools are often rewarded by how well they control the behavior of students: the fewer violations of the negative

47

sanctions, the better the school. Reward does not mean financial reward, rather, the praise and acceptance by the community that the principal runs a "tight ship." Most principals have been prepared to retain the status quo. They are also rewarded for not rocking the boat. Superintendents and school board members don't look with favor on principals who try to experiment or innovate. Faidley and Musser (1989) describe school leaders as "agents for stability rather than visionaries, adapters as opposed to transformers and maintainers rather than champions" (p. 9). Moreover, teachers feel safer with a principal who does not stir things up (McCall, 1988). That is the primary mark in the community of a good administrator. Such an attitude obviously reinforces the efforts of the administrator to make sure that the students know and follow the rules, the negative rules. These policies and procedures convey very directly to the students how they are perceived by the authorities of the world — they are expected to be "bad" and only the imposition and strict enforcement of many rules can keep them within appropriate boundaries of behavior. Pellicer studied high school principals and their jobs. He found that they averaged more than 55 hours a week and spent more time on school management than any other task. They averaged only four hours per week observing teachers informally.

This negative focus on adolescence makes one question the priorities of secondary schools and the messages these priorities convey to students. The organization and administration of secondary schools seem to indicate that student needs are not the reason for schools' existence. From the way schools are organized and the things that are emphasized at school, students may perceive that learning and academic development by all students are not a high priority. What priorities of the school are emphasized when they see a football coach assigned two class periods of algebra each day? What is this coach rewarded for, his effectiveness at teaching algebra or his win-loss record? Is it possible that the coach devotes more time and effort to learning to teach algebra more effectively than to preparing his team for the Friday night game? This is not to deny the importance of athletics in secondary schools. Athletic competition, in both team and individual sports, plays an important role in adolescents' lives. Some schools seem to place a higher priority on athletics than on providing an atmosphere conducive to learning. A school budget that goes to support athletics, as opposed to support of such activities as foreign language clubs, drama and debate clubs, indicates clearly the priorities of the school. It is probably safe to conclude that most secondary schools convey to students, through direct and indirect means, that learning is only one reason, and probably not the most important reason, that schools exist.

Secondary schools are not currently organized or administered to promote an emphasis on learning or to maximize learning. They are organized to make administration easier, following from theories of administration and principles of management, neither of which have anything to do with how students learn or what they should be learning. A typical secondary school will have a principal, one or more assistant principals, a teaching faculty (usually divided by departments) and some auxiliary personnel, such as guidance counselors, cafeteria workers, janitors, etc. This complement varies according to the number of students enrolled and attending. Teachers are assigned to classes by subject, grade level, students' ability level and, at the very end of the scheduling process, by closeness of the teachers' course work to the classes that still need coverage. With very few exceptions, classes last 45-50 minutes, even though all subjects do not lend themselves well to being taught in 50-minute segments and even though adolescents' minds may not respond well to 50 minute segments. But in most schools, the class schedule, the organization of content, and students' learning rates are all organized according to the same artificial time clock.

However, in most schools, students' and subjects' styles and needs are allowed to interfere with the smooth operation of the school that demands a uniform time schedule, all day, every day. Does this organization of time maximize learning? No, clearly not. The fact that teachers of English could probably do a better job of teaching *Macbeth* in 90-minute periods three times a week, or Algebra III in two 45-minute periods every day for nine weeks, or typing in 30-minute sessions four times per day cannot be allowed to interfere with the 50-minute clock. Having a non-uniform schedule would be messy. It would be very difficult to organize and schedule; it is impossible to run biology labs after 2:30 in the afternoon, because the school bus drivers have to leave to keep the schedule. To most principals, factors that would maximize learning — learning patterns, rates, and styles and teaching techniques based on an understanding of these factors and a knowledge of the content area — cannot be allowed to take precedence over the need for a uniform set of class periods each day. However, principals have no problem scheduling a pep rally the day of the "big game" and altering class schedules to accommodate this important event. After all, the priorities must be kept in mind. How many secondary schools have athletic booster clubs and how many have academic booster clubs?

Another aspect of secondary school operation that is not conducive to maximizing learning is the departmental organization of most of these schools. Does such an organizational format best promote learning in secondary school students? The answer to this question rests on the answer to the question: "What type of learning for these students is desired?" If the answer to this question is a type of learning which promotes study of a specialized nature, of learning subject by subject without regard to the interactive, integrative aspects of various subjects, then the answer is yes, a departmental structure probably serves to promote this type of learning as well as any. On the other hand, if the type of learning that is desired is the ability to integrate material, to synthesize information, to learn the processes of pattern recognition and relationships, as well as to learn the content of specific subject areas, then the departmental structure is probably not the most productive format.

The departmental structure is a university creation, forced by the growing amount of specialized knowledge in disciplines. The amount of this expanding knowledge base in discipline areas, particularly the natural and physical sciences, has increased to the point in which specializations within current disciplines, e.g., biology, exceed the knowledge base of the entire discipline of only a few years ago. It now takes extensive graduate education to learn these discipline specializations. At the undergraduate level, studying the entire knowledge base of a discipline exceeds the time capacity for a student to become adequately familiar with, to say nothing of understanding, a few of the basic principles of the discipline.

As the knowledge base of these disciplines continues to expand, it will take longer and longer to learn the fundamental principles of each. Three possible consequences could follow. First, students could be forced to begin specializing in a particular discipline earlier and earlier in order to have sufficient time to learn it well. This process could well be forced back to the secondary school level or below. Such a consequence could well mean the end of a comprehensive liberal arts education.

Second, the format of undergraduate and graduate education could change. Undergraduate education, with an emphasis on liberal studies, could shrink to two or three years, thus allowing specialized graduate education to begin a year or two earlier. The impact on secondary schools would be to a need to better prepare students for a liberal arts college education. In some ways this format offers the most advantages. It would allow secondary schools and undergraduate programs to concentrate on liberal studies and the integration of subject matter. However, this consequence seems unlikely because too many colleges and universities have invested too much capital on the basis of four year undergraduate programs and are too dependent upon students paying four years of tuition. Also, college and university faculty members would not appreciate having to truncate their discipline at the undergraduate level. They especially would not like having to learn how to integrate and synthesize their

50

discipline with others since they really do not know how to teach such integration.

There is, of course, an alternative within this consequence. That is to make the four years of undergraduate education a truly integrating liberal arts education. This would mean specialized graduate education, probably for a greater period of time than such study now requires. It would also mean that secondary schools could concentrate, at least for those going to college, on preparing students for learning how to integrate various disciplines, and an introduction to each major discipline, or group of disciplines.

The third possible consequence could be to re-conceptualize the purposes and methods of secondary school education. Note that, in the two scenarios described above, the consequences to secondary schools were depicted only for college-bound students. Secondary schools have many students who are not going on to college, and the schools' responsibilities to these students are as great as to those preparing for college. This is one of the great dilemmas of secondary education: How to deliver quality programs to meet the needs of a diverse student population. A program design for delivering equal quality programs for all students — those desiring to learn a specific vocation, those desiring to go to college, those who have no specific plans, those who will marry immediately after graduation, those who have failed at everything — must be developed for secondary schools. It will not be an easy task. It would require re-framing and re-thinking how secondary schools are organized and administered to achieve their objectives. The key to this problem is identifying a clear set of prioritized objectives. When the mission is clearly in focus, the organization and administration of secondary schools begin to fall in place. The objectives must drive and orient the administrative theories, the organization, and the operations — not the reverse.

It is because the knowledge bases in most disciplines are expanding that the departmental structure of secondary schools must be questioned. A need now exists to formulate new structures and procedures for teaching this ever-increasing amount of knowledge. Outmoded organizational structures and administrative practices cannot be allowed to continue to shape and design the means by which this knowledge will be transmitted to students. Rather, the reverse is true. The mission of the schools and the means by which it will be implemented and achieved must shape the organizational structures and administrative theories and practices. This will call for a new conceptualization of the role of secondary schools. Such is provided in following chapters *(Chapter 12, Second-Order Changes 4, 5, 6, 7, 11, 12, 13, 15, 16 & 17)*.

51

Personnel preparation

Given the unique and difficult period of transition between childhood and adulthood, one would expect secondary school education and administrative education programs to spend considerable time studying adolescence in their preparation programs. This is not the case. Rarely has a student preparing to teach in secondary schools had more than one course in adolescent development and psychology. Many times this topic is only one of many touched upon in a course in educational psychology. Secondary school principals spend even less time studying adolescent development and behavior.

Secondary school teachers

Many of the national reports [e.g., *A Nation at Risk* (1983)] issued in recent years have commented upon secondary teachers' lack of knowledge about their major areas of concentration. Unfortunately, these reports recommended that prospective secondary school teachers take additional courses in their content area, although most secondary teachers have a major in their subject area. These prospective secondary school teachers generally have taken the same courses in their major as students who are not preparing to teach. Perhaps the faculty members teaching these disciplines (English, political science, history, etc.) are unable to integrate their disciplines' knowledge base in a coherent manner. In any event, education students often end up with a random array of non-integrated courses and bits of knowledge, which presents a problem for public education. The solution lies with school of education faculty and university administrators to force arts and science faculty to improve their teaching. The point is, secondary teachers have majored in an academic discipline, English, mathematics, biology, etc. Their depth of knowledge of that discipline is predicated on the knowledge and teaching skill of the faculty of that discipline, not the faculty of the school of education. This is a point that should not be overlooked. If secondary school teachers have an inadequate amount of subject area content, it is the arts and science faculty members responsible for these disciplines who have not adequately prepared them.

There are two flaws in believing that requiring more work in an academic discipline will improve content learning at the secondary school level. The first flaw is the belief that more knowledge of a discipline on the part of a teacher will lead to improved learning or understanding on the part of secondary students. That is not necessarily true. These teachers already have taken approximately one third of their college course work in their chosen disciplines. It hardly seems logical that to take more work will result in significant increments of learning on the part of secondary school students. However, it is possible that the same amount of work taken in a more organized and integrated fashion would result in a better understanding of the structure of the discipline. That could well lead to improved understanding of the subject area by teachers.

The second flaw relates to the emphasis on content itself. It is the difficulties of adolescence and the social factors accompanying these difficulties that cause learning problems. It is not additional work in a discipline that is needed. It is additional courses in adolescent development and behavior. The national and state reports that addressed the issue of preparation of secondary school teachers recommended that these teachers need more preparation in their discipline. Secondary teachers have an adequate amount of preparation work in their disciplines. What they lack is sufficient knowledge of their students. They know how to impart their knowledge to them. The study of adolescence should form a major portion of a secondary teacher's preparation program. But when only 21 credit hours of a 128-credit hour program (Corrigan, 1986) (or 16% of a secondary teacher's program, including student teaching) are spent in education courses, it is difficult to devote sufficient time to adolescent development, learning, or any other education topic. It is not that secondary teachers have too much work in education. Rather, they have far too little. William Bennett, former Secretary of the Department of Education, gave elementary schools higher marks for meeting student needs than are generally accorded to secondary schools. Elementary teachers take much more work, usually a third of their college program, in education courses and are generally considered to be much more student-centered than secondary teachers. In essence, they know more about the developmental needs and patterns of their students. (This topic is discussed more completely in later chapters when the type of changes necessary to improve teacher education programs are discussed.)

It is not entirely the fault of secondary teachers that they operate within a non-student-centered environment. In fact, the organization of secondary schools and preparation programs of secondary teachers seriously impede a student-centered approach regardless of a teacher's orientation toward his/her students. Two reasons account for this.

First, the funding of secondary schools, like other schools, is on the basis of enrollment *(Chapter 12, Second-Order Change 16)*. So many students attending so many days result in X number of teachers. These teachers must be apportioned across grade and ability levels and by subject area. As a result there are many teachers at the secondary level who are "teaching out of field." In addition, *A Nation at Risk* (1983) found that half of the newly employed mathematics, science, and English teachers are not qualified to teach these subjects. This means that the credentials they possess to teach that particular subject are less, often considerably so, than a teacher who majored in that subject at college. The number and percentage of teachers teaching out of field are greater in high demand fields such as math and science. The percentage is less in such fields as business, history, etc. The point is, secondary schools are currently funded on an enrollment basis. This method does not provide sufficient funds to allow comprehensive quality academic programs to be delivered to all students, especially within smaller high schools.

The second reason why secondary teachers are not student-centered involves both the nature of their preparation programs and the interactive organizational nature of secondary schools. Secondary teachers, because of their preparation programs, are taught to identify with an academic subject. Their primary identification is with an academic discipline, not with the profession of education or with children. Secondary teachers take education courses late in their college program, and then only to a minimal extent. This process does not afford the opportunity to identify with the profession of education. Ask a primary school teacher what his/her job is and he/she is most likely to respond that he/she is a teacher. Ask a secondary teacher what his/her job is and he/she is likely to respond that he/she is an English teacher, a math teacher, etc. The difference is subtle, but critical. The primary teacher identifies with the profession of education, with teaching. The secondary teacher identifies with a discipline. Does this difference in professional identification make a significant difference in the process of schooling at the secondary level? Obviously, the answer can be argued from several perspectives. Such an identification does make a significant difference. It makes a difference in terms of attitude, in terms of knowledge, and in terms of thinking about the purposes and methods of schooling.

What makes a difference is how the secondary teacher thinks about himself and about the students he teaches. Just as it makes a difference whether a physician thinks of himself or herself as a pediatrician or a neurologist, it makes a difference whether a teacher thinks of himself or herself primarily as an English teacher or a teacher who happens to teach English. The way one orients oneself professionally, the professional literature one reads, the professional meetings one attends, the way one thinks about one's job and profession are all affected. If a teacher identifies primarily with a discipline, for example English, this teacher is much more likely to be involved with professional activities which revolve around the discipline of English. The discipline is paramount. Students' learning patterns, styles, rates, and needs will tend to be subordinated to the discipline. If, on the other hand, the teacher identifies first with the teaching profession, then the learning patterns, styles, rates, and needs of students predominate. How one teaches English is based on educational factors, not the structural aspects of the discipline of English. If the objective is to assure the learning of English, then one fits English to the learning styles and needs of the students. One does not achieve this objective by forcing these various patterns, styles, and rates to accommodate to the artificial structural aspects of the discipline of English.

One's professional identification also makes a difference in terms of the amount of knowledge one gains about the profession of education. As was indicated earlier, a secondary teacher takes about 16% of his/her college program in education courses, versus 30% of the college program taken in the major field (assuming a 36-39 semester credit hour major in a 124-credit hour college degree). Many disciplines require more than 36 hours in the major. The 16% represents 21 semester credit-hours, or seven, three-credit-hour courses. If three of these courses, or nine semester hours, are devoted to student teaching, then only four courses, or 9.6%, are left for learning the knowledge base of education versus 12-13 courses for learning the knowledge base of the discipline. Of the four courses in education, one is usually devoted to methods of teaching the particular major area, one to educational psychology, one to a historical or sociological review of education, and perhaps one to a course in adolescent growth and development. These courses are just too few to cover in adequate depth the expanding knowledge base of education. It is not only that they are inadequate for coverage, but it is also a disgrace that so little coverage of education is required of prospective secondary school teachers. One wonders why schools of education are blamed for the lack of quality in America's secondary schools when they have so little contact with potential secondary teachers.

This discussion should not be interpreted to mean that prospective secondary teachers should receive less grounding in their major field. That is not the intent, nor would it be desirable. It may be that some academic majors could be taught in a more integrated fashion. That would be desirable. But today's secondary teachers do not need less content knowledge. They do need a greatly expanded knowledge base of education — one taught in a more and better integrated fashion.

One's professional identification also affects how one thinks about the purposes and methods of schooling. If a secondary teacher's primary identification is with a discipline, e.g., English, then the purposes and processes of education will tend to be framed and interpreted from the perspective of that discipline. This means the overall purposes of education, its mission, its objectives, hopes, and aspirations will be filtered and distorted by the strengths, weaknesses, politics, and needs of the particular discipline. Multiplied by the number of discipline areas within the schools, this results in a kaleidoscopic view of the profession of education and the processes of schooling. A secondary school student must find it all very confusing.

On the other hand, if a secondary teacher's primary professional identification is with the profession of education, then the perspective of the purposes of education and the processes of schooling would be much wider, much more encompassing. The various sub-disciplines of education — English, math, history — would be perceived as critical elements of the profession and its purposes and processes. The profession would be perceived as an integrated whole, focused on fostering learning in children. The role and contributions of each of these disciplines would be perceived and framed from this broader and more integrated perspective of education.

The combination of these three differences, i.e., attitude, knowledge, and purposes and processes of schooling on the part of secondary teachers, has a powerful cumulative effect. Secondary teachers frame the profession of education and their students through the eye of their academic major, rather than framing their academic specialty and their students from the perspective of the education profession. Would such a difference in perception lead to significant improvements in learning? This is an empirical question, and to date there is no direct data to suggest a conclusion. There is, however, some indirect evidence. We know from the national reports issued in the past few years that secondary education is perceived as being of poor quality, while elementary education received higher grades. We know that achievement test scores have been improving at the elementary level but declining at the secondary level. We know that the way in which elementary teachers are prepared differs significantly from the way secondary teachers are prepared, primarily in the amount of education coursework taken. We know that elementary teachers tend to be far more child-centered than secondary teachers. The evidence seems to point clearly to a logical conclusion: Secondary teachers need to be trained differently, both in content and in professional identification *(Chapter 13, Second-Order Changes 21, 22, 23, 24, 30, 32 & 33).*

Administrators

It was mentioned earlier in this section that secondary teachers do not generally take more than one course on adolescent psychology or growth and development during their preparation program. The same is true for most principals of secondary schools. In fact, most principals do not study adolescent development at all during their administration preparation program. They do spend a considerable amount of time studying theories of administration and school law. The inference is obvious. Theories of administration and school law become the focal points for administering the schools, but the study and understanding of the group for which the schools exist is lost. If the objective of the secondary schools is to promote learning, to increase understanding of oneself as a maturing adult, then secondary schools should be organized and administered in ways that promote such objectives. Theories of administration for secondary schools that are not derived from the mission of secondary schools and from an understanding of adolescent psychology and development should be abandoned.

Administrator training programs, departments of public instruction, and local boards of education must equally share the blame for this situation. Administration training programs are at fault because they do not require a study of adolescent psychology or development. State departments of public instruction are at fault because they generally issue administrator certificates, not specified as to level or type of school, i.e., elementary or secondary principal. These departments are also to blame because they do not require the study of adolescence in their program approval guidelines. Local boards of education are at fault because most have a policy of hiring or promoting principals to secondary schools without requiring them to demonstrate evidence of studying and understanding adolescence as a basis for administering a secondary school *(Chapter 12, Second-Order Change 3, 6, 7 & 17; Chapter 14, Second-Order Changes 34-36).*

Summary

In summary, secondary schools are beset by a host of problems impeding delivery of the most effective learning programs to their students. These problems include the mission, organization and administration, as well as the quality of professional preparation teachers and administrators of these schools receive. These criticisms go to the very heart of today's secondary schools. They tear at their most sacred assumptions and are not to be taken lightly. But, if we are serious about achieving significant educational reform, which will be long lasting, and which will be more than cosmetic, then these are the basics that must be re-designed.

4 Problem identification in teacher education

The problems of education in America are usually perceived to be those of public education. These problems are often thought to be the result of marginally prepared teachers who manage to graduate from inadequate and non-rigorous preparation programs. To some extent this is a valid and accurate perception. There are teacher preparation programs that should not be in business. As in any profession, some students who are inadequately prepared do manage to graduate and obtain teaching positions. This is not, however, the most serious problem of teacher preparation.

The most critical and serious problems of teacher preparation are complex, subtle and insidious. They involve the reward culture of universities, the lack of coordination of teacher preparation with the mission of public schools, the objectives and program control of teacher preparation, the resources made available to teacher preparation programs, and the quality of teacher preparation program faculty members. These factors have not been recognized or addressed in efforts to reform teacher education. *(Third-Order Changes 1, 2 and 4)*. The reform efforts implemented in teacher education have, in fact, increased the very problems which stand most in the way of improving the quality of teacher preparation programs. As in the case of public education, there must be a change in the change process which has marked efforts at reforming teacher preparation programs. In addition, a new perception must be developed of the need to coordinate public and teacher education program improvement efforts.

Schools, colleges and departments of education are, in most instances, held captive, dominated and controlled by a university culture which does not hold teacher preparation in high regard. *(Chapter 10, Third-Order Change #3)*. As a consequence, efforts at substantial reform of teacher preparation programs have usually intensified the conditions preventing the needed changes. In much the same fashion that public education is held captive to external social, political and economic forces, teacher

59

preparation programs are held captive to an archaic, political and intellectually rigid university culture.

These problems which afflict teacher preparation and impede development of improvement efforts can be examined from at least two perspectives. The first includes those generic problems which pervade most universities and colleges with teacher preparation programs. The second perspective involves an examination of problems specific to preparation programs for elementary teachers, secondary school teachers, and teachers who work across the K-12 spectrum. This chapter discusses the generic problems. The problems associated with specific levels of teacher preparation are discussed in Chapter 13, along with necessary changes for both the generic and specific problems.

The context

A widely held view of education is that the quality of teacher education programs is not good. Unfortunately, there appears to be some truth and validity to this perception. It is important to examine this perception in an attempt to ascertain the extent of its validity, to determine the "what" of the problem, and to recommend changes which would improve the quality of preparation programs and the quality of the graduates these programs produce.

Two factors drive this need for change of preparation programs. First, there is a need to improve many, although not all, of the current 1200-plus teacher training programs in the United States. This need for improvement has been well documented in the numerous national and state reports published in recent years. Although the recommendations for change which accompanied these reports left untouched many of the most fundamental areas needing change, the perception that change and improvement are necessary is a valid one. *(Chapter 13, Second-Order Changes 18, 19, 20, 23, 25, 30)*. It is important, however, to distinguish between the need for change and improvement and the probability of success of the recommendations proposed by the reports dealing with educational policy and practice. None of the reform reports and recommendations that dealt with public education the need to change the solutions attempted previously.

The second factor driving the need for change of educational personnel preparation programs is one consistent with the theme of this book. The current structure, objectives, and content of elementary and secondary teacher education programs do not prepare teachers to produce significantly improved learning outcomes. It will require a series of second-order

60

changes of these programs to bring about the improvements necessary, and to prepare graduates with the knowledge base and skills necessary for assuming the responsibilities outlined in Chapters 11 and 12.

What is the "what" of the problem of teacher preparation programs? There are several, depending on which programs are being examined. There are some generic problems in teacher preparation programs which affect all such programs, regardless of the level, e.g., elementary, or the specific content area, e.g., music, history. These are largely problems of the university context in which these programs are embedded. These problems will be discussed first.

There are also changes specific to each level of preparation program. *(Chapter 13, Second-Order Changes 21, 22, 26-30)*. Problems in elementary programs differ from those in secondary programs (Confrey, 1982). These programs have a different set of problems from those which prepare students to work with all 12 grade levels, e.g., music. Programs which prepare teachers have different problems from those designed to prepare administrators and supervisors, and those programs which prepare support personnel, e.g., school counselors or psychologists, have yet another set of problems associated with them.

Generic problem identification

The basic questions for teacher preparation programs are "What they should be prepared to teach their students?" and "How should such programs be structured?" *(Chapter 13, Second-Order Changes 21, 22, 23, 24, 26-31)*. The answers to these questions demand a forward-looking attitude, a futuristic view of what children will need to know when they complete their public education. This perspective is consistent with Morrish's (1976) notion of creative change. As with public education reform, attempts to reform teacher preparation have been based on a deficit perspective. However, reform of teacher preparation based on a deficit model is almost sure to fail in the long term. Such a reform process is focused on curing a specific problem, not on designing a framework and process which will enable the educational system's structure and functions to achieve clearly specified goals.

Previous efforts to improve teacher preparation programs have been based on a deficit perspective of problems in public education. This has hindered the development of a perspective that includes public and teacher education as inter-related elements of the same system. It has also prevented the realization that, in addition to these inter-related problems, each also has a unique set of problems brought about by their specific political, social and economic contexts. Efforts to improve public and teacher education must address both the inter-related and specific contexts in a coordinated fashion.

In order to do this most successfully, a specified mission priority for the public schools is needed. This mission priority can then serve as a guide for decision-making in improving teacher preparation programs. The effective achievement of the public schools' mission would become the goal of teacher preparation programs.

There must be a sense of what education wishes to achieve for the betterment of children, and, thereby, society. Without such a mission, education will continue to resist change. Without such a mission, teacher preparation programs will continue as they have in the past, preparing students to do more of the same as they have done previously. In order to achieve second-order change, teacher preparation programs must have a common sense of *the primary purpose of education.* — to foster the most effective learning and personal development in all children in the most efficient manner possible. Schools do not exist primarily to teach reading, history, music, or any other specific subject. Schools exist to enhance learning. These various subjects are critical for learning, and to learning, but individually, no one subject exists as the prime purpose of education. *(Chapter 13, Second-Order Changes 21-22).*

The purpose of teacher education programs should be to produce graduates who are able to foster learning and personal-social development in each child they will work with during their professional life. The basic barrier to accomplishing this goal in most universities is one of values. Many university faculty, particularly those not directly involved in applied or professional programs, are more concerned with advancing their discipline's knowledge base than they are with the educational success of students in the classroom. There may be nothing wrong with this attitude as long as it does not prevent equal recognition, support and rewards of faculty and professional programs concerned with successfully preparing students to teach children.

There is another perception in universities, including many schools of education, which handicaps the development and improvement of sound teacher education programs. This is a perception that is concerned with the goals and purposes of a school of education, and the allocation of resources for program development within a school of education. Most, if not all, schools, colleges, or departments of education began with the primary purpose of preparing teachers for the public schools. As time went on, other professional training programs were added to these initial programs of teacher preparation. Many current education units now include a variety of programs to prepare students to assume many different roles within the public schools. Many of these more recent programs also prepare students to assume positions in agencies outside the schools. For example, many counselor education programs prepare students to become school counselors, but also to assume positions in mental health agencies, or to enter private practice. Many programs in educational research and evaluation were added which do not lead to teacher certification, but are necessary support programs for graduate and, particularly, doctoral training.

The addition of these and other programs, many at the graduate level only, may well have been a logical step in the development of a school of education program at one time. However, such programs are costly and demand significant resources if they are to be effective. There is nothing wrong with adding these programs to a school of education, but they tend to dilute the prime focus of the education unit, that of preparing teachers. In many of these programs the faculty members are more interested in attracting resources for their own program than they are in developing the teacher education programs around which the school of education revolves, and which give meaning to the term, "a school of education." The basic dilemma is this: Should a school of education's priority for resource allocation and development be given to programs which are not directly involved with the preparation of teachers, or should available resources for development go to those programs which are the strongest, regardless of their involvement in teacher preparation? This dilemma is made worse by three critical factors — the university culture, available resources, and program quality.

The university culture

As matters stand now, teacher preparation programs are primarily responsible to the institution of higher education within which they exist. *(Chapter 13, Second-Order Changes 32 & 33)*. Such institutions pride themselves on being independent in determining the appropriate objectives for their students and the means by which these objectives will be achieved. University faculty do not typically allow consumer needs to determine either the goals or the methods by which teacher candidates will be educated. To be sure, many schools, colleges, and departments of education have practitioner representatives sitting on their coordinating councils. In fact, such representation is a requirement for accreditation from the National Council for Accreditation of Teacher Education (NCATE), and many states' accreditation criteria require such representation. Such representatives do not, however, see their role as effecting concordance between the goals of the school, college, or department of education. Even

63

if it were, two major obstacles stand in the way. First, such representatives are usually from one school system. In many instances, these representatives are chosen from different school systems on an annual or biannual basis, so that the teacher education unit at the university will not offend those systems who are not asked to provide a representative in any given year. Thus, these representatives could not speak for any school system except his/her own in seeking a concordance of objectives. Secondly, these representatives are often from the ranks of teachers and, as such, present particular discipline biases, not an overall view of the profession of education.

A much larger and more significant obstacle exists — the very purpose of the teacher education unit itself. The current purposes of teacher preparation programs represent the most significant barrier to achieving second-order change and improvement in teacher preparation programs. Most universities encourage and reward research and publication by faculty members. Academic respectability and advancement are gained in each department according to the prestige of the faculty and the amount of research and publications these faculty generate. Such research is undeniably a critical aspect of a university's role in our society. The continued expansion of our knowledge base in all disciplines enables universities to exist with few restrictions. Such unfettered pursuit of knowledge, as critical and important as it is, also brings with it a set of problems which have been only minimally addressed, and not solved in university debates. It is assumed by many university faculty and administrators that engaging in research makes one a better teacher, although there is little evidence to support this assertion. A counter perception which is heard much less often seems to have equal validity: That those qualities and characteristics which make for the best *researcher* are not those which make for the best *teacher*.

(Chapter 13, Second-Order Change 19). Academic units which are concerned with advancing the knowledge base of the discipline (and which are not concerned with the application of this knowledge, or the training of practitioners of the discipline) tend to dominate and control the criteria which all faculty must meet in order to be promoted and gain tenure. Jencks and Riesman (1968) addressed this issue some twenty years ago. They described the manner in which graduate schools, research scholars, and the academic profession itself had come to dominate higher education and faculty promotions with their emphasis on research, publication, and national reputation. Keller (1983) observed that the past 30 years of higher education has not been marked by great teaching or dedication to student growth. Hodgkinson (1986) asserts that faculty members who devote themselves to quality teaching can usually count on being denied tenure.

64

Many university administrators actively support and reinforce the application of research-oriented criteria. Thus, a faculty member who wishes to be promoted and/or gain tenure must meet these criteria. In an applied program, such as education, this presents a serious and difficult dilemma for faculty members. This is the dilemma. Education is an applied program. It prepares students to assume positions of great responsibility, teaching our children. But education, unlike other professions where the entry level to the profession is after graduate education, allows entry to the profession after the undergraduate level. The vast majority of teacher preparation programs require only four years. Thus, education faculty are faced with taking 18-year-olds and preparing them to assume full responsibility for a classroom by the time they are 22. This requires a tremendous amount of dedication on the part of the faculty, and a commitment of time, energy, and involvement that would probably not be necessary if these students were at the graduate level.

Education faculty must supervise undergraduate students in the field as they practice observing children and learning how to teach them. This supervision requires more time, energy, and involvement by the faculty. Schwebel (1982) found that education faculty reported spending 10% of their time doing research and scholarly writing and 31% of their time with administrative matters. In contrast, faculty in agriculture and the biological and social sciences reported 22% and 14% for these same activities respectively. Education faculty must spend significant amounts of time supervising and preparing young undergraduate students to assume responsibility for a classroom. An applied program, e.g., education, requires more administrative time for program coordination, and student placement, than does a non-applied program. These activities are necessary if the program is to run smoothly and students are to receive the attention they need and deserve. Most universities do not recognize these responsibilities as worthy for meeting the criteria for promotion and tenure. Yet, if an education faculty member is to do his or her job properly, these are the responsibilities that must be carried out. And if they are carried out properly, there is not much time left to conduct research.

An education faculty member is faced then with a cruel dilemma, to choose between doing what is responsible for his/her students, or doing what is necessary to remain in the university. This is an especially cruel choice for young faculty members who have not yet earned tenure or a professional reputation. If a faculty member does earn tenure and the job security that goes along with it, then there is more freedom to choose how he/she will spend his/her professional time. The data on this issue seem rather clear. Most tenured education faculty do not engage in research or publish beyond a limited amount.

65

Clark (1978) found that the median level of institutional productivity of schools, colleges, and departments of education was zero! Clark pointed out that this was partially a function of type of institution. Virtually all of the baccalaureate institutions offering teacher education programs were low or non-producers, and only eleven percent of the doctoral institutions were so classified. At a Colloquium held in 1984, "Increasing Research Capacity in Schools of Education: A Policy Inquiry and Dialogue," Gideonse and Joseph (1984) concluded that this state of affairs had not changed significantly between 1978 and 1984.

Champion (1984) asserts that research involvement and activities are not usual behaviors of education faculty. Those faculty who do manage to conduct research usually do so "out-of-hide." Champion concluded that research is considered of no more value than other information sources and that teacher educators did not appear to be grasping for scientific evidence to develop principles or rules for teaching.

Schwebel (1982) concluded that education was less productive in generating knowledge than agriculture and the biological sciences. He also questioned the low knowledge productivity in a profession that accounted for 20% of the doctorates conferred annually in the United States.

The conclusion seems clear. Education faculty produce less research than faculty in other disciplines. The reasons for this are less clear. They are complex. Serious and significant alterations in teacher education programs and university structures will be needed to remedy this situation. Education faculty do spend significant amounts of time in teaching and with their students. The result? Most education faculty members receive low academic respectability from their university colleagues because they choose to spend their time preparing their students to teach our children, rather than engaging in research which may or may not be useful to the larger educational community.

Astin (1985) attributes this perception partially to the history of teacher colleges. In the 1950s there were more than 200 teacher colleges in the United States . Today, there are few, if any. Most of these teacher colleges were converted into state colleges or state universities. Astin asserts that since teacher colleges were lower in status than flagship universities, they received a lower amount of funding. In order to achieve more funds, they attempted to copy the value structure of the flagship universities, including minimizing teacher education, a low prestige symbol, and increasing graduate and research capabilities.

Dunham (1969) was more direct in his conclusions. He asserted that, because of teacher colleges' attempts to emulate flagship universities, many first-rate teachers colleges became third-rate universities. Dunham also attributes the problem of low status of schools of education to the value

66

system of most college/university professors and administrators. According to Dunham, one of the major elements of this value system is a higher value on the *demonstration* of intellect over the *development* of intellect. At the same time "pure" knowledge is valued over "practical" knowledge. This suggests that these academicians place greater value on *having* knowledge (the academic department), rather than on *applying* knowledge (a professional school such as education).

Clifford and Gutherie (1988) make this point clearly. Their book contrasts the schools of education at Berkeley and UCLA. Berkeley was noted for its faculty's research and knowledge production, while UCLA had developed around professional schools, and, although it had developed a commitment to research and scholarship, it maintained a professional practice and public school orientation that permitted it to survive and thrive. At Berkeley, which focused on the arts and science disciplines and their reward structure, the school of education struggled noticeably and nearly failed.

Dyer and O'Connor (1983) concluded that university administrators tended to support programs that: (1) attract large numbers of students, (2) pay their way through grants and contracts, and (3) bring prestige to the university based on the caliber of the faculty's research and reputation.

Another significant factor, perhaps the most troublesome of all, affects educational units in university settings. This is the attitude displayed, mostly by arts and sciences faculty members, toward the quality of the educational faculty and the programs of the educational unit. This attitude is usually a negative one (Ducharme, 1985), or worse, one of indifference. These faculty tend to decry the quality of the education faculty, students, and programs. They condemn the lack of academic rigor, program quality, and research. They blame the poor quality of students they have in their classrooms on the poor quality of the secondary schools and secondary school teachers and the schools of education in universities that allowed these teachers to receive teaching certificates. They criticize the reasoning skills, math skills, and poor writing abilities of these students in their classrooms, blaming everything on the poor quality of the schools of education.

What these criticisms reveal is the ignorance of these arts and science faculty about the educational system. They fail to realize that it is not the schools of education that teach English and composition; departments of English in colleges of arts and sciences do. Schools of education do not teach mathematics. Departments of mathematics in the arts and sciences do. The critics forget how many times arts and sciences faculty have argued that one of the major strengths of the arts and sciences is the ability to teach students to think clearly and rationally and to express themselves clearly in both written and oral communication.

This attitude on the part of many arts and sciences faculty is a substantial barrier to improvement of school of education programs. It significantly impedes the development of cooperative programs that are necessary and desirable, not only for change and improvement of educational programs, but also for improved program integration, teaching, and research on the part of all concerned. Schwebel (1985) attributes this attitude on the part of arts and science faculty to a clash of cultures. He perceives the mission of the arts and science faculty as producing the leadership of the nation and to produce new knowledge. The mission of education faculty, according to Schwebel, is to produce teachers who would then produce the mass of workers and the unemployed. Although Schwebel's perceptions may be a bit extreme, he does raise a valid question. The mission of colleges of arts and sciences and that of schools of education are quite different. It is unfortunate that neither universities nor their administrators have been flexible or creative enough to develop a philosophy and set of operating principles that are broad enough to encompass more than one mission for the university.

What arts and sciences faculty must realize is that public school teachers in America, particularly in the secondary schools, must teach all subjects, not just the particular one with which a university professor is concerned. And they must do so under appalling conditions of employment and for a meager salary. University professors have a far easier professional life than do elementary and secondary school teachers, and they are far more richly rewarded.

In recent years the purpose of school of education faculty members and the programs for which they are responsible has been simply survival. They have been faced with too many students, too few resources, and too little respect or understanding from their professional colleagues, while attempting an impossible job under impossible conditions. It is to the credit of these faculty that they have done as well as they have under recent conditions. Some education programs are not only below par, but a disgrace to the profession of education. Such programs should not be allowed to exist. Regardless of the reason for sub-par performance, such programs should be put out of business and prohibited from graduating and recommending students for teacher certification.

The resource situation

Diminished respect for education units within the university setting has caused most education units to be denied resources to fund their programs adequately (Peseau, 1980, 1982; Ducharme, 1982). *(Chapter 13, Second-*

Order Change 25). The data on this issue is quite clear. Professor Bruce Peseau has been collecting data on the financial situation of public doctoral programs of education for a number of years. Although his surveys and reports (1980, 1982) have been restricted to these institutions, there is no reason to suspect that his conclusions are not equally valid for education units which do not grant the doctorate.

Among other results, Peseau concluded that the average direct cost of instruction for a teacher education student was 65% as much as for a public school student, and only half as much as the average cost for students from all university disciplines. In addition, Peseau found that, in less than 18% of the institutions responding to his surveys, the direct cost of instruction equaled the average provided for a public school student. He concluded that university administrators who govern academic affairs and who allocate university budgets were responsible for this inadequate funding of teacher education programs.

Schools of education enroll large numbers of students, primarily at the undergraduate level. As Peseau's data indicate, the funds from these students are often used to support other, less well enrolled programs, not teacher education programs. In order to conduct research effectively, significant numbers of qualified, full-time graduate students are necessary. Most graduate students in education are part-time, more interested in advancing their professional skills than in learning to conduct research, which is neither highly supported nor valued in the public schools. Schools of education do not meet the criteria for attracting support from university administrators suggested by Dyer and O'Connor.

The resource base for education units within most universities is much less than other units within the university, and it is inadequate to meet the responsibilities of these units. Most university administrators have used the education unit within their campus as a source of funds for supporting other academic units on the campus. Thus, educational units on many university campuses have not been funded in direct measure to the number of students and/or the number of student credit hours they generate. Too few faculty members work with too many students. And if educational units attempted to limit the number of students entering its programs, university administrators cut the number of faculty because the unit was losing students. This is a Catch-22 situation, one that educational units are bound to lose.

In such circumstances program units within a school of education will demand and fight for scarce resources to assure their own survival and development. Decisions concerning resource allocation in such circumstances are not likely to be based on concepts and visions of long-term development, but rather on the basis of short-term need and individual

69

program maintenance. Faculty who are responsible for individual programs within an educational unit, or any other for that matter, cannot be expected to generate rules which would give their programs less support than programs they perceive as inferior or lacking in academic quality and rigor.

Teacher education program quality

The question of program quality in teacher education preparation programs is a major issue in teacher education. As valid as they may be, the issues of faculty member perception, resource availability, and administrative support are not the prime issues for concern. It matters not whether a university president or chancellor will provide the resources necessary to develop a quality program, or if university administrators do not comprehend the importance of working with undergraduate students who shortly will be responsible for the learning of hundreds of students. It matters not the attitude of faculty members who are ignorant of the complexity and difficulties of working in today's public schools. What should matter is that the faculty and programs of schools of education be the very best that can be developed. Our children deserve the best teachers, and if an education unit cannot assure that their graduates measure up to this goal, they should get out of the business. Unfortunately, this would affect many of our teacher education programs. The truth is, there are many teacher education programs operating today that should not be in the business. The report of the National Commission for Excellence in Teacher Education (1985) concluded that many criticisms levied against teacher education programs were valid. The writers of this report recommended teacher education programs move beyond the very best currently in existence.

The reasons for this poor quality are many and complex. *(Chapter 13, Second-Order Changes 21-24)*. This assertion should be taken neither as an indictment of all teacher education programs, nor of all teachers. There are very good teacher education programs and there are very good teachers that graduate, even from poor programs. The goal should be to assure that all teacher education programs are as good as possible, and that all graduates from these programs are "safe to teach."

As indicated previously, this is not currently the case. Lack of resources, administrator perceptions of the usefulness of these programs, and faculty perceptions from the arts and sciences each play a role in limiting the quality of many teacher education preparation programs. However, none of these reasons explain the poor quality in these programs. Educational faculty in teacher education preparation programs must assume the major

70

responsibility for this lack of quality. The five major reasons for poor quality in teacher education preparation programs include: (1) lack of program purpose; (2) lack of coordinated program objectives; (3) lack of appropriate curriculum and content; (4) lack of an appropriate structure for program development and change; and, (5) faculty inadequately prepared for instituting program development initiatives. Not all of these problems are inherent in every teacher education preparation program. Some programs have none of these; others may have one or more. Obviously, the more of these problems that are inherent in any program, the more likely the program is deficient and the more difficult it will be to accomplish change and improvement of such programs.

Lack of program purpose

In the first years of programs specifically designed to prepare teachers, the purposes of such programs were clearly defined. The responsibilities of graduates of these programs were specific. Graduates of these programs were responsible for teaching the basic skills of reading, writing, and mathematics plus religion and moral behavior (Douglass and Grieder, 1948). Since the time of these basic, yet complex responsibilities, the world has become much more complicated and the responsibilities of teachers have become more uncertain. *(Chapter 13, Second-Order Changes 21, 22, 26-30)*. Obviously, teachers' current responsibilities still include the basic skills of reading, writing, and mathematics for all students. But beyond this level there is confusion. What courses for which students for what purpose? Should students of public schools be taught to get along with each other? Should all be expected to master the beliefs of equal opportunity for all, regardless of what they may be taught in the home, or see in the behavior of adults or on TV? Should all students be taught to master the necessity for, and intricacies of, social interaction and reform? Should all students be taught the politics of international relations? The list could go on and on.

What is the prime role of the schools? The first objective of the schools is to teach students how to learn and what to learn, and equally important, to foster their personal-social development. It is imperative that the goals of public schools coordinate with the objectives of teacher preparation programs. Unless the schools are clear about their mission priorities (which means that the general public must be sure of their priorities for the schools), teacher preparation programs will not be able to focus their efforts. They will continue to dilute their efforts. There will be unnecessary and counterproductive allocation of limited resources to non-critical programs, and there will be no standard purposes and priorities for teacher preparation. To improve children's learning and development, the purposes of public schools and teacher preparation programs must be established and brought into concordance so that teacher education programs can have a clear focus and set of priorities for their programs.

Lack of coordinated program objectives

If the mission priorities of teacher education programs are obscure, then the specific objectives of these programs are also uncertain. *(Chapter 13, Second-Order Changes 21-22)*. This tends to be the case in most teacher education preparation programs. In the absence of clearly defined and discernible program purposes, the objectives of such programs tend to become a series of disconnected and unrelated tasks that students are expected to master. This is the logical end result when there is no overall guiding purpose to teacher preparation programs, and no common knowledge base and set of skills which teachers are expected to foster and assist public school students to attain.

Without overall program objectives in teacher education programs, education has become a splintered profession. Each sub-specialty in the education profession defines its own purposes after developing the specific program objectives that continue and develop the discipline. Thus, history, physical education, music, English, etc., each develops the objectives it wishes to instill into the overall purposes of education. And so education as a profession incorporates all such objectives and purposes without a unifying or integrating conceptual framework, purpose, or objectives. Without such an underlying and unifying purpose and set of objectives, teacher education programs each tend to go their own way, resulting in teacher education programs on individual university campuses with no common denominator, except requiring a liberal studies background and some courses in professional education.

Efforts on the part of professional education faculty to change this situation usually ends in defeat for the educational faculty (Ducharme, 1985; Schwebel, 1985). *(Chapter 13, Second-Order Changes 32 &33)*. Educational faculty suffer from a lack of status and prestige on most university campuses (Borrowman, 1956; Schwebel, 1985). Many times their efforts are seen as attempts to generate more student credit hours without any improvement in the academic rigor or substantive aspects of the education programs. Unfortunately, many times this perception is valid. At other times, such efforts end in defeat because no other program wants to give up credit hours to any other program, especially education, since program funding is supposed to be based on the number of student credit hours generated (Freeman, 1980). Still other times, such efforts end in defeat because education faculty cannot agree on what the common knowledge base for all teachers should be, regardless of the sub-specialty within education. The end result is that there are any number of teacher education sub-unit programs, each attempting to achieve its own objectives and fulfill its own purpose. The lack of consistency between the purposes and objectives of public schools and teacher education preparation programs, and among teacher education preparation programs themselves continues to grow wider.

Many people will defend this situation as desirable, citing the rights and prerogatives of academic freedom for the faculty of each program area or discipline to determine what is in the best interests of their students. At least two arguments to this view may be made. First, the same courtesy is often not extended to the faculty of the school, college, or department of education. Secondly, and far more importantly, the rights of academic freedom must be balanced against academic responsibility and the needs of our children and society. When children's needs are greater, then academic freedom must give way. The development and implementation of a common knowledge base for all teacher education preparation programs illustrates this situation. Without a common, core knowledge base to support discipline-based specialization, education will remain a many-splintered profession, with each sub-discipline of education defending its own turf, rather than developing a common program core which would better serve teacher education students and our children.

Lack of appropriate curriculum and content

The curriculum of teacher education programs has not changed much in the past few decades (Corrigan, 1985). *(Chapter 13, Second-Order Change, 30)*. To be sure, there have been some additions, generally brought about by some legal mandate with which schools of education have had to comply. The addition of a course or two in response to the dictates of PL 94-142 is a case in point. Left to themselves, it is unlikely that many schools of education would have instituted a required course on handicapped children for all teachers. Again, the laws of second-order change. Few schools, colleges, or departments of education can generate their own change. Thus, the curriculum has remained relatively static in most schools of education for decades, except, as noted above, when there has been a response to an external force mandating some change, usually through adding a requirement of a course. The difficulty in approaching change through this type of add-on process is, of course, that change and improvement of the

73

teacher education curriculum does not proceed from any conceptual base, purpose, or set of coherent and internally consistent set of program objectives. Thus, the curriculum reflects a patchwork of individual courses designed to deal with a specific problem or topic, but without an integrating conceptual base.

In the latest round of reform recommendations, major changes in the curriculum of teacher education programs were not mentioned. There are two reasons for this. First, many reform committees and task forces may have felt that curriculum matters were best left to the faculty, and, secondly, they may not have perceived the importance of curricular change for teacher education programs.

The latter of these possibilities is understandable. The former reason, and by far the most dangerous, is also understandable. Faculty in these programs are unable to generate the rules necessary to achieve second-order change of their own programs. If such change would cancel a faculty member's favorite course, change is unlikely to occur. Faculty do not like to recommend that another faculty member's course be deleted. After all, the same may happen to them someday. It is also understandable that a faculty member would not accept his/her course being deleted from the program. A faculty member has usually invested years in developing and refining a particular course. The faculty member's ego and a good part of his/her professional life is invested in the course. It is not easy in such circumstances to accept that such investment may no longer be considered vital for the education of students. Yet, second-order change of teacher education curricula is a vital need if teacher education programs are to significantly improve. Without a dramatic change in the curriculum, it is unlikely that significant improvements in the learning outcomes of children will occur.

Lack of an appropriate program development structure

Most schools, colleges, and departments of education have no formal structure or process for considering, recommending, or requiring program change and development. Many do have an executive committee or teacher education coordinating committee. These committees generally deal with problems of administration and coordination. Most educational units do have a "curriculum committee." Any of these committees may be responsible for staying abreast of changes and developments in teacher education and for recommending appropriate changes in program content or curriculum. For the most part, however, these recommendations are seldom issued and less often heeded. There are few educational units that have program development committees, or program review committees, or committees specifically charged with recommending appropriate changes in program format or content.

There is usually also a similar committee at the university level. The responsibility of these committees, at least in theory, is to review proposals for new courses submitted by individual faculty or program units. These committees spend a great deal of time making sure that the reference list for these proposed courses are up to date, that the course title is short enough to fit into the catalogue description, and that the course number proposed is not already assigned to another course. Seldom, if ever, do these committees spend time attempting to understand how the proposed course is logically related to the existing program or how it extends the program's conceptual base. In most cases, each course is considered as an item isolated from any conceptual base of the program or the relation of the course to others in the program. Efforts, oftentimes requirements, are made to assure that the course does not overlap significantly with any other course in the university, or that other academic units on the campus do not object to the course being offered. It is, of course, rational on the part of these committees to assume that the faculty member or program unit proposing the course has developed the course from the conceptual base of the program. Education units, without a sense of purpose or a conceptual base from which to operate, usually cannot describe the relation of the course to a conceptual or knowledge base of the program.

Another feature of these curriculum committees is that they generally review course proposals submitted by departments. However, they are not charged with *initiating* reviews of the curriculum of various program units or with *recommending* changes in the curriculum of various programs. This is left to the faculty of each program area or academic unit. As discussed earlier, this is not usually a viable option, since faculty are very reluctant to recommend a change which may result in another faculty member's course being denied or deleted from the curriculum.

In educational units, most changes in the curriculum come about as a response to external mandates. The conclusion seems inescapable. Educational units, without a conceptual base, do not have a logical structure or process for assessing the need or direction of program improvement. The review mechanisms of most schools, colleges, and departments of education do not provide for the initiation of change. Neither do the review mechanisms of universities provide the impetus for such change within the educational unit. Faculty within these educational units have demonstrated neither the capacity for initiating second-order changes, nor significant change of program format or curriculum.

75

Lack of an adequately prepared faculty

The common denominator to the issues and problems in teacher education programs described above is the quality of the faculty involved in teacher education preparation programs. *(Chapter 13, Second-Order Changes 18 & 20).* Faculty quality is an extremely elusive concept, almost impossible to measure. The measures for assessing faculty quality vary significantly, and many of these methods are suspect. Perhaps the single most common measure of faculty quality is his/her rate of publication, preferably in prestigious refereed journals.

However, few faculty in schools, colleges, and departments of education conduct research, unless they are seeking tenure or promotion. Corrigan (1985) perceives education faculty as more interested in attempting to gain the rewards of the system, and to satisfy the promotion and tenure criteria of arts and science faculty, than in working to improve the working conditions and curriculum within schools.

Education professors are generally good teachers, although their lectures are often out of date. They spend enormous amounts of time working with their students, and most have a heavy load of supervision. They tend to be an aging teaching force. Most were hired during the high enrollment days of teacher education during the late 1950's and early 1960's. In 1975, 53.5% of the males and 54.6% of the females teaching in post secondary institutions were over age 41. In 1984, these figures were 71.1% and 59.6% respectively (Carnegie Foundation for the Advancement of Teaching, 1985). Many gained tenure early in their academic careers and have had job security for much of their professional careers. For the 1986-87 academic year, 63% of all faculty in public institutions were tenured (Ottinger, 1987). Many are within a year or two of reaching the age bracket of 60-65. Keller (1983) estimated that, by the year 2000, over half of U.S. faculty members will be over the age 55. This should bring sounder judgment, maturity, and experience to institutions. It will also bring a larger percentage of faculty who do little, who abuse tenure, and who do not keep current in their field. As Keller (1983) has described it, U.S. institutions could well have a geriatric faculty.

During the high enrollment days of the 50's and 60's, many faculty made a career of changing jobs every few years. This was a real benefit for program development and change, for it kept new ideas circulating and under review. However, as enrollment began to drop, new jobs became harder and harder to find, families were growing, and constant moving was less possible. Many of these faculty located in a university setting where they have remained for the past 15-20 years.

Another significant impact of the declining enrollment was that new positions in teacher education units were not available because enrollment decreased. Therefore, new and younger faculty were not being employed, and their new ideas and continual input of vitality were lost.

In recent years another change in the educational environment has had an impact on education faculty. There has been a dramatic drop in the grant funds available from the federal government for education. The loss of these funds reduced significantly the ability of education faculty to obtain support for experimenting with new ideas, new programs, new means of increasing learning, and improving the means of delivering educational services.

The cumulative effect of these developments has shaped the current faculty composition in educational units. They are an older group, protective of what they have, proud of what they have accomplished, and resistant to change if such change would mean that they would have to learn new concepts and change the way they are currently operating. One wonders whether they have the interest, energy, or time to develop and/or implement significant changes in format or curriculum of the programs for which they are responsible.

This is a critical observation and question, for it is upon the shoulders of existing faculty that changes in teacher education programs rest. Although the increasing enrollment in teacher education programs, and the demands for reform, will undoubtedly result in increased faculty positions for these programs, it is to these older faculty that the burden of leadership for change will fall.

There is also a question of attitude and behavior from these faculty. If Corrigan (1985) is correct in observing that education faculty are more interested in obtaining system rewards than working to improve conditions of schooling, where will the leadership for change efforts come from? What about the reality that promotion and tenure criteria do not favor the work necessary to improve teacher education programs or public school efforts? What attitude and behavior will education faculty display when called upon to exert leadership for significant change when such change may well require that they exclude what they have been doing all their professional life, in order to include something entirely foreign to their way of thinking? Very few universities have faculty development programs which address this need. Attitude change is a very difficult goal to accomplish. Yet the probability of achieving significant change in teacher education programs rests on just that change.

Summary

The preceding discussions have outlined the generic problems associated with teacher preparation programs. These problems pervade the context of most teacher preparation programs. Problems of university culture, the priority activities for reward and prestige, attitudes of indifference towards teacher preparation programs by many university faculty members and administrators, and the lack of adequate resources each contribute to the failures of teacher preparation programs. Cumulatively, they constitute a significant barrier to improvement efforts of teacher preparation, and they have neither been recognized as such, nor addressed in reform agendas.

However, faculty members of schools, colleges and departments of education must assume the major responsibility for the failures of teacher preparation. Allowing themselves to be maintained within a captive condition, (1) they have not addressed the relevant issues successfully, and (2) they have not proposed or implemented those changes which would provide them the freedom and flexibility to design the necessary improvements to program design and function.

5   The flaws of educational reform

Educational reform in America is a cyclical process dating back to the late 17th century. Since that time at least eight periods of major educational reform have been identified. The reform emphases of these periods have varied from the growth of the common school to the current emphasis on excellence, standards and economic productivity. Each of these periods of reform have emphasized a particular issue and each was motivated by a combination of social, political and economic interests (Elmore and McLaughlin, 1988).

A variety of explanations have been offered for the cyclic nature of these reform efforts. These explanations include a variety of reform purposes. Chubberly (1934) perceived schooling as an appropriate extension of democratic ideals and the basis of early reform efforts. Kaestle (1983) perceives the school reforms of the 18th and 19th century as the development of a Protestant, capitalist majority against various minority groups. Katz (1968, 1975) saw the development of secondary education as a means of exerting control over the working class. Tyack (1974) suggested that the "administrative progressive" reforms of the 19th and early 20th centuries were efforts to solidify control of public education by urban elites. Ravitch (1983) dealt with more recent reform efforts and described current endeavors as clumsy attempts by political interests to shape schools, and thereby society, according to their own perception. She suggested that these attempts have failed at the central task of improving student learning. Bruner (1983) agreed that the latest round of reform is "enormously political." Whatever their particular perspective, these authors share in common the conclusion that educational reform efforts have not been successful. In addition to these critics of educational reform, many other authors cited that specific reform projects have not demonstrated significant long-lasting effects on teacher behavior or practices or on student learning (Cuban, 1984; Welch, 1979; Popkewitz, Tabachnick, and Wehlage, 1982).

Both Miles (1967) and Dalin (1978) described educational reform efforts as lacking consistent, specific, and clearly articulated goals, which they perceive as a necessary condition for achieving successful educational change. Kantor (1987) has argued for targeting the [reform] issues which will make a difference in the classroom. He asks, "To what extent have school reform proposals actually moved beyond political expedience and platitudes to take into consideration the actual conditions under which teachers work?" (p 179). Mitchell and Gallagher (1987) echo this concern when they argue that the current reform efforts are centered around the issue of who will control the schools. These authors suggest that the early reforms of the 1900s were an effort to adopt business and industrial values and practices indiscriminately and to apply them with little consideration of the educational values, purposes or consequences for children. Callahan (1962) demonstrated that this application of business values was not to provide the best product but to keep down the cost of education. Today's current educational reform attempts are another example of a similar effort with the interests of children as inconsequential today as they were in the early 1900s.

A number of authors have concluded that current educational reform attempts have not learned from these previous reform efforts, that they are seriously flawed and will not achieve their goals. Almost a decade and a half ago, Leiberman (1977) observed that the more about schools that is discovered, the clearer it becomes that improvements must be initiated, nurtured, and supported at the local level. However, he found that the reform efforts of the 1970s centered around "mandating specifics, linear procedures that tie money and support to precise objectives and their outcomes" (p. 265). This process of reform in the 1970s set in motion the form of reform that is currently being utilized.

Albrecht (1984) concluded that *A Nation At Risk* contained within it the seeds of "immense mischief" (p. 684). Dodd (1984) concluded that none of the proposals to fix the public schools confronted the basic issue that schools were expected to accomplish so many tasks at once that they could do no single job very well for very long. He also concluded that the current efforts to patch the present system were not likely to bring about fundamental reform. Eisner (1992) suggests that a major assumption of both *A Nation at Risk* and *America 2000: An Education Strategy* (see below) was that the state of the schools influenced the state of the economy. He raises serious concerns about the validity of this assumption and points out that the state of the economy was more a product of the decision-making by industry leaders than anything the schools have done.

A number of authors have questioned the validity of the national reports' perception of educational quality in America (Graham, 1984; Hacker, 1984;

Peterson, 1983). Peterson, in particular, has provided an insightful critique of these reform reports. He concluded that, instead of substantive answers to education's problems, the current reform efforts offer little more than rhetoric. Cornbleth (1986) concluded that the reform reports omitted consideration of serious and critical issues of reform including "the purposes of public schooling . . . the processes of teaching and learning, and the possibility of organizational or structural changes to improve schooling" (p. 6). Many educational reforms that did target changing the basic organizational and administrative structures and practices of education have met with little success (Cuban, 1988). The common conclusion from these reports is that past educational reform efforts have had little effect on teaching and learning in the classroom (Elmore and McLaughlin, 1988) and that current efforts will not enjoy any more success. Fuhrman, Elmore, and Massell (1993) concluded that the reform efforts since 1983 have not achieved their goals, that there is confusion about the various interventions that have been implemented, and that there has been limited improvement in student learning. McCarthy (1990) concluded that there is little evidence to support the notion that changes in teacher policy have led to significant improvment in teachers' knowledge.

McDonnel (1989) identified four features common to educational innovations focused on restructuring the schools: (1) The proposals were not new. (2) The solutions proposed depended on the definition of education's problems. (3) The restructuring proposals ranged from the radical to the incremental. (4) The particular strategies for restructuring tend to focus on factors other than student achievement.

Elmore and McLaughlin (1988) have reviewed the history of educational reform. They state about the current reform effort,

> Given what we know about the historical record of educational reform, about the effects of attempts at reform, and about the nature of educational practice, what then can we say about the prospects of the new reform agenda? Few things are certain about the new agenda, except that (1) it relies heavily on standard-setting and regulation as the major implements of reform, (2) most policymaking occurs at the state and local level, (3) the dominant theme of reform is quality, and (4) secondary schooling is the major target of reform (p. 53).

Bruner (1983) suggested that today's reform efforts deal with abstractions such as accountability, testing teachers' knowledge, and the relation between federal and local responsibility. He acknowledged that these are all important, but he pointed out that none of them can be shown to impact directly on what happens in a classroom between a teacher and his/her students.

81

Penning (1989) reports from an Education Policy Forum in Washington, DC, that Clark indicated that the central problems of our educational system will get worse, not better in the years ahead. He indicated that during the Regan years the economic investment of the federal government declined by $15 million, although the gap was more than made up by the states. He observes that the lack of federal investment in education has left a significant deficit in education. In order to make up this gap, education will have to compete with a host of other social needs, and it will not fare well.

Sarason (1990) suggests that educational reformers in the past have been unable to break through the rigidity of schools and that this inability dooms present efforts. According to Sarason, the reformers have failed to come to grips with the existing power relationships that exist within the educational system. Ignoring, or not addressing these power relationships, dooms educational reform efforts to failure.

The weight of opinion on reform efforts since 1983 is that they have failed, and particularly, that they have not produced noticeable improvement in the learning of children. Pellicer and Stevenson (1991) concluded that the results of these reform attempts have been disappointing. Fuhrman, Elmore, and Massell (1993) concluded that an evaluation of recent educational reform efforts is that they have been broad and with out substantial improvements in education, particularly in the ways in which they have improved student learning. They stated, "by virtually all aggregate indices of performance, schools have shown little improvement since the beginning of the current period of reform" (p. 8). McCarthy (1990), concluded that there is little evidence to support a claim that reform efforts have led to significant improvements in the knowledge that teachers bring to the teaching-learning process.

Elmore and McLaughlin proposed solutions for education's problems that converge on four major items: (1) clarifying goals and curriculum content, (2) improving the quality of teaching, (3) improving the organizations of schools, and (4) clarifying the standards of student performance. These authors indicate that, if their analysis of previous reform efforts is correct, all roads lead to the classroom and the school. Their review concluded, as does the Goodlad's (1984), that the school system unit which must be improved is the school itself.

The argument for this focus is three-fold. The quality of education improves as the quality of classroom instruction improves. The quality of classroom instruction improves as the schools function more effectively. And the schools function more effectively as all features of the larger system concentrate on the prerequisites of effective school performance.

However, Elmore and McLaughlin are not certain that the new reform will achieve its objectives. They suggest that the main appeal of the new agenda is that it has not yet failed. They raise good questions about who will get the blame when the current reform efforts fail. They conclude that the blame will fall on people who work in the schools. They warn that a reform agenda based on improving the schools can generate hostility and indifference toward schools and the people who work in them. They state in this regard, ". . . that making the school the unit of improvement doesn't solve the problem of reform, it simply redefines the target" (p. 59). There is great danger that, having defined the problem so narrowly, every policymaker in a position to influence schools will attempt to do so.

Educational reform at the national level

These failures in reform attempts since 1983 even forced the President of the United States and the nation's governors in 1989 to set forth six national goals for education. This was the first time ever that educational goals at the national level had been recommended. *America 2000* was the educational reform strategy President Bush supported to achieve the six goals.

National goals and America 2000

These six goals, to be achieved by the year 2000, are difficult to argue with. They are:

1. Bring all children to school ready to learn.
2. Raise the graduation rate to at least 90 percent.
3. Demonstrate student competency in selected subjects and prepare students to be responsible citizens, productive workers, and lifelong learners.
4. Make the United States No. 1 in math and science.
5. Achieve 100 percent adult literacy.
6. Ensure drug-free, violence-free schools. (U.S. Department of Education, 1991)

Certainly, no one can state rationally that achieving these goals would be bad for either the schools or society. However, it is in the "how do we get there question" that problems begin to arise. There are also problems that arise out of this movement towards national goals that need to be addressed.

83

There was some support for *America 2000,* President Bush's strategy to achieve these goals. Ravitch (1992) expressed the view that the movement to national academic standards was an effort to develop higher expectations for all students and that public support for the six National Education Goals was expressed. (It should be noted that Dr. Ravitch was an assistant secretary of education for the U.S. Department of Education at the time these thoughts were written.) Sewall (1991) suggested that *America 2000* was an effort to increase student achievement and educational freedom through a parental choice program. He concluded that if successful, *America 2000* would lead to improved mechanisms for quality control in education. Cuban (1990) supports establishing national goals if they lead to the improvement of big-city school systems and help re-shape curriculum subject matter and teaching practices.

Congress had many reservations about the President's reform strategy. Both the House and the Senate modified significantly the president's recommendations and the House began to consider establishing national subject standards, opening the door for voluntary national tests (Penning, 1992). Hudelson (1992) commented that the President's proposals were not well received by Congress. Both the House and the Senate rejected the President's proposals and passed their own reform bills. Again, children and education were caught in a web of political fighting and compromise.

The majority of thought seems clearly to indicate that this reform effort has failed, however. Many more authors argue that *America 2000* was flawed from the beginning and will not lead to improvement in the schools. Pellicer and Stevenson (1991) concluded that the need for *America 2000* arose from the poor results that had marked the reform efforts in the United States since 1983. They also concluded among others, (e.g., Schneider, 1992) that even the *America 2000* educational reform strategy of President Bush was a "thinly veiled" effort to restructure schools in a way that would make them more competitive in today's marketplace.

Clinchy (1991) suggests that the reform strategy of *America 2000* is flawed by a major educational/political blunder and a major internal contradiction. The blunder is allowing educational vouchers to be used in private, as well as public schools. Clinchy maintains this would lead to a well-funded public, private, and parochial system, and a minimally funded public system serving primarily urban poor and minority students. The internal contradiction is that instead of leading to a radical re-restructuring of our schools suggested by the reform strategy, it is more likely that the efforts will fix in place the hierarchical, top-down control of schools that has marked them for decades. These two problems, according to Clinchy, could ruin the plan altogether, and may cause it to be dangerous to the academic health of students and education.

84

Harold Howe (1991, 1992), a former U.S. commissioner of education has severely criticized *America 2000* on several grounds. First, he suggests that the origins of the plans for *America 2000* were not made available to the public. Second, he suggests that the plan assumes no significant additional funding is needed to finance the poorer school districts. Third, the plan says nothing about to serve the many communities, families, and youth that live in poverty or how to make the social and cultural diversity of American society a positive factor. In general, he submits that America 2000 identifies educational issues that need attention but that these are shrouded by inadequate policies and funding, and a rhetoric that suggests local control of schools while really advocating a national control of educational policy, standards, testing and goal setting.

Krepel, Grady, and Paradise (1992), writing in the *American School Board Journal*, reports the results of a survey of local school board members concerning *America 2000*. After noting that national goals suggest a more centralized structure for American education, they indicate the goals need to be understood in terms of their implications. Their first implication, drawn from their survey results, indicates a problem between policy makers and citizens. Secondly, they suggest that local school board members, although aware of the goals prefer to keep education goal setting at a local level. A strong preference was reported for keeping goal setting as a rightful responsibility of the local community.

Darling-Hammond (1991) perceives two of the major supports of the *America 2000* plan as flawed. These are the elements of choice and national testing. According to Darling-Hammond these ideas are based on the notion that schools need to be pushed to compete and that the threat of lost students and/or dollars is required for improved schooling. She suggests it is not that school personnel lack purpose but that the system of schooling in which they work is dysfunctional.

Schneider (1992) described *America 2000* as a political effort to assure middle-class Americans that the president was addressing the economic woes of the country. Goodlad (1992) raises the question of how an educational movement that is claimed to be sweeping the country is barely recognized by many educators and most parents. The general conclusion seems to be that *America 2000* has goals that few could argue with. However, it is flawed in many respects and seems to be more a danger to quality education then not.

America 2000 also raised the specter of several other implications concerning national testing, standards, curricula, and by implication the probability of uniform teacher preparation programs. Goodlad (1992) states that the plan explicitly calls for national tests. The chain seems to be as follows. The country sets world-class standards for all students. These standards are to be measured by individual achievement tests which will motivate students to achieve at the levels expected. Thus, educational quality and outcomes will be raised to the standards desired.

Nystrand (1992) concluded that a general theme underlying the process of implementing the strategies of *America 2000* was a strong, centralized approach to educational reform in areas previously reserved to the states. *America 2000* proposes a voluntary, national testing program tied to the standards established for each of the subject areas proposed in Goal 3 (Nystrand, 1992). What apparently was not known, or deliberately overlooked, was the fact that standardized educational tests leave much to be desired. They simply do not measure the kind of thinking or cognitive processes that are needed to assure a student will be successful (Darling-Hammond, 1991; Fiske, 1991)

The SCANS report

Another indication of the perceived role that education should play in promoting the economic productivity of the country is the SCANS report. SCANS stands for the Secretary's Commission on Achieving Necessary Skills and was issued by the U.S. Department of Labor. This Commission was asked to examine the functions of the workplace and assess whether young people were able to fulfill these functions (U.S. Department of Labor, 1992). Specifically, the Commission was given four charges;

1. define the skills needed for employment,
2. propose appropriate levels of skill,
3. recommend ways to assess the skill level, and,
4. develop a dissemination strategy for schools and businesses (U.S. Department of Labor, 1992).

The report focused on "workplace know-how" that defines effective job performance. This know-how included two components, "competencies" and a set of "foundation" skills. The five areas of competencies were resources, interpersonal, information, systems, and technology. The foundation skills consisted of three elements, basic skills, thinking skills, and personal qualities. This report speaks directly to the National Goals described above, particularly Goal #3, and to the reform strategy of *America 2000* (U.S. Department of labor, 1992).

Lewis (1991) reported that the SCANS report will plunge the vocational educational establishment into confusion because these educators were just beginning to implement federal vocational education legislation with its new requirments.

A number of other national movements that seemed designed to cement a nationalization of educational standards and testing requirements have been developed. From the six national goals for American education, A National Education Goals Panel was formulated, initially composed of governors and administration officials, and later broadened to include congressional leaders (where are the parents and teachers?). This group was to develop means by which each of the goals could be measured and then issue a report card to the nation.

Out of this Goals Panel arose the National Council on Education Standards and Testing. This Council was supposed to develop national standards and achievement tests to measure the five core subject areas identified in the National Goals. Eisner (1993) describes many of the problems and pitfalls associated with national standards. He suggests that the emphasis on standards may move schools in the direction of fixed and uniform goals and away from diversity of learning and that a simple emphasis on standards will not solve the problems of education.

The difficulties inherent in attempting to use tests to measure achievement were described above (Hudelson, 1992). Sizer (1992) has criticized both the goal setting and the reliance on tests to measure whether students have achieved the standards. Nystrand (1992) also speaks to the limits of current standardized testing to measure the success students. Fiske (1991) summarizes, tests "measure the wrong things in the wrong ways for the wrong reasons" (p. 117P.

Trotter (1991) writes that before national tests become a reality there is a need for new approaches to assessment. He describes the conclusions of a meeting held by the American Educational Research Association including that not only would a national test fail to achieve reform goals, it would also hinder the reform efforts. Additional conclusions included that such a test would limit the scope of the curriculum, that current tests are based on out-moded theories of learning, that current tests do not afford students the opportunity to develop reasoning skills. In fact, the conference concluded, the results of the national Assessment of Educational progress show that current achievement tests demonstrate a small increase in rote skills at the expense of teaching students to reason.

A further national movement is a national system of voluntary certification for teachers. The National Board for Professional Teaching Standards was set up in 1987 in response to the recommendations of the Carnegie Forum on Education and the Economy (Lloyd, 1991). The danger, of course, in such a system is developing a uniform set of teacher education program curriculums that will lead to uniformity in public school programs. As Lloyd points out, the lack of mandated federal standards may have helped preserve academic freedom, and that Americans over the years have rejected national standards for teachers in addition to a uniform curriculum.

It is not just that national goals, national standards, or national testing programs are bad in themselves, it is when they are taken as a package that the real damage occurs. As Darling-Hammond (1991) has indicated, when we have highly regimented and regulated schools, mandating curricula, texts, standards, and test scores, we do not have good schools. One of the problems she points out is that if we only institute more regulations and requirements we lose the chance to develop new types of schools that will effectively lead to higher quality education.

It is not far of an imaginative leap to perceive that if there are national goals and standards, and a national testing system to measure whether the standards are being achieved, a national curricula will not be far behind. Once there is a national set of standards and a national curricula there will have to be national teacher preparation program standards, curricula, and measures of performance. The outcome will be a uniformity of schooling that (1) can not succeed, and (2) would result in a centralization of educational control at the national level. Uniformity cannot tolerate diversity so experimentation, novel approaches to instructing students with various needs, and local and state needs will be largely neglected.

Apparently the authors of these reports recommending nationalization have not realized that (1) the nature of the relationship they perceived between economic investment and education was flawed from its inception and by the programs this relationship spawned or, (2) that the quality of life in a society, including its economic status, is determined more by the personal-social competence of its members than by the expansion of its material possessions.

Outcomes of the nationalization movements

Two major outcomes have resulted from these moves to institute a nationalization of education. The first was a move to move educational decision making to the local level. The second, and it is just beginning, is a move to develop a "systemic" educational reform effort.

Hess (1993) has suggested that there is occurring at the same time a move to centralize educational decision-making (the nationalization move) and moves to decentralize this decision-making, to bring it down to the school level where it can be more practical [sometimes called school-based management, (SBM)]. This move to SBM is perceived by some as a reaction to the move to nationalize control of education. What both of these movements have in common is an effort to take control of education away from the current bureaucrats at the local board level and move it either upward through the state level to the national, or down to the school level. Local school board members have responded by indicating the goal setting is a local responsibility (Krepel, Grady, & Paradise, 1992).

Goodlad (1992) suggests that there is a sizable and strong "grassroots" movement that rests on the belief that "homegrown" school improvement efforts are the most valid. He also notes that these local efforts are frustrating to those who want quick-fix answers for educational improvement. Goodlad also suggests that these grassroots efforts are more concerned with educating our children then they are with "restructuring" the schools. At least half the states have instituted policies that would allow parents and students some increased measure of choice in their educational experiences (Fossey, 1992; Nathan, 1989).

One of the results of such a grassroots approach has shown some dramatic results as reported by Clinchy (1991). He describes the approach in new York City where the basis of the reform rests on a "creation of diversity" approach that has as its objective the development of schools that fit the needs of every student. This is in opposition to trying to fit every student into some standardized school.

Another important ingredient in the national versus local reform debate is the sense of teacher efficacy. Efficacy has to with the beliefs that teachers have about whether they can affect student learning (Dembo and Gibson, 1985). Lieberman (1989) has sensed that a sense of purpose arises in teachers and principals when they have the authority to design programs that best serve their students' needs. Such feelings are going to be enhanced when teachers have some voice in the matters such as curricula, assessment, etc., which are not likely to be part of a nationalized education system.

Fuhrman, Elmore, and Massell (1993), have suggested that since 1993 there have been three waves of reform in the United States. The first of these dealt with state standard setting and increased rules and regulations. Darling-Hammond and Berry (1988) have indicated that over 1,000 pieces of legislation were enacted to change teacher policy between 1983 and 1988. The second wave of reform, according to Fuhrman, et.al. focused on school-level change, basically designed to provide school level planning and improvement of instruction. The third wave of reform is "systemic", which is an attempt to pair in a coordinated way state policy development with restructured governance at the local level (Fuhrman, Elmore, and Massell, 1993; Smith and O'Day, 1991). What these authors have omitted from in describing these three waves of reform, obviously, is the wave of effort directed towards national control.

In the past decade America has seen four waves of reform. They have not produced the results desired, nor are they likely to in view of the many conflicting political controls and lack of knowledge about educational change and improvement evident in the reformers' efforts.

What must be avoided, according to Elmore and McLaughlin, is the explicit recognition of the limits of policy as an instrument of reform. Policies are useful, but blunt, instruments. Under the best of circumstances, they can influence the allocation of resources, the structure of schooling, and the content of practice. But those changes take time and often have unexpected effects. Under the worst circumstances, they communicate hostility or indifference to the very people whose commitment is required to make them work; they fragment organizations in ways that make them more responsive but less effective; and they initiate demands at a rate faster than the system can implement them. Fullan (1982) makes the point that, in previous attempts to engineer social change, the tendency has been towards limiting variation and maximizing faithful implementation. As will be discussed in later chapters, the act of faithful implementation by captive audiences leads to a defeat of the efforts to improve practices and conditions. If the new reform agenda is to avoid the mistakes of the old, it must explicitly deal with four major problems underlying the use of policy as an implement of reform: (1) the gap between policy and practice, (2) variability, (3) the function of rules, and (4) creating effective organizations.

Closing the gap between policy and practice

Policymakers initiate; administrators and practitioners implement. In the process of reform, the mode of transition from one structure to another is critical. The process must be better attended to. Policies must be used less to mandate resource allocation, structures and rules, and more to initiate development. The process requires commissioning people who work in real schools to fashion workable solutions to real problems, and allowing those solutions the opportunity to fail and the time to succeed.

Accommodating variability

Learning to accommodate variability on all dimensions of the current reform agenda must be achieved. Policy deals at a high level of abstraction. This attribute of policy can be an advantage when it accommodates diversity and variability in practical solutions. It is a disadvantage when it limits the development of solutions and imposes rigid constraints on variations in practice.

Variability is a reality — whether it occurs in response to uniform policies or in response to developmental efforts to encourage it. The question is not whether variability can be tolerated, but how to use it in developing solutions to the problems of the new reform agenda.

Learning the function of rules

Simply put: Rules should set expectations, not dictate practice.

Learning to create effective organizations

If schools are dismal places to work and learn, it is because we have made them that way. They can be remade, but it will take time, accommodation, and tolerance for error.

Why, despite hundreds of millions of dollars being allocated to achieve the goals of reform, has educational reform in the past had so little effect on improving student learning outcomes? Why are current reform efforts probably doomed to repeat the failures of previous reform attempts? There are four primary reasons: (1) Educational reformers did not understand the nature of the educational system they were attempting to change, nor did they properly understand the nature and limitations of educational change processes. (2) Reform recommendations did not address the problems of mission, organization and administrative practices of the schools. (3) There was no coordinated and cooperative effort to integrate changes in public schools and educational personnel preparation programs. (4) They did not address fundamental elements of educational preparation and practice, e.g., mission, organization, administrative practices. The processes utilized and recommendations generated during the current reform movement will not achieve the goals desired.

Therefore, educational reformers of recent years have failed in their primary assignment of identifying root causes for the perceived faults of education. Roemer (1991) argues that the process of implementation is as important as the reform itself. It is in the process of implementation that the reformeers have failed. This failure can be attributed to several causes.

First, they did not engage in a systematic problem identification process which tracked symptoms to the cause. They tended to address the symptoms rather than invest the time necessary to identify the cause of the problem. As a result, they developed recommendations for change which may ameliorate the symptom(s) but not cure the disease.

Second, the goals of reform were unclear. The reform reports and accompanying recommendations seldom explain who should benefit from the reform proposals and in what way. Seven national reform reports[1] identify a combined total of 15 areas of reform needed. However, none of the seven reports list the exact same change areas. The areas targeted for reform include: (1) elementary and secondary schools, and the federal government; (2) the public sector and the private sector; (3) secondary schools; (4) elementary and secondary schools and state and corporate leaders; (5) the federal government, state and local officials; (6) school boards, principals, superintendents, citizens, educators, parents and students; (7) higher education and schools, political leaders, and elementary and secondary schools and local communities.

Third, the failure to recognize the root causes of educational symptoms caused most reformers to overlook the complicated set of interdependent elements of education which needed to be addressed if structural elements of education are to be improved.

Finally, educational reformers tended to perceive educational reform as a product, not a process. They tended to operate from a basic assumption that, if they could develop a new curriculum, a new set of student performance standards, and new criteria for entrance to teacher education programs, the system would respond positively.

Toffler addressed this issue in his 1970 book *Future Shock*. He forecast severe psychological and sociological consequences that would be brought about by increasingly rapid social change. In this regard he was highly critical of education because its orientation was to the past, rather than to the future needs of society's members. He perceived the mission of education to be increasing the individual's "capability," the speed and effectiveness with which s/he could adapt to continual change. In Toffler's view, a curriculum was needed that helped students learn how to learn, how to relate to others, and how to clarify their values so that they could choose effectively from among competing alternatives.

This chapter describes the consequences of reformers' failure to address the issues of (1) mission, (2) organization, and (3) administrative practices of education. It relates these lacks to reformers' lack of knowledge about how education operates as a system and about educational change processes. It also examines four flaws in the present design of educational reform efforts and recommendations and identifies four issues that must be addressed if current attempts are to have a reasonable chance of success.

[1]*The Twentieth Century Fund, America's Competitive Challenge, Academic Preparation for College, Action for Excellence, A Nation at Risk, Meeting the Need for Quality: Action in the South, and The Paideia Proposal*

Mission

The root cause of education's problems is its mission. Actually, the cause is the lack of clarity and agreement concerning education's mission and the resulting goal confusion and role uncertainty on the part of educators. The goal confusion, role uncertainty and lack of a clearly focused mission leads to individual teacher and organizational attempts to impose and achieve their idiosyncratically developed goals for students and the school organization. As will be presented in Chapter 8 *(Chapter 11, Second-Order Changes 1 & 2)* in the discussion of a knowledge base for education, individuals attempt to impose order on their environment. In the absence of a system-defined structure for ordering mission priorities, individual members of a system will impose their own definition of mission priority. The result in education is disorder, if not chaos, as individual teachers, parents, and others attempt to impose their own definitions of what the mission of schools should be.

Many authors and observers of education (Cornbleth, 1984; Dodd, 1984; Lapointe, 1984; Wassermann, 1984) have noted the wide range of missions that education is expected to fulfill. These writers concur that the multiple roles education is expected to fulfill seriously detract from its capacity to accomplish any at a superior level.

The problem is not only the wide range of goals that schools are expected to achieve, but also their increasing complexity. Greater emphasis is being placed on mastering increasingly complex technological skills and learning increased amounts of knowledge. These increases require that schools not only value and agree on this more complex mission, but also teach students to master the these new requirements (Leithwood and Jantzi, 1989). Given that education is attempting to achieve too many missions, it would only be logical to assume that educational reformers would have paid this issue considerable attention. This was not the case. Educational mission was not addressed in educational reform reports, certainly not as a problem worthy of attention.

This lack of attention to education's mission was a serious and perhaps fatal flaw in the reform reports. If the mission of education is not addressed, then other serious problems of education will not surface as issues of concern.

A related problem is the failure to prioritize the various elements in education's mission. This results in educational goals which are general in nature, often characterized by ambiguity and vagueness (Miles, 1967). Over the years, education has been expected to serve both an academic-learning and social maintenance role (Dalin, 1978). Other purposes for education have been identified as enabling the individual to achieve greater personal

93

fulfillment, informed active citizenship, economic self-sufficiency, upward social mobility, a deeper humanity, and a caring for others (McDonnell, 1989). In addition, education has served an economic mission and other unspecified goals that serve the national interest (Coombs, 1985; *Time, October, 16, 1989*). Within each of these major functions, there are many sub-functions. Which of these should receive priority has not been specified. No processes have been defined for prioritizing education's mission elements. There has been no discussion of what mission elements education could actually achieve. There has been no recognition or attention given to teachers' needs for self-development or setting and achieving goals. The resource needs and allocation bases for an ordered set of mission priorities have not been addressed. Educational reform reports have not addressed either the mission priorities of education or these critical issues.

The process by which these issues should be addressed is crucial. As Dalin (1978) points out, the process of educational change is one which involves political, economic and social interests. It is a process which requires understanding the school as an organization involving conflicts over values, and a "systemic view" of education as a social system. In order to address these issues appropriately, one must begin by identifying the mission of the schools. What should the schools be expected to achieve,? What can they achieve? Once the "should" questions are answered, an examination of the "can" question must be undertaken. The "can" question essentially deals with an examination of the current capacities of teachers and other professional educators to implement the procedures necessary to carry out the mission *(Chapter 12, Second-Order Change 5)*. If the answer to the "can" question is "no" under existing circumstances, a determination of the personnel-development needs and additional resources necessary must be specified to implement programs needed to achieve the desired goals.

A specified and prioritized mission for schools is an essential first step for achieving significant improvement of educational outcomes. Specifying a set of mission priorities for schools also has important derivatives for other elements of educational operations, including school organization, administrative practices, and resource allocation. Educational reform reports did not address this issue of mission, and they addressed other elements of educational need without seeming to understand the complicated problems of achieving educational change of other elements in the absence of a focused mission.

School organization

The organization of a school system or an individual school is a complex affair and should be based on achieving the mission of the schools.

94

Presumably, a school system or school is organized to achieve the goals of the institution. However, an examination of the organization of schools quickly shows that the school is operated to maintain order and ease administrative paper work (Elmore and McLaughlin, 1988). Schools are a haven for bureaucrats where shuffling paper, filling out reports, and making sure every thing runs smoothly. As was described in Chapters 4 and 5, schools were not designed with the intent of improving student learning. Class schedules, teachers' working conditions, the 50-minute class period, the authority of principals and lack of authority for teachers, all contribute to a variety of organizational problems (Elmore and McLaughlin, 1988). In addition, even though the research has identified a number of organizational factors that impact student learning, such as team teaching (Rosenhotz, 1989) and matching teachers' preferred teaching methods with students' preferred learning styles (Hunt, 1981), these organizational variables were not addressed by reform recommendations.

A number of authors (Boyer, 1985; Conant, 1964; Goodlad, 1984; Sizer, 1984) have commented on the need for fundamental restructuring of schools. Some 25 years ago Conant asked for drastic changes in the way educational policy is shaped. He argued for including classroom teachers, in addition to those usually involved, in forming educational policy. Mary Futrell (1989), former NEA president, has indicated that the present structure of schooling has been with us for more than a century and is obsolete. *A Nation Prepared* (1986) probably spoke the strongest on the need for restructuring of the schools. These proposals include reducing the bureaucratic responsibilities of principals, implementing higher standards for promotion to principalships, training principals to become better "instructional leaders," and creating simple, more flexible structures (Elmore and McLaughlin, 1988). However, there was not a set of proposals for re-organizing the schools within the context of prioritizing the schools' mission elements. Proposals for organizational reform of schools did not include such obvious elements as the system organization, coordinating any such changes with administrator and teacher preparation programs, describing the process by which current educators would be re-trained to operate within a new organizational environment, or dealing with the attitudes of resistance and uncertainty on the part of teachers and/or educational administrators that will unquestionably accompany any significant organizational change *(Chapter 12, Second-Order Changes 4, 9, 10, 11, 12, 13, 15, and 17).*

Administrative practices

A critical element of school organization is the administrative practices utilized to operate schools. Although educational reform recommendations did speak minimally to educational administrators, few spoke to administrative practices. In the absence of a well-defined and -focused set of mission priorities for schools, administrative practices seem more oriented toward assuring that procedures for processing paperwork are followed, that buses run on time, and that troublesome students are contained. These other activities are important for smooth school operation, but they do not advance the cause of student learning.

Again, the reformers did not identify the appropriate problem. The reports focused more on teacher competence and reducing the rules and regulations of school operation than the relationship among mission, school organization and administrative practices. The problem with administering the schools is that there is not a clearly defined mission from which schools can develop an effective organization and focus their efforts and administrative practices *(Chapter 12, Second-Order Changes 5, 6, & 7).*

Resource allocations

A growing national trend appears to be developing concerning the attendance formula basis on which schools are financed *(Time,* October 16, 1989). An increasing number of states are seeking ways to equalize the funds allocated to each school. These states include Alaska, Minnesota, North Carolina, North Dakota, Montana, Oregon, Tennessee, New Jersey, Texas, and Kentucky. This trend appears to based on the assumption that equalizing funding levels among schools will result in equalized educational opportunities and/or equalized educational outcomes. Once national performance standards for students are set *(Time,* October 16, 1989), and standardized tests are implemented, it will be easy to compare the outcomes of students from different schools.

The problem with this effort is that, once again, educational reformers have identified and attacked the wrong problem. The problem is not the unequal funding of schools, but the distribution of funds based on the wrong factors. Funding of schools is primarily based on the number of students attending a particular school, regardless of the needs of the students or the programs necessary to provide them the experiences required for their development as mature learners. It is not the *number* of students which should determine the funding level of schools, but the *type* of learning experiences needed by students. These needs should be addressed within given deadlines so that specific programs can be designed to achieve the desired outcomes on the part of students. Implementing equifinality requires freedom and authority of local educators to specify students' learning needs. Funding should be provided on the basis of what programs and learning experiences will be required to meet these needs. For example, a small group of students may need to improve their reading readiness skills. Local educators may decide that these students could best master the skills required in an intensive six-week immersion reading readiness program outside the regular classroom. If this was a high enough priority, then the local school should have the authority to allocate resources for such a purpose *(Chapter 12, Second-Order Change 16)*.

Conclusions

In sum, educational reformers either did not address the critical elements of mission, school organization, administrative practices, or resource allocation, or they addressed the wrong elements of these issues. They did not address the interdependence among these factors. Perhaps they did not understand the process of educational change, or school system functioning in general (Sarason, 1990). There appeared to be a significant lack of a problem identification process, a lack of understanding of the need for an integrated and coordinated plan of reform, and a fatal lack of understanding of the educational change process. These lacks by themselves suggest that the goals of educational reform will not be achieved. However, in addition to these lacks there were serious flaws in the recommendations most commonly made by educational reformers.

Flaws of reform recommendations

Most national and state reports recommended changes in similar areas. There is more emphasis on one aspect or another, depending on the particular report, but on balance they are fairly consistent. There are four major categories targeted for change:

- Improved working conditions and salaries of teachers;
- New and stricter requirements to enter and continue in the profession of education;
- Incentives to attract brighter young people to the education profession; and,
- Restructuring of the profession of education.

Each of these will be considered in turn, but all are considered crucial to achieving the goal of reforming American education.

It is widely recognized and accepted that, if high quality teachers are to be attracted to and retained in the education profession, the conditions under which they work must improve. Schlecty and Vance (1983) examined the credentials of many teachers who had left the profession in recent years. They found that, as a group, those teachers who left the profession were identified as the best among their peers (best being defined on the basis of admission test scores, achievement in college, and success in student teaching). Darling-Hammond (1984) found that the teachers who scored the highest on the Scholastic Aptitude Test (SAT) were more likely to leave the profession after only a few years. These findings are a strong indictment of the conditions of teaching. [See also discussion of the studies by Foreman (1985 and Pechman (1987) in Chapter 3.]

These professionals left teaching because they lacked professional autonomy to do their job in the manner in which they deemed best for their students. Boyer (1983) observed that teachers felt demeaned by having to do a host of things which had nothing to do with teaching and which took time away from their primary job of teaching. Teachers, really good teachers, are tired of having to do bus duty and cafeteria duty, of having to take up lunch money, and of not having the time to go to the bathroom.

Teachers also resent not having the autonomy to exercise professional judgments regarding their students' needs. They are tired of not being able to choose the materials and resources they consider best for their students, and they are tired of having too many students per day to do their job properly. They are tired of trying to motivate students who are more interested in working after school to pay for their cars than in doing homework. They are tired of dealing with students who come to school drunk, or physically abused, or who must sleep all day because a drunken father kept the family up all night.

Good teachers are tired of trying to do their job effectively under these conditions. They are especially tired of doing these things for 30 years and then receiving a minimum retirement salary. Good teachers are tired of receiving the same salary increases as the worst teachers do. There is no merit salary differentiation between effective and non-effective teachers. Good teachers are tired of trying to raise a family on a salary that will not stretch from one month to the next. Therefore, they leave the profession. Instructors in high demand and critical areas, such as mathematics, physics, and chemistry, go to industry where they earn double their teaching salaries, work on interesting problems, gain professional respect, and receive salary increases based on the quality and contributions of their efforts.

Practically all the national reports have addressed the imperative need to improve the conditions of teaching because of these conditions. Prospective reforms include more professional autonomy for decision-making, less time spent on non-professional activities in the schools, and improved starting and continuing salaries. The specifics of each of these improvements are left to the states. Many states are developing ways of identifying lead or master teachers who will be used to assist younger teachers, develop curricula, and improve the professionalism of educators. In addition, most states are attempting to find ways of reducing class size. It is too early to determine the final outcome of these efforts. Most of these efforts are in an embryonic stage. What is clear is that the conditions under which teachers work and the salaries they earn will probably improve. Whether they will improve sufficiently to make a significant impact will only be known in time. The Holmes Group (Evangelauf, 1987) concluded that, unless school teachers are respected as professionals, efforts to reform education will probably not succeed. Futrell (Evangelauf, 1987) addressed this issue directly when she indicated that teachers must be allowed a significant voice in the design of curricular content, schoolwide objectives, and standards for teacher education. The Carnegie's Task Force on Teaching as a Profession (1986) indicated that the key to successful reform of education was teacher empowerment. *(Section 3, Introduction; Chapter 12, Second-Order Changes 3, 5, 6 & 7; Chapter 13, Second-Order Changes 21, 22, 26, 29 & 30).*

This author predicts that current efforts to reform education will fail because they have not addressed the right "what" of the problem: how to design and implement the appropriate educational change processes which will empower teachers. The educational change processes mandatory for such redistribution of power are complex and difficult because such empowerment requires a redistribution of the authority to control education *(Chapter 10, Third-Order Changes 1-4; Chapter 12, Second-Order Changes 3, 6 & 7).* Harris (1986) supported this prediction and found that leadership groups are twice as likely as teachers to think that the impact of recent educational reform efforts have been positive for teachers.

Requirements for entering and continuing in the profession of education

The second category of recommended change concerns improving the quality of those individuals currently in or currently entering the teaching profession. These reforms urge higher admission requirements for teacher education students, improvements in programs these students must endure, higher standards for exiting the preparation phases and becoming certified to teach, and stricter requirements for maintaining certification as a teacher. The percent of states requiring standardized or proficiency tests for program entry more than doubled between 1980-81 and 1984-85

(Holmstrom, 1985). These strengthened entrance requirements for the profession include higher test scores on the SAT, successful completion of a number of program entry tests, a higher GPA during the first two years of general college work, passing new entrance tests to enter the professional education curriculum, achieving a higher GPA during professional course work, and passing new exit tests in professional knowledge and competence areas.

These requirements are designed to restrict those who now enter the teaching profession to the most able. Unfortunately, these requirements come at a time of an increasing teaching shortage in the United States. Nearly 40% of the teachers in America will reach retirement age within 5-7 years. Harris (1986) found that there was an increase in the number of teachers seriously considering leaving the profession, and that between 1984 and 1986, job satisfaction among teachers declined by seven per cent. In order to replace those leaving, one in every five entering college freshman will have to enter teaching. The stricter requirements, as needed as they are, will make this a difficult task.

These new program requirements will probably mean extending the length of teacher preparation programs to at least five years, although the merits of such extension are still being hotly debated in many quarters. It is difficult, however, to see how all the requirements, both old and new, for teacher education programs can appropriately be met within a four-year period. There is simply too much to learn and practice. Also, it is difficult to understand how an 18-year-old can become a fully qualified professional practitioner of education after only four years of preparation.

A frequently heard argument against increasing the length of programs is the additional cost to students and to their parents. This is a ridiculous argument. Veterinarians are required to study for three years after college to take care of our cats and dogs. Do we think more of our pets than our children's learning? If it requires five years to prepare our children's teachers, money must be found to fund this preparation.

The induction of teachers into the profession and their continuing professional development is the third element involved in improving the quality of professional educators. Many of these support programs require an individual plan for professional development based on an assessment of the teachers' strengths and weaknesses. The successful completion of this professional development plan leads to continuing certification. Failure to do so leads to dismissal. It is hoped that these induction and support programs will lead to more qualified teachers who are more competent and professional.

Continuing professional development for teachers is also being improved and strengthened. Currently, such activities are required by most state education agencies, but the choice of content is usually left to the discretion of the individual teacher. This often leads to random, non-productive activities which are not based on an assessment of teaching need. To improve this situation, two coordinated activities must take place. First, these efforts must be coordinated with other needed changes in the educational system. Second, these efforts must be focused equally on improving the knowledge and competence of new professionals and improving the professional orientation and teaching behaviors of the current two million teachers. The success of that effort is much in doubt as is the re-design of teacher education programs because, again, reformers have not dealt with the appropriate "what" of these programs.

Incentives to attract more qualified personnel to the profession

The third category of change for improving education is to attract more and better qualified students to the profession. In order to do this, the conditions and rewards of the teaching profession, as described earlier, have to improve significantly. But, to attract the brightest students to education, the profession must compete against the allure of more glamorous, higher-paying professional occupations such as medicine, law, and business. In recent years, education has been losing many females and minority members to these other areas. These two groups, females and minorities, both represent special recruiting problems for education. Females used to view education as the primary profession to which they could aspire. This is no longer true. Affirmative action programs, higher salaries, and more professional autonomy in other professions have attracted many of the brightest females away from education.

The same holds true for minorities. At one time, particularly among blacks, education was perceived as the highest profession to which they could aspire. This also is no longer true. Blacks and other minorities compete very successfully for positions in all professions, to the extent that there is considerable and growing concern and alarm in educational circles that the lack of minority teachers and administrators in America's schools is a very significant and growing problem. The numbers of minorities entering the teaching profession do not nearly match the numbers reaching and nearing retirement age, and the percentage of minority children entering the schools is rapidly increasing. A recent report (Foreman, 1986) issued by the North Carolina Association of Education warns of the many serious problems confronting education in the areas of recruitment, preparation, employment, and retention of minority personnel. Recommendation 3 of the National Commission for Excellence in Teacher Education (*The Chronicle of Higher Education*, March 6, 1985) addressed

101

this issue and warned of negative outcomes if the decline of minority teachers continued. We ignore these warnings at our children's peril.

In order to compete against the allure of these other professions, some states are considering packages of special inducements: scholarships and benefits to attract more and better qualified students to the profession of education. It is unknown at this time whether these plans will result in increased numbers and higher quality of applicants. It is much too early to tell if such plans will work. If they do not, the schools will be faced with a rapidly increasing student population and a decreasing number of quality teachers for the classrooms. In such a situation, the schools, as they have in the past, have no alternative but to find warm bodies where and however they can. As a result, the quality of instruction will decline, not improve *(Chapter 12, Second-Order Changes 5 & 7)*.

Restructuring the profession of education

The fourth major category targeted for change and improvement is restructuring the educational profession. This is the area of change which is the most ambiguous in the current reform movement. The difficulty, of course, is that the critical elements, mission, organization and administrative practices, necessary for re-structuring the educational system, were not addressed. Everyone talks about reforming the education profession and agrees that it must be done, but no one knows exactly what to do, how to do it, or what is meant by restructuring the profession. The problem is (1) the right "what" of the problem has not been addressed and/or (2) no one wants the responsibility of attempting to re-structuring the schools. Focusing the mission of education must be accomplished and coordinated with the systematic change of other elements of education, or any other changes and improvements in education will be short-lived.

Unless the profession of education is provided the authority and incentives to produce substantial change in education's mission and organization, it is likely that only change imposed from outside the profession will result in substantial, fundamental change of the educational structure. Change brought about in this manner will produce only short-term changes and improvements at best. It will not provide a process for establishing and maintaining change and program quality improvement on a sustained and controlled basis. Until this change is achieved, education will not have the capability to modify its own structure as such becomes necessary in the future.

Some of the national reform reports (*A Nation Prepared, 1986*) discussed restructuring the profession. They did so only in a peripheral manner, primarily, perhaps, because the prospect of trying to restructure such a huge, complex enterprise as education is a mind-boggling proposition. How does one go about trying to conceptualize change for the fundamental nature of an enterprise that expends over a hundred billion dollars a year, has overlapping lines of responsibility and authority, and is composed of over 16,000 separate units? The first step of course is to define the primary mission of the schools. Once that is accomplished, the task of how to resolve the other problem becomes more focused and can be approached on an incremental and coordinated basis.

As mentioned earlier, the control of education seems to be shifting from the local community to the state level. An article in *Time* (October 16, 1989) concluded that the once sacred principle of local control appeared to be rapidly going the way of *McGuffey's Reader*. The State of New Jersey has taken control of operating the Jersey City schools because of educational failure. Five other states now have laws permitting such take-overs (*Time*, October 16, 1989). Boyer (*Time*, October 16, 1989) suggested that, although the nation was once committed to the idea that local communities should operate their schools without reference to larger, national purposes, the trend now appears to be moving toward the issue of how national interests can be served by the schools. Some signs are emerging of control of certain elements, such as national certification of teachers (Evangelauf, 1987) and national performance standards for students (*Time*, October 16, 1989), moving to the national level. (Can a national curriculum be far behind?) These movements again address the wrong elements of needed school change. It is not by centralizing the control of educational operations that improvement of student learning will occur, but rather by the provision of authority to the local school.

Restructuring of education is necessary to achieve long-lasting substantial improvement of education. However, it will occur only if the education profession (the teachers) and representatives from the public share responsibility and authority to determine how the purposes and priorities of education can best be achieved and fulfilled. As long as professional educators are not permitted to have a significant voice in the design of educational policies and practices, its restructuring will be a long, difficult, and probably losing proposition.

The structure of the schools must follow from their functions, and their functions must follow from their purpose and objectives *(Chapter 11, Second-Order Changes 1 & 2; Chapter 12, Second-Order Changes 3-17)*. What are the purpose and objectives of the schools? None of the reform reports or recommendations addressed this question. The schools should have only one prime mission — to teach children how to learn and to teach all children how to learn to the maximum of their ability.

In sum, the changes being recommended for educational improvement by current reform reports are significant, and they are also highly interdependent. Achieving change in one or two areas may be helpful in the short-term, but the necessary long-term change and improvement will be possible only if all four areas of indicated change are achieved.

Probability of achieving reform goals

The chances of current educational reform goals being achieved is not great. The lack of a coordinated plan of quality improvement for public and teacher education and the problems inherent in the areas discussed above contribute to weaknesses in the current reform efforts. Four fundamental elements of education must be more fully addressed if the current recommendations for reform are to succeed. Even then, the chances for long-term improvement are small. These four areas include:

- The Content of Learning
- University Faculty Training & Development
- Retraining the Administrative Leadership
- Allow Sufficient Time

The content of learning

What will our children learn and how will they learn it? The answers to these questions are among the most critical in education. Fortunately, recent advances and developments in cognitive science offer new opportunities for education. This subject area deals with the content, processes, and interactions among human development, learning, intelligence, and motivation. The advances made in these areas and their applications to education allow a departure from well-worn paths of curriculum theory and development. They have allowed scientists to map processes used by young children in language acquisition, second language learning, reading proficiency, and the development of mathematical skill and understanding. These advances have formed fundamental understandings of individual differences in abilities to learn and have shaped theory and practice in psychological testing and educational measurement. New developments have yielded new understanding of human mental functioning. Work on information processing, human and artificial intelligence, and cognitive processes such as memory, attention, and problem-solving offer powerful new perceptions of the nature of the learning process and of the acquisition of knowledge and intellectual skills. These new developments provide the foundation for a knowledge base of education. They will allow educators to reformulate the curriculum of learning for children and their teachers

(Glaser, 1984; Resnick, 1984). Cognitive science also allows us to redefine the organization and administration of schools along lines that maximize learning, without impeding it as so many of our current practices do.

The chances of these new developments being used to train the vast new numbers of teachers about to join the profession are small. However, the opportunity is there and the effort must be made. This needed emphasis on cognitive science forms one of the major components of conceptual framework for education and is discussed extensively in Chapter 8 *(Chapter 11, Second-Order Changes 1 & 2)*. The processes by which these advances can be implemented in teacher education preparation programs are described in Chapter 10 *(Chapter 13, Second-Order Changes 21, 22, 24, 27, 28, & 30)*.

Retraining university faculty

At the current time practically all national and state reports have focused their recommendations for change on elementary and secondary school teachers. Very few have mentioned the teachers of teachers, the university faculty. Long-term fundamental change in the quality of instruction provided children will not be achieved if we do not change how and what our children's teachers learn, no matter how bright they might be. We would only wind up with brighter teachers doing more of what teachers have been doing for years. To change the quality of instruction we must change the university faculty.

Most of today's teacher education faculty are tenured (Ottinger, 1987) and have been for many years. They are an aging group; many, if not most, are in their late 50's and early 60's (Carnegie Foundation for the Advancement of Teaching, 1985). They were initially hired during the 1960's when there was a faculty shortage, at a time when many faculty were needed to train huge numbers of teachers. Few have impressive credentials. Most do not conduct research (discussed more fully in Chapter 10). Many are not current in their fields or knowledgeable about conditions in today's schools. A large percentage of university education faculty are adequate teachers, but they badly need updating. Most academic subjects have changed dramatically in the past decade. So also has research on learning and instruction. Yet many teacher education faculty have kept up with neither. We must find ways to either update or get rid of those faculty who will not improve themselves to make way for younger, more vigorous faculty.

As noted earlier, America is beginning to experience a teacher shortage. It is expected to become worse during the next decade. This trend has been noticeable for the past several years. We are experiencing a baby boom at the early grades, a bubble of enrollment that will rise through the schools over the next 20 years. This enrollment increase will demand many new teachers, and it happens just when 40% of our current teaching force is reaching retirement age. Schools of education will have to train vast numbers to fill these positions. Who will train them? Many will be trained by older, worn-out faculty who themselves need updating. University faculty must improve the quality of their teaching and act as better role models for prospective teachers *(Chapter 13, Second-Order Changes 18, 19, 20, 25, 32 & 33).*

Retraining the administrative leadership

Few of the national reform reports dealt with the issue of the administrative leadership of the schools, although, since 1980, papers and reports have paid attention to the problems of educational administration (Hoy, 1982; Fogarty, 1983; and Pitner, 1982). Recommendation E of *A Nation at Risk* (1983) did address the question of leadership in America's schools.

Few others mentioned anything, except perhaps in a peripheral manner, about the administrators of our schools, or the need to retrain them, until the 1987 publication, *Leaders for America's Schools* (National Commission on Excellence in Educational Administration). This document was followed in 1988 by a companion report, *Leaders for America's Schools* (Griffiths, D., Stout, R. and Forsyth, P., 1988), which contained, not only the NCEEA recommendations, but also many of the data and working papers. The recommendations of this report and the work of the National Policy Board for Educational Administrators (1989) are beginning to exert an influence on educational administrator preparation programs. But these efforts appear to be more concerned with preserving the "respectability" of administrators than in promoting more effective learning on the part of students. These reports have resulted in most states establishing committees and task forces to generate improvements in school management (Hoyle, 1989). However, the recommendations generated by the committees have done so with little research to validate their recommendations (Hoyle, 1989).

The general lack of concern with the issues and problems of educational leadership is surprising. Over the past 20 years, countless studies have documented the profound influence and importance of capable school leadership. These studies have documented time and again the characteristics of effective school leaders. These characteristics are clear, and most can be taught. In view of such findings and understandings, one wonders why the leaders of schools (the principals) were not more prominently mentioned in these national reports and recommendations. It is obvious that if we were successful in improving the teachers of our schools but did nothing about the schools' leadership, we would accomplish very little in the long run. To improve our schools, we must improve their leadership. However, this does not necessarily mean the administrators *(Chapter 12, Second-Order Changes 3, 6 & 7; Chapter 14, Second-Order Changes 34-36)*.

Allow sufficient time

Americans in general are impatient and suffer from a quick-fix mentality, particularly with regard to education (Florio, 1983). They perceive a problem on Monday, they develop a solution on Tuesday, and they want to see results on Wednesday. In education, it does not work that quickly. The time span between implementation and performance outcomes is often considerable (Elmore and McLaughlin, 1988). It usually takes years from the time a solution is implemented until results in education are demonstrated. The allocation or re-allocation of resources, the training of personnel, the organization of service delivery are but some of the factors that must be developed and in place before a solution can be validly evaluated against student performance (Elmore and McLaughlin, 1988).

Education, by virtue of the individuals it serves, is a developmental process. It takes a minimum of four years to train a teacher new methods, and many more years for the results to show up in children's learning. Time must be allowed to see these results, otherwise, we run a very strong risk of destroying positive benefits and results by being too impatient. The pace of change in American education has increased in the past 40 years. We have often leapt from fad to fad and lost time, energy, and positive learning outcomes. We must allow the time for the developmental nature of education and children to take effect.

At an Excellence Forum held in the summer of 1984 (College Board News, 1984), co-sponsored by the Far West Laboratory, the College Board, the California School Boards Association, and the Association of California School Administrators, one thing that was stressed was that schools had a "strategic window" of only two or three years to make reforms. It was felt that if schools did not institute their own reforms within this time period, new reforms would be imposed on them. This quick-fix mentality toward education poses a severe threat to being able to implement significant quality improvement changes, which are bound to take more than two or three years to design, implement and evaluate.

Summary

Despite the political and turf issues surrounding educational reform, educational reformers had the best interests of children in mind when they established their agendas and made their recommendations. However, many of the reform recommendations were inadequate, and few address the most critical and glaring aspects of education. By and large, educational reform reports did not address the fundamental problem of American education — the need for a clearly specified and focused set of mission priorities. Without mission priorities, other aspects of educational need can not be adequately addressed. These needs include the content of learning, the re-training of teacher education faculty, the administrative leadership of the schools and the re-structuring of education. Equally important, a sufficient amount of time to design, implement and evaluate outcomes was not provided.

Section Two

Section Two

SYSTEM THEORY, EDUCATIONAL CHANGE AND EDUCATIONAL DEVELOPMENT

The next chapter of this book deals with the topic of system theory and contrasts characteristics of education as a system against selected principles of system theory. The following chapter provides an introduction to the concept of change followed by a chapter which discusses an overview of principles and variables critical to an understanding of educational change processes. The final chapter of this section presents a framework for an educational development process.

Education in the United States is a vast, complex and expensive enterprise. It includes nearly 16,000 local school systems, 50 state education agencies, some elements of the federal government, hundreds of colleges and universities, private companies, research and development centers, untold political leaders at the federal, state and local levels, millions of parents, and even more millions of students. These elements of education do not operate in a coordinated or cooperative manner. The lines of authority and responsibility are ill-defined, overlapping, and often more concerned with protecting presumed territorial rights than improving the conditions and processes of learning. These various elements of education are loosely connected, and often only by informal connections.

American education supports one of the largest bureaucratic organizations in the world. The number of personnel required to develop, implement, adhere to and monitor the incredible number of rules and regulations of education number in the hundreds of thousands. It is also one of the most expensive organizations in the world. The annual cost of operating America's educational systems amounts to billions of dollars. Any attempt to conceptualize, and possibly improve, an operation of such size, complexity and cost requires an integrating framework. Currently, no such framework exists.

System theory offers one such integrating framework. System theory offers a means of identifying and improving the critical elements of education and the links and connections among system elements. It provides a framework for identifying, characterizing, and understanding the operations of education as a system. This understanding, in turn, provides a means for identifying areas needing improvement and designing the changes necessary.

The process of educational change is a poorly understood topic, despite the more than 1,300 references identified in the professional literature since 1973. There are many aspects to the process of educational change. However, perhaps none are more critical than the realization that significant educational change as a process must be understood apart from any particular change in content. Significant educational change takes considerable time to demonstrate results. It is a process, also, that must be perceived within the context of the educational system that is either attempting internal change or having change imposed on it. It is important, therefore, to approach the process of educational change from an understanding of both system theory and educational change theory.

System and educational change theory suggest that reform efforts in American education have violated many of the basic principles of these interdependent processes. Efforts to improve American education have suffered greatly from these violations. If American education is to enable students to learn more effectively, an extraordinary set of attitudinal and conceptual shifts must take place. The framework for these shifts are presented in the final chapter of this section.

6 Systems theory and education

American public education, which is supposed to be an open social system, differs in significant fashion from the expected norms and predicted behaviors of such systems. These differences occur because outside agencies control the mission- and goal-setting procedures for schools and the relationship between an educational system and its larger environment of systems. In response, education has maintained its system structure and developed regulatory mechanisms designed to avoid structural change to environmental demands. The pace of environmental and expected educational change and adaptation has exacerbated this situation. As a result, education has not developed the capacity to respond to environmental changes by modifying its policies, mission priorities, or structures to assure more effective response to such changes. Its energy is focused on maintaining the existing structure.

These factors, variables and processes are a function of the manner education operates as a social system. This chapter will explore the nature of educational systems from a system's perspective and propose a conceptual framework within which the basic and structural problems of education will be examined, and from which recommendations for educational change will be proposed. It is not the intent or purpose of this chapter to provide a comprehensive review of system theory. The purpose is to identify those elements and considerations of system theory which permit an analysis and understanding of American public education, considered as an open social system, with the various characteristics, definitions, and processes typical of open social systems.

The history of education dates from the dawn of the human race. Only through education, i.e., learning and change, has mankind been able to develop social and educational systems designed to maintain and improve the human condition. Toffler (1970) stated that change and adaptation is not new. It began with the earliest forms of life, and mankind's survival has depended on individuals' ability to adapt. Through continued learning and change, and learning to learn more effectively, has mankind continued to develop. The system of education implemented by a particular country reflects the manner in which the cultural mores of the country will be transmitted to future generations. The process of learning and change, once halted, leads to stagnation, and stagnation leads to atrophy and ultimately to death.

This process is certainly true of biological organisms — if not of the entire organism, then of the particular organ involved with the atrophying process. We know further, that if an *open system*, either biological or social, does not adapt to a changing environment, it perishes (Burns & Stalker, 1961 1966; Cadwallader, 1968). Burns and Stalker indicate that within static environmewnts, closed systems work well. In changing environments, however, characterized by numerous changes, demands, and politics, closed systems tend to be increasingly entropic, and eventually die. Open systems work much better and have a greater probability of survival in changing environments.

King and Cleveland (1980) have extended this line of thinking. They classify environmental changes as either random or systematic. *Random changes* are those unexpected changes in the system environment to which the system members react. Most educational reform can be characterized as a response to random environmental change. *Systematic change* implies planning for change and continuation. Systematic change can also be sub-classified as temporary or permanent. *Temporary systematic change* requires adjustment by system members. *Permanent systematic change* requires system adaptation. Systematic educational change and reform has been primarily temporary in nature. Failure to control educational improvement efforts has produced no permanent systematic change.

Miles (1964a) points out that permanent systems find it difficult to change themselves. He argues that a major portion of energy available to the system goes to carrying out routine operations with little energy left over for diagnosis, planning and innovation. He argues further that all organizations tend to achieve, maintain and return to a state of equilibrium which is perhaps a means of preserving identity, character, institutions and culture.

Brickell (1964) supports Miles by arguing that institutional stability ensures maximum production at a given moment. Any change automatically reduces production, at least until new habit patterns are formed.

Watson (1967) argues that, according to systems theory, social systems are stable and homeostatic. After minor disturbances, they return to a state of equilibrium resembling their previous state. This provides them a sort of self-regulating character allowing them to meet the demands of the environment without being permanently disturbed.

This is a most critical point with respect to examining the history of change and adaptation of American public education. It helps to explain why public education in America has kept its form, basically unaltered, for so many years and why it has remained so resistant to change and so consistent in its form, appearance and operation.

There is a curious situation that operates with respect to education and a few other social systems in American society which permits this paradoxical situation. A look at these circumstances will provide a necessary framework for understanding the conditions and forces governing educational change in America. It will also provide a framework against which the recommendations for educational change and improvement made later in this book can be examined.

This framework is premised on systems theory, of which only a very brief introduction will be presented. [For a more complete treatment of this subject, the reader is referred to Bertalanffy (1968), Berrien (1968), Buckley (1968), and Schoderbek, Schoderbek and Kefalas (1985).] The principles of system theory to be discussed here, besides basic definitions, include the those of entropy, equifinality and regulation. Studying these principles will help the reader understand how education operates as a social system and how the principles effect appropriate educational change procedures.

Social systems

Berrien (1968) defines a "*system*" as "a set of components interacting with each other and a boundary which possesses the property of filtering both the kind and rate of flow of inputs and outputs to and from the system" (p. 14). Berrien describes an *open system* as one which can accept and respond to inputs such as stimuli, energy, and information. In contrast, a *closed system* is one which functions within itself. It should be noted that Berrien's definition of an open system does not assume stability of the system as some other authors do (Bertalanffy, 1968). According to Kast & Rosenzweig (1985) closed systems receive their inputs only from internal agents and all their operations are contained within the organization and internally focused. Closed systems receive direction partially from external agents and are externally focused.

An equally important aspect of this theory is the notion of *environment of systems.* According to Hall and Fagan (1968):

115

For a given system, the environment is the set of all objects, a change in whose attributes affect the system and also those objects whose attributes are changed by the behavior of the system (p. 83).

In relation to school systems, the community in which the school system is embedded, the state board of education, and teacher preparation programs can each be an element of the environment of a given school system at a particular time. Obviously some elements are part of the system, but also at times are part of the system environment. Their actions at that time have no direct bearing on system functioning unless they are interacting with system components. Parents and school board members are examples of these overlapping elements. When school board members are not dealing with school system operations are not part of the environment of the system. In the sense of Berrien (1968), they are boundary personnel, and as such, particularly critical persons in the educational change process.

Although their influence has waned recently as initiators of educational change, local boundary personnel can impede, and even block, the successful implementation of change mandated by higher levels of boundary personnel, e.g., state school boards, state legislatures. The control of which groups have the authority to institute significant change in educational policy and practices has shifted. Although local boards of education can still institute some changes which may affect local schools, the group with the greatest impact on education — personnel preparation, curriculum, and resources — has increasingly been state-level boards.

Local system boundary personnel have lost the opportunity to control and institute change in such policy matters as curriculum, personnel preparation, and educational objectives for the schools. However, they maintain the power to impede, delay, and, in some situations, block the successful implementation of changes mandated by higher authority. They do this by failing to act, or by acting in a way that clearly signals to system members that they are opposed to the change. Unless these boundary personnel several levels removed institute change through legislation, local system members (principals and teachers) may be more influenced in their actions by the local boundary personnel than by boundary personnel several levels removed.

Miller (1977) and Reilly (1969) have pointed out there is a hierarchy of systems, ranging from minute biological organisms to complex international organizations. As Reilly previously indicated, each of these system levels is ordinarily more heavily influenced by the next highest level of system in the hierarchy than by those more removed.

According to system theory, any system — biological, social, or other — must have inputs in the form of direct energy or material that can be transformed into outputs, a product of some type which is related to and a function of the amount of inputs. These inputs must come from the environment because, for all practical purposes, there are no systems, except perhaps in a particular chemical reaction, where the inputs and outputs are self-contained (Bertalanffy, 1968). Certainly, there are no closed social systems. All open social systems draw their inputs from the environment and project their outputs into the environment, either the same from which came the inputs or another. This is an "open system" because it is not self-contained.

There are, however, different characteristics associated with open systems. There are several key concepts which are crucial to understanding social systems. Measuring educational systems against these concepts will provide an understanding of the educational change process as it operates in American education. Defining these characteristics of an open social system will provide a framework for (1) contrasting the educational system against these characteristics and (2) understanding better the nature of the educational system so as to improve its structure or functions or, preferably, both. In developing this understanding of the educational system, we are seeking to develop a conceptual framework for education and the educational change process.

The principle of entropy

Entropy, from the second principle of thermodynamics, is a process in a closed system that must increase to a maximum where a state of equilibrium is reached and the process stops. Entropy is also a measure of probability and, in a closed system, tends to a state of *probable distribution*, which is the tendency to maximum disorder (Bertalanffy, 1968). In open systems, this tendency is the reverse. Human evolution and development demonstrate a tendency toward increased order, complexity, organization, and homogeneity. This tendency toward order operates through negative entropy. Although this tendency is not demonstrated by all social systems in an open educational system, a tendency toward increased centralization of policy development, decision-making, control of resources, accountability standards and procedures, and control of personnel is likely to occur over time.

The principle of equifinality

The *principle of equifinality* states that, in any closed system, the final state of the system is unequivocally determined by the initial conditions. In an

117

open system, however, the final state of the system may be reached from different starting points and conditions as well as by different routes (Bertalanffy, 1968). This principle has profound implications for school organization, classroom organization, planning operations, and instructional strategies in the development of programs for teaching students with different learning levels, patterns, and rates. It also has important connotations for one's philosophy and expectations when working with children from different cultural and economic backgrounds.

The principle of control

Derived from the field of communication, or information theory, the *principle of control* concerns the principles of feedback and regulation. Actually, both of these principles can be subsumed under the concept of control. *Feedback* is defined as that process which is used to detect a disturbance between the desired state of affairs and the actual state of affairs (Ashby, 1968). If these two states are harmonious there is no need for action. On the other hand, if these two states are sufficiently discordant, the organism or system becomes aware that some action is necessary to return to or to re-establish a harmonious state. The purpose of feedback is to achieve stabilization of a certain action (Bertalanffy, 1968) or to achieve a state of homeostasis.

According to the *principle of regulation,* the process of regulation provides control of the feedback mechanisms (Ashby, 1968) and is designed to maintain a homeostatic condition in the organism. Although Ashby (1968) is concerned with regulation in biological systems, certain aspects of this concept have considerable relevance for social systems. According to Ashby, the process of regulation is primarily concerned with controlling the flow and variety of information that enters and leaves the system. It is the regulator's task to control the flow of a variety of information to the system. An effective regulator controls the flow of information to minimize disturbances to the larger system. Ashby uses the example of air-conditioning. If the regulator is effective, a person in the room will be unable to tell how hot it is outside. If the regulator is not effective, the person will soon notice that the room is becoming hot.

Another essential feature of the principle of regulation is that a regulator acts as a channel of communication. As such, it has a finite capacity to absorb and transmit information. However, it cannot transmit information of a nature it was not designed to detect or transmit.

If control is perceived of as a controller of the regulatory processes, and there is a perfect regulator, then the controller mechanism has complete control over the outcome if the desired outcome is to maintain a homeostatic condition (Ashby, 1968).

A *homeostatic condition* is the generally desired state of biological organisms. Homeostasis requires a regulatory process that counteracts deviation or change. Marvyama (1968) has presented the concept of deviation-acting and -amplifying systems which are processes of mutual causal relationships that counteract or amplify deviations between the original conditions of the systems. Both deviation-counteracting and -amplifying systems are mutual causal systems. Elements within each system affect each other simultaneously or alternately. The difference between the two systems is that the deviation-counteracting system has mutual negative feedback between the elements, and the deviation-amplifying system has mutual positive feedback between its elements. A system which is deviation-counteracting seeks to reduce disturbances among system components or between it and other elements within its environment.

Complex adaptive systems

Buckley (1967, 1968) presented the concept of a social system as a complex adaptive system. He argued that the mechanical equilibrium model and the orgasmic homeostasis model are inappropriate and inaccurate descriptions of an open social system. According to Buckley, a sociocultural system is a complex adaptive system. Buckley holds that an equilibrial system is relatively closed and entropic and that, in going to equilibrium, it loses structure and has a minimum of free energy.

Such systems are affected only by external events and have no internal or indigenous sources of change. The system's main function is to maintain the given structure of the system within predetermined limits. Its feedback mechanisms are geared primarily to self-regulation (structure maintenance; first-order change) rather than adaptation (change of system structure; second-order change). These system features will be discussed further in later sections and chapters because they describe the condition of the American educational enterprise.

Complex adaptive systems are open internally as well as externally. This means that system components exchange information internally that may result in component change as well as system change. This internal and external exchange of information, i.e., self-regulation, provides for self-direction so that the system may change or elaborate its structure for either survival or increased effectiveness of function. However, Vickers (1968) raises strong issues regarding the endless interaction between and among individuals, systems, and their environments.

The first of these issues is that biological evolution determines future growth and development patterns by shaping such patterns in human genes. Further, although the theory also allows for differences, cultural development and conditioning mold and shape a particular value structure which may be shared by a number of societies. The influence of this cultural conditioning is immense, but not absolute for any individual or sub-group of individuals. This fact is important because biological patterns of development are pre-determined by the interaction of certain gene combinations. The value structure of a society is a function of its history, environmental context and objectives. Gene pattern is not open to change, although the extent of realization of the particular biological pattern is also dependent upon the nature of the environment. The cultural pattern is open for total change, at least theoretically.

This line of reasoning can be applied to the structure and functioning of open social systems. Biological systems display an equilibristic characteristic because of the limitations of their gene characteristics. Social systems, on the other hand, are an artifact of a particular society and its interaction with a specific environment. Therefore, the laws governing social systems are not fixed as they are with biological systems. With social systems, systems theory is restricted to description rather than providing fixed, immutable laws of system function. Further, this suggests that social systems may display characteristics which differ from the expected, either on the basis of equilibrial models or the current state of knowledge about social system models.

A second aspect of Vickers' propositions concerns the regulating process of social systems. According to Vickers, this process has three functions. It must (1) receive information about how things are going in relation to how they should be going, (2) be able to initiate behaviors, and (3) select the appropriate, or "best fit," behavior from among those available in the circumstances.

At this point we must digress from Vickers' thinking and revisit Marvyama and his distinction of deviation-counteracting and deviation-amplifying systems. The distinction between these functions holds that the functions of the regulating process of each system provide entirely different results for system operations. In the case of deviation-counteracting systems, the regulating process is focused on minimizing disturbances between two or more systems. With deviation-amplifying systems, the regulating process is aimed at maximizing such disturbances. Thus, how system members interpret the information concerning Vickers' questions depends to a great extent on the type of the systems' regulating process.

The implications of Vickers' questions and the type of regulating process raise critical problems concerning system functioning. How does the system know that action is needed? How does it decide what to do? How does it make its decision effective? In a deviation-counteracting system, the necessary decision is to choose that behavior most likely to reduce system disturbance to an acceptable level. The converse is true in a deviation-amplifying system.

One final aspect of Vickers' thinking must be considered. How do systems learn to choose possible alternative courses of action and how is this experience transmitted to future system members? The answer to this question involves learning by experience and passing this knowledge to future generations. Generally, future system members will respond to a given situation in much the same way previous system members responded. Two results of this knowledge-passing are possible. First, the knowledge may allow the system to make an appropriate decision. Second, the knowledge may produce an inappropriate decision and the system is faced with failure, or even extinction.

This latter situation is usually caused by a significant change in the environment which the previous system members had either not encountered or anticipated in their sharing of knowledge. Four possible reactions by the system are usually possible in such a situation: (1) the system can alter itself; (2) the system may alter the environment; (3) the system may leave the environment; or (4) the system may alter its relation with the environment. Each of these possibilities is dependent upon the system's capacity to judge, initiate, and complete the appropriate action. Choosing these alternative courses of action is a function of the regulating process and its controller mechanisms.

The controller mechanisms may be exercised by one of three means — error, rule, or purpose. *Control by error* occurs when the system receives signals through the regulating process to control (modify) future behavior. *Control by rule* occurs when a behavior is chosen because of similar situations in past circumstances. *Control by purpose* exists when a behavior is chosen because it is likely to have an expected and desired outcome. Again, the presumption is that such control is governed by the particular system.

This control by a system may not always be possible. The pace of change in industrialized countries may be faster than a system's rate of adaptation can match. When such an overload occurs, the usual response may no longer be available or viable in the new circumstances. In such a situation the regulatory mechanisms tend to become over-occupied with short-term behavior at the expense of more important long-term objectives of the system. This creates to a vicious cycle which Watzlawick and his colleagues (1974) have described as the "Game Without End." Further, a system which is constantly under heavy pressure to change may severely limit its rate of change to accommodate its capacity for regulation, i.e., amount of information transmission.

Buckley (1967, 1968) offers three other important considerations. The first is the expectation that stress and strain are ever-present among systems and among system components. The way the system responds to these tensions is one measure of its capacity for successful adaptation. Second, the *state* of a system should not be confused with the system *structure*, since the structure itself may need to be changed to maintain the state of the system. Third, an adaptive system should not be confused with a system structure since continuity of the system may require change of structure. This change is a complex process involving the internal condition of the system, the nature of its environment, and the functional relationships between the two.

It was not the intent or purpose to provide a comprehensive review of this field. The purpose was to identify those elements and considerations of systems theory which permit an analysis and contrast of American public education, considered as an open social system, with the various characteristics, definitions, and processes typical of open social systems.

Education as a system

The American educational system is a vast conglomeration of some 16,000 school sub-systems existing in a loosely connected relationship.

Sergiovanni and Carver (1980) describe the educational system as composed of three connected, sub-systems: political, organizational and human. The *political sub-system* makes decisions about system inputs will converted to outputs through policies and legislation. The *organizational system* is composed of a formal unit with its own survival goals of eliminating uncertainty and maintaining the present equilibrium, plus any additional goals and purposes that society gives it. The organizational system works through people (the *human system*) to achieve its goals and purposes. It is hierarchical in structure, and each of the three major sub-systems includes its own structure of sub-systems corresponding to the levels of governance (national, state, local and building level).

These sub-systems are governed by ill-defined and overlapping lines of authority from the federal, state, and local levels (Dalin, 1978). These overlapping controls create confusion over who is responsible for determining the mission, policies, and practices of school systems at either a school or state level. The decentralized nature of education under local control is changing to a trend toward a higher degree of centralization with control at the state level. In some states, such as North Carolina, increasing state control, as evidenced by a mandated set of learning objectives, teacher preparation standards, and accreditation procedures, may co-exist with minimal local option for determining educational procedures.

The lack of clearly defined lines of responsibility and authority for determining school system policies and practices result in diverse opinions of appropriate educational outcomes and the means for achieving them. The definition of appropriate educational outcomes are equally diverse.

Sarason (1982) argues that school personnel will lead one to believe that there is *a* system, that it is run by somebody in some central place, that it tends to operate as a never ending source of obstacles to those within the system, that a major goal of the individual is to protect against the harmful influences of the system, and that any one person has and can have no influence on the system. In one sense, the system works — teachers teach, students attend classes, and administrators administrate. But rarely does an educator believe the system is working well or that his own job could not be done better if the system operated differently. Sarason points out that each individual's conception of the system determines his role performance, even though the conception may be invalid.

Sarason pays particular attention to the role of principals and their perception of and relation to the system. He indicates a tendency among principals to anticipate trouble in relation to the system. This attitude is one of the most frequent and strong obstacles against trying anything new. The role of the principal cannot be understood by a listing or description of what he or she can or cannot do. Any job description of a principal consists essentially of a set of generalizations, which, if anything, states or implies the minimum limits or scope of the position. It does not describe the maximum limits or scope of the position. According to Sarason, the model urban school system does not provide the climate in which new ideas or innovative ventures can be easily attempted.

Sarason also believes that the center of control, internal or external, felt by educators is important in attempting to bring about educational change. He wonders if a principal (teacher, student) believes that s/he controls his/her own professional destiny, or whether his destiny is determined by the system or other external forces? He believes there are four interrelated factors which affect this belief.

- There is a marked tendency for school personnel to view the school system in negative terms.
- In the case of the principal, there is an equally marked tendency to view the system as the primary determinant of role performance.
- The principal's view of what the system will permit or tolerate tends to be faulty and incomplete, and it obscures the diversity in role performance.

123

- An important factor shaping the principal's view of his or her role and the system is in part at least, determined by the degree to which the principal feels he or she, rather than external factors, will govern the course of action.

Sarason also describes a school system as bounded, largely autonomous in determining its functions, structure, goals, distribution of power, personnel and role definitions. A part of this bounded system is that it may have all kinds of contacts with outside forces, but those contacts do not and should not alter the characteristics of the system. The fact is that the absorption of school personnel with the internal nature and workings of the school system, in addition to an historical stance that prevents questioning the traditional concept of a school system, has had the effect of blinding them to what was happening outside the system. This latter assertion by Sarason appears to be valid. However, a school system is controlled by many outside sources whose dominant control of educational structure, procedures, personnel preparation, curricula and resources clearly indicates that a school system is to controlled by external sources.

Sarason asserts also that the view of the school as an autonomous system has long been the basis for the belief that schools were mechanisms for social change. He questions how one could hold such a belief unless it rested on the assumption that schools were independent of outside forces? Quite obviously, schools are not independent systems. Nor have they been effective as mechanisms of social change (Dalin, 1978). Although schools have not been expected to be leaders of social change, they have been expected to be mirrors of society.

Sarason also raises the issue of who has the right and responsibility to determine the rules under which a school system will operate and be governed. Educators feel, "How can we do our jobs if everybody has the right to control and criticize us?" On the other hand, parents, political and business leaders feel that they have every right to tell the schools what and how to achieve the goals that have been established. Sarason notes that the question of who has responsibility for the schools too frequently comes up after conflict, failure, and polarization, a situation that is not likely to lead to or support change.

In order to develop educational change strategies to alleviate these problems of education, an improved understanding of how education functions as a system is necessary. Each of the system characteristics discussed below are displayed by school systems. Some systems will display more or less of these characteristics, but, overall, each is typical of the system configuration described. It is important to understand this configuration, for it determines the nature and type of change necessary for long-term improvement in education conditions and performance.

Education and entropy

The first consideration of an educational system, within the context of an open social system, is that of *entropy*. As indicated earlier, open systems tend over time toward increased order, organization, and homogeneity. This occurs in educational systems with centralization of educational policy development and other critical elements, such as personnel preparation standards, accountability standards, and curriculum mandates, increasingly being assumed at the state level. Although states have had the legal right to exercise such control, in the past eight years state legislatures and state school boards have increasingly assumed such powers. Less and less control of policy and decision-making in critical areas, e.g., curriculum, accountability, resource allocations, is being left to local boards of education. This trend to increased centralization is consistent with system theory leading to increased order, organization, and control.

Education and equifinality

The second consideration concerns the principle of *equifinality*. This principle states that, in an open system, the final condition of its formation can be reached from different initial conditions and by utilizing different procedures (Bertalanffy, 1968). Application of this principle to educational systems yields three important understandings. First, it requires that the final condition of the system be specified, so that its goals are clear and acceptable to a majority of its members. Second, it insists that the various routes to this final condition can be mapped and that under optimal conditions the desired procedure can be chosen. This presumes the direction and movement of the system is under conscious control and regulation. This factor has important implications for the discussion of control of regulation and feedback which follows this discussion. Third, this principle indicates that not all school systems have to take the same route to reach a specified outcome. Thus, required state curricula, accountability procedures, or resource allocation procedures may deny achieving the very educational goals that are desired. Local school districts may better achieve realistic goals if they have the authority to design educational programs on the basis of local conditions.

This raises the question of who decides and controls the educational route to be chosen. Educational decision-makers in America today appear to be ignoring this principle of systems theory. They are attempting to assure that all local districts achieve minimal standards of achievement by requiring uniform curricula and standardized procedures to implement such

125

curricula. These efforts ignore the principle of equifinality. Because school systems neither establish the goals for education, nor have a clearly stated mission or purpose for their efforts (Boyer, 1985; Dalin, 1978), nor control the means by which the poorly conceptualized goals of the larger society are to be achieved, education fails the test of the principle of equifinality. As such, it fails to meet one of the major criteria for an open social system.

It can be stated that the extent to which a school system tolerates, allows or promotes diversity is an indication of its capacity to incorporate change and risk improvement efforts. This statement is consistent with the principle of equifinality. One would expect to find more internal locus of control, more experimentation, higher morale, more incentives and rewards for improvement efforts, and less criticism for risk taking in schools and communities that can tolerate diversity.

Education and the principle of control

The third consideration is that of *control*, which includes the elements of *feedback* and *regulation*. As indicated earlier, if control is conceived of as a controller of the regulatory process, providing control of the outcome, it must be assumed that the system has knowledge of the desired outcome. It must be further assumed that the system has control of, i.e., can regulate, the information flow and feedback related to movement of the system toward the desired goal. Education also fails this test of being an open social system. Educational systems do not determine their own goals. Goal-setting for educational systems is established by community, state and national agencies, each with its own sense of priorities, needs and desired outcomes. Obviously, in a democracy the educational system cannot be an entity unto itself. However, under current conditions the mission priorities of schools, their procedures, and the necessary resources to achieve the goals are constantly subjected to a lack of clarity and disruptive, unnecessary and confusing changes. At best the profession of education is afforded minimal input into the goal-setting process and its associated implementation programs. An improved mechanism for developing educational policy and achieving a more coordinated articulation between the educational needs and goals of society and the expertise of professional educators is needed.

Educational systems meet the criteria for open systems in the sense they have inputs and outputs and interact with their environments. They do not meet the criteria for open social systems in the sense of controlling the mechanisms of establishing their own goals and, therefore, they do not control the regulatory mechanisms necessary to advance towards the goal.

In the absence of controlling mechanism to establish system goals and those regulatory mechanisms for moving towards mission priorities, educational systems feedback loops are more typical of the equilibrium or organismic model of system functioning than an open social system model.

Without the capacity to establish its own goals, an educational system must strive for self-preservation of the system. Any sociocultural system must have a sense of purpose for which it exists, and this motive must be under its own control. Further, a system will establish those control features necessary achieve this purpose. Protection of these features will be a first priority in its operations and responses to environmental changes. Generally, any system that does not control its own purpose or control mechanisms quickly begins the process of entropy. Therefore, without the capacity to establish explicit goals, an educational system will establish self-preservation as its implicit goal.

This goal explains why educational systems function as they do and resist structural change. First, an educational system's first priority is to maintain the structure of the system. It has no indigenous motive for system structure change to provide for increased effectiveness of function. The lack of this capacity is a serious handicap in responding to environmental changes.

Second, the lack of structural change capacity seriously inhibits internal exchange of information among system components. This internal sharing of information and feedback exchange is a necessary component for detecting significant differences between the desired and actual state of affairs. The absence of such information sharing prevents the system from determining when change of structure is necessary to improve system functioning.

Third, the basic goal of an educational system, i.e., maintenance of structure, often conflicts with the purpose(s) established by a larger environmental system, (i.e., community, state, or nation). If meeting the state's purpose requires modification of the educational system structure, the educational system responds by changing function but not structure. Thus, there are times when an educational system's priority is to achieve a homeostatic condition and it becomes a deviation-counteracting system.

This occurs when America moves through one of its countless periods of educational reform. New educational goals are established and thrust upon the schools by each reform movement (Elmore and McLaughlin, 1988). The schools have not established these goals and their achievement would require the educational system to modify its structure. This it cannot do, because the first law of system survival is system structure maintenance. Thus, education seeks to counteract reform goals and priorities by a series of functional changes which leaves the system structure unchanged.

127

Thus, by a series of functional deviation-counteracting responses, an educational system is actually maintaining deviation-amplifying differences between it and its larger system environment. These responses are an effort to maintain its structural integrity and purpose, which is primarily avoidance of structural change.

Such a response is seen in a school system's response to PL 94-142. Left to its own devices, a local school system would not likely develop and implement the programs of special education mandated by this public law. Because of the law, there are now many special education programs available for handicapped children. Seemingly, the education enterprise has assumed the responsibility for these programs. Yet, special education programs have not really been integrated into the mainstream of education activities, and the current form of special education does not seem to be achieving the results desired. However, education can point to the funds expended, the number of children served, the number of teachers involved and so forth as evidence of its accommodating these children. The point here is that special education children do not conform to uniform raw material on which the structure and processes of education are built. Therefore, programs for special education children are grafted onto the basic structure of education, only to be rejected as soon as feasible. It was not the educational establishment that developed the demand for these programs. They were imposed from the outside and, as such, were not program priorities or goals established by the schools.

As was pointed out earlier, the regulating process of a social system has three main functions. When the mission priorities of a system are under its control, these functions, based on appropriate feedback, serve to continuously orient the system toward these goals. However, when a system's goals are not under the control of the system, the regulatory functions providing feedback and goal orientation are not under its control either. In such a situation, a system has no effective means for assessing progress towards the goal.

An educational system does not have the capacity within its regulatory mechanisms to select the "best fit" behavior between its current and desired goal because it does not control the definition of the desired outcome(s). This circumstance is made even more difficult for educational systems because the larger system environments (community, state and national agencies) are constantly changing the definition of the desired goal (Dalin, 1978).

Being unable to choose "best fit" behavior is further complicated by the rapid turnover of policy managers. Each time there is an election, a new slate of decision-makers wants to alter the agreement of desired outcomes for education's objectives. In such a situation, educational systems are faced with a constantly changing array of goals. Two major consequences result. First, educational systems' responses and efforts to achieve a certain goal are constantly frustrated. There are four possible theoretical responses (Vickers, 1968) to such a situation. However, for an educational system, changing of the relationship between the educational system and its larger system is the only one of the four responses which can result. The nature of this change is to offer short-term functional responses to outcome demands and definitions which require structural modifications. As described here an educational system lacks the capacity for this structural change.

Secondly, when the demand and pace for change outstrips a system's capacity for change, the regulatory mechanisms of the system focus on short-term behavior at the expense of the more important long-term objectives of the system (Watzlawick et al., 1974). This has certainly occurred with education during the past three decades. Education's response to this overload situation has been to curtail regulatory functions to assure maintenance of system structure. This reaction has prohibited education's ability to adapt constructively to the environmental demands for change. Because education does not establish the goals or outcomes for its behavior, it has no other option. Broudy (1975) described this situation more than a decade ago when he claimed that, as institutions act to protect their functions and functionaries, they respond with confusion, hesitation, and ad hoc improvisations. Broudy further described education's adaptations as transitory and superficial. Almost two decades ago, Fantini (1970) said that schools simply do not have the capacity to deal with diversity and have been given too many missions for which they are unprepared. Nothing in the past 20 years has changed to correct these observations. Schools have become captive systems constantly seeking to maintain structural homeostasis, by relying on functional adaptations to environmental changes and pressures.

Innovative systems

Another feature of system functioning must be addressed within the general context of educational system operations — the extent to which the system demonstrates the characteristics of and capacity for innovation. Much of the literature about innovative systems or institutions comes from sociologists and industrial psychologists. A typical description is that of Steiner's (1965) creative organization which encourages idea men, has open lines of communication, is decentralized and diversified, encourages contact with outside sources, employs heterogeneous types of personnel, uses an objective and fact-finding approach and is willing to try out new ideas on their merit, regardless of their originator. In short, a creative organization is a collection of creative personnel who do not get in each other's way.

Mort (1964) described schools with high adaptability as those in which (1) teachers are more highly trained and more receptive to modern educational ideas; (2) administrators provide active support for adaptations rather than remaining neutral; and (3) the public's attitudes favored modern practices. Hilfiker's (1969) study demonstrated that innovative schools have open climates, higher expenditures, younger staff members, larger professional staffs, and staff members who remained in the system a shorter period of time.

Huberman (1973) stated that many of these characteristics can be grouped around Miles' (1964c) ten dimensions of organizational health. In general terms, a healthy organization not only survives its environment, but continues to cope adequately over the long haul, and continuously develops and extends its surviving and coping abilities. Of the following list of ten, many of which were drawn by analogy from the behavior of persons or small groups, the first three are related to tasks, organizational goals, the transmission of messages, and the way in which decisions are made. The second group (4-6) refers to the internal state of the organization. The third group (7-10) deals with growth and changeability.

1. Clarity and acceptance of goals. Members are reasonably clear about goals and their acceptability. Goals are achievable with available resources and are appropriate or consistent with demands of environment.

2. Adequacy of communication. The movement of information is crucial. Internal feedback and communication for regulation purposes is crucial. Personnel can obtain the information they need without exerting undue efforts. This communication must be among all parties involved in the system.

3. Optimal power equalization. Subordinates can influence upwards, and they can perceive that their superiors can do the same with their superiors. Units stand in a dependent relationship with each other. There is less emphasis on one unit being able to control the entire operation.

4. Resource utilization. The organization works to its potential. Personnel are neither overloaded nor idling. They have a sense of learning and developing while making their contribution to the organization.

130

5. Cohesiveness. The organization knows who it is. This is obviously related to the first condition. Personnel want to stay with the organization, be influenced by it, and have an influence on it. Lippittt (1967) also stresses this point. Teachers who feel they had an influence on other teachers and on school policy are more likely to share information, new ideas, and their own problems with others. Those who feel alienated from colleagues see no point in communicating since they are convinced no one would listen.

6. Morale. Referring to the sense of well-being or satisfaction of the group, morale includes psychological safety, trust, psychological freedom, and openness. Schools with qualities of openness or trust tend to create a climate favoring change and innovation.

7. Innovativeness. A healthy system will tend to invent new procedures, move towards new goals, produce new kinds of products, diversify itself, and become more differentiated over time. Such a system will grow, develop, and change, rather than remain routine and standard. There are a number of implications for the structure of education here. School systems with these characteristics could be expected to institutionalize innovation, to devote space, time and money for individual and organizational development programs, to set up change-generating and experimental units with a research and development function, to provide rewards for innovators, and to install environmental scanning units.

8. Autonomy. A healthy organization is independent from its environment because it does not respond passively to demands from without, nor destructively or rebelliously to perceived demands. Like the healthy individual, the school system would not treat its responses to the community as determining its own behavior. This is related to the Systematic Learning Organization described by Dalin (1978). [This type of organization is discussed more fully in Chapter 8.]

9. Adaption. The term adaptation implies that the healthy school is realistic and has effective contact with its surroundings. Its ability to bring about corrective change should be faster than the change cycle in the community.

10. Problem-solving adequacy. All systems have problems. But a healthy system is able to cope with the problems. In an effective system problems are solved with a minimum of energy. They stay solved, and

the problem-solving mechanisms are not weakened, but maintained and strengthened. Conflicts are treated as an indication that changes are needed.

Society has created systems called schools to attain goals and more specific objectives that could not easily be achieved without such organization. The schools organize themselves in certain ways to achieve these goals in a systematic and effective manner. The most common organizational forms in education are professional, collegial, and bureaucratic, with the latter being the most common. The objective of the organization is to facilitate a series of interactions between teachers and students via formal instruction in the classroom. Innovative schools monitor those interactions more closely and will attempt to modify them to look more closely at the structural characteristics that distinguish these innovative systems from those which more often resist or reject improvements. Bureaucratic organizational formats hinder implementing innovative attempts and stifles creativity of the system personnel.

Why don't school systems display more creative and innovative characteristics? Why don't these characteristics occur more frequently in schools? Is it due to system factors, personnel preparation, political interference, economic factors, the ever changing cast of leaders, or some combination of these? As interesting as these questions are for study and analysis, it is far more important to address the "what" question.

Since most school systems display characteristics opposite of creative, bureaucratic, hierarchical, deviation-countering, etc., "what" processes can be utilized to encourage school systems and their personnel to move to one which displays the characteristics described by Stiener. The answer to this question requires an understanding of the educational change process and the development of a framework which would allow educational systems to develop their potential and capabilities for continually improving student outcomes. These issues are addressed in the next three chapters.

Summary

An analysis and comparison of education with the factors and considerations outlined above leads to two major conclusions: (1) American public education exhibits few of the characteristics of open social systems. (2) The American educational system exhibits characteristics that differ significantly from those expected in open social systems. In fact, it does, display more characteristics typical of an equilibrial system. These component and procedural differences are a function of education's history and its relationship with its larger environmental systems. These differences have also severely limited education's effectiveness and capacity to respond to critical needs, particularly on a long-term basis, and prevented it from developing and implementing the conditions and procedures necessary for fundamental changes in its structure and functions.

7　Introduction to change

The previous chapter addressed several key issues of system theory and contrasted education as a system with those principles. It concluded that education operates as a unique form of system, displaying some, but not all, characteristics of an open social system. These system characteristics of education serve as a backdrop against which educational change efforts must be perceived. A knowledge of how education operates as a system will make change and improvement of education much more likely. This chapter will examine fundamental aspects of educational change theory and outline a framework of educational change which will serve as a basis for (1) examining current educational reform efforts and (2) developing recommendations for an educational change process.

One must examine and understand the process of educational change for attempts at improving education to succeed (Dalin, 1978). Fullan (1982) argues that, in theory, the purpose of educational change is to help schools accomplish their goals more effectively by replacing some programs or practices with better ones. However, neither the process of educational change nor the characteristics of education as a system is very well understood. The lack of understanding the key elements involved in this change process — schools as organizations (systems), the process of change, and the management of change — has prevented education from achieving its full potential (Dalin, 1978).

The process of educational change can be examined and understood apart from the content associated with any particular change. According to Dalin (1978), efforts at educational change have been unsuccessful because of at least one of the following reasons.

- Lack of a systematic problem-identification process.
- Lack of clearly defined goals and benefits.

135

- Practical factors embedded in the setting or environment.
- A failure to view schools and the educational process as part of a complex social system.
- The tendency of educational reformers to be *content*-oriented rather than *process*-oriented.

The forces of environmental (social, political, economic) change have caused alterations in educational policy, practice, and direction (Dalin, 1978). Professional educators must understand these forces and contexts if they are to initiate educational changes of their own, to respond adequately and appropriately to educational changes initiated by others, and to direct the means by which our children will be educated.

A background on the types and nature of change is helpful in understanding educational change. Several aspects of the change process must be considered, regardless of the complexity of the system. Although the more complex systems have more factors to consider, the characteristics and processes of change are similar.

Change does not necessarily involve instability. If alteration is gradual and innovations are reliably evaluated and gradually absorbed, the stability of any social system is not seriously affected. In fact, change can have a very positive element. Mankind's development and history shows that change is essential to expansion and greater adaptation to life and the environment. However, this change is best accomplished in a gradual and steady manner (Morrish, 1976).

[Educational literature describes a number of models of change, as well as types and dimensions of change. Not all will be discussed here. Only several have specific relevance to this chapter. Table 7.1 provides a summary of those discussed.]

Table 7.1
Dimensions and types of change

(Dalin 1973) Typology of Innovations Category of Change	(Rand Corporation 1975) Target of Change	(Dalin 1978) Critical Dimensions
1. Objectives and Functions	1. Centrality (CPC1)[2]	1. Technological
2. Organization and Administration	2. Complexity (CPC2)	2. Behavorial
3. Roles and Relationships	3. Nature and amount of	3. Organizational Change
4. Curriculum Change	4. Social Evaluation	4. Consonance of Change (NCP)[3]

Dalin (1978) described a *"typology of innovations"* with respect to educational change. The four dimensions of this typology include: (1) objectives and functions, (2) organization and administration, (3) roles and relationships, and (4) curriculum. According to Dalin, all educational change efforts are characterized by one of these four dimensions.

Havelock (1971) suggested four categories relating to how much change is required in a given system: (1) change in both the size and scope of operations, (2) the acquisition of new skills, (3) changing system goals, and (4) changing values and orientations. Havelock suggested that there may be six types of change required for adaptation or adoption:

- Substitution, as substituting one textbook for another;
- Alteration, the changing of guidance functions from teachers to a professional staff;
- Addition, as when computers are added to a curriculum;
- Restructuring, providing work space for smaller classrooms;
- The elimination of old behavioral patterns and habits; and
- The reinforcing of old behavioral patterns.

[2] CPC1--Counterpart, Category 1.
[3] NCP--No Counterpart.

Williams, Wall, Marin and Berchin (1974) have identified three types of educational change. *Enforced change* results from pressure from outside the school. *Expedient change* is based on alterations devised by the school to avoid true change. This type of change is resistance or counter pressure to enforced change. These two types of change are the most common in education. Change is enforced from the outside and school systems tend to respond with expedient change. The third type of change identified by Williams, et al., is defined as *organizational renewal* that builds on the needs, initiative, and imagination of individuals within the school. It is neither an accommodation to external pressure nor a tactic for resisting second-order change. It is also not very common in educational change efforts.

Fullan (1982) has suggested that educational change is multi-dimensional, with three components: (1) the possible use of new or revised materials, (2) possible use of new teaching approaches, and (3) the possible alteration of beliefs. Fullan suggests that all three are necessary because they represent the means of achieving a particular educational goal. Fullan also suggests there are three difficulties in approaching educational change. First, there is no assumption about who develops the materials, defines the teaching approaches, and decides on the beliefs. Second, there is a dilemma and tension that runs through the educational change literature in which two different emphases or perspectives are evident: (a) the *fidelity approach* to change, which is based on the assumption that innovation exists and the task is to get people to use it as intended by the developer, and (b) *Multi-adaptation*, which stresses change is and should be a result of adaptation and decisions taken by users as they work with a new approach. Third, according to Fullan, it is difficult to define the objective dimensions of change.

In a study of educational change in federally supported programs conducted by the Rand Corporation, Greenwood, Mann, & McLaughlin (1975) described five dimensions of change critical for its success. These programs were the outcomes of federal policies developed in the late 1960s and local system programs implemented in the early 1970s. The dimensions are (1) centrality, (2) complexity, (3) nature and amount of change, (4) consonance, and (5) visibility.

Certain commonalties can be perceived in the lists of Dalin and Greenwood, et al. Dalin describes *objectives* and *functions* in much the same manner as Greenwood and his colleagues describe *centrality*. Each is concerned with the objectives, goals, and norms of the institution. Dalin's organization and administration is similar to that of Greenwood, et al. Although not entirely similar, each is concerned with the extent to which a particular change affects groups and decision-making processes within an

138

organization. The dimensions of *roles and relationships* (Dalin) and *nature and amount of change* (Greenwood, et al.) are each concerned with the effect on individuals and the roles they play within an institution. The remaining three dimensions, Dalin's *curriculum* and Greenwood's *consonance* and *visibility* do not seem to have counterparts in each other's scheme.

Dalin's *dimensions of change* are concerned with the focus of the intended change. Those of Greenwood et al. are more descriptive of elements of change which can be utilized to assess the causes of success or failure of a particular change effort. However, the first three dimensions of Greenwood, et al., can also describe the target of an intended change. The following four target dimensions to educational change appear to result: (1) objectives/goals/norms, (2) institutional groups and decision-making processes, (3) individual roles and development, and (4) curriculum goals, methods, and outcomes. The final two dimensions of Greenwood and his colleagues appear better suited for determining the reasons for failure or success of a particular change effort.

In addition to the focus of the intended change, there is also the *type* of intended change to be considered. Dalin (1978) has proposed four such types: (1) technological, (2) behavioral, (3) organizational, and (4) social. There is evidence that technological change can affect organizations, but also that such change tends to maintain the societal status quo (Aldrich, 1972; Travers, 1973). Most change efforts require individuals to change some aspect of their behavior. This change can range from simple to complex. Generally, the more significant the intended educational change, the more complex behavioral change is required, which often depends on change of attitude. *Organizational change* can involve a wide range of categories. For example, a group of teachers, leadership behaviors, decision-making processes, and change of an educational structure can each affect organizational change. These changes are generally quite difficult to achieve and have met with little success in education. *Social change* is an effort to redistribute power, resources, or opportunities within a society (Dalin, 1978; McDonnell and Elmore, 1987). Efforts to achieve such social change through education have not been effective.

King and Cleveland's (1980) definition of change classified it as *random* or *systematic*. These were sub-classified as *temporary* or *permanent*. These are important concepts. *Random change* is that which is not expected and must be reacted to by those individuals affected. This is the typical type of change in education. Rarely is change in education developed from within. It is usually developed from outside the educational system. Morrish (1976) attributes this to the fact that school systems are normally not responsible for the evaluation of their practices in order to determine whether changes are necessary; so most educational changes are forced from the outside. Change in education is dependent upon external forces fostering a reaction by education. When educational change has been systematic, it has usually been temporary, because the time frame allowed for development, implementation, and evaluation of the change outcomes has been too short (Dalin, 1978; McDonnell and Elmore, 1987).

As should be apparent from these dimensions and types of change, a process for achieving educational change can be extremely complex and difficult. Without comprehending and/or understanding the full nature of the educational enterprise, and the inter-related elements that are involved with any effort at educational change, it is not surprising that most attempts at planned, significant educational change have failed. Most efforts at educational change, and most that have been successful, have been targeted on individual roles and development and curricular goals, methods and outcomes. The type of change desired with these efforts has been primarily behavioral. There have been relatively few change efforts targeted on the change of objectives/goals/norms or institutional groups and decision-making processes. Where there have been such efforts, they have generally failed, or at best, have been short lived.

Efforts to significantly improve education through a planned-change process have not yielded impressive results to date. The causes for these failures are found in an incomplete understanding of several aspects of education. These include a lack of knowledge of education as a system, the educational change process, and the difference between first- and second-order change. *First-order change* is focused on changes which maintain the status quo, while *second-order change* seeks to understand and develop new methods for resolving problems by re-framing the perspective of what constitutes the problem. Second-order change also seeks to introduce new goals, organizational arrangements, and/or roles that significantly alter the usual means of solving difficult and persistent problems (Cuban, 1988a).

In order to achieve sustained educational improvement, it is necessary to understand the elements involved in the educational change process, to identify goals and problems of education, and to provide recommendations for resolution of the problems and achievement of the goals. The first step is to understand critical elements involved in the educational change process.

The first aspect of change — indeed a requirement — is that feedback is necessary at lower levels of system functioning. This is necessary in order to maintain system stability. To avoid change at a higher level of system functioning, feedback (the basis for change) is required at a lower level of system functioning. Although higher levels of system operation may be aware of the feedback to lower levels and of actions taken by lower levels

140

in response to the feedback, the higher levels of system operation usually do not become involved at this level of operation unless the feedback responses do not maintain system stability. In many cases such lower level responses may be automatic and taken without awareness at higher levels of system functioning, unless, of course, the responses do not maintain system stability or homeostasis.

This is a critical point for understanding educational change. As the previous chapter stated, the first law of any system, biological or social, is to preserve itself. This effort involves maintaining a homeostatic condition except under conditions of significant environmental change when maintaining the status quo would lead to system atrophy. Preservation of the system demands this, and, in a non-changing, unaltering environment, it is highly improbable that an open system would alter or change itself except in minor ways to maintain a homeostatic condition. It is only when conditions in the environment change to such an extent that the system cannot maintain homeostasis that it is forced to either adapt or stagnate and perish. In such situations, the feedback at lower levels of system functioning may be sufficient to maintain system stability, but system stability is a choice for death.

Thus, higher levels of system functioning must institute more drastic measures in order to survive. Such measures usually involve alterations in the structure, as well as functional operations of the system. Various system components or functions may be ceased in order to allow the system to redirect its energies and strengths to meet the new demands imposed by the environmental change. Those systems which change are able to survive; those that are not, do not. One gross measure of system intelligence may be the ease and success with which a system adapts to environmental change and new demands. Some may describe this as the ability to realistically assess environmental change and then the willingness and ability to make those alterations in system structure and function that provide the highest probability of survival within the new environment.

Two types of change have been described in the preceding discussion. Watzlawick and his colleagues (Watzlawick, Weakland, and Fisch, 1974) have termed these two types first- and second-order change. *Change of the first-order* addresses the issues confronted by the system, and although it may lead to improvement of function or system operation, it is primarily designed to bring the system back to a homeostatic condition. These efforts are made to make what already exists more efficient and more effective, without disrupting the structure of the organization, or altering significantly the roles of individuals within the organization. First-order change efforts proceed on the assumption that existing organizational structures are adequate and desirable, needing only some minor adjustments (Cuban,

141

1988a). This type of change occurs when the system's feedback mechanisms have noted that some aspect of the system's functions is in need of corrective action. An example of such provided by Watzlawick, et al., is that of a bike rider. Small changes in steering, braking, and pedaling are based on feedback and are necessary if the larger system is to remain stable, that is, if the bike rider is not to fall off, come to an undesired stop, or crash.

Minor variations in the environment may be adapted to by first-order change efforts. For example, with the bike rider, minor variations, such as change in the road surface, a small hill, or a dog passing, may be responded to by variations in braking, pedaling, and so forth. The larger system, the bike rider, remains stable and probably at times is unaware of the first-order change efforts being made to maintain the stability of the larger system. Many first-order change efforts become automatic. Thus, first-order change efforts are also designed to avoid the necessity of resorting to change of the second-order.

Change of the second-order is that change whose occurrence changes the structure of the system itself. It involves an alteration in the state or structure of the system. Second-order change seeks to alter the basic structure of the organization, reflecting major discontent with the outcomes of the current organizational arrangement.

As long as the environmental changes are minor, first-order change efforts can be effective in maintaining the stability of the larger system. If, however, the bike rider should come to a very steep hill, pedaling harder will maintain the rider's stability for only so long. At some point the rider will slow down and, if the hill continues long enough, with a steep enough gradient, come to a stop. The stability of the system is disrupted; the system has, in fact, ended. In such a situation, the only two alternatives are to stop or to adapt to a significantly changed environment by utilizing a change of the second-order. This could involve shifting to a different gear to make pedaling easier, or switching to a car. In either event, the state of the system has been significantly altered. Because of a significant alteration in the environment, the system has been forced to choose from among three alternatives, all of which may be easily perceived as undesirable. The first, to continue pedaling harder, ultimately leads to disaster. This is generally the first choice of a system when faced with a significantly altered environment — to do more of what had been done previously and which had previously been proven effective in responding to minor variations in the environment. The second choice is to allow the system to come to a stop. Self-preservation usually forbids this. The third choice is to alter the state of the system itself so that an effective response can be made to the new environment.

It is obvious why the first of these three alternatives is usually the preferred, but incorrect, choice. It allows mechanisms to be utilized which have proven effective previously and, more significantly, does not require a significant alteration to the system structure. Most systems attempt to avoid such significant alterations. An educational system is dedicated to preservation of system structure, thereby greatly inhibiting its capacity for change and improvement. Such changes are costly. They are disruptive. In social systems, they invariably cause some persons to lose power, and they can result in the loss of system components. In such social systems, those persons in components that might be discarded tend to argue strenuously against the proposed changes to the system. This is understandable; but if these arguers against change are sufficiently persuasive, they may sway the system response to continue first-order change efforts to a second-order change problem. In education, this has occurred time and time again.

One additional point needs to be made regarding how a system develops a response to a changed environment. It is the system's ability to anticipate and/or detect changes in the environment (the regulatory process) which determines or necessitates either first or second-order change efforts. In a perfectly static environment, or under circumstances in which a system completely controls the environment, neither type of change would be required. Of course, neither of these situations exists, at least for any social system. Therefore, a system's ability to survive is, to a large extent, dependent upon its ability to anticipate or (failing to anticipate) to detect as quickly as possible any changes in the environment that may require a response by the system. A system's detection apparatus is a complicated affair, and in complex social organizations it can account for a substantial portion of the system's budget. The lack of an adequate detection apparatus can be a dangerous state of affairs, for either the lack of one or an inadequate one can prevent timely and appropriate responses by the system, or, in extreme cases, can lead to the system's death (Weick, 1976).

As in the case of the bike rider pedaling up a steep hill, if the rider detects early enough that continued pedaling will not allow him to gain the crest, he can shift to an easier gear, hook a ride behind a car, or switch to driving a car. A number of alternatives become possible that will allow him to gain his objective. Of course, he can always turn around and go back down the hill. In that event he avoids the necessity for second-order change and does not achieve his objective.

By detecting early enough that the hill is sufficiently steep to negate the usefulness of continued first-order change, the rider is in a position to consider and choose from the available second-order change alternatives. The importance of this point cannot be overstated. The rider must detect the amount of environmental change, decide if continuing first-order change efforts will continue to be effective, and, if not, determine what second-order change alternatives are available, and choose the most appropriate one which will provide the highest probability of success at the lowest cost. Cuban (1988b) addressed this issue with regard to educational reform. He asserts that most educational reforms have failed because their implementation design and/or management was flawed. In addition, the use of inappropriate target dimensions of education to bring about the changes desired have resulted in flawed reform processes and outcomes.

Because this book is concerned with educational change, not bike riding, it may be useful to supply some examples at this point of first and second-order change from the world of education. In most states and school systems, there is considerable concern about the reading levels of many students. In fact, the great number of children unable to read at an appropriate level of comprehension has been described as a national problem and a national disgrace. Former Secretary of Labor William E. Brock has termed the fact that 700,000 high school graduates a year cannot read their own diplomas, an "insane national tragedy" (Applebee, Langer and Mullis, 1987). This same report, issued by the Educational Testing Service (ETS), concluded that only a small percentage of children and young adults could reason effectively about what they read or wrote. As this problem became more visible and as more demands were made to correct it, schools made more efforts to ameliorate it. These efforts consisted primarily of doing more of the same, e.g., more reading teachers, more instructional time devoted to reading, more curriculum materials devoted to reading, etc. — all changes of first-order magnitude. The problem has not been corrected. If anything, it has become worse in recent years, a fact that has led to more intensive first-order change efforts, similar to the bike rider who pedals harder as the slope of the grade increases.

In our example of the reading level, the problem has not gone away, but the schools can point to increased teacher time, increased expenditures of funds, task forces and committees who have studied the problem and proposed increasing the numbers of teachers, the amount of instructional time devoted to reading, etc. Many educators conclude that, if, after such expenditure of time, energy and effort, adequate results have not been obtained, the fault must lie with the children, their parents, or both. Reading experts, psychologists, principals and others will describe in educational jargon why, after so much investment of time, energy, and funds, the fault must lie with too much TV time, lack of motivation on the part of students, too little role modeling of parental reading, the socio-economic status of the parents, split families, and so on and so on and so on. There is no doubt that any or all of these may explain some of the problems some children experience with reading. However, the reality remains that too many students continue to experience severe problems in reading.

Seemingly, it has not occurred to educators that the problem may not be the reading level of students. The problem may be the types of solutions utilized in attempts to solve the problem. What is understood to be the problem determines the solution to be attempted (Dalin, 1978). First-order change efforts have been utilized when changes of the second-order have been necessary. The above situations attributed as the causes of the reading level problem have not been recognized for what they really are, manifestations of a changed environment. These changes have rendered obsolete any efforts for improving reading that may have been successful in a previous environmental context.

In this reading example, instead of endless attempts to do more reading which leads to more reading problems, the solution (second-order) is to modify the system's definition of and response to the reading situation and its inherent problems. In this example, such a second-order change might be to delay the teaching of reading until the fourth or fifth grade and to do something more useful instead, like teaching children to learn, with the instructional time thus left in the first three years.

At this point educators are shocked and parents dismayed. Both are alarmed. What kind of solution is this? Can the author really be serious about such a suggestion? Yes! Extremely so.

Consider for a moment the process of reading. It represents one of the most complex cognitive and reasoning tasks any person must master if he or she is to be able to survive and live successfully in our increasingly complex, technological society. The ETS report mentioned earlier found that only one fifth of young adults were successful on tasks measuring the advanced reasoning skills similar to those found in college, professional, and technical working environments.

Seemingly, the most logical time to start this process of learning to read is as early as possible in the infant's life, thus giving him/her a head-start in mastering this complex process. For those who are successful early, proud parents can tell prouder grandparents and disbelieving neighbors (especially those with children of their own of a similar age) at what age their offspring had mastered the alphabet and were able to read their first words. Parents are not likely to accept easily the suggestion to delay instituting the teaching of reading.

Teachers are dismayed, especially those who teach kindergarten or one of the first three grades. What would they teach during these years if not reading? Fourth and fifth grade teachers want nothing to do with the teaching of reading, even though they spend increasing amounts of time doing so anyway to the increasing numbers of children who have not been successful during the first three or four years of school.

What thinking could prompt such a radical suggestion? What possible benefits could there be if it were implemented? The following discussion

145

attempts to respond to these questions. Previous efforts (first-order changes) have not solved the reading level and reasoning problem. If anything, the problem has become greater. This is a strong indication that previously attempted solutions are not achieving the desired objective. Such a situation demands a new look from a different perspective. This new perspective must include an examination of previous problem resolution efforts and an analysis of the contextual factors (the environment) in which these efforts have been embedded. If, after such examination, it is clear that the problem still remains, then one can hypothesize that a second-order change effort may be required.

This is the case with the reading level problem. The environment has changed dramatically. The factors cited earlier as reasons why students are not learning to read at the desired levels provide ample evidence of this fact. In addition, the level of reading and reasoning proficiency needed to adapt to a more complex, increasingly technological environment has grown significantly. Thus, consideration of a second-order change is warranted.

This example of inadequate recognition of the need to replace previous solution efforts to reading problems with a new perspective is only one manifestation of a larger educational problem. This is the problem of recognizing the extent to which a changing environment demands new educational perspectives. There is no doubt that our environment has changed. Our physical, social, and educational environments are each much more different, complex and technological than they were just a few years ago. At the same time, paradoxically, these environments are more interdependent but with increased isolation and fragmentation among individuals. Much more will be discussed about our changed and changing environment in the next chapters, because environmental change is a cornerstone for understanding education's response to such change.

Environmental changes have resulted in a need to better understand how education functions as an organization. This understanding is necessary to address educational change procedures to the appropriate educational situation. Miles (1967) and Schmuck & Miles (1971) have provided a number of characteristics of schools that illustrate why many educational change efforts have failed. The following characteristics of these efforts are of particular importance:

- Goal confusion. Educational goals are usually general, ambiguous, and vague. As a result, it is difficult to measure educational outcomes unless some narrow aspect of the teaching-learning process is measured by test scores.
- Vulnerability. Schools are vulnerable to outside influences, particularly in a period of economic decline.

- Low Internal Interdependence. Teachers generally work in self-contained classrooms with little integration of responsibilities.
- Weak Knowledge Base. Most educators know very little about how children learn or about organizational functioning.
- Non-competition. There is little incentive or pressure to innovate, and therefore there is a low investment in research and development activities.

These characteristics of schools must be kept clearly in focus, for they describe basic and critical barriers for achieving educational improvement. Further, they represent problems which can only be overcome by changing the current structure of education and providing for an integrated and comprehensive program of educational change.

In order to provide the background necessary to develop such a comprehensive program, it is important to understand more fully the types of change and the elements involved in the educational change process. As Watzlawick and his colleagues (1974) point out, the real problem is often the attempted solutions to the original problem. The solution to the problem is often change of the change process. Reilly and Starr (1983) have commented upon the need for this type of change in education in a previous paper. House (1974) and Travers (1973) argue that attempts at innovation and change are often attempts to maintain the status quo, that a technocratic structure maintains equilibrium by constant innovation. Change of the change process is a second-order perspective that must be realized in seeking new solutions to educational problems.

What type of second-order change? And what process does one utilize in developing such an effort? An examination of previous efforts will often provide important clues. An examination of the reading level problem as such reveals that more and more time has been devoted to teaching reading at earlier and earlier ages. This provides a significant clue for a second-order change effort. Often a second-order change effort requires the reverse of what had been previously attempted. Therefore, the consideration of delaying the teaching of reading opposed to attempting to teach it at ever earlier ages is an appropriate second-order change consideration.

Two further considerations are necessary: (1) consideration of the positive consequences of instituting the second-order change being proposed, and (2) consideration of any negative consequences of doing so. Both of these considerations require that the objective for making any such change be kept clearly in focus. The reading level example may serve to illustrate this point.

The objective of reading instruction is to teach children to read so they can learn to learn, and to reason effectively about more complex tasks and

147

decisions. The objective is not to teach them to read as young as possible. Hence, *when* a child learns to read is not as important as assuring *that* he/she learns to read. Also, teaching a child to read is a function of the interaction between and among the child's maturation level and those social factors mentioned previously. We know from previous studies (for example, Reilly, 1971, Reilly, 1972, Reilly, 1973, among others) that both sex and demographic features play a role in determining auditory-visual integration skills in children. This is an important component of reading readiness ability. In many cases, to require a child to successfully master a task before he/she is maturationally ready to do so, or when the social environment of the child is not supportive of those activities and conditions necessary for task mastery, is to condemn the child to failure.

Attempting to force a child in such a situation to master the task at an ever earlier age is to doom the child to failure at an ever earlier age. Delaying the teaching of reading until the child is at least maturationally ready to master the skill removes one major cause of non-reading. Also, by delaying the teaching of reading, the child's experiential base is increased substantially, causing comprehension to be gained more easily and quickly. Keep in mind the objective is to teach reading as an asset for learning to learn comprehension; the mouthing of words is not the criteria.

Further, by delaying the teaching of reading, the pressure to succeed is removed and the stigma of failure is avoided. In addition, children who begin to learn to read at grade four should learn to do so at a far faster rate because of their more developed cognitive skills and conceptual development.

Thus, the positive consequences of delaying reading seem to warrant its consideration, at least for those who might have difficulty in mastering this skill at an earlier age. But what about those children who have no difficulty in learning to read at an earlier age? Would the negative consequences to them outweigh the positive ones gained by delaying reading for the others? Probably not. It would be expected that these children would learn to read anyway and, in any event, would be expected by grade six to achieve the reading level they would have obtained anyway. Pressure on these children to achieve and excel would be removed, thereby reducing the probability of failure.

In addition, Americans, and educators especially, claim to believe in individual differences. There is nothing to prevent introducing reading at one age to some children, and to others, at a different age. This would result in alterations of classroom operations, scheduling, and so forth. If the goal is to teach children to learn to learn, and not to continue condemning so many to failure, then the change and effort would be worth it.

There is one further consideration for this example. If the teaching of reading was delayed until third, fourth, or fifth grade, what would teachers

148

teach during the time previously devoted to the teaching of reading? The answer, briefly stated here and more fully developed in Chapter 10, is to teach children how to learn by teaching teachers to understand far more completely how children learn.

School systems are prime examples of what Watzlawick and his colleagues (1974) call the *Game Without End.* That is, they run through any number of internal changes without effecting a second-order change. On the whole, a school system cannot generate the rules for its change from within itself under current conditions. Often, educational systems have very little energy for attempting change. Most of their energy is spent in maintaining the existing structure (Dalin, 1978). This is also consistent with what would be expected from an equilibrial system (Buckley, (1967). The impetus for second-order school system change and, at a higher level of consideration, educational change must generally come from the external environment rather than from the system itself. Dalin (1978) indicates quite clearly that current educational change is largely a function of social and economic forces. This is clear from a historical perspective. Such changes as New Math, Open Classrooms, Union Schools, Back to Basics, and Teaching Centers have come from the system environment, not from the system itself. This understanding reveals the importance of boundary personnel.

Dalin (1978) describes the problem well. He asserts that, in educational change, the groups most concerned with the change — those who benefit, those who decide, and those who have to change — are usually groups with different roles. Since they often have little in common and seldom meet together, the result is alienation and lack of change.

Thus, a critical aspect of educational change is that second-order change must be introduced from outside the system, given the current conditions and procedures for establishing education's mission and goal-setting. Watzlawick and his colleagues (1974) and Buckley (1968) espouse this conclusion. Buckley indicated that an equilibrial system has no internal sources of change and the system's main function is to maintain the given structure of the system. This is not to deny that some first-order changes may result in increased effectiveness of functioning of some components of a system.

An example from Watzlawick, et al., (1974) may serve to demonstrate this point. As summer leaves and winter arrives, people make functional changes to adapt so that their functioning is not impaired. They raise thermostats, they dress warmer, etc. This is first-order change; it probably does not impair the functioning of the individual, but it also probably does not increase it either. Functional or first-order change is designed to maintain a homeostatic condition. If, however, we were to enter another ice age, or some other equally severe climatic condition, these efforts would not suffice. We would have to develop a second-order change effort in order to adapt or we would not survive.

In applying this premise to a school situation, the recent emphasis on competency testing may be used. Although school systems might institute any number of first-order change attempts (primarily instructional) to ensure that students achieve a minimum level of achievement, it is highly unlikely that schools would mandate required competency testing and levels as a graduation requirement. Yet, well over 30 states have passed laws requiring such mandatory testing. These laws were mandated from outside the individual school system. This is an example of second-order change mandated from outside the system because of a perceived significant environmental change — in this case, the number of students graduating from high school with unacceptable levels of academic competence. In this case also, it was the environment that detected an unacceptable condition in the system and imposed a second-order change on it.

Watzlawick and his colleagues (1974) point out that one of the critical elements of second-order change is that it examines the question, "What?" and focuses on finding a solution to a problem. As in mathematical analysis, which does not ask "why" but "what," and whose statements are best understood as interrelated elements within a system, the question of "what" is critical. To again borrow freely from Watzlawick and his colleagues (1974), the question "what" is concerned with examining what is being done at present to perpetuate the problem and what can be done at present to effect a change. In this sense, the question of problem continuance or change is the extent to which the system is able to generate the rules for change of itself.

Summary

Educational change is often a misunderstood concept, and certainly its processes are not well accepted by most educators. The notion of change often brings fear to the individual who must change. This is usually because the person feels (1) the need to change implies s/he has not been doing the best job, or (2) she/he does not fully comprehend what the change will demand of him/her for new behaviors. Unless change, growth, and adaptation are part of an individual's and organization's repertoire of behavior, improvement cannot occur. Change is also a process that can be viewed from many different perspectives. This chapter has provided some views not often found in source materials related to educational change theories or models. The most critical dimension is that the source of the problem demanding change is often the solutions that have been previously attempted to resolve the original problem.

8   Overview of educational change

Despite the implication in Chapter 7 that few educational reformers adhere to the principles of educational change, a great deal is known about the process of educational change. The following sections deal with different aspects of educational change theory and the findings of various educational change efforts.

Deficit- and improvement-based change

Huberman (1973) offers the concepts of deficit-based change and improvement-based change. It may be that *deficit-based change* is change imposed from external forces perceiving a deficit in level of achievement (whereas the internal system is focused on system maintenance). *Improvement-based change* may arise from unique situations in which the internal system perceives a need for improvement of level of achievement. These concepts form an important component of the discussion of a framework for educational improvement in the next chapter.

These forces of change are related to Fullan's (1982) description of change that comes about because it is imposed by natural events or deliberate reform, and that change that is voluntary because of dissatisfaction, inconsistency, or intolerability in a situation.

It is possible to graph these forces or reasons for change as depicted in Table 8.1.

Table 8.1
Reasons and forces of change

	Deficit Based Change	Creative Change
Imposed Change	3	3
Voluntary Change	2	1

The numbers in each quadrant indicate the ranking of presumed probability of a successful educational change effort under each set of conditions. It is presumed that the highest probability of a successful change effort occurs when change is voluntary and focused on improvement efforts. Change which is voluntary and based on deficit correction has a lower likelihood of success, but still higher than change that is imposed, whether it be deficit or creative. This poses a difficult dilemma for educational change specialists. If, as suggested earlier, second-order change must be introduced from outside sources, but externally imposed change has a lower probability of causing successful change, how can significant and successful change of education be achieved? This dilemma is amplified by the concept that school systems, under the assumptions of second-order change, cannot develop the rules from within to significantly alter their practices. Thus, a school system cannot change itself significantly, and change imposed from outside has a low probability of success. The answer is a shared responsibility and authority for change between internal and external forces. This idea is developed in the next chapter and expanded upon throughout the third section of the book.

Agents and variables involved in change

Both the participants and the processes involved in the change are important considerations when analyzing the process of change. Huberman (1973) has identified three levels of participants. These are:

- The individual as adapter. Studies related to this level have come primarily from psychology, rural sociology, consumer research, and public health.
- The group as the key parameter. This level has been identified primarily from studies in mass communication, social psychology and sociology.
- The institutional and cultural framework. This level has been studied most in anthropology and political science.

It is important to note that all three levels are involved in any important educational change effort.

Huberman also notes that, in analyzing the process of change, individuals must study a wide and complex range of variables operating in a highly integrated system. These variables include:

- Individual perceptions
- Group process norms

- Organizational structures
- Pressures from community
- Pressures from ministry
- Cultural codes.

There must also be a means for classifying the affiliations that exist among the following elements:

- The internal and external participants of the system involved in the change effort,
- The formal and informal structures that exist within and among the system, and
- The roles and relationships that exist among the participants of the system.

Internal and external participants

The *internal participants*, those directly concerned with the legal or social system in education, include students, teachers, school principals, supervisors, parents, and legislatures. The *external participants,* exerting indirect influence through dissemination of information, raising expectations or invoking sanctions, include non-educationors, foundations or research agencies, academics, industry and mass media (Marsh, 1964). More precisely, these external classes of individuals should be classified as *boundary personnel*. They are able to exert influence on the educational system and its change efforts but only indirectly and in specific ways.

Formal and informal structures

The formal education system (state, local school system) is only a part of the education structure. Change efforts must take into account ancillary structures and institutions. *Ancillary structures* are formally organized systems contributing to, but not part of, the formal system: PTAs, textbook publishers, mental health organizations. The third type of structure is the *autonomous group* made up of individuals within the education system: friendship groups or cliques. The final type, *institutions*, is made up of in-school relationships which follow prescribed norms: informal rules of conduct, status differences among teachers and administrators, treatment of parents.

153

Classification by role and relationship

The school system is composed of interlocking positions and interacting roles. Each position requires a role performance with other positions. As roles interact within the system and in response to larger systems, they change relationships. The key relationships must be examined to gauge the direction and effects of change (Miles, 1967).

The change process can also be examined from the perspective of individual or system change.

Individual Change

New educational techniques, technologies and policies introduced in a change effort are personalized by the individual teacher. The change initiator must consider how the prospective adopter will respond to the type of personalized change of the type being effected. The self-system comes into prominent play at this point. The result is usually high anxiety, prolonged resistance, and a greater need for "unlearning" and "relearning" than is caused by simply giving out written instructions. The critical factor appears to be the teacher's concept of what changes she/he will be required to make, rather than the nature of the change or its potential for improving learning (Morrish, 1976). Fullan (1982) reports that there is no reason for a teacher to believe in change, and there are few incentives (and high costs) to find out whether a given change will be worthwhile. New practices are generally encouraged, but educational systems usually have not taken the steps necessary to facilitate the appropriate changes in attitude and behavior that must accompany them.

Initiators of change must judge the significance of the change for the meaning it has for the *adopter*. This is not necessarily the meaning it has for the *introducer*. The individual teacher's personality or value system is a less adequate indicator of his attitude toward change than is his perception of the effects of the innovation on his interests and institutional goals (Atwood, 1964). The planning and introduction of the change must be a developmental process. This is particularly important since we know little about how and why people change their attitudes, about group behavior and about how to effect such change (Chin and Benne, 1961), and the fact that many recent changes in American education involve similar variables and require important adjustments in the way school personnel interact with each other. According to Fullan (1982) many attempts at policy and program change have concentrated on product development, legislation, and other "on-paper" changes that ignored the critical variable of what people did and did not do.

Whereas the teacher is the key figure in the final implementation of any innovation directly affecting the learning process, she/he is much less significant in organizational change efforts. As structures, schools outlast teachers. For the administrator, schools are essentially bureaucracies, and the teacher is not a professional but a functionary. The teacher usually feels helpless to influence the larger organizational structure.

The school, in turn, is closely linked to its environment, to the influence of parents, community organizations, media, universities, etc. As a highly vulnerable, visible, community-dependent agency, the school can only initiate changes as long as the changes do not conflict with the community's concept of what education should be.

Therefore, it is unlikely to have a more developed school system in the sense of child-centered, non-directive, or highly individualized teaching than the social context in which it is embedded. Political, cultural and economic settings that discourage innovation, placing stress on education as a religious activity, with a general hostility towards social and cultural change. Such communities place a high value on the past and often have low educational attainments and little contact with outside communities.

Schon (1967) writes that we are a technologically, but not emotionally, adoptive society. It is precisely this type of change, however, that must be made if schools are to significantly improve their efforts to assist students.

Administrators perceive schools as bureaucracies and the teacher, not as a professional, but as a functionary. Few innovations can be introduced by the teacher since she/he runs into the bureaucracy when she/he needs more space, equipment, etc. Since schools operate within a community, they cannot make changes that would conflict with community codes except under certain conditions. These include those school systems operating within a centralized state system where local options, codes, and concerns are generally not considered when larger, more imperative state interests are perceived to be at risk. This raises again the question of who *actually* controls and who *should* control the policy development, goals, procedures and desired outcomes of the schools.

Inhibitors of change

Educational systems are more resistant to innovation than industrial or business enterprises, and teachers are more difficult to change than farmers or physicians. It is interesting to address the factors that account for this. Havelock (1971) has provided three types of inhibiting factors: *input,* which inhibits change from entering into the system; *output*, which prevents the genesis of change from within; and *throughput*, which limits the spread of new ideas and practices through the school system.

Input factors

- Resistance to change from the environment. The community does not expect or encourage change in the system unless there is a perceived crisis in the system's functioning. In addition, most people believe that children should not be used as experimental subjects.

- Incompetence of outside agents. Most parents, political leaders and other community officials know too little about teaching or learning to judge any innovative effort that is not a policy matter.

- Over-centralization. Power is usually concentrated in the hands of a few senior officials. This drastically slows down the rate of change and filters all efforts at innovation through a bureaucratic, rather than professional, agency.

- Teacher defensiveness. Teachers, like others, resent changes brought into their school without their participation in the planning process.

- Absence of change agent or linking pin. There is no recognized agent responsible for bringing and demonstrating new practices to the teacher or administrator.

- Incomplete linkage between theory and practice. Educational research is underdeveloped, and there is no direct way of getting research findings from the lab into the school and classroom. Much of the research available is unrelated to practical problems, and experimental conditions have little in common with normal classroom life. Practitioners in the schools have a reduced knowledge base about new practices or developments.

- Underdeveloped scientific base. Inventions in education do not have the proven validity of scientific inventions. Most learning theories are not highly developed. Many are incompatible. New practices can seldom be justified on a scientific basis before being tried out, and they are seldom evaluated carefully. Technological inventions, in particular, have not had exaggerated claims.

- Conservatism. The school has traditionally seen its role as one of resisting pressures from external sources. Socialization is principally a matter of conservatism, of ensuring cultural continuity rather than promoting cultural change. Finally, changes in the environment are only implemented into school programs after they are fully stabilized.

- Professional invisibility. Most school-teaching takes place behind closed doors. As a result, it is hard to obtain accurate information whether the teaching and learning activities are in need of change. Criteria for judging teacher effectiveness usually depend on the values of a particular administrator.

Output factors

- Confused goals. There are two aspects to this problem: (1) the contradictory goals within the school system, and (2) the fact different members (teachers, administrators, parents, educators) stress one set rather than another, and thereby support certain changes while combating others. Miles (1967) noted in regard to this issue that educational goals are usually vaguely stated, multiple in nature, and conflicting, in the sense that different publics may want mutually incompatible things.

- No rewards for innovating. Rarely are teachers or administrators rewarded for initiating or carrying out innovations. Rather, they are rewarded for stable, dependable, behavior. Those adopting change are paid the same as those who reject change, and they run the added risk of possible failure. Promotions are usually made on the basis of seniority, personal influence, popularity, or by obtaining advanced degrees or earning additional credits at a university.

- Uniformity of approach. With such a diversity of backgrounds in both teachers and students, schools seek to install methods and procedures applicable to the greatest number. Innovations for small groups are generally resisted by one party or another.

- School as a monopoly. Because they face no competition, schools have no economic motive to innovate and improve their services. Reichart (1969) notes that schools are in the unique position of "having been created as a monopoly by society to do what society has mandated." Clients are not free to accept or reject the services of an obligatory educational system. As a result, schools' organizational environments are more stable than that of other types of institutions.

- Low knowledge component. There is a low investment in research and development efforts. For an institution whose central task is the dissemination of knowledge, there is little investment in knowledge acquisition or dissemination within the school itself. There is a limited awareness and little direct use of relevant areas of knowledge, such as learning theory, etc. This may be due, in part, to the fact that policy decisions are made by lay people rather than professionals.

- Low technological and financial investment. The amount of technology per worker in the schools is relatively low. Systems that can barely provide the necessities of education can hardly be expected to invest in innovation because of the cost (Sussman, 1971).

- Difficulty in diagnosing weaknesses. The school is defensive towards external criticism. The diagnosis of weakness — usually a pre-condition of change — is stifled. Neither the school as a whole nor any of its personnel is rewarded for admitting that changes are needed.

- Product measurement problems. It is difficult to identify the product of educational organizations. Many of the results are delayed over a long span of time. This difficulty can be used as a defense against external criticism. Why should teachers change their methods if it cannot be proved that one method is better than another?

- Focus on present commitments. Few teachers or administrators are sufficiently detached from normal operations to probe weaknesses or learn about promising practices. Administrators are generally overburdened. Teachers are responsible for fixed numbers of students in fixed periods, with little time for creative work.

- Low personnel development investment. Little money is spent by school systems on the development of personnel. However, experience has shown that major innovations in school systems only come about as a result of personnel development efforts, often with outside funds and facilities.

- Lack of entrepreneurial models. The school system is usually not a place where one finds individuals who sense needs, develop practices suited to meet those needs, and push them through the organization. The teacher is generally not an innovative character. Most assessments depict them as restrained and deferential, lacking in social boldness, eager to please, more passive and less competitive than professionals in other jobs. This picture not exact in developing countries.

- Passivity. Miles (1967) indicated that in many school systems the stance of the administrator is a withdrawing and passive one. The schools believe they have little power to initiate, develop, grow, push things, or be disagreeable to anyone.

Throughput factors

- Separation of members and units. The different parts of the system are not as interlocking as those of industrial firms and other organizations. This lack of interdependence, according to Miles (1967), makes the system much more difficult to alter, since changes occurring in one part are not transmitted to other parts. This low level of coordination constricts the flow of information about new thought and practices. In other occupations, for example, farmers and physicians, practitioners discuss new ideas and imitate one another.

- Hierarchy and differential status. Most professional organizations have a higher rate of innovation than bureaucratic organizations, stressing expertise rather than rank, encouraging greater flexibility of members, having more precise goals and output criteria, and making high demands for production.

- Hierarchies discourage or distort information flow. Organizational members hesitate to send information upward unless:

  1. it is firmly substantiated by hard data, which can seldom be the case with innovations,
  2. it reflects only a favorable evaluation of themselves,
  3. it is directly relevant to the receiver (Havelock 1971).

The school structure has a more stultifying effect on initiation than on adoption of an innovation. In an authoritative system,

159

anyone can be ordered to adopt something new, but no one can be ordered to create something new. Enforced adoption, however, is likely to be superficial and unstable, an act of compliance rather than of identification and internalization.

- Lack of procedures and training for change. Teachers have no institutionalized procedures for learning about the new practices of colleagues. School personnel do not enjoy human relations training to stimulate awareness and gain acceptance of new ideas and methods.

Implementation rates in educational systems lag behind those of industrial, agricultural, or medical systems. Miles (1964b) mentioned three reasons for this:

- Absence of valid scientific research findings,
- Lack of educational change agents to promote new educational ideas,
- Lack of economic incentive to adopt innovations.

Mort (1964) states that change in American school systems takes an extremely long time and follows a predictable pattern. It takes 50 years for a change to spread throughout the education system once the need is recognized. Another 50 years is required for diffusion or full adaptation. During this second phase, it takes 15 years for the practice to appear in 3% of the systems in the country, followed by a period of 20 years of rapid diffusion, followed by a final 15 years of slow diffusion through the last small percentage of schools. The rate of change in education has increased greatly since Mort's studies in the 1930's. Mort estimates an increase in tempo of about 20% (Huberman, 1973). Mort also argues that the major discovery at the turn of the century — that the theory of formal disciplines is untenable — will lead to a long period of adjustment characterized by thousands of innovations that, later in the century, will merge into new designs.

Huberman (1973) has plotted the an S-curve for the adoption process of an educational change:

- Innovators - 2/3%
- Early adopters - 5%
- Early majority -
- Late majority-combined majority - 68%
- Laggards - 12%
- Small group that never give in - 4%

160

Havelock provides an S-curve for individual adoption of a particular change:

- Slight involvement – beginning awareness
- Moderate involvement – information seeking
- High involvement – active information seeking, try-out
- High involvement – efforts to adapt the innovation
- Decreasing involvement with accustomization and internalization
- Innovation becomes routine, an accepted and automatic part of the adopter's behavior

Educational change process variables

To reduce the time lag of innovation adoption, the variables and factors involved in the change process must be isolated and understood. Our understanding of the change process, models of change and the strategies for implementation that emerge all depends on the interactions of the following factors:

- Inherent in the innovation itself,
- Situational or connected to the school system and its personnel, and
- Inherent in the environment.

Variables associated with the innovation

A number of variables are a part of any attempt at educational change. These variables are inherent to the particular type of change or innovation under consideration. These include:

- Proven quality of the innovation. This variable is particularly difficult, since education, as a science, is less scientifically verifiable than other physical sciences.
- Cost. There is a need to identify the initial start-up costs and the continuing costs of any change.
- Divisibility. Havelock (1971) and Rogers (1962) define this variable as the degree to which an innovation may be tried on a limited basis. Innovations that are adopted on a small scale basis or for a limited time have a higher probability of being diffused. Divisibility also can refer to the number of individuals or the proportion of a community to be involved in the adoption. Thus, group consent means a slower diffusion rate than individual consent.

161

- Complexity. This variable refers to (a) the number of parts of the innovation, (b) the number of behaviors or skills to be learned or understood before adoption is possible, or (c) the number of procedures required for effective maintenance over time (Havelock, 1971). The more difficult it is to understand and use, the more slowly an innovation will be adopted.
- Communicability. How easy or difficult is it to explain or demonstrate the innovation? Material items, such as a new textbook series, find more acceptance than ideas, because their utility is more easily demonstrated.

Situational variables

Situational variables are associated with factors involved with the system itself:

- Structure of the instructional system. Structure involves a multitude of variables, including:
    1. Size. Both the largest and smallest systems are the most difficult to change since institutional mass and tight cohesion are highly resistant forces.
    2. Organization. Hierarchical institutions initiate change more slowly but adopt it more quickly than decentralized institutions. The key factor in a hierarchical institution seems to be the amount of dependence on authority felt by the potential acceptor.
    3. Tenure. The longer the chief administrator has been in office, the less likely she/he is to initiate changes.
    4. Cost. Communities giving higher financial support tend to have more innovative schools.
- Leadership and sponsorship. It is important to specify the relationship between the sponsor of the change and the persons being helped to change, particularly with the power and prestige levels of those involved.
- School environment. This is an indistinct factor. However, the institutional climate in which a specific innovation is to be introduced can be measured — by personnel attitudes, views of the proposed change as a threat or panacea, and familiarities with changes of the same sort. These factors can determine whether the climate is favorable, neutral, or opposed to the change. A special case is that of change caused by crises. Crises tend to loosen structures and value systems and, thereby, speed the rate of adoption

or at least lessen the forces of resistance. Such changes tend to be temporary unless the institution is effected long enough for new patterns to take root.

- Group norms. Depending on which target group is most affected by the proposed change, the probable reaction of existing reference groups, clique structures, and vested interest groups can be predicted. In particular, group norms concerning value placed on security and on the assumption of risks should be examined in this context.
- Personal characteristics of the adoptees. Although adopters probably differ little from initiators, perhaps they are more prone to conforming, deferring to authority, and feeling insecure. Such factors as age, education, income and SES status should be examined.
- Rewards and punishments. The profitability of an innovation can be judged by its educational quality, administrative efficiency, and psychological satisfaction. What matters the most is what the potential adoptee thinks she/he stands to gain or lose.

Environmental factors

Except in times of crisis, two factors in the environment are usually blocking or inhibiting forces to educational change. These factors include:

- Innovation system congruence. The willingness of the community to support specific changes depends on cultural values. Culture is a filter that rejects certain changes and allows others to be implemented. These cultural norms and what will be accepted or allowed must be understood if educational change efforts are to succeed.
- Readiness. Perhaps the best way to measure this variable is (a) estimating the weight of public demand or (b) analyzing the properties that the innovation has in common with other changes already in acceptance.

Sources of change

Case studies have shown that the initiative for educational change comes from outside the system. School systems are more preoccupied with the operation of the existing program, in keeping with the organizational tendency to stability.

Griffiths (1964) maintains that changes made in response to those inside the system are concerned with clarification of rules and internal procedures. Those made in response to those outside the system are concerned with new rules and procedures, and possibly with changes in general purpose and direction.

In a large number of studies, the decisive figure in the change process is the chief administrator of the school or local school system. However, the chief administrator is neither inside nor outside the system. She/he stands between the functionaries of the system and the representatives of the community. As such, she/he has balancing role to play. This is also true of a school principal. Spindler (1963) claims that, for this reason, school administrators are rarely outspoken protagonists of a consistent and vigorously profiled point of view. Given the nature of our culture and social system, and the close connection between the public and schools, administrators cannot alienate significant segments of that public and stay in business. Whether the administrator can effect changes within the system depends on whether the nature of the system (hierarchical or decentralized) suits his/her leadership style.

Planning and executing change-models of change

A questionable aspect of the literature on educational change is that most analyses have been conducted on changes that have already taken place. The studies are based on change, mostly unplanned change, from which models are made to show how the process took place.

The literature contains three models illustrating how change takes place.

- A theory into practice model — The research and development model. This model views the process of change as a rational sequence of phases by which an innovation is invented or discovered, developed, produced and disseminated to the user. The innovation is not analyzed from the viewpoint of the user (who presumably is passive). Nor does the research begin as a set of answers to specific human problems, but rather as a set of facts and theories that are then turned into ideas for useful products and services in the development phase. This is basically an American model in its emphasis on the translation of basic research into applied knowledge. Eastern European and Latin European systems are characterized by research and development activities that are centralized at the ministerial level. Dissemination takes place only after a number of carefully controlled experiments. There is an assumption that links exist between the research and practice.

- Social interaction model. This model emphasizes the aspect of diffusion, the movement of messages from person to person and system to system. It is widely used in medicine and agriculture. It stresses the importance of interpersonal networks of information, of opinion leadership, personal contact, and social integration. The idea is that each member in the system will proceed through the awareness-adoption cycle through a process of social communication with his/her colleagues. In a number of decentralized systems, for example, Great Britain, this strategy takes the form of convincing a respected administrator of the usefulness of a new device or practice, and then facilitating the process whereby colleagues encounter the new practitioner while he is using the new practice.

- The Problem-solving model. This model is built around the user of the innovation. It assumes that the user has a definite need and that the innovation satisfies that need. Thus the process is from problem to diagnosis of a need then to trial and adoption. Very often an external change agent is required to counsel individuals on possible solutions and implementation strategies, but the emphasis is on client-centered collaboration, rather than on manipulation from without.

These models differ on the source of initiative in the change process. The research and development model stresses the developer; the social interaction model stresses the communicator; the problem-solving model emphasizes the receiver. One model is highly natural (social interaction); another is highly planned (research and development). The research and development model studies in particular the activities of the resource person or system, whereas the social interaction model focuses on the user person, and the problem-solving model on the change agent in interaction with the user. Havelock (1971) points out that the dissemination strategies in each model are different: One-way media for information and training (research and development), two-way involvement between sender and receiver (problem-solving), and a variety of transmission media (social interaction).

None of these three models are very adequate for dealing with the complexities of the educational change process, although each has its benefits and advantages. For example, the research and development model is essential for basic research, but it fails to take into account the political-economic-social-cultural interactions that affect major educational change. The research and development model may provide useful, specific innovations for classroom practice, but yet the research arm of American education has not developed the theories, concepts, or mechanisms for dealing with major change of the educational structure.

The problem-solving model has several advantages over the research and development model. For example, it offers the opportunity for theory to be based on actual problems, and, with careful attention and follow-through, would allow for the development of theories that are practice-based. It has two major disadvantages: (1) It is problem- or deficit-based and, as such, probably will generate efforts to modify existing practices rather than develop new ones. (2) It assumes that the problems of education can be developed from expressions of need. Also, it does not take into account the political-economic-cultural-social interactions. It offers no mechanism for analyzing such interactions.

The social interaction model is hopelessly outmoded for initiating change of American education. Its chief advantage is that it offers a mechanism for disseminating positive feedback on the effectiveness of any particular change. As a model for initiating significant and substantial change, it is neither necessary nor sufficient.

To be effective, a model (theory) of educational change (improvement) must first be concerned with the purpose and goals of American education. It must also consider the political-economic-cultural-social interactions, and the appropriate timing for any particular type of change. It must be developed from a particular theory of education, and it must account for the structure of education as either an aid or obstacle for achieving a particular change. It must keep the focus on the *learner* and not the teacher or system. It must be improvement-based, not deficit-based or basic research. (Although that, too, has its place, as does the practice into theory approach.) It must focus on the local level and must account for all elements that affect the functioning of the school at the local level, such as teachers, SES of students, teacher preparation, staff improvement, and the principle of equifinality.

Strategy considerations

Strategy involves a set of policies underlying specific actions expected to be useful causing the lasting installation of a particular innovation. This set of policies must conside:

- the innovation itself,
- the process of change,

- the characteristics of the target individuals or groups, and
- the nature of the system adopting the innovation.

No one strategy can be applied to all types of innovations, processes, adopting groups, or adopting systems. However, certain combinations or sequences are more effective than others, and certain pre-conditions must be met if progress is to be made. For example, Watson (1967) argues that structural approaches achieve the best results. Effective change sequences in schools usually involve structures first, altered interaction processes next, and attitudes last. Watson also believes that all strategies should consider both the resisting forces in the adopter and the tactics for causing adoption. Watson provides five pre-conditions for any particular attempt at institutional change:

- Participants must feel that the project is their own and not wholly devised by outsiders.
- The project must have the wholehearted support of senior system officials.
- The project must be in fairly close accord with the values and ideals of participants.
- The participants should experience support, trust, acceptance and confidence in their relationships with one another.
- Participants must feel that their autonomy and security are not threatened.

The strategy adopted by a highly bureaucratic, centralized system must be different from that used in a decentralized, more professional framework. Similarly, the potential adopters will be sensitive to different tactics in the two systems.

Guba (1967) provides a list of strategies that depend on the nature of the adopter. These strategies include different types of motivation and intimidation:

- Value strategy. The adopter is viewed as a professional to whom an appeal can be made in terms of value priorities.
- Rational strategy. The adopter can be convinced on the basis of hard data and logical arguments of the utility, feasibility and effectiveness of the innovation.
- Didactic strategy. The adopter is willing, but untrained.
- Psychological strategy. The adopter has needs for acceptance, involvement and inclusion which can be used to influence him.
- Economic strategy. The adopter is compensated for agreeing to adopt or is deprived of resources if he refuses.

167

- Authority strategy. The adopter can be compelled by orders from hierarchical superiors.

Each of these strategies is then related to six diffusion techniques — telling, showing, helping, involving, training, and intervening.

What should be told about a rational strategy would be different from what would be told in a psychological strategy. Decentralized systems must rely more on the indirect methods (rational, psychological, value priority), while more centralized systems might use the authority or economic strategies. Guba suggests strongly that techniques be consistent with the strategies they employ.

Chin and Benne (1961) have regrouped these categories into basic types. These types are closely allied to the process models described and can be referred more specifically to different kinds of administrative or policy-making traditions.

- Empirical-Rational Approach. The implication here is that men are rational, and they will follow their rational self-interest once it is shown to them. The innovation will be adopted if it can be rationally justified and if the adopter can be shown that he will benefit from the change. The assumption is also that reason determines the process of initiating innovations. Thus, scientific investigation is the best way of extending knowledge. Such a strategy has its best results when the public is ready to accept a new invention.

- Normative-Re-educative Approach. The assumption here is that the adopter is not passive, waiting for solutions from without, but rather is in an active search for a solution to his problems. The strategy is based on a psychotherapeutic model of change-agent and adopter in which the adopter, with the collaboration of the agent, works out his changes for himself. The aim is less technical training than changing of attitudes and values with two principle objectives:

  1. To improve the problem-solving capabilities of the adopter or system, and
  2. To bring self-clarity and personal development to the individuals within the system.

- Power-Coercive Approach. The strategy here is to use political and economic sanctions to enforce change. This approach is necessary when legislation is involved, but it is also the common manner of causing less sweeping changes in countries where teachers are expressly hired as civil servants. It should be kept in mind that making an order does not mean that the decision can or will be carried out successfully.

To be adopted at the individual level, most innovations require new knowledge, skills, attitudes, and often new value orientations on the part of the individual. At the social level, there must be changes in norms, roles, and relationships.

Many of the same problems associated with the models of change apply to these approaches. Basically, they do not take into account the importance of the context, the political-economic-cultural-social situation, in attempting to formulate strategies for change. With each approach, the emphasis for change is on the school unit. The problem with this is that, with fundamental and structural change, the decision is not made at the local school or system level. It is a political decision for these types of changes, not an educational one. Although the characteristics of the local school and system are important, it is the political decision-making process within the social, economic and cultural context which determines if the change will be made. The extent to which change is carried out, and how well it is carried out, is determined at the local level. It is then that the strategies discussed become more important.

Characteristics of resisters and innovators

When an attempt is made to introduce an educational change into a school system, it is important to keep in mind that there will be individuals who will resist the attempt for various reasons. Each school system will also have its share of innovators. It is important to keep the characteristics of these groups in mind.

The Resisters

Anthropologists maintain that resistance to change is proportional to the amount of change required in the receiving system. Psychologists note that individuals resist most strongly at the point where the pressure of change is greatest. The change becomes perceived as a threat, and the individual reacts defensively. In general, teachers tend to resist all changes that leave them with less control over the classroom or over the students in it.

Most educational change strategies concentrate on facilitating change by lowering resistance. It is also possible to examine resistance in terms of curves. A resistance curve is the mirror image of an adoption curve, or it can be put into a formula where [Innovation=Demand-Resistance] (Havelock, 1971).

Watson (1967) has set out a stage theory of resistance to typical innovations. These are:

- Massive, undifferentiated resistance. Few individuals take the change seriously.
- Pro and con sides regarding the change are identifiable. The resistance level can be defined and its power appraised.
- Direct conflict. The resistance is mobilized. (This is the critical stage.)
- The changers obtain power. Wisdom is needed at this point to keep latent opposition from mobilizing. Resisters are now pictured as cranks.
- The first circle, old adversaries, are as few and alienated as advocates were in the first stage. Advocates now resist new change.

Watson (1967) has identified eight forces or motivations prompting most forms of resistance:

- Homeostasis. The desire to maintain balance and revert to previous forms and patterns of behavior.
- Primacy. The way an organism first successfully copes with a situation tends to persist.
- Habit. Unless the situation changes significantly, an individual will continue to respond in his/her accustomed manner.
- Selective perception and retention. Individuals tend to admit only such information as fit an established outlook.
- Dependence. Educators tend to rely on the views of peers and hierarchical superiors.
- Superego. There is an enforcement of moral standards acquired in childhood, for example, a blind respect for authority.
- Self-distrust. Educators tend to hesitate to correct existing malpractice.
- Insecurity and regression. Educators tend to flee change by seeking security in the past or in fantasy.

Morrish (1976) reports that, from seven contested attempted innovations, four types of resisters were identified. These included:

- Those who favored the change but were opposed to the particular form it should take;

170

- Those who created independent groups of their own to defeat the change;
- Those who were inspired or coerced into opposition by this second group; and
- Those whose resistance was only incidental or situational but whose real interests lay elsewhere.

Guskin (1980) has reported on individual variables in knowledge utilization among educators. These factors have relevance to resistance found to many efforts at educational change.

- The individual's sense of competence and self-esteem. Individuals with less confidence in themselves are less willing to try innovations.
- Authoritarianism and dogmatism. The authoritarian personality has a strong tendency to accept directives from dictatorial leaders and rigidly rejects any changes from outside sources.
- Feelings of threat and fear. A person has a need for consistency in his self-concept and tends to distort new information to maintain that image.
- Self-fulfilling prophecies. Expectations of success or failure, effects of early experiences, and others' expectations of failure or success affect an individual's attitude toward change.

Eicholz and Rogers (1964) studied resistance to new educational media on the part of elementary school teachers. They found eight types of resistance responses. These were:

- Rejection through ignorance,
- Rejection through default,
- Rejection by maintaining the status quo,
- Rejection through social mores,
- Rejection through interpersonal relationships,
- Rejection through substitution,
- Rejection through fulfillment, and
- Rejection through experience.

These authors have developed a framework for the identification of rejection responses. They provide typical responses for various types of rejection and differentiate between real and stated reasons for rejection.

It should also be noted that there may be good and sufficient reason for rejecting an innovation. As all changes are not necessarily warranted, resistance may be justified.

171

Miles (1964a) describes innovators as strong, benevolent, high in intelligence and verbal ability, less bound by local group norms, more individualistic and creative. Harvey (1967) relates that innovators are characterized by a high degree of abstractness, a more complex, enriched meditational system with greater ability to depart from immediate situations. They tend to be less absolute, use more relativism, are freer to solve problems, and have high task-orientation, risk-taking, and independence.

Lippitt (1967) makes some interesting observations about teachers. He found that teachers were more likely to be involved in the innovation diffusion process if they felt they had authority to direct their own classroom, were confident they could do so effectively. They were also willing to share information about their classrooms with their peers with a minimum of fear or rejection, were highly committed to the profession and willing to engage in discussions about professional matters.

Rogers (1962), drawing on research on diffusion of innovation in rural sociology, industrial engineering, and anthropology, developed a "world" picture of the innovators. *Innovators* tend to have the following characteristics:

- They enjoy relatively high social status in terms of education, prestige and income.
- They are generally are young.
- Impersonal and cosmopolite sources of information are important to them.
- They are cosmopolite.
- They exercise opinion leadership.
- They are likely to be viewed as deviant by their peers.

Katz (1963) claims that in traditional or underdeveloped communities, the most marginal and disaffected are the innovators, whereas, in most industrialized countries, the situation is reversed. The implications for the politics of educational innovation are obvious.

Barnett (1953), in a study of acceptors and rejecters, described four categories of *acceptors*. These included:

- The dissident. These individuals consistently refuse to identify themselves with some of the conventions of their group.
- The indifferent. These are individuals who are prepared to accept new ideas because they have not committed themselves to a custom or to an ideal of their society.

172

- The disaffected. Some individuals begin by being active participants in particular aspects of their culture. Later they acquire a distaste and may experience a change from a positive to a negative attitude.
- The resentful. These are individuals who are the have-nots, and they have little to lose by acceptance.

Evaluation of educational change efforts

Berman and McLaughlin (1978) report that federally sponsored evaluations reveal inconsistent and generally disappointing results of federally sponsored educational change efforts. Despite considerable innovative activity on the part of local school districts, the evidence suggests that:

- No class of existing educational treatments has been found that consistently leads to improved student outcomes (when variations in the institutional setting and non-school factors are taken into account).
- Successful projects have difficulty sustaining their success over a number of years.
- Successful projects are not disseminated automatically or easily, and their replication in new sites usually falls short of their performance in the original sites.

All the federal programs have funded some successfully implemented projects, as well as dismal failures and many projects in between. The difference between success and failure depended primarily on how school districts implemented their projects, not on the type of federal sponsorship. The guidelines and management strategies of the federal change agent program were simply overshadowed by local concerns and characteristics.

Few districts in the Berman and McLaughlin review planned for the long-term stability of projects. The end of federal funding generally resulted in a reduction of resources, particularly expensive ones. Budget and personnel decisions typically perpetuated the "special project" status of innovations, thereby leaving them particularly vulnerable to the financial and political fortunes of the district.

Factors affecting implementation and continuation

Berman and McLaughlin examined how characteristics of projects and school districts affect the outcomes of innovation. They studied the projects' educational method, resource levels, scope, and implementation strategies. The district characteristics they examined included school climate and leadership, teacher attributes, and district management capacity and support. They found:

- Educational methods. A project's methods determined its implementation, effect, and continuation to only a small and limited extent. This was because projects with essentially the same educational methods can be, and usually are, implemented very differently and with varying effectiveness. In short, *what* the project was mattered less than *how* it was done.

- Project resources. Funding does not make much difference. More expensive projects were no more likely than less expensive ones to be effectively implemented, to elicit teacher change, to improve student performance, or to be continued by teachers.

- Scope of project. Teachers must clearly understand the project's goals and precepts; such clarity comes during implementation. The authors doubt if projects aiming at significant change can be effectively implemented across a whole system at once.

- Implementation strategies. Implementation strategies are the local decisions and choices, explicit or implicit, on how to put the innovations into practice. These strategies could spell the difference between success and failure, almost independently of the type of innovation or educational method involved. Moreover, they could determine whether teachers would assimilate and continue using project methods or allow them to fall into disuse. The following strategies were frequently *ineffective* because they were not consonant with the conditions of school district life or with the dominant motivations and needs of teachers:

  1. Outside consultants,
  2. Packaged management approaches,
  3. One-shot, pre-implementation training,
  4. Pay for training,
  5. Formal evaluation, and
  6. Comprehensive projects.

Effective strategies promoted mutual adaptation, the process by which the project is adapted to the reality of its institutional setting, while at the same time teachers and school officials adapt their practices in response to the project. Effective strategies provide each teacher with necessary and timely feedback, allow project level choices to be made to correct errors, and encourage commitment to the project.

The following were *effective strategies,* especially when applied in concert:

- Concrete, teacher-specific, and with extended training programs,
- Classroom assistance from project or district staff,
- Teacher observation of similar projects in other classrooms, schools, district,
- Regular project meetings that focused on practical problems,
- Teacher participation in project decisions,
- Local materials development, and
- Principal participation in training.

School organizational climate and leadership. Three elements of a school's organizational climate powerfully affected the project's implementation and continuation: (a) the quality of working relationships among teachers, (b) the active support of principals, and (c) the effectiveness of project directors. The importance of the principal to both short- and long-run effects of innovation efforts can hardly be overstated. This support is for moral support and giving the project legitimacy, not how to do it.

Characteristics of schools and attributes of teachers. Change was typically harder to obtain and continue at the secondary level.

Three teacher attributes significantly affected projected outcomes:

- The number of years had negative effects: The longer a teacher had taught, the less likely was the project to improve student performance. Furthermore, teachers with many years on the job were less likely to change their practices and less likely to continue using project methods after the end of funding.
- Teachers' sense of efficacy. The belief that the teacher can help even the most difficult or unmotivated students. This factor showed strong positive effects on all outcomes.
- Teachers' verbal ability had a positive correlation only with improved student achievement.

District management capacity and support. Districts differ sharply in their ability to manage change and in their receptivity towards it. Although these factors could not be measured precisely, observations and interview data left little doubt as to the importance of constant and active support from district officials and specialized staff for the project's short-term outcomes and particularly for its long-term fate.

Sarason (1982) has summarized three of Berman and McLaughlin's conclusions:

1. The way in which the change process is conceptualized is far more important for success or failure than the educational method or content one seeks to implement. The significance of this conclusion is that it invalidates the step-by-step process of how-you-do-it-social engineering.
2. The time perspective. There was uncritical acceptance of the assumption that the adopted time perspective was appropriate to the goals of change. In almost every instance, the time perspective was determined, not by people in the schools, but by federal policy-makers and legislators, for example, by the assumptions underlying funding policies. That the schools willingly accommodated to such a time perspective indicates the widespread tendency to oversimplify what is involved in cultural and institutional change. It also demonstrates how desperate the schools were to obtain federal funds.
3. If the effort at change identifies and meaningfully involves all those directly or indirectly affected by the change, the effort stands a chance to be successful. Educational change efforts cannot ignore the needs and self-interests of significant people.
4. The third major finding is the most discouraging and instructive of all. Whereas a very small percentage of efforts at change was judged to have been successfully implemented, a smaller percentage was sustained after funding ended. Sarason reports this finding demonstrates the importance of developing project support from a number of constituencies. Change initiators need powerful constituencies in order to stand a chance for continuation of the project, particularly in a time of limited and competitive resources.

A 1990 (McLaughlin, 1990) review of the Rand Change Agent Study in view of today's changed practices and perspectives underscored some of the original conclusions and modified others. The findings that were reinforced included:

- Implementation dominates outcome. This indicates that the choice of implementation— the decision about how, or whether, to put a policy into practice — has more influence on program outcome than do

176

features such as program design, funding level, etc. This finding reinforces the concept that successful educational change is best accomplished when it is a decision of the local authority.

- Policy cannot mandate what matters. Policy outcomes are determined most by local capacity and determination. This is a complex issue with key players including teachers, administrators and local policy-makers. The environment must be supportive of the change and provide the resources necessary to carry out the program, and all players must be committed to the plan.
- Local variability is the rule; uniformity is the exception. Variability is often a sign of a healthy system. It suggests that the system is shaping and modifying policy directives to fit local circumstances.

Miles, Fullan, and Taylor (1978) reported that, of those school districts where no federal money supported the program, 57% had decisive institutionalization; but in cases where the program was supported by a majority of federal money, only 40% were institutionalized. Unless the school district is using a part of its money, it is unlikely to be committed to continue a new program.

Levine (1980) suggests that the institutionalization-termination decision regarding an innovation or change is a critical period for the organization and the life of the change. He indicates that this decision is usually the result of a political process and determined by two concepts, compatibility and profitability. Compatibility is defined as the degree to which the norms, values, and goals of a change are consistent with those of the organization. Profitability is subjective and consists of two types, self-interest and general. It is defined as the degree to which the change satisfies the organizational, group, and personal needs of the organization.

Why planning fails

According to Wise (1977, 1979), educational change policies often fail because the assumptions of policy-makers are frequently hyperrational. Wise suggests that one of the initial sources of the problem is the commitment of reformers to see a particular change implemented. Commitment to what should be changed often varies inversely with knowledge about how to work through a change process. In fact, Wise observes, strong commitment to a particular change may be a barrier to setting up an effective process of change.

Lighthall (1973) suggests that leadership commitment to a particular version of change is negatively related to the ability to implement it. He argues that educational change is a process of coming to grips with the multiple realities of people who are the main participants in implementing the change. Unless policy-makers and change agents are able to do this, the process of change will likely fail. Fullan (1982) makes the observation that one of the great mistakes in the late 1960s and 70s was the assumption that involving some teachers on a curriculum committee or in program development would facilitate implementation because it would increase acceptance by other teachers. The fallacy in this thinking is that the planners did not distinguish between change and the change process.

Implications for educational change efforts

Berman and McLaughlin suggest that federal policy has often been based on misconceptions about the reality of school districts and the factors that produce change in their organizational and educational practices. In a sense, school districts were thought of as black boxes. Federal inputs would be supplied to change and control district behavior so that desirable educational outputs would occur. This research and development point of view was embodied in the following assumptions:

- Improving educational performance requires educational technologies.
- Improving educational performance requires the provision of missing resources to school districts.
- Improving educational performance requires a targeted project focus.

These authors indicate that they believe that federal officials should set aside the largely ineffective research and development point of view and consider an approach that assumes that school districts are ultimately responsible for improving their performance but require both short- and long-term aids to achieve this end.

The following premises might provide building blocks to formulate this point of view:

- Educational performance could be improved if more attention were paid to all stages of the local change process.
- Educational performance could be improved with adaptive implementation assistance.
- Educational performance could be improved if the capacity of school districts to manage change were enhanced.

Berman and McLaughlin suggest that federal efforts to improve the change process within districts should take precedence over their past concern with improving educational products. Sarason (1982) suggests that the Berman and McLaughlin report indicates that we can no longer talk about change at the local level without discussing changes at the state and federal levels. The problem of change is no longer a local one.

Sarason also reviews the Experimental Schools Program (ESP). He indicates the ESP (early 1970's) was based on several considerations:

- Past federal efforts to improve and change schools were ineffective.
- Federal programs had a "buckshot" quality about them, a separate program for separate parts of the school system.
- The federal program should provide resources for comprehensive change.
- There was merit in the complaints of local personnel that federal imposition of programs denied local personnel of creativity, initiative, and control.
- Federal efforts to evaluate past reform efforts had been inadequate and they bore no relationship either to changes in federal policy or to local program management.

Sarason indicates that the ESP was a disaster and that it did not escape the fate of other federal programs. Comprehensive change failed; the principle of local autonomy also failed; and so did the federal evaluation program. Sarason suggests that the significant point is that failure is not explainable only by factors internal to the schools. Therefore, any conception of the change process has to start with the modal ways in which a school system ordinarily relates and responds to outside forces.

Power and educational change

Sarason (1982) proposes that, concerning federal efforts at educational change, there can be little doubt that many federal programs had as their goal an alteration in the distribution of power. More specifically, they sought to give more power to parents and community groups. He indicates that, in doing so, the federal government itself became a source of power. He maintains that it is difficult not to overestimate the issue of power within the schools. Although the failure of federal efforts had many sources, one of the most significant was the superficial understanding of the role of power within the schools. As was discussed in Chapter 5, recent efforts at educational reform have made many of the same errors that have been identified in previous reform attempts. Unfortunately, current reformers did not study the results of the federal efforts at educational change of the 1970's. Perhaps, if they had, the same errors would have not been repeated. As it is, the federal mistakes are simply being repeated at the state level, and one can predict that the results will be similar. Efforts at educational change in the current reform initiative have lacked a productive conception of the educational change process.

Analysis of change effort

Downs and Mohr (1976) and Berman and McLaughlin (1976) have both suggested possible schemata for analyzing an innovation. Downs and Mohr (1976) classify the attributes of innovation into two categories: *primary attributes,* which allow an innovation to be classified without reference to a specific organization, and *secondary attributes* with which classification depends on the organization. In a 1979 article Downs and Mohr provide a list of several dimensions of the innovation.

Dimensions of the innovation

- Benefits
    1. Programmatic benefits
    2. Prestige benefits
    3. Structural benefits
- Costs
    1. Decision costs
    2. Implementation costs
- Resources
    1. Wealth
    2. Manpower, both expertise and time
    3. Equipment
    4. Information
    5. Staff tolerance for change
- Discounting factors
    1. Risk
    2. Average cost of discontinuance
    3. Uncertainty
    4. Instability of future benefits
    5. Venturesomeness.

They provide a hypothetical relationship between innovation and these dimensions: $I = B/C*R*D$.

Berman and McLaughlin's (1976) approach is different. They provide four innovation project characteristics that can affect the success of the project. Their research indicates that educational treatment or technology and resource level have had little effect on project outcomes. However, the scope of the proposed change was found to have major impacts.

Project characteristics

- Educational treatment or technology
  1. Classroom organizational changes
  2. Enrichment techniques
  3. Intensive traditional staffing
  4. School administrative changes
  5. Behavior modification techniques
- Resource levels
  1. Funding level
  2. Number of students served
  3. Concentration of funding
- Scope of proposed change
  1. Centrality of project goals to district goals
  2. Nature and amount of change required
  3. Complexity of treatment
     A. Structural complexity
     B. Complexity of treatment
     C. Integration into ongoing procedures
  4. Consonance or fit between the project goals, values, and practices and those of the school and district
- Implementation strategies

These approaches and variables not only provide a means for analyzing an innovation, but they also allow the process to be evaluated to ascertain which elements of an innovation effort have contributed to its success or failure. Further, in order to assess the potential probability of its success or failure, these various dimensions can be assessed prior to instituting an educational change.

Summary

Change is a process that is a necessary attribute of any system if it is to thrive over a long time. The need for change comes primarily from some change or development in the environment of the system. An open social system can ordinarily respond to new environmental demands by changing its functions (first-order) or its structure (second-order), or both. Education, meeting some but not all criteria for an open social system, has not developed the capacity to respond to environmental change with second-order modifications. Since education does not control the mechanisms necessary to establish its objectives, it has not developed the capacity to regulate its behavior to achieve the objectives established by its external controlling systems. As a result, (1) education seeks to preserve its existing structure, and (2) it does not achieve the constantly changing goals established for it. The institutionalization of the former of these has negated external efforts to improve educational outcomes that require new structural arrangements within education. Because the basic principles of education as a system have not been understood, the principles of change as a process, applied to education (themselves not generally understood), have been doomed to failure. This is so particularly when the objectives of an educational change require a modification of the educational structure or power relationships within the system. It is precisely these elements of the educational system, however, that must change if improvement of education is to be achieved over a sustained period.

9   Toward a framework for a continuing educational improvement process

The first section of this book examined problems of public and teacher education and the failures of educational reform efforts to address and ameliorate these problems. The three previous chapters of this section provided an overview of systems and educational change theory. When contrasting the problems of education and reform efforts with system and educational change theories, we see that educational reformers have either ignored or violated the principles and processes of system and educational change with the highest probability of achieving successful educational reform.

The conclusion seems clear. First, educational reformers have not used effectively the principles and procedures that have proved to be successful in bringing about planned educational change. Second, unless the change process accounts for educational reform effort leaders being unfamiliar with effective principles of educational change, it will not be an effective framework for achieving long-term educational change. Thus, a change of educational reform efforts is warranted.

The theories and forms of educational change existing today fail to consider the complexities of achieving substantial reform of educational structures and functions. In many cases, current educational change theories address the wrong issues or are based on faulty assumptions of education and/or change. In some cases, current knowledge is not utilized in reform efforts. Whatever the reason, the processes of educational change currently available and utilized have not proved effective in achieving educational change or improvement. A different perspective — a second-order change of the reform process — is required.

The reason for the ignorance and violations can be attributed to a fundamental difference in values concerning the appropriate role of education in our society. This value difference is expressed most directly in the question, "Who should control our schools?"

As Kirst's (1988) review points out, (discussed in Chapter 2), the control of American schools is a many-fingered enterprise, although state-level control is obtaining dominant control. The point is, education is a profession dominated and controlled by many forces, causing it to respond spasmodically to each new dictate and fad from local, state and national sources. What must be realized is that this random- and multiple-sourced control of education denies achieving the very goals that many of these efforts hoped to accomplish.

The reasons for the failures of educational reform can also be seen in these externally-sourced controls of education. It is quite clear that the most effective schools and the most successful educational change efforts occur when the local participants are significantly involved in determining both the goals and the processes of change. This has occurred only rarely in recent reform efforts. Thus, the leaders of educational reform are faced with a difficult dilemma. To achieve a successful reform effort, control of the process must be given to those who are perceived to be the cause of the failures—the teachers. This is a difficult decision. Over the past twenty years, the public's trust and confidence in professional educators has eroded considerably. However, this is an unwarranted loss of trust. Education has achieved well those tasks assigned with the resources provided. The failures of education are not due solely to inept educators. They have been caused more by social, political and economic conditions of the times. There were unnecessary intrusions into educational operations by political and lay community leaders and inappropriate and inadequate attempts at reform initiated by these personnel.

If political leaders advocating for reform were serious about achieving successful change, they would demand that professional educators guide the reform process. This would mean, however, that these political leaders would have to remove themselves from the spotlight of the reform process. That is a difficult decision for a political leader. It seems that few have the capacity to do so.

In a democratic society, the control of education and other social institutions is a public responsibility exercised through elected officials. This is a responsibility the public cannot ignore. However, a process of improvement must be devised to protect the educational system against the constant demand for alteration and reform of educational policies and practices. This process must also ward off unwarranted and inappropriate intrusions into educational operations.

This system of improvement is necessary for several reasons. First, education is a developmental process. Periods of stability and no change must be built into the change process. These periods are necessary so that the educational system has an opportunity to incorporate and evaluate

184

improvement efforts and practices. There is a need to allow teachers the time to focus on their students. There is a need to allow staff development programs to be planned, implemented and evaluated over a sufficient time to determine whether they have been successful in achieving their goals. In short, schools, like individuals, need regular periods of quiet time to consolidate advances, plan to meet new needs, and better achieve existing objectives.

Second, professional educators must have a significant voice in determining appropriate goals, policies and practices the profession may be asked to carry out. This is necessary so that no goals, policies and/or practices are imposed on the profession that it has neither the capacity nor resources to achieve. Currently, school superintendents and other administrators are supposed to play this role. However, these administrators are political creatures in their educational roles and subject to the dictates of local and state school boards. They do not have the authority to reject inappropriate demands made on teachers or the schools.

Finally, and most importantly, education is a transmitter of our social and cultural heritage and a reflector of contemporary trends and issues. To realize these goals successfully, education as a profession, and professional educators, must be free to raise any issue, discuss openly any event, free to critique any decision, and free to object to unwarranted intrusions that curtail the profession's right to determine the policies and procedures best suited for meeting students' needs. A democratic society needs its education profession to reflect and discuss contemporary events and issues. To carry out this democratic ideal, the profession cannot be subject to a constant barrage of whims, fads, and changes. The profession must have the capacity to resist external forces that seek to dominate and control it. Once education as a profession is dominated by external local, state, and national spasms, it fails to serve the nation's best interests. The role of education as an analyzer of historical themes and reflector of contemporary issues must not be subverted by short-term economic or political issues. Education must be free to speak to any issue. It must be able to respond negatively to inappropriate demands for reform, from those issues that detract from its primary mission, or limit the capacity of education to comment upon any issue relevant to the education of its students or the nation's needs.

At the same time, education must be held accountable to elected officials and the general public. A totally independent profession would not be in the best interests of the nation or of student learning. Thus, a mechanism for providing education with increased freedom and improved methods of political oversight is needed. A balance must be sought and achieved which will enable education to respond appropriately to legitimate social, political and economic trends, while providing shared responsibility, authority, and accountability for educational activities and outcomes.

To achieve this balance, the system aspects of education must be integrated with an effective process for achieving continued and coordinated improvement of educational structures, teacher preparation programs, learning activities, and learning outcomes. Achieving this goal depends on a change of the reform process and a framework that uses principles of system and educational change theory in a new design for educational improvement.

This chapter provides an overview of such a framework. The next section identifies and discusses key differences between educational reform and an educational improvement process. The following section identifies and discusses the five critical features of the framework. These features provide the rationale for the second- and third-order changes to be made in the remainder of the book. These changes identify the elements of educational structure which must be modified so that a continuing educational improvement process may be instituted. The changes also address specific aspects of educational activity that must be altered if a developmental process is to be successful.

Educational reform versus educational development

There is some confusion in the literature about whether the terms *educational reform*, *educational change* and *innovation* are synonymous or represent different concepts, processes and outcomes. Miles (1964) and Moorish (1976) agree on a distinction between *change* and *innovation*. They assert that *innovation* is clearly more planned, deliberate, routinized and willed. *Change*, on the other hand, tends to be more spontaneous. Moorish further defines *innovation* as something that is introduced that is new and different. It may be good, bad, or neither. The definition of each is an individual value judgment. Moorish suggests that distinctions can be made between novelty innovations and those which provide improvements and between creative and deficit change. These two aspects of change will be discussed more completely in the next section of this chapter. The most appropriate improvements for education come about from a combination of those that are based on creative change, are voluntary, and which are sincere in their efforts to improve the teaching-learning interactions between teachers and students. Creative-based change is a key principle of a continuing educational improvement process.

Fullan (1982) distinguishes between *change* and *progress*. According to Fullan, *change* implies doing something different. Only change which leads to improvement is *progress*. Fullan also agrees with Lighthall (1973) that educational change is a process of understanding the realities of the main participants in the change process.

186

Dalin (1978) suggests that *innovation* implies a conscious effort to improve practices or programs in an attempt to achieve desired objectives. Dalin also uses *innovation* interchangeably with *change*, as well as with *renewal* and *reform*.

Sarason (1982) offers another perspective on change. He asserts that, for all practical purposes, change is mandated and that the strongest pressures for change come from outside the system. These pressures imply that there is something "wrong" with the schools and that legislation will "fix" what is wrong. This concept is strikingly familiar to Fullan's notion of deficit-based change.

The terms *change*, *reform* and *innovation*, therefore, may be interpreted as meaning the same thing. They may also represent different concepts or processes, or one or another may subsume the others. What they do have in common is that they imply a need for an alteration of current educational practices because there is a perceived disparity between the desired and actual state of educational outcomes. This perception is related to the premise advanced by Coombs (1967, 1985). He suggested that there is a significant and adverse disparity between the changes undergone by society and the lack of educational systems to adjust appropriately to these changes.

This commonality of perception is based on a deficit framework and perspective for achieving improvement of educational outcomes. That is, educational improvement is considered to have been achieved when the cause of the problem resulting in the current undesired actual state of affairs has been "fixed." What has not been realized in this perspective is that an educational system does not have, under current conditions, the authority or capability to generate the rules for second-order changes that would allow it to modify its structure and functions to adapt successfully to the environmental changes around it. This deficit perspective leads to (1) mandated changes, which invariably are not successful, and (2) an imposition of reform tactics which are not successful because they do not emanate from an understanding of educational systems and change processes. This is because they are rooted in attempts to cure the problem as opposed to setting in place a process for continuing educational improvement.

This perspective results in unfortunate consequences for educational improvement efforts. First, the educational practice targeted for improvement is usually isolated from its contextual system components. This reduces the benefits of the proposed change because all affected system elements are not dealt with in a coordinated fashion. This consequence results from an imperfect knowledge of education as a system. For example, attempts to improve curriculum standards tend to focus on mandating certain curriculum objectives to be achieved at specific grade levels. On the face of it, there appears to be little wrong with this approach. The state certainly has a right to specify what it believes are appropriate standards to be achieved. This approach fails to recognize that:

- Achieving certain standards can be achieved through a variety of methods. These methods are best determined by the teacher by his/her knowledge of his/her students.
- The achievement of these standards may not be possible for all students within the same time period.
- All teachers may not have the capabilities to provide the instructional methods necessary to achieve the standards within a particular time frame. Thus, before imposing a set of standards, a period of capacity-building for teachers is necessary.
- Those who are expected to carry out the change — the teachers — have not been adequately involved in the planning of either the standards, or the methods to be used in achieving them. It is not enough to include a couple of teacher representatives and expect them to act for all teachers from all communities.

Second, such a perspective demands a retrospective view of the educational process. This means that, in order to perceive a need for change, an individual must be dissatisfied with current educational outcomes. This results in an examination of possible factors from a historical perspective that may have contributed causally to the current state of the outcomes. The consequence of this type of perspective is that one is attempting to correct situations of the past that *may* have contributed to the current outcomes. There is no sure way to determine if the educational component identified in the past contributed to the current situation in a meaningful way. Such actions lead to several consequences.

First, the wrong educational element may be identified as the causal agent, that is, the diagnosis is wrong, and therefore, the prescribed treatment is wrong and fails.

Second, such a perspective concerns itself primarily with an examination of the "why" question. This leads to attempts to understand what went wrong, and why it went wrong. This procedure focuses on an analysis of previous procedures in an attempt to fix them. It would be far more fruitful and beneficial to ask "what." What can be done now to move the system as it is to a desired state. What procedures, what improvements, what alterations, what resources, will be necessary to develop the system to enable it to provide a desired process of educational quality.

Third, and perhaps more importantly, such a retrospective approach to educational change means that education will never be able to achieve its potential or satisfy its critics. This is because education is told to correct some perceived deficiency. During this period of correction of one element of the system, developments have been taking place in other system components, society has changed, the resource picture has altered, new political officials have been elected, and a new round of deficiency identification has begun. The result of such a process of deficiency identification is that education is told to correct the newly noted deficiency and the cycle repeats itself. Education is thus placed in a position of constantly attempting to correct perceived deficiencies, not to improve its functions.

This deficit perspective of educational change is caused by a lack of understanding of education as a developmental process. Many educational reformers seem to have the idea that improving education is like fixing a car — if a part does not work as someone thinks it should, it is fixed or replaced. Education is not a car. It is a process of carefully assisting children develop into responsible adults. This is a process that does not lend itself to quick fixes or replacing parts of a brain or behavior.

Third, a deficit perspective of educational change results in models of change that are based on correction of perceived disparities and deficiencies. These models of change are thus oriented towards how education has attempted to change from one type of practice to another to correct a deficiency. Most theories of change have evolved from this type of perspective. There are two notable exceptions.

Dalin (1978) describe forms of organizations that have evolved as a result of two major developments: (1) Societies are moving from a state of stability to rapid change/dynamism and (2) Systems are moving from simple to complex organizations. Education, as an organization, can be categorized as complex because it reflects a complex mission in a rapidly changing environment. Our society can be categorized as dynamic. According to Dalin (1978), the most appropriate type of complex organization within a dynamic society is a "Systematic Learning Organization" (SLO). An SLO is one that moves away from a mechanistic tradition towards an organic organization that allows for democratic control of educational development in complex environments.

A *mechanistic organization* is described (Burns and Stalker, 1966) as one that is complex but best suited for a stable society. It is characterized by a hierarchical structure, standard operating procedures, and precisely defined rights and obligations. These authors assert that it is the most frequent form of educational organization. They describe mechanistic educational systems as having the following tendencies:

- Differentiated tasks are assumed by system sub-units, e.g., elementary education vs. special education.

189

- There is a concentration on specific means rather than on educational objectives.
- There is a hierarchical nature of responsibilities/control manifested in a hierarchy of positions.
- Roles/positions are regulated by precise definition of rights/obligations.
- Interaction tends to be based more on vertical level than among peers.
- Work is guided primarily by instructions and decisions from above.
- The location of knowledge is primarily at the top of the hierarchy.
- There is a high degree of loyalty; there is little radical criticism of existing conditions.
- There is a higher value placed on internal knowledge (experience and skills) than on general knowledge.

In contrast to mechanistic organizations, *organic organizations* are simple and found in dynamic societies. They are characterized by a constant process of re-defining individual tasks. They have collective ownership of problems, and a network structure of control and advice, rather than a vertical hierarchy of instruction and decision-making. Burns and Stalker (1966) ascribe the following characteristics to organic organizations:

- The environment determines challenges/tasks; objectives and methods are relatively easy to define.
- There is built-in flexibility, which is the norm of the organization.
- There is greater utilization of individuals who are not bound to tightly defined roles or positions.
- Responsibilities are shared; there is less specialization and more holistic understanding of task requirements.
- System sub-units have a high degree of autonomy with the capacity to relate directly to problems and tasks.
- Problems are solved in several ways depending on who has the problem and the capacity to solve it.

According to Burns and Stalker, the organic model does not easily fit educational organizations for the following reasons:

- Today's educational system is highly complex; responsibilities are defined by the political level representing the highest democratic institutions in society.
- It is difficult to see how greater autonomy for individual schools can be combined with political control of the educational process.

190

- Confusion and difficulty for teachers, students, and staff would be caused by creating autonomous schools and maintaining the current hierarchical staffing structure.
- The organic model was developed for industry, where accountability is related to market needs which can be fed back to the company relatively quickly.
- The organic tradition uses the change agent concept who builds on consensus. This is problematic in school systems, where conflict resolution and priority-setting are needed.
- Recently there have been more autonomous educational institutions developed for specific purposes and organized according to the organic model. Experience has shown that these institutions — research centers — have been phased out rather quickly.

Dalin suggests that both the mechanistic and organic organizations developed within or as educational systems when the environment was relatively stable, i.e., when environmental change developed slowly. According to Dalin, although the environment is no longer stable, efforts to develop or reform educational systems are based on rather simple organizational models. Buckely (1968) agrees regarding the demise of the appropriateness of the mechanistic and organic models. He asserts that they have outlived their usefulness and that a more viable model, which more accurately reflects the type of system that society is today, is needed. He suggests that more than an equilibrium or a homeostatic system is needed. He recommends a complex adaptive system. Both Dalin and Buckley are asserting that previous models of systems (organizations) are outmoded because their adaptive speed, both actual and potential, has not kept pace with that of environmental change. This is essentially the point that Coombs (1985) made when he spoke of the disparity between educational systems and their larger environment. The essential point is that, currently, there is not a viable model of educational organization that will allow educational systems to interact successfully with its larger environment of systems.

In contrast to the mechanistic and organic organizations, there does not currently exist an example of an educational system that meets the criteria of a Systematic Learning Organization. However, some of the components of such an organization have been specified (Dalin, 1978). These components include the following:

- Political control of the educational system is maintained; however, allowance is provided for individual (school system, school and teacher) choice among alternatives.

- There is recognition of the legitimate needs for both stability and change.
- The possibility exists for taking alternative perspectives into account.
- Effective schools balance the need for both equal opportunity and autonomy.
- Alternatives to centralization of technical skills are developed.
- Openness to the environment is maintained; however, an effective process for protecting the system from powerful outside interventions is also operative.
- The system structure operates to limit future uncertainties and optimizes the possibilities for learning about the future.

No blueprint for developing a Systematic Learning Organization in a complex and dynamic environment currently exists. In such an environment the schools reflect a complex social mission in a rapidly changing set of interdependent variables. What educational structure will best allow the educational system to achieve its mission(s) within such an environment and how can such a structure be developed? Unfortunately, the outline of a Systematic Learning Organization does not provide the answers to these basic questions, although it does describe some of the characteristics of such an organization if it was to be developed.

Watson (1967) has outlined ten steps constituting a design for a self-renewing school system. These steps include: sensing, screening, diagnosing, inventing, weighing, deciding, introducing, operating, evaluating, and revising.

Sensing is defined as sensitivity to unmet needs in individuals and to changing social situations affecting education. It might best be characterized as awareness of a need for improvement. A primary characteristic of a self-renewing school system is a constant and widespread sensing of problems and new possibilities.

Screening is a process of determining priorities of problems so that attention can be focused on the more urgent. A self renewing school system has an established set of criteria against which to measure the priority of a problem. In today's terms, this would be called *environmental screening*.

Diagnosing is a critical step in the formulation of constructive remedies. Watson makes the point that it is important to understand the "why" of a problem so that appropriate corrective action can be directed towards the heart of the problem.

Inventing is the process of developing remedies based on adequate and appropriate diagnosis. A mechanism for permitting wide participation in the production of possible solutions is recommended.

Weighing is the process of evaluating the merits of each proposed solution. Watson suggests that a small group of possible solutions be evaluated by a small group who must assess the advantages and disadvantages of each proposal.

Deciding is the selection of a particular innovation or set of actions to address the diagnosed problem. Those who will be involved in implementing the solution should be a part of the decision-making process.

Introducing is the process of inserting the solution into the system. Watson suggests that this step requires artful strategic planning, particularly for dealing with those who have not yet been a part of the process, but who would be involved by the solution.

Operating is the process of implementing the solution for a long enough time so that its success or failure can be fairly judged. Decisions on revisions or rejections should be held in abeyance until the solution has a chance to demonstrate its merits.

Evaluating includes both formative and summative elements. The criteria, procedures whose responsibility it is for the evaluation, should be specified at the onset of the implementation.

Revising is the process of improving the solution on the basis of the evaluation results.

Watson suggests that a structure for the implementation of a self-renewing set of procedures is essential. The process of self-renewal includes an internal and external perspective. It is intended to serve as a model that can be modified as circumstances suggest.

These two models of educational improvement, the Systematic Learning Organization and the Self-Renewing Educational System, each represent significant departures from other models of educational change. Each focuses on the developmental aspects of educational improvement. Each provides for significant components that an adaptive educational system must include. However, each suffers from critical flaws. For example, neither accounts for the interactive role that teacher preparation and retraining must play in any serious effort to improve educational outcomes. Also, neither describes the process by which the organizational, administrative, and training changes must be implemented if either model is to be successfully instituted. Neither provide a process by which the type of organization recommended might be implemented. Neither recognize the political-social-economic interactions that must play a vital role in the development of any educational improvement process. Finally, each characterizes the type of system (organization) recommended as an outcome, given the type of environment we live in. Neither recognize that the system (organization) type that is necessary, given our society and environment, must be a constantly developing and improving process, not an organizational entity, the maintenance of that soon becomes a goal in itself.

Toward an educational improvement process

In contrast to the concepts and processes represented in the term's *reform*, *change* and *innovation*, a continuing educational improvement process uses positive and goal-oriented concepts and processes. It represents a significant departure from most existing theories and models of educational change. It does include some of the principles of a Systematic Learning Organization and Self-Renewing Educational System, but it also provides for a process of how to implement the improvement process. It goes well beyond the principles of either a Systematic Learning Organization or Self-Renewing Educational System, however.

An educational improvement process focuses on the system and human requirements for implementing a continuing improvement of an educational unit, be it at a classroom, individual school, school system or state level. It does not expect or assume that a stable organizational structure for education is the goal of development. Rather, it assumes that a continuing process of development provides the best means for achieving continuing educational improvement. The key features of the process are discussed next.

Features of a continuing educational development process

There are four major components to the process. The first two are concerned with conceptual and attitudinal shifts that must occur in the thinking of professional educators, political leaders, and the public about how schools can be improved most significantly. The third component deals with the structural transformations of the educational system that must take place to allow an educational development process to be implemented. The fourth component deals with the specific features of the development process.

Component 1: a paradigm shift

The first conceptual shift that must be made is for those concerned with the improvement of education to stop thinking of it as an entity that can be reformed and to start thinking about education as a process that can and

194

should constantly improve over time. On the face of it, this may seem like a simple shift for people to make. It is not, for the consequences of such a shift are substantial.

The first consequence is that such a shift would force people to stop thinking about educational outcomes as a product. Most individuals tend to regard appropriate educational outcomes as the scores' students achieve on a test. These are not the most appropriate educational outcomes. The most appropriate educational outcome is the successful institutionalization of a process of thinking in each student about life, problems, self, the future, and a host of other topics and issues. This cognitive process orientation as an educational outcome is much more highly related to determining the quality of life of an individual and society than are the scores a student achieves on a test battery. It is the successful school that can assist each student to develop such a process of cognitive analysis and decision-making.

The second consequence of this paradigm shift is that it forces a futuristic orientation in thinking about education and its improvement. Because education is a developmental process, it must proceed in an integrated, progressive series of increments towards achieving its objectives. Just as it would be totally inappropriate to expect the average five-year-old to master geometry, so also is it inappropriate to expect all schools and school systems to be able to carry out all aspects of a successful educational improvement plan. The focus for such a school should be on the process of capacity-building in order for the school personnel to achieve its objectives. This process of capacity-building takes time to implement and achieve its goals and it must go through a developmental process, the same as a student must progress through a series of mathematics preparation before s/he is ready for geometry.

The third consequence is that of a longer time perspective for educational improvement. Most educational reformers, particularly those who are not professional educators, have an unrealistic time perspective about improving education. Often, so do many educators. If educational improvement is thought of as a developmental process, rather than as a reform product, the time perspective must become longer. An educational improvement process is an on-going activity, one that does not stop, because there are always aspects of the educational program that can be improved. However, some take longer than others to achieve so the on-going process of improvement is a constant effort at capacity-building.

Component 2: system interactions and shared responsibility

The second paradigm shift that must take place includes three inter-dependent elements. These are, first, the recognition that there must be a more appropriate, positive, and trusting set of interactions established between an educational system and its larger environment of systems. Second, there must be recognition that educational improvement is a function of successful inter-actions of the various sub-units of public and teacher education, and successful internal communication within and among each of these sub-units. Third, educational improvement must provide for shared authority of decision-making. Each of these will be considered in turn.

External system interactions

One of the most frequent and serious observations of education examiners has been that there is a lack of trust and confidence in the profession of education and professional educators by the general public. This condition has developed to the extent that the education profession has lost confidence in itself (Dalin, 1978; Coombs, 1985). This is a damaging and debilitating condition to overcome as education seeks to improve its ability to adapt to the needs of its environment of systems. It is a condition that leads to a self-fulfilling prophecy and a Game Without End (Watzlawick, et al, 1974). It is a condition that can be overcome only by a display of confidence in education by its larger environment, by establishing a jointly developed, achievable mission, and a shared authority and responsibility for developing the policies and practices from which the goals of the mission will be sought.

Internal system interactions

Although public education and teacher preparation programs exist in a symbiotic relationship, their inter-dependence is rarely noted or accounted for in educational reform efforts. Their relationship and inter-dependence must be accounted for if educational improvement efforts are to be successful. Successful public education obviously depends on highly qualified teachers. Thus, changes and improvements in public education depend on successful and synchronized changes in teacher preparation programs. Each system unit, public and teacher preparation programs, has a different environment of system sub-units, constituencies, and issues with which to contend in achieving successful improvements. This makes it extremely difficult to coordinate changes and improvements in each. Reformers and educators must recognize that teacher preparation programs should exist for the sole purpose of providing teachers for the public schools. Thus, it is public education that must be the leader, and teacher preparation programs the follower, in developing the desired capacities and capabilities of the teaching force.

Another aspect of teacher preparation that often is overlooked in school improvement efforts is the continuing development of teachers' capabilities. If educational improvement is considered to be a developmental process then a continuing process of teacher capacity-building will be necessary. This capacity-building must be coordinated and synchronized with the improvement goals of individual schools.

Shared authority

This paradigm shift of shared authority may be the one that most non-professional educators will agree with the least. Education in America has always been considered to be under local control, with elected school boards responsible primarily for determining policy. As Kirst's (1988) review indicated, there are currently numerous groups from the national, state, and local levels affecting educational policy decision-making. There is one notable exception to these groups. That is the education profession. Professional educators are, with a few exceptions nationally, excluded from policy development at the state and local levels and are without vote when decisions are reached concerning the mission, procedures, resource allocations and the alterations of educational structure and function deemed necessary to improve educational outcomes. This is a scandalous treatment of a profession. What is more important, two substantial aids to educational improvement are lost because of this exclusion.

First, the knowledge and expertise of teachers are lost to the decision-making process. The professional advice, counsel, and wisdom that teachers — those most intimately concerned and involved with the education of students — could provide concerning educational improvement are lost to decision-makers. The cumulative storehouse of teachers' knowledge concerning educational matters is a resource that, under current conditions, is being lost to efforts to improve education. It is not a loss that can continue if significant educational improvement is to be realized.

Second, and perhaps more significantly, it is the teaching force upon which efforts depend to dramatically improve education. Thus, the responsibility for improving educational outcomes ultimately depends on teachers. However, teachers do not have the authority for decision-making concerning the most vital aspects of educational activity which will affect improvement efforts. The review of educational change (Chapters 7 & 8) revealed clearly that those who must change to cause the improvements desired must be involved in the improvement process from its inception. Further, it is clear from Chapter 5 that teachers have not been significantly involved in the current reform attempts. It is also clear from Chapter 8 that educational change has its highest probability of success when such efforts are focused at the school level. The combination of these findings strongly suggests that the highest expectation of educational change occurs when such efforts are (1) focused at the individual school level, and (2) when the teachers of a school have a shared authority for determining improvement processes.

Component 3: transformation of educational system elements

The current system of public and teacher education in America does not include those processes and structural elements that would allow educational improvement efforts to have a high expectation of success. In fact, the current form of governance of education, the structural elements of both public and teacher education and the reform agenda and processes, each operates against the very alterations in the educational system that must be instituted if improvement efforts are to be successful. The basic alterations in governance of education and the structural alterations that must be instituted before a continuing process of education development can be implemented are presented and discussed in the remaining chapters. These alterations would require modifications of education on an epic scale. For that reason, among others, they may not be seriously considered by educational reformers. However, they are the very adjustments necessary for continued educational improvement.

Component 4: key features of an educational improvement process

There are six key features to the Educational Improvement Process. Each of these will be considered in turn.

A futuristic orientation

A futuristic orientation towards education implies that the focus of educational improvement must be process-oriented. This process requires that a school system and its environment of systems be more concerned with developing the instructional capacities of a state, school system, school, and classroom to achieve an on-going process of improvement than concerned with remedying perceived problems. This difference is crucial. A deficiency- and problem-orientation negates the interaction and involvement of system components that must be a part of any on-going improvement process.

A futuristic orientation also requires the identification of a desired end-state of the process that can be constantly refined, improved, and provided for succeeding classes of students.

Beeby (1966) has developed a four-stage model for measuring the quality of primary education as it is related to teacher education. It can also serve as a framework and guide for a desired end-state of an educational improvement process. The four stages are:

Stage 1 — Teaching activities are primitive or loosely organized. They typically and often involve transmission of symbols without meaning, or memorization rituals on the part of students.

Stage 2 — Classrooms are organized rigidly. Teaching methods and examinations are highly standardized. There are frequent inspections by administrators or evaluators.

Stage 3 — This stage is characterized by greater initiative on the part of students and more flexibility in teaching practices.

Stage 4 — Pupil problem-solving and self-initiated behaviors are common. Personal-social development as well as cognitive development becomes an important aim, as does a positive relationship between students and teacher.

The goal is to have each classroom in a school system have as its goal the consistent demonstration of practices and behaviors that characterize Stage 4. To achieve this goal, a teacher must be able to characterize his/her teaching practices and to alter them as necessary to move his/her students toward Stage 4 behaviors, and be able to maintain these over time.

Mission and acceptance of variability

This component involves two inter-related elements, each of which is also related to Component #1.

Mission of the schools

The mission of the schools involves two elements. These are:

- Foster the academic-intellectual growth of children;
- Inculcate in them those values appropriate for living in a democracy.

The first mission is to develop the cognitive-academic capacities of students. The second is to prepare them to live in a democratic society. The issue of the schools' mission will be more fully discussed in the following chapter, for it has significant implications for organizational structure, administrative practices, curriculum focus and development, teacher preparation, and resource allocation priorities and procedures. There is little doubt that these two elements of schools' missions have always been included in any treatment of the purpose of schools, there are differences, such as knowledge base, between them. Although not always receiving the same emphasis (Sarason, 1982), and although there have been many other responsibilities assigned to the schools, these have practically always been considered to be the prime purposes of schools.

The emphasis that these two purposes have received has generated major differences in instructional focus. These differences should not, however, confuse the fact that they are equally important in any effort to improve educational outcomes.

Each of these mission elements has at least two stages. The first stage is a realistic and achievable level of expectation for each element of the mission. The second stage, which should accompany each achievable level, is an aspirational level. The aspirational level goes beyond that which can be realistically achieved to specify the ideal level of accomplishment. This level should characterize the goal of each classroom for each mission element.

The mission of the school is obviously related to a futuristic orientation. A school, or any organization for that matter, must have a sense of its purpose and the goals it is attempting to realize. A futuristic orientation and the mission of the schools must be in harmony. They must be consistent and related, for they provide the conceptual and decision-making framework for organizational structure and development, curriculum development, administrative practices, personnel development needs, and resource allocation priorities.

Respect for variability

It must be recognized that each classroom will have students who are at different levels of functioning concerning each element of the mission. Not all will respond in the same manner, or at comparable rates, to any one method used to assist them in their cognitive or personal-social development. Thus, there must be acceptance of and respect for a variety of methods to assist students in developing their skills in these areas. The recognition of which methods are most appropriate can best be determined by the teacher in consultation with each student's parents. The critical point is that teachers should have the authority and flexibility to use different approaches with different students, and that not all students should be expected to display comparable rates of improvement.

Just as teachers must have the authority and flexibility to use different approaches to assisting individual students, so also must individual school systems have the flexibility to develop and implement various means to improve instructing and learning conditions within the system. This means that there cannot be an imposed set of time requirements or grade-level expectations by the state or a higher authority. The school system, and each individual teacher, are in the best position to assess and determine which approaches will yield the best possible results in the shortest amount of time. This time will probably not be the same for all systems, and certainly not for all students.

A shared authority and responsibility

One of the most critical elements of an effective educational improvement process is the implementation of a shared responsibility and authority for educational decision-making. Educators have the responsibility for educational outcomes, but are not given the authority to determine either appropriate and achievable results or their criteria for success. A significant disparity exists between the environment's pace of change and the capacity of educational systems to adapt to the rapidity of the change. This disparity has resulted in a loss of confidence in education, and about education's capabilities by educators. However, fundamental and successful change of education cannot be accomplished without educators' cooperation and involvement in the change effort. These points argue for a mutual, cooperative, and equal power authority effort between educators and external agents to develop and implement an improvement effort.

A significant aspect of this type of improvement effort must be the recognition and reliance on capacity-building of teachers to implement the improvement effort developed. An educational improvement effort that relies on mandating change or attempting change through inducements may achieve short-term improvements, but generally the costs will greatly exceed the benefits. Long-term, significant educational improvement is best achieved through a process of capacity-building in which teachers develop a wide repertoire of skills that can be applied to a variety of educational situations and conditions.

A system perspective

A perspective of educational improvement based on a knowledge of the environment of systems of any given system of education provides for an analysis and understanding of which system elements must be involved in any improvement effort. Generally, the larger the improvement effort, the more sub-systems that must be involved. It is more than just a recognition of which elements will be involved in any change effort. There must also be a recognition of what changes will be required from each element, the time necessary to allow for any capacity-building, the coordination of timing when each system element will be involved and the delivery of resources at the appropriate time. The coordination of all of the above must be achieved according to an established time schedule.

A system perspective of educational improvement also provides a more realistic time perspective to be developed before tangible and significant improvements can be expected. Most educational change efforts are geared to an unrealistic set of time expectations. Understanding which system elements must be involved in any improvement effort, and how long it will take to prepare and coordinate the timing and development of each element, should provide a more realistic expectation of the time that will be involved before improvement efforts are noted in educational outcomes.

The political-social-economic context (PSEC)

The PSEC of any educational improvement effort is a dynamic aspect of any change attempted. The PSEC can exert an influence that ranges from catastrophic to triumphant. Each of these three elements of the environmental context exerts an influence on an educational change effort. The larger and more complex the change attempted, the more involved and influential each of these dimensions becomes. The conditions of each of these dimensions that lead to certain types of reaction to educational change efforts are understood fairly well.

When the political situation is fairly stable, there is less likelihood of achieving substantial educational change, because political leaders do not like to introduce controversy when things are fairly quiet and stable. There is a greater probability of introducing significant educational change when the political context is fairly quiet and stable. However, chances of sustaining long-term educational improvement efforts are enhanced when the political context is relatively stable and there is neither significant change in the political players nor significant issues of political debate. Thus, an unstable political context increases the probability for introducing change, but decreases the probability of sustaining it. A stable political context reduces the probability of introducing change, but increases the probability of sustaining it.

The economic context favoring the introduction of educational change is a declining one. When economic indicators suggest that the economy is faltering, there is usually an outcry for change in the educational system. This is because economic and business leaders typically blame education for the failure of economic procedures, i.e., poor work skills, lack of motivated workers, etc. This is the context in which economic leaders prod political leaders to do something about the schools. The recent round of educational reform is a classic example of this situation.

When the economy is strong and growing at an acceptable rate, there is generally little pressure from business leaders to do much about the schools. This is because they generally perceive and treat the mission of the schools as the production of workers who will fuel the growing economy. Such leaders tend to be reluctant to ascribe any other prime mission or purpose to the purpose of the schools.

The social context that most favors educational change efforts is a crisis one. When the social context is calm, there is little pressure or expectation that the schools should embark on program of educational change. In truth, there are few educational leaders who would advocate significant change at such a time. However, when the social context experiences substantial change, there is heavy pressure for educational change.

When, however, the social context is tranquil, there is generally little pressure for change. In fact, there may be an expression of "don't rock the boat," or "if it isn't broken, don't try to fix it."

The common denominator to these three dimensions is that educational change efforts are most favored when there is upheaval in any one of them. Often, upheaval in any one signals upheaval in the others. When the PSEC is calm, there is little pressure to change educational activities, and there may be resistance to attempting change during such a period.

The irony, of course, is that educational change attempted during or as a result of upheavals in any one of these dimensions is likely to be self-defeating. This is because such efforts under taken at such a time are likely to be narrowly focused, problem-centered, rather than improvement-centered, and more concerned with short-term results than long-term improvement.

An educational improvement effort, however, can operate irrespective of the conditions of the PSEC. This is because it requires a cooperative effort on the part of the educational system and representatives of the PSEC. This acts as one safeguard against an educational system constantly being deluged with demands of change at a time when the PSEC argues more for stability than narrow, short-term change efforts. In all probability, an educational improvement process would probably work best in a period of PSEC calm. This is because there would be less pressure for immediate changes and the expectation of dramatic, immediate results from political and business leaders.

Program improvement plans

Any educational improvement plan should describe how the school system, each school, and each classroom will go about developing its instructional capacities and practices to bring each to Stage 4 and sustain each at that Stage. Such a plan should include learner characteristics and needs, capacity-building needs of teachers, classroom approaches to be used, resource requirements, and evaluation procedures. The time for developing each of these should be sufficient to allow each to be adequately refined. The time for initial implementation should be no less than three years, following the development and refinement phase. The rationale for this time period is explained in Chapter 12 with Second-Order Changes 9 & 10.

Evaluation procedures require a special note. Currently, the most frequent measures of school effectiveness are the results from various national- and state-normed tests. These are inappropriate measures of classroom effectiveness when the emphasis of instruction is process-oriented, i.e., the development of thinking skills and personal-social competence. This issue is addressed more fully in Chapter 12, but it should be noted that the primary outcome of an effective school is a process of cognitive analysis and synthesis and socially acceptable behavior.

Summary

This chapter has addressed the differences between educational change efforts and the development of an educational improvement process. An educational improvement process has six major components that provide a framework and set of principles for decision-making by educational systems. The intent of an educational improvement process is to reduce the disparity between an education system and its environment of systems. This is achieved by focusing on the development of cognitive-academic and personal-social competence skills in students, providing a futuristic orientation to educational improvement instead of a problem-centered approach, and recognizing the importance of the PSEC to educational improvement efforts.

Section Three

SECOND- AND THIRD-ORDER CHANGE

This section contains the remaining chapters of this book. There are three sub-sections. The first (Chapter 10) presents four proposals for third-order change. The second section (Chapters 11-15) presents 43 proposals for second-order change. The final chapter (16) discusses the prospects for achieving fundamental change of education and outlines the process elements that must be attended to if significant improvement of education is to occur.

The current system of education in the United States has serious problems that must be addressed and altered if significant improvements in student outcomes are to occur. Previous efforts to improve the educational system have not met with significant success. A signal characteristic of these attempts is that the structure of the educational system has not been altered in any meaningful manner. However, the re-structuring of the system has been mentioned many times. The most salient obstacle to re-structuring the schools is that such an effort would require a significant redistribution of the control and power of educational policy development and practices. It is essentially a dilemma of a state versus local versus professional control of education. Obviously, no one of these should have complete control over all aspects of education. It is, therefore, a question of how much control over what aspects of education should each of these groups command. The goal is to establish a mechanism for developing shared responsibility and authority for ensuring desired educational outcomes among these groups.

When repeated attempts to achieve a goal have failed, it usually means that an inappropriate solution(s) to the problem has been utilized. In the case of educational reform, it means that a different means of conceptualizing education's problems is required to identify a solution more likely to achieve a desired and acceptable solution. Fuhrman, Elmore, and Massell (1993) suggest that a different way of thinking about school change is required. The solution to education's problems is not to be found solely in improving the working conditions of teachers, raising the entrance requirements for teacher education preparation programs, or in the other state-controlled efforts to improve educational outcomes. The solution lies in changing the control of education and the means by which educators go about their business.

This solution requires understanding what groups control the structure of education. This control does not rest in the hands of educators. It lies in the hands of those who command the power, decision-making authority and resources that shape the structure of education. These are the political leaders at the state and local level. Therefore, the solution to the re-structuring of education lies outside the domain of professional education and in the hands of political leaders, parents, and the rest of the general public. What has not been realized, apparently, in efforts to re-structure education, is that re-structuring will require a redistribution of the control, power, and decision-making authority of education. It will not be until such redistribution has occurred that the re-structuring of education will occur.

There are three fundamental understandings that must be developed for this redistribution to occur. The first is that the alignment of educational policy-making and decision-making authority must be re-designed and re-structured for significant improvements in student outcomes to occur. There are many ways that education can be re-designed. Some of these do not require re-structuring the educational establishment. However, if the re-design of education is based on a re-structuring of education, a second understanding must be developed.

The second understanding is that any significant re-structuring of education will require redistributing the current power, authority, and resources that control educational decision-making. The redistribution of control of these forces among any group is not an easy task. In education, it would be an extremely difficult task because of the traditions affecting education, the loosely connected organization of education, and, particularly, because control of these factors presently resides in the hands of many political leaders at the federal, state, and local levels. These political leaders are not likely to give up such power easily. However, they are the leaders who could most effectively implement a process of educational change that leads to a redistribution of the power and control of education.

The recommendations for change proposed in this book do not require these leaders to give up such control entirely. The proposals do recommend a sharing of power among the three groups most intimately involved and concerned with the effectiveness of education. These three groups are the political leaders, parents, and teachers.

208

The third understanding that must be developed is the relationship among re-structuring education, redistributing control of education, and second- and third-order change. The second- and third-order changes proposed in the following chapters require a redistribution of the power to control educational policies and practices. The basis of these changes is that re-structuring education is necessary to make it more effective. To re-structure education, a redistribution of the power to control it is necessary. This power currently resides outside the educational system. Therefore, the changes proposed focus on elements external to the educational system as the sources of resistance to change of its structure.

Chapter 10 addresses the third-order changes that must take place at the state level. These are concerned with change of governance and coordination of public and teacher education. State legislatures are the appropriate bodies to initiate such changes. They must establish the conditions and mechanisms required for second-order changes to be developed.

Chapter's 11-15 present the second-order changes that are considered necessary for the redistribution of authority to shape and direct educational activities. Chapter 11 deals with the mission and knowledge base of education at the public school level. Chapter 12 addresses the organization, program design, and resource allocation mechanisms of public education. Chapter 13 addresses changes in teacher education programs and conditions that must be coordinated with those proposed for public schools. Chapter 14 addresses the changes in education administrator preparation that must occur. Chapter 15 addresses the changes necessary in both the practices and preparation of support service personnel. Chapter 16 focuses on the processes of educational change that must be considered if the second- and third-order changes proposed are to have a reasonable prospect of success.

10 Governance and coordination of public and teacher education: third-order changes

Chapter overview

This chapter begins the presentation of the changes deemed necessary to resolve the problems of education addressed in previous chapters. A definition and overview of third-order change are presented, followed by a discussion of the rationale for the need for third-order change. Legal and legislative considerations in implementing third-order change are presented. The chapter concludes with a presentation and discussion of four third-order changes.

The changes proposed in this and following chapters are premised on the material presented in Chapters 6-8 that dealt with systems and educational change theory. These changes address the problems of education that have been discussed. These changes are consistent with what Honig (1990) suggests, that reform strategy must be strategic, it must be comprehensive, and it must be based on an understanding of what students need to learn. Nathan (1990) suggests that how children learn must be the basis on which schools are re-structured. The changes proposed in this chapter deal with third-order changes that are focused on achieving the conditions that must exist so that schools can be re-organized on the basis of how children learn. Hess (1993), citing Chicago's reform effort, asserts that although that effort was characterized as a change in governance, it was really an effort to develop the conditions necessary for school level program changes to take place. The changes recommended here serve a similar purpose.

Third-order change involves instituting the appropriate educational governance structure and mechanisms necessary to coordinate public and teacher preparation programs and to provide the change climate prerequisite for design and maintenance of second-order change efforts. The intent of third-order change is to design and implement those changes in governance structure and mechanisms necessary to allow second-order

211

changes to be established, maintained, and modified as educational outcomes indicate. It is also the intent of third-order change to maintain those characteristics, structural components, and mechanisms of the current structure and governance controls that have proved useful, and would continue to be so under a new system of structure and governance. It is not the intent of third-order change to dismiss and discard all aspects of a previous structure and governance system.

Third-order change is a logical and necessary step in the development of an improved educational system. Just as second-order change is necessary to modify those aspects of the current educational system so that improved learning can be achieved by students, the development of third-order change is necessary to cause the changes necessary in the education structure and governance control mechanisms to ensure that learning improvements will continue. Current educational governance structures and mechanisms do not permit or encourage the design and implementation of second-order changes at the local school system or individual school levels. The need to re-distribute authority for control of education is necessary in order to provide the climate for second-order changes to develop at the local levels, and for schools to implement the principle of equifinality. Thus, changes in the governance mechanisms of education that stifle local systems and schools from implementing these changes are necessary.

Education is a developmental and adaptive process, and changes in its form and functions are a logical development if education is to appropriately adapt to a world of changing social, psychological, technological, and other environmental conditions. Just as the tremendous increase in knowledge in recent years demands changes in the means of teaching, so are changes in the structure and processes of education demanded to allow this knowledge to be more effectively learned by students. Second- and third-order changes are logical steps in the developmental progression line of improving and adapting education so that it can carry out its responsibilities more effectively and efficiently. These changes must include modification of existing structures of governance and control of education, because it is the current framework of governance and control that most impedes achieving significant improvements in students' learning.

It is possible to consider third-order changes occurring at any one of three levels, local, state, or national. The state level has been chosen as the most appropriate level for implementing third-order changes. The rationale for this decision follows.

Two primary reasons account for the decision to exclude the local level. First, third-order changes at the local level would be restricted to implementing changes only at the local level. They would not affect or be coordinated with third-order changes occurring in other communities.

212

Second, they would not effect those changes that must be instituted at the state level, and they would have no authority to effect changes necessary in teacher education preparation programs.

The federal level was not considered as an appropriate level for instituting third-order changes for two reasons also. First, the Constitution reserves to the states the right to legislate and determine educational policy. This situation presumably could be modified, but probably only after long, tedious, and unnecessary discussion and debate. It is simply not necessary to have control of education centralized at the national level. Second, transferring control of education to the federal level would mean bypassing the state level. This would call for development of a set of educational policies and the knowledge and skills necessary to govern and coordinate education at a level with which the United States has had no experience. This would not be worth the risk.

At the state level, however, those problems associated with attempting to institute third-order changes at the local or national level are avoided. The state has the authority to regulate education at both the public and higher education levels. States currently have policies and mechanisms in place that increasingly are controlling, but not coordinating, education at the local and higher education levels. Establishing control of education at the state level means that citizens would have easier access to educational leaders and decision-makers than would be possible at the national level. States have had experience in regulating the current separate components of the state educational system. Thus, it seemed warranted to choose the state level as the most appropriate for instituting third-order changes.

Rationale for third-order change

This chapter deals with two of the most significant aspects of education. They are the governance and coordination of educational policy development and practice. These two factors currently represent the core policy development obstacles to improving educational outcomes. Significant and long-term improvement of educational outcomes cannot be expected until these two aspects of educational activity are changed in such a fashion that they become strengths of educational improvement efforts. Chubb and Moe (1990) write that a system of control of education that is "almost beyond" the reach of public authority must be devised. Wise and Leibbrand (1993) suggest that teacher organizations must set the standards for the profession and reverse the current practice os allowing state legislatures to set educational standards.

The governance and coordination of educational activity must be concerned with public education and teacher education programs. Each is

213

obviously dependent on the other, and their governance, as well as other aspects of their activity, must be coordinated. It does not make educational, management, or programmatic sense to have them operating relatively independent of each other. They must coordinate their efforts to maximize the probability that appropriate learning experiences will be provided to all students by all teachers. However, such coordination will require changes in state governance mechanisms. These changes would involve legal and legislative considerations, consideration of the problems common and unique to public and teacher education, and consideration of the attitude changes necessary to allow the necessary alterations of governance that would create a sufficient degree of coordination.

Public education and teacher education each have serious, severe, and long-standing problems. These problems are not those referred to in recent national and state reform reports. The most serious and fundamental of education's problems and difficulties have not been adequately addressed in these calls and recommendations for educational reform. Five conditions of education are most in need of change: (1) the lack of a state-level structure for coordinating the purposes and activities of public education and teacher education programs, (2) the lack of a conceptual base for education, (3) the inappropriate control, structure, and administration of public education, (4) the lack of authority, resources, and rewards available to most teacher education programs, and (5) the rigid structure of most universities that strongly inhibits achieving second-order changes in educational personnel preparation programs. Each of these major areas of difficulty subsumes a number of critical problem areas.

Future chapters will describe these problem areas and suggest coordinated and internally consistent second-order changes designed to resolve and remedy these problem areas. These second-order changes are embedded in a change of the third-order. This third-order change is the primary focus of this chapter. It deals with the changing the governance of public and teacher education and proposes a state-level structure for coordinating and maintaining change and quality improvement efforts in public and teacher education.

These recommended changes will not likely be received warmly, nor will they cause policy-makers and decision-makers to rush immediately to implement them. More likely, they will be dismissed as unrealistic, naive, or idealistic; and these will be the flattering descriptors. The changes recommended in this book challenge long held assumptions and traditions of and about education. The changes would reverse positions of power, rewards, and authority. Most damaging, perhaps, they would hold to task as agents responsible for education's problems many who have considered themselves immune from, and not a factor in, the causes of education's problems.

Many who have assumed that they were reforming education are the very individuals who have perpetuated the continuing, fundamental, most serious problems of education. Although educators must hold themselves equally accountable for these problems of education, the majority of professional educators probably will not object too strenuously to most of the changes recommended in following chapters, with a few exceptions, such as doing away with tenure. It is the parents, public school administrators, school board members, arts and science faculty, college administrators, and legislators who will object most strenuously to these recommended changes. The changes recommended would require change of the legal framework concerning education, changes in the governance mechanisms and reward structure of public and higher education, and changes in attitudes, beliefs, and behaviors on the part of the groups mentioned. These are difficult changes to consider, and their achievement will be made more difficult by the number of groups involved, and the deep emotional attachment and commitment these groups have to the issues involved.

What is it that binds individuals to maintaining the status quo in controlling education? Certainly, the complex nature of the educational enterprise in America, with its decentralized structure that encourages overlapping and layered control of policy and practice, is one significant factor. The commitment to maintaining this overlapping control appears strong, even though control of education is in the process of hidden, and generally non-publicized, change.

The issues involved in ceding power from elected officials to others is a serious one. How much power, and under what conditions of accountability should be ceded? How to ensure that a new crop of elected officials will not interfere with developing improvements in education is a serious one. These issues will be resolved only with a fuller understanding of the factors involved. (See Chapter 16 for this discussion.)

The commitment to avoiding fundamental change of the control of education goes deeper than these points suggest. There is not a commitment to maintaining the status quo. There is a commitment to reform, as long as each power and special interest group does not lose the share of the educational power base it currently commands. It is a commitment to power. This power currently resides in elected state legislators, appointed or elected state school board members, higher education governing bodies, local school board members, other state and local political groups, federal agencies, professional organizations, and special interest groups at all levels. Each of these groups controls a certain portion of the overall educational enterprise. This control often overlaps but without clearly defined lines of responsibility and authority. As a result these groups are often in conflict about the means by which an educational improvement effort should be implemented and who is going to be in charge of it.

As Corwin and Edelfelt (1978) point out, it is not so much that one group of this power structure controlling education can change the entire education scene, as much as it is any one group's power to exercise a veto over the proposal of another group. Although one of these groups can, and in the past, has achieved some of its special interest goals, it must be careful to do so without diminishing the power of one of the other groups. When this is likely to happen, the fine art of negotiation and political compromise must be introduced to the process. Thus, any changes in education must give the appearance, if not the substance, that each group will retain a share of its current power base and decision-making authority. Although some may describe the proposals of this book as unrealistic and naive, it is because, if implemented, they would alter significantly the current power structure and control of education.

The changes recommended in this book offer sufficient potential and promise for significantly improving learning on the part of children. The American public should be aware and understand the real reasons these solutions are not being implemented. These reasons are the interdependent factors of the current power hierarchy that controls education, the veto power that elements of this hierarchy can and do exercise, and the uncoordinated nature of this power structure. Given these factors, and if the changes recommended would result in improved learning outcomes for children, is there a way to bring about these changes? There is. It begins with the third-order changes discussed below.

The remaining portions of this chapter deal with third-order change of the educational power hierarchy. There must be no misunderstanding of the implications of this point. The changes would cause a significant alteration of the current power hierarchy controlling education, the manner by which educational services are delivered to children, and even the social and economic spheres, with largely unforeseen and unpredictable consequences.

The third-order changes proposed (as well as the second-order changes proposed in following chapters) would require alterations of state laws and the legal framework surrounding educational policy and practice. Significant changes in the governance procedures currently in place in public and higher education, as well as other educational and social institutions, and alterations of attitudes and behavior on the part of many individuals and groups would also be required. Change of any of these factors represents a distinct challenge to the affected groups. Changing all in any type of coordinated manner has never before been tried, much less accomplished. Thus, before proceeding to a discussion of a change process for these areas, it may be useful to explore each of these areas, and the difficulties each presents in attempting to achieve change.

216

The context

In any discussion of educational change, the question of control must be considered as a major issue. There are several agencies and groups involved, including local and state boards of education, universities and the various components within each, state departments of public instruction, professional organizations and associations, parent interest groups, state legislatures, the federal government, and economic and business enterprises.

Many of these agencies and groups operate on an independent basis, each seeking to maintain and increase its power and sphere of influence in education in order to achieve its goals, which may, or may not, be beneficial to all children. Each of these groups has its set of objectives, perceives the mission of the schools from its perspective, and is primarily concerned with lobbying for its special interests. This is a consequence of the decentralized nature of the American educational system.

Control is not only vested in many groups, but these groups exist with varying amounts of power at the federal, regional, state, and local levels. No one group, except for state legislatures, has the constitutional authority to cause change in both public and higher education. It is not likely that state legislatures would act to cause the changes recommended in this book unless there was strong support from the American public, professional educators, and corporate leaders. Even if one or more of these groups acted, it is not conceivable that a majority would act in concert to cause these changes.

Thus, one of the major strengths of the American educational system, its decentralized form of control, is also its greatest weakness. This decentralization of control prohibits concerted and coordinated action from being taken to cause change, to implement reform improvements, or to discard unnecessary policies or practices. This decentralization of control is also a major reason for the uneven nature of educational achievement and attainment, evidenced in various regions of the country, within states, and even within communities. Decentralization is obviously not the sole reason for this uneven pattern, but it is a major one. It is within this context of decentralized control of educational policy and practice that a discussion of the three critical areas — the legal framework, educational and social governance mechanisms, and individual attitudes, beliefs, and behavior — must take place.

To understand educational reform, one must be aware of the role education has played in the social history of America, particularly its recent history. Altbach (1985) asserts that education has been a part of virtually every social change in recent American history and that educational policy

217

and social policy are interactive. According to Altbach, the recent crisis in education reported in the national reports was directly caused by social policy and public opinion, and that, again, educational policy-makers had to follow, because they seldom lead. Altbach believes that, if reform and improvement in American education are to be achieved, the basic fact that education is a follower to social policy and change must be understood.

Altbach supports this position by pointing to the complex process required to achieve change in American education. He attributes this complexity to the many competing constituencies and interests relating to the decentralized nature of American education. He contrasts the nature of the educational change process in France, where it is only necessary to convince the prime minister and the minister of education that a change is needed, with that involved in achieving change in the United States. He describes the checks and balances, the constitutional permissions and limits, and the wide variety of special interest groups that must be satisfied if change is to be achieved. Altbach pays tribute to the concept of "excellence" that many of the current reform reports and recommendations seek to achieve.

However, Altback does not carry his analysis far enough and examine the recommendations that are provided to achieve "excellence." It is with these recommendations, their strength, validity, and appropriateness, that the concept of "excellence" will be achieved or not. As will be discussed in later chapters, it is the contention of this author that the reform recommendations currently being promulgated in almost every state (U.S. Department of Education, 1984) will not achieve the desired results of improving all children's learning outcomes. These desired results are potentially within the grasp of education, assuming the type of changes recommended in this book are implemented. Without these changes, it is unlikely that the reform goal of excellence will be achieved. Dalin's (1978) assertion that education has not been successful when it has been used as a vehicle for achieving social change supports this contention.

However, Altbach does raise a serious concern. As indicated above, he asserts it is necessary that educational policy-makers accept the fact that they follow, not lead. This is related to the famous question of William H. Kilpatrick, "Dare the Schools Change the Social Order?" (Altbach, 1985). This question really has two parts. First, *should* the schools attempt to lead the social order, and second, *could* the schools lead the social order? According to Altbach, as well as many others, the answer to the first question is no. Therefore, the second question has never really been addressed, much less tested. Certainly, under the conditions and vested interests currently controlling and governing education, this author would agree that education should not lead social change, because under current conditions education could not lead social change. The education profession does not control its destiny, and certainly it does not possess the concepts or personnel to achieve social change leadership. Neither has it demonstrated the courage necessary for such leadership. It has been held captive so long, and by so many, that any vestige of the knowledge, skills, or risk-taking necessary to exert social leadership has long vanished. However, under different conditions, such as those recommended in this book, it is conceivable that education eventually *could* be a leader of social change and improvement. Whether it *should* include such a goal within its agenda is a much different question. We come back again to the question, "What is the mission of the schools?"

So, if the question of whether education should attempt to lead social change is addressed, the answer is no. One can justify this response on philosophical grounds alone. But, even if one's philosophical perspective allows the answer to this question to be affirmative, the answer must still be no, based purely on pragmatic considerations. Education currently does not have the where-with-all to provide such leadership. However, if the answer, based on philosophical grounds, is affirmative, then one can begin to consider means by which this objective could be included within education's agenda and begin to work toward education achieving a position of social leadership.

Such a goal would certainly run counter to the historical role of education in American society. It is not probable that this objective would be accepted by the American public, or by many of the vested interest groups currently controlling education. It also is an objective that would reverse the current prime focus of education, which is economic development. If education were to become a leader of social change and improvement, it would quickly find itself returning to the decade of the 1960's, when social reform was its prime focus, and social services in the schools rewarded more than academic attainment and responsibility. This is the cost that America must pay for having educational policy play the follower's role to social policy. Education will constantly be a political football, on the defensive, trying to maintain a homeostatic balance among changing and shifting missions, goals, and objectives as long as the current governance structures and mechanisms exist. First-order responses will continue to mar both society's and education's attempts to improve student learning outcomes.

The follower and leader roles are not, however, the only two alternatives available to American education. Therefore, it is necessary to use a new perspective to perceive other alternatives for an appropriate role for education, acceptable for achieving education's prime goal of improving students' learning and for education serving as an instrument of social

219

improvement. This new perception of realizing the school's potential, which forms an important component for introducing third-order change, will be presented following the discussion of the three areas of the legal framework, social and educational governance mechanisms, and individual attitudes, beliefs, and behaviors that must be changed in order for third-order changes to be implemented.

Legal and legislative considerations

The legal framework surrounding education has grown significantly in the last three decades. During this time, it has been particularly responsive to the previously unmet rights and needs of minority groups, the disadvantaged, the handicapped, and other groups with appropriate, but unmet, educational aspirations. Most of these gains came about as a result of the social reform and improvement efforts of the 1960s. Whether these gains will continue to be achieved under the current conditions and mood of those governing education is debatable.

Along with these gains, court decisions, primarily at the state and federal levels, have recently demonstrated an increasing inclination to intervene in local educational affairs. These have included such matters as attendance requirements, hiring policies, school district boundaries, teacher certification, teacher preparation, and academic program design at both the public school and higher education levels (Corwin and Edelfelt, 1978). On the whole, these issues have been brought to the courts by special interest groups. This does not make these concerns invalid, or inappropriate, but they have often been concerns for a relatively small group. This is consistent with the finding of Selznick (1949) who found that, in an agency of the federal government, operating in a local community, citizens would use the local programs to satisfy their own private interests that were often at variance with the larger society's interest.

Besides these court decisions serving individual or relatively small group needs at the possible expense of a larger social need or purpose, recent decisions and actions by many state legislatures have had two inhibiting effects on educational improvement. First, these decisions, for example, mandating high school competency tests, have demonstrated often that the profession of education is perceived and treated differently than other professions. It is the only profession where legal mandates, not the profession itself, determine who is considered competent to enter and practice within the profession. It is the only profession in which legal decisions tell the practitioner how many clients must be served in how many hours for how many days. It is the only profession where legal decisions tell the practitioner what tools must be used to carry out his/her responsibilities and determine the rewards for such effort without regard to the merit, task difficulty, or success of the practitioner. The list could go on, but the truth of the matter is, the legal framework and processes affecting education have inhibited and hindered education's efforts to improve and, thereby, they have lessened its achievements. Thus, education has been held hostage without regard for its capabilities or the potential it would have for achievement if it were treated as a profession, not a captive.

The second inhibiting effect the legal framework and recent court decisions have had on education relates to the restrictive and/or mandating, as opposed too permissive, nature of many legal actions and court decisions. On the whole, legislative action has prescribed not only policies, but also specific practices, that the education profession must follow. A case in point is the action taken in New Jersey in 1983, at the initiative of Governor Thomas Keene, to not only permit, but encourage, non-certified individuals to teach in the public schools (Council of New Jersey State College Locals, 1984). The problem identified was to find a means of addressing and solving short-term teacher shortages in certain areas by an "alternative certification route," which by-passed the usual teacher education preparation programs. Such a procedure by-passes the profession in an attempt to solve a very real education problem. Such a procedure demonstrates a contempt for education's ability to solve educational problems, and it demonstrates vividly the impotence of education to deal with the political aspects of such situations. Similar actions have been repeated in many states. It is highly unlikely that a similar proposal would be considered, much less proposed, by a state official for any other profession. Education, however, is fair game for intrusion and interference by almost any special interest group, agency, or individual. Such actions restrict initiative and innovation and prescribe policies and procedures that keep education captive. This, in turn, leads to psychological resentment by the captive, which, in turn, leads to, and results in, first-order responses to the proposed policies and recommendations for reform.

It must also be noted that court decisions are taken in response to actions initiated by specific groups or individuals. These actions usually affect a relatively small percentage of the population, but they may be extremely costly, in terms of funds, time, or energy, far in excess of the numbers and percentage of students affected. Legislatures, in contrast to court decisions, usually initiate actions. These actions include policy statements and/or specific procedures and practices that are usually intended to bring educational outcomes back to some previous state of equilibrium, to some remembered state of years ago. The "Back to the Basics" movement is an example of such a nostalgic effort. These actions are seldom sufficiently

221

forward-looking. They do not consider the entire state of education or the potential ripple affects of any particular piece of educational legislation.

These piecemeal efforts to improve education are a manifestation of random incrementalism at its worst. It should not be inferred from these remarks that these legislative actions are intended to restrict or downgrade education. Such actions are usually taken with the belief that they will result in an improved educational system. However, these actions and efforts are usually initiated by lay people charged with the responsibility for making decisions about education, which they really do not understand in all of its complexities. The decisions they render, and the actions they take, are often made on political grounds and to achieve a political agenda, not educational ones. Corrigan (1985) made this same point when he observed that the teaching profession has not had support to make the fundamental changes in policies necessary to improve education. He characterized the policy-makers' responses to the crisis in education as symbolic; education appeared to be more important in political campaigns than in appropriations. Corrigan's conclusion was that "education is not influenced by politics, it is politics" (p. 8).

Without a guiding conceptual framework for education, or a clear understanding of the prime mission of the schools, or an understanding of the developmental and interdependent nature of the components of education, many of these legislative actions not only inhibit, but disrupt, educational improvement efforts. If education is to thrive and deliver the quality of programs and services to students of which it is capable, the political control of education, and the use of education to serve political purposes and achieve political objectives must cease, or, at least, be brought under responsible control. State legislatures must stop meddling and interfering in education. They particularly must stop changing directions and objectives for education every time the party in control changes. Education must become a profession that is free of both partisan politics and of political interference. This does not mean that education should be free from responsible state or national level oversight. Education serves too vital a national and state interest to have unrestricted freedom, but the structure and mechanisms of this oversight must change. A recommended structure is provided at the end of this section.

Court decisions and legislative actions have increasingly played a major role in shaping and directing educational activities in recent years. The courts must continue to serve as a forum for addressing issues of concern to the American public. However, it would benefit all children if a more balanced perspective between the needs of the individual and the needs of the many were established.

Legislative action is a different story. There seems little doubt that the intent of educational legislation has been to improve education policy and practice. Yet, this intent has not been realized, and, although it would be of academic interest to discuss the reasons legislative action has not improved educational and learning outcomes to the extent desired, it is far more important to discuss the "what" of the question, which is what and how legislative action can lead to these improved outcomes. This is a question that must be considered at several levels, but primarily at the state and federal level. It is also a question that must be considered within the context of other third-order recommendations for change. These recommendations are presented following the discussions of governance mechanisms and attitudes.

Governance considerations

The central and critical problem relating to governance of public and teacher education, as it relates to improving educational and learning outcomes, is three-fold and interdependent. These three aspects of the problem are (1) the separate, but overlapping, tiers of governance control for public and teacher education, (2) the lack of coordination between and among these various tiers, and (3) the captive status of education maintained by these governance structures and mechanisms. Public and teacher education have separate but similar problems of governance. In this regard, the problems are common but separated by different lines of governance authority. In some instances the problems are unique to the specific area, i.e., public or teacher education. The common problems of governance will be discussed first.

Common problems

The first common problem of educational governance concerns the many-layered, overlapping agencies and groups that all have a voice, and, more importantly, a veto, in governance efforts to modify and improve education. In public education at the local level, these groups include the school board, parent groups, school administrators, professional organizations, teacher unions, and community business leaders. At the state level, these groups include the state school board, the state department of public education, the governor, the state legislature, special interest and lobby groups, business leaders, professional organizations, parent groups, and unions. At the federal level, the President, the Congress, any number of federal agencies, national professional organizations, teachers' unions, special interest groups and lobbies, business leaders, and parent groups can influence

223

educational policy and practice. Given this myriad of groups, agencies, and individuals all striving to advance their special cause and protect their portion of control and power over education, it is no wonder that education is in its current state. Educational policy becomes a political game using compromise as the avenue of resolution. Compromise may be the name of the game in politics, and a necessary means for achieving a portion of one's objectives in a political arena, but it does not make good educational sense or lead to those programs and activities that would most promote improved learning on the part of all students.

Fuhrman, Elmore, and Massell (1993) speak to this very point. They assert that policymakers and educational agents operate independently of each other, each with a separate agenda, and without an overall guiding agenda for reform. Further, they indicate those teacher education programs that are controlled by higher education authorities have a particularly difficult time coordinating their functions with expectations for student learning.

There are educational policies and practices that, if enacted, would lead to improved learning outcomes on the part of students. However, such policies and practices would require that these many groups and agencies give up much of their current degree of control and power over education. This would be a difficult goal to accomplish. There are simply too many vested interests involved in educational decision-making to encourage or permit rational educational policy and practices to be developed and implemented. Not only are there too many layers of decision-making, there are groups within each layer, but often these groups have parochial and competing interests that reinforce the practice of compromise. As a result, there is not one group that has responsibility and authority for overall development, implementation, and evaluation of educational policy and practice.

At the teacher education level, the situation is similar although the groups are different. At the university level, where the individual campus is analogous to the local school system, there are several groups which control and/or can veto development and implementation of educational improvement efforts. These include the various departments within a school of education, the coordinating curriculum committee of the school, the campus teacher education committee, the university curriculum committee, review committees of the graduate school, the campus administration, and, at times, the university system's administration. At the state level, there are legislatures and state program approval guidelines and reviews with which to contend. At the national level, there are the voluntary professional associations' accreditation guidelines and reviews to consider. Coordination of policy-making and decision-making is severely handicapped because of this many-layered hierarchy.

One of the differences in governance control between public and teacher education is that public education is controlled by more groups at the local and state levels. Control of teacher education historically has been exerted primarily at the local campus level, with some control being exerted by state program approval guidelines and reviews. In recent years, however, this has changed dramatically as state legislatures increasingly have moved to legislate educational policy and practices at both levels (U.S. Department of Education, 1984). For example, states have increasingly mandated entrance and exit requirements for students of teacher education preparation programs.

A second common problem of governance of both public and teacher education is that the control is exerted primarily, although not exclusively, by non-educators. This is seen most dramatically at the local school level where lay school boards operate. These lay boards control resource allocations and are responsible for personnel decisions and other decisions that are better left to professionals. Most state school boards are also composed primarily of lay people. At the teacher education level, the observation that control of teacher education is primarily by non-educators may come as a distinct surprise, particularly for those who teach in an academic discipline and consider themselves educators to some degree. These individuals, at least in the definition of this author, are not professional educators. They have not been prepared to teach, although they do. They are not well versed in understanding how learning occurs in their students, and they tend to be more concerned with pursuing research and publication in their discipline than with ensuring their students are comprehending the structure of their discipline and integrating its knowledge with that of other disciplines. It is these individuals, at campuses across the nation, that have had primary control of teacher education through their membership on university committees. Their indifference to teacher education and their lack of understanding of and respect for the needs of both public and teacher education has exerted a negative control of education that is one of the major and most difficult obstacles to appropriate reform of education.

Certainly, one of the hallmarks of American education has been its control by lay people. However, the complexity of the education enterprise in America, and its potential for the future, has far surpassed the ability of most lay people to comprehend its intricacies. They do not understand the complexities of learning and the human mind that are the real foundations and understandings necessary for successful educational programs. The governance and control of education by non-educators, at both the public and teacher education levels, are significant handicaps to the development and implementation of meaningful educational reform. Undoubtedly, many

225

people believe that it is preferable to sacrifice some improvement in learning outcomes to preserve the principle (actually a myth) of local control of education. This is a matter of debate. It is also not an either-or question. As will be discussed in the next chapter, there is a structure and mechanism that would allow both lay, and professional governance of education at the public school level. The situation at the teacher education level is different, but even at this level there is the potential for a structure that would allow for increased authority and accountability for their programs on the part of teacher educators.

An especially difficult problem of governance control of public and teacher education is the lack of coordination and cooperation between the separate tiers of authority for public and teacher education areas.

The structure of separate lines of authority for each of these areas leads to two inherent and related problems. The first of these problems deals with separate routes for authority — there is no coordination of effort, goal setting, need assessment, and outcome evaluation between these two separated components of the education system. Obviously, coordination of effort between the education system components of public and teacher education is desirable. The current structure of governance for these two system components in many states not only discourages such effort, it inhibits it. For example, a state board of education may mandate a required curriculum for all grades. However, the state board of education does not have any control over the curricula of teacher education preparation programs within the state. Thus, graduates of these programs may not be prepared to implement the requirements of the state mandated curriculum.

North Carolina is one of the few states where an effort at such coordination is under way between the NC State Board of Education (public education) and the NC University Board of Governors (teacher education). Although this effort was begun within the existing governance structure and mechanisms, and there has been insufficient time to assess the results of this effort, preliminary review is encouraging. North Carolina's plan includes a Professional Practices Commission, revised state program approval standards, partnerships between schools and preparation programs, and statewide programs of school-based research (Southern Region Educational Board, 1989). (However, the Professional Practices Commission is limited to an advisory role to the State Board of Education.) Thus, North Carolina is attempting to implement some of the activities necessary for improving educational outcomes. It is, however, attempting to do so within the framework of existing governance mechanisms.

There are inherent problems with using existing structures and mechanisms for such an effort, primarily dealing with sustaining cooperation and coordination over the long term, which subjects those individuals involved in such efforts to the same political pressures that have so long handicapped educational reform efforts. Using existing governance structures and mechanisms also prevents the emergence of other groups, such as teachers, from developing a significant voice in determining educational policy and practices.

The second problem involved with separate lines of governance for public and teacher education is that both become enmeshed with separate political pressures, situations, and turf battles. It often happens that these battles become the groups' focus of effort within each of these separate governance channels, while the needs of students and teachers and improving education become secondary, and almost incidental, activities. Observing these groups in battle brings to mind the "hyperrationalization" described by Wise, (1979). *Hyperrationalization* is said to occur when a group becomes so involved with the process of a task that the objective for the task is lost. It is not so much that these groups have to deal with the political aspects of their positions and responsibilities, but that, with so many groups involved, the potential for many unrelated political problems is increased significantly. Each of these governance groups takes on a life of its own, and coordination within each of the areas of public and teacher education, not to mention coordination between these areas, becomes almost impossible.

Another problem common to both public and teacher education arises out of these separate lines of governance. This problem is the lack of a common conceptual framework for education agreed upon by these two major education system components. This situation is exacerbated by the lack of coordination among the various governance groups. Obviously, there is no assurance that an agreed upon conceptual framework would be arrived at by these separate governance authorities if there was increased and improved coordination between them. The chances for such a framework would certainly be enhanced if there was improved coordination and cooperation. However, given the vested interests of the groups composing current governance chains at the local and state levels, it is unlikely that such coordination and cooperation will occur.

Unique problems of governance

Public Education

Among all the professions, public education stands alone in that its practitioners possess no authority for determining how their profession can and should best implement its theories and techniques. The best teacher can have his/her plans and/or efforts negated by one uninformed lay person on a local school board. This school board member may not have completed high school, or even the 8th grade, yet he or she can prevent implementation of the most desirable program for a class or group of students. This does not make good educational sense. Local involvement in educational planning and programming is desirable, particularly by parents. And, certainly, parents have the right and responsibility to stay apprised of what is being planned for their children. However, the desirability of this knowledge and involvement does not equate to control of educational plans and programs. In actuality, parents are seldom sufficiently informed or educated about learning and educational developments, theories, and techniques to warrant having sole control. These efforts at control by parents at the local and state levels probably do more to handicap educational improvement efforts than they do to assist such efforts. This does not mean that educational improvement efforts should not be held accountable to parents at the local level. Again, however, such accountability does not equate to control.

At the teacher education level, the unique feature of governance most in need of reform is the prevailing attitude that everyone in the university is an expert on teacher education (except for the faculty charged with the responsibility for these programs). This is an attitude analogous to that displayed by parents at the local school level. Many campuses take absurd pride in stating that teacher education is an all-campus responsibility and receives all-campus involvement. What does a faculty member in a school of business know, even if he or she cares, about what is needed in teacher education programs? Certainly, this faculty member may know the field of business, but how to increase high school students' learning of this field is a knowledge not likely to be found in most faculty members at a school or department of business. The only time a faculty member in a school of business is likely to become interested or involved in a teacher education matter is if a faculty member in the school of education proposes a course in management theory. For some strange reason, faculty members in a school of business believe that all knowledge of management theory and techniques should reside solely in a school of business, even though management of educational programs and personnel requires a far different knowledge base and technique than does management of a business. Faculty members of most other disciplines exhibit a similar attitude. This attitude has a serious and debilitating effect for the efforts of education faculty members to improve teacher education programs. Teacher education programs are not accorded the same rights and responsibilities to govern their programs as are accorded to faculty of other university programs, even though on the surface the structure and mechanisms for governance appear similar.

228

Education has been held captive to the dictates of a number of non-professional education groups, boards, and agencies. It has, also, been held captive to some groups within its profession as these groups sought to protect their limited spheres of influence and control. These various groups, at both the public and teacher education levels, have viewed education from their particular sphere of interest and influence. Over time, these groups have developed governance and control mechanisms, as well as understandings and accommodations with other groups that allow each to maintain its particular sphere of influence. It is through these governance and control mechanisms that these groups maintain their power and prevent the professional educators from assuming a position of influence in determining educational policy and practices. Although the governance and control mechanisms used are different in public and teacher education, the results are similar. The profession of education has not been free to develop as a profession or to use the knowledge and skills of its practitioners to maximize student learning.

Considerations of attitude

The problems outlined above result from deeply embedded attitudes and long held beliefs about public and teacher education. These attitudes and beliefs are the products of the history of American education, reinforced by continued expressions of the conviction and need to maintain local control over education to have quality schools. Although the governance and control of education, primarily at the public school level, but also at the teacher education level, are increasingly being assumed by state legislatures and other state-level agencies, there is the continued myth that education is and should be controlled at the local level. This is partially good; some minor aspects of education should remain under local control. However, the most critical aspects for determining the quality of an educational program (personnel, curriculum, and resources) are increasingly under the control of state-level agencies. Certainly, since the quality of education is perceived as the key to improved economic development and conditions, it is highly improbable that control of these important determinants of educational quality will be left to the whims, fads, and beliefs of each local school district.

Centralization of control of education at the state level, if not at the national level, is occurring as business leaders seek to install the same centralized style of management in education that they have used (with not such very successful results) in business. Most business leaders seem to believe that centralized management allows profit-making decisions to be made most effectively. This prevailing attitude has not worked too well in business, and it would be disastrous if implemented in education. The American public does not seem to be aware that centralization of control of education is occurring to the extent it is. It would be interesting to see their reaction when they discover that local control of education is restricted to only minor aspects of educational activity.

The belief in local control of education by parents and lay people has hampered the development of education as a profession. Although there is no evidence to support this claim, this author is convinced that corporate America believes that educational quality cannot be left to local decisions, and that, to improve the quality of American education, centralization of control must be instituted, using corporate decision-making and management styles. If these two scenarios are a valid observation of attitudes and beliefs about control of American education, then there exists significant potential for a clash of fundamental values about education.

Neither of these two movements (local control and centralization of control) is likely to produce the standards of excellence in education each would like. Proponents of local control overlook that education is too complex to be managed successfully by local dictate. Such a view also overlooks that it is in the state's best interest to have coordinated education improvement efforts, a situation that can best be accomplished at the state level. Otherwise, a profile of uneven academic attainment will surely emerge. Proponents of centralized control overlook the fact that education is a developmental process that cannot be successfully managed by current corporate management styles.

Some aspects of both the local control and centralization of control movements are necessary conditions for achieving increased and improved learning on the part of children. It is imperative to have the positive interest and involvement of parents in their children's education if the chances for a successful educational experience are to be maximized. Centralization of control of education at the state level offers some advantages for coordination and development of curriculum at the public school and teacher education levels, meeting the continuing professional development needs of teachers and ensuring that prospective educators have met appropriate standards. Thus, proponents of both scenarios are partially correct in their attitudes and beliefs.

However, proponents of both movements are also partially incorrect about what they believe is necessary to achieve excellence in education. Both movements ignore the input of the very group needed to achieve the level of excellence they desire — the teachers. Essentially, it is the teachers who will determine the excellence of any education program. To ignore these personnel, and to exclude them from having a significant, if not major, voice for determining how educational excellence should be achieved is the height of folly. Without a change in attitude towards the role teachers should play in determining educational goals and how they should be achieved, education is doomed to a continuous Game-Without-End, one that will continue a series of first-order responses to second-order problems, never achieving the standards of excellence desired.

The American public appears largely unaware of who governs higher education and how. However, the popularity of such works as Bloom's *The Closing of the American Mind* (1987) may well direct the public's attention to one of the major criticisms this book will make: The manner in which liberal education in this country's colleges and universities has failed generations of students (discussed in Chapter 10). A large percentage of college and university graduates lack critical thinking skills. The individuals responsible are the university faculty, mostly arts and science faculty, and university administrators who allowed this situation to develop. Both the current governance mechanisms and attitudes of university administrators suggest that it will be a very difficult problem to resolve. The problem may reinforce the common belief that professional educators, as well as university faculty in general, cannot responsibly govern themselves. The spread of this idea could lead to increased control of university practices by legislators or others outside the profession. Such increased control would almost certainly result in decreased learning, rather than leading to the improved learning desired.

Unfortunately, the attitude that university faculty are unable to govern themselves is not totally invalid. Since second-order change cannot be generated from within a group, university faculty can not be expected to seek new methods of providing education to their students without external impetus, particularly when the reward structure of most universities does not encourage or promote such activity. Starr (1987) reported that a study by Bowen and Schuster (1986) indicated that an increasing conflict between research and teaching reflected a trend of junior faculty to view publication as the only means of professional survival. This conflict could not have developed unless the reward structure supported by university administrators approved of the publication side of the conflict. Too many university administrators are unwilling to support a balanced reward system among teaching, service, and research, to force innovation among reluctant faculty; or to encourage, promote, and reward a flexible mission for the university. This situation may explain why higher education is the stilted and rigid intellectual activity it is today. Too many university administrators have hidden behind the facade of faculty governance in an attempt to maintain a myth that is not realistic. University faculty do maintain some control over curriculum, but even this is evaporating. They

231

certainly do not control resource allocations, and they are increasingly losing control over criteria for selecting faculty and students. Governance and control of university functions by faculty has largely been lost, and such works as Bloom's will only speed the process, unless university faculty themselves act to change current conditions. Control of higher education is increasingly being centralized and taken out of the hands of university faculty and is increasingly being assumed by university administrators, boards of trustees, university system administrators and their governing boards, governors and state legislatures, and specialized accreditation agencies. These various groups will likely fight for control soon.

The root of the problem is that education is held captive at all levels. Teacher education programs are also held captive to some of these boards and agencies, but even more alarming, on most university campuses, faculty members are in danger of losing what little authority they currently possess to govern themselves.

To free education from this captive status and allow it to achieve educational excellence, a series of coordinated changes isnecessary. The ingredients of these changes are a structure and mechanism of governance and control that will liberate teachers and allow them to exert their expertise for increasing students' learning, provide for appropriate local involvement, and centralize control appropriately and to an appropriate degree. The framework and structure of education currently existing in most states do not lend themselves to easily accomplishing this goal. These changes are necessary to permit the second-order changes proposed in this book to be achieved. These second-order changes would lead to improved learning on the part of students. However, in order to assure that long-term improvement of education continues to occur, with attention paid to teacher control, local involvement, and centralization for coordination of appropriate educational activities, third-order changes would have to be implemented.

Third-order changes

The following third-order changes are those considered necessary to provide the governance and coordination structure and mechanisms for implementing and maintaining second-order changes. Each third-order change is followed by a discussion of its rationale and implications.

Third-Order Change #1. Each state should, by action of the state legislature, establish a state-level Educational Policy and Coordination Committee (EPCC). The responsibilities and authority of this Committee are described below.

232

This Committee would have jurisdiction over public and teacher education policies and practices, with the authority and responsibility to coordinate all educational activities of these two components of the educational system. This means that several current governance bodies would have to give up some of their powers, or, in some instances, be disbanded altogether. For example, many states have state-level boards to oversee higher education within the state. Under Third-order Change #1, the responsibilities of these boards would not include teacher education programs for curriculum development. Coordination of teacher education curriculum would be a responsibility of the EPCC so that a concordance of teacher preparation curriculum and that of the public schools could be developed and maintained.

A second state-level board that would be severely affected by Third-Order Change #1 would be the State Board of Education. In fact, there would be no need to have a State Board of Rducation as all of their responsibilities and authority would be assumed by the EPCC. The State Department of Public Education would become the administrative arm of the EPCC, with its duties and personnel determined by the EPCC.

Summary

Third-Order Change #1 would establish one group with responsibility for controlling and coordinating educational policy and improvement efforts. The EPCC would have the responsibility, authority, and accountability for coordinating the curriculum of both public and teacher education programs. It would establish and evaluate standards for certification of professional educators and conduct assessments of continuing professional improvement needs at both the public and teacher education levels. It would have responsibility to develop programs to meet these needs and to mandate national accreditation for teacher education programs and local school systems.

Third-Order Change #2. The composition of the EPCC should be as follows: One-third of the membership (total membership no more than 15) should be elected by local boards of teachers; one-third should be elected by full-time tenured education faculty from public and private institutions of higher education; and one-third of the membership should consist of two legislators appointed by the legislature or governor, and three should be parents appointed by the state parents' association.

The rationale for this EPCC composition is that the decision-making authority for development of educational policy should be a shared responsibility by those most concerned with its effect on children's

233

learning. These are the teachers, the teachers of teachers, parents, and the state legislature, which also has the responsibility to protect the state's interest in education. The major implications of this composition follows: (1) It places the decision-making authority for development of educational policy, and coordination of public and teacher education improvement efforts, into the hands of professional educators, with sufficient input and control from parents and the legislature to assure that all concerned bodies are represented. (2) It re-distributes the power and control for development of educational policy among those who are most vitally interested in improving the quality of education.

Third-Order Change #3. Educational units on each college and university campus should be re-configured as free-standing professional schools, responsible for the preparation of all personnel who seek professional employment in the public schools. These units should be headed by a Vice-President for Educational Affairs who reports directly to the president or chancellor of the campus, with authority equivalent to a Vice-President for Academic or Health Affairs.

The rationale for this Change Order is to provide a climate and the on-campus conditions which would allow all education programs the opportunity to develop unfettered by the current unnecessary restrictions prevalent on most campuses. This is not likely to occur under current conditions. Providing for the coordination of curriculum, faculty and student selection, rewards for teaching, service, and research, and other matters critical for developing an excellent teacher education program under a vice-president will help to ensure that the necessary changes and improvements in teacher education can be made.

The implications of Third-Order Change #3 are these university education units and their programs would have a level of authority, responsibility, and right to determine curriculum and standards comparable to those in the health affairs professions and academic disciplines in the arts and sciences. This change should enhance the potential for education units to obtain and attract the level of resources necessary to mount effective professional education programs. It would also allow these units to develop their programs free from intrusions by non-professional educators. Under this change, teacher educators would assume the responsibility and have sole accountability for the adequacy of their programs. Programs that do not achieve a professionally determined level of excellence should not be permitted to continue operation.

These three third-order changes would do more to allow educational improvement efforts to develop than any other series of changes proposed by either the current reform movement or the second-order changes proposed in this book. They go to the heart of the obstacles that are impeding the development of improved means of student learning in both public schools and teacher education programs. They remove the separate and convoluted lines of governance authority currently impeding educational improvement efforts in public schools and teacher education, and they place the majority of responsibility, authority, and accountability for improving the education system and children's learning where it belongs, in the hands of professional educators. These changes also provide for adequate input and oversight from the two groups with primary interest in how effective schools are in producing the quality of outcomes desired — parents and members of the state legislature.

Besides placing the major responsibility for educational improvement in the hands of professional educators, these changes also recognize the need for centralization of educational control at the state level. Significant educational improvement efforts cannot be accomplished at the local level. There are too many local school systems to allow a coordinated improvement effort to occur, and the interest of the state in improving education demands coordinated efforts. Otherwise, the unevenness of educational attainment would severely handicap the academic attainment of many students. The implementation of improved methods of education, the basic value structure of the schools, and the economic needs of the state would vary tremendously. Increasingly, state control of education is occurring, but in an uncoordinated fashion. Such current efforts are also being directed largely by economic needs and managed by political and educational bureaucrats. The third-order changes proposed would erase such control and management by non-professional educators.

These third-order changes also call for the coordination of the improvement efforts of public and higher education under one authority. Such coordination does not currently exist in most states, and, in those states where such efforts are being made, it is not so much the result of coordination among education professionals as it is an effort of a few people in decision-making positions. Current results are not encouraging.

There are four groups that could provide such impetus. Working in concert, parents, teachers, business leaders and state legislators would be an extremely powerful coalition. Parents would be an extremely powerful group in causing the changes recommended. If parents are convinced that such changes would result in a better education for their children, they are more likely to demand the type of change suggested. Teachers are obviously concerned about the quality of education provided students and about the development of conditions that would allow them to improve the quality of instruction. Business leaders are obviously concerned about the quality and level of educational attainment of prospective employees, and it is probable that they would support changes that would improve the quality

235

of their workers. State legislators have the responsibility for ensuring that the state's interests in education are protected. Each group has a self-interest in developing an educational change that would lead to improved learning outcomes.

The rationale for this Change Order is that, because the appropriate education of teachers and teacher educators is so important to the welfare of the state and society and to the host of vested interest groups, it is unlikely that they would initiate such action for fear of losing their political life. It is not likely that the second-order changes proposed in this book will be considered on the basis of their educational merit, and/or the potential they have for improving education and the academic and intellectual attainment of students. It is far more likely that these proposals will be considered on the basis of their political and power implications for the incumbents in educational decision-making positions. This is unfortunate, as it leads then to denial or to imposed mandates from the existing power hierarchy to maintain their positions.

The reality is, of course, it is within the authority of current political leaders to cause the changes proposed. They have much to gain from such changes. The educational system, its structure, processes, and outcomes would be improved substantially. Students' knowledge, thinking skills and citizenship abilities would be increased substantially. These leaders are unlikely to propose the legislation necessary to cause the changes proposed without considerable support from teachers and parents. The responses and importance of business leaders to these changes are indeterminate. However, the support of teachers and parents, as members of a coalition effort, would be indispensable. It is not probable that the changes recommended could be implemented without the support of teachers. Their professional stature and opportunity to practice their profession as their expertise indicates would be well served by the changes suggested. Except for Second-order Change #9 (doing away with tenure), the second-order changes would provide them the opportunities to exercise their professional knowledge and skills in ways that are not possible under current conditions. Of the four groups, the teachers, as a single group, are the most impotent to initiate and cause the changes recommended. By themselves, they just do not have sufficient clout to force the level of changes needed. However, their interests in improving children's education, and their own professional pride in improving children's learning, combined with parents' concern for their children achieving a better life and future, could exert a significant pressure that state legislatures could hardly ignore.

If teachers were given the power to affect change, their student's learning and ability to learn would be improved significantly. Most importantly, a structure for continuous educational improvement would be

236

established, hopefully eliminating the many vacillations in educational objectives and effectiveness that have characterized education in recent decades.

The fourth group, state legislatures, are the key element to implementing the third- and second-order changes proposed. They could enact legislation that would mandate both levels of change. They could enact legislation that would put in place only the third-order changes recommended and leave to the EPCC the determination of which second-order changes need to be implemented. Legislators could enact either of these types of legislation, with or without the support of parents, teachers, business leaders and/or any other groups. Legislatures would probably not take such action, however, without the active support of at least the three groups mentioned above. Nor should they. Legislatures generally turn to the established educational governance structure for study and advice when they are considering educational legislation. Such a process has considerable merit, but in a situation where changes of the type recommended here are being considered, such a process is ill-advised, as it is not likely that the established structure would recommend or support legislation which would result in either loss of power, or being put out of business. Therefore, Third-Order Change #4 is proposed.

Third-Order Change #4. State legislatures that are interested in reforming the structure of education should establish a Study Commission, chaired by a state legislator knowledgeable about education, and composed of members representing parents, teachers, and business leaders. No member of this Commission should be a member of a group, board, or association that represents a vested interest in the current decision-making chain of education. Representatives of current education boards and associations should be invited to attend Commission meetings as observers only.

This type of approach would allow a state legislature to establish control of educational change, and it would enable such changes to take place outside the power structure currently controlling education. The suggested membership for the Commission is representative of the groups most concerned with the improvement of education, and without the vested interests' characteristic of current decision-makers of educational policy and practice.

The third-order changes proposed have as their core the establishment of a structure and mechanism for redistributing the authority for control of educational. This redistribution will not occur easily, but the changes proposed are those necessary if education is to be re-structured and achieve lasting improvement of students' learning. The political considerations of such changes cannot be dismissed. They are considerable and the lead must be taken by state legislatures.

237

Conclusions

Educational reform efforts currently under way in the United States are concerned with improving learning outcomes in children. The recommendations made for reform, and the reform efforts currently under way, are not dissimilar to those that have been made in previous times of perceived crisis in education. These efforts will surely not achieve the levels of reform or standards of excellence desired because they fail to alter those areas of education most in need of change to significantly improve the learning of America's students.

The recommendations for second- and third-order change proposed in this book address the necessary issues of the conceptual base of education, the problems of public and teacher education, and the need for coordination among these three areas. The changes proposed in this chapter address the structural, governance, and control issues of education that have proven to be the primary obstacles to achieving appropriate fundamental reform and change in education.

It is these latter issues that have proved to be the most resistant to change in the past. They are likely to remain so in the future because they deal with the psychological and social variables of pride, power, control, prestige, and public image, most of which would be lost by incumbents if the changes recommended in this book were implemented. The second- and third-order changes proposed in this book provide radical and drastic suggestions for change. Ultimately, only the American public can determine if the improvements desired in education and student learning are worth the changes recommended. If they decide negatively, then our education system will continue to fail as new objectives, fads, and quick-answer solutions are constantly proposed for problems that are only symptoms of greater problems of education.

11 A conceptual framework for second-order change of education, part one: mission and knowledge base

Previous chapters discussed the systemic problems of education and educational reform's failure to deal satisfactorily with the problems. These chapters presented the ideas of systems theory and educational change processes as a conceptual base for understanding the types of alterations that should be made if sustained improvement of education is to occur. A framework for a continuing educational development process was introduced. The preceding chapter presented a series of proposals for third-order changes that are necessary for coordinating and governing changes in both public and teacher education. The initial focus of such coordination in the public schools should begin with the mission and core knowledge base necessary for accomplishing the mission. The organization of schools at the system and individual school level, the program design for elementary and secondary schools and the resource allocation rationale must all be logically related to the educational mission and knowledge base. Teacher education and educational administrator preparation programs must also be modified to coordinate and integrate their activities with the mission and knowledge base of the public schools.

The remaining chapters of this book present an integrated series of second-order changes designed to address these issues. This chapter addresses the issues of educational mission and a core knowledge base for educators. The following chapter addresses organization of public education, program design at the elementary and secondary levels, and a rationale for resource allocation.

The conceptual framework

At present, no agreed-upon mission priority exists around which a knowledge base can be developed. Bruner (1966) made this same

239

observation when he referred to the lack of an integrating theory in pedagogy and a body of maxims. Without such a unifying structure, it will not be possible to develop a coherent and comprehensive conceptual framework for educational improvement. Such an infrastructure must include a knowledge base that forms a foundation for the formation and implementation of an organizational and programmatic design which maximizes student learning outcomes. To address these issues, a conceptual framework must be developed in which the interdependent elements of a knowledge base for education, system and school organization, and program design are coordinated to achieve the schools' mission.

The purpose of a mission priority is to provide a comprehensive, unifying, and integrating base on which to build the various components of education and to which they can contribute. This integration must occur on at least two major levels. The first, or the "mega" level, is concerned with three major categories — a conceptual framework, changes that allow the elements of the conceptual framework to be implemented, and the preparation of educational personnel. Each of these mega level components must be integrated and logically related with the other two and perceived as part of a mutually causal and interdependent system.

The second major level is within each of these categories and must incorporate the same integration. Each category sub-component must be integrated and logically related to all other sub-components and perceived as part of an interdependent system. This and the next chapter are concerned with the first two of these at the second level of integration.

Five major interactive and interdependent elements compose the proposed conceptual framework and content base for education. (1) The first element of the framework is *defining the primary mission* of the schools. (2) The second element is *establishing the most appropriate knowledge base* that will allow the schools' mission to be realized. This means that the learning processes of children at different developmental levels and those factors that affect such learning must be well understood, for it matters not what "content" is taught if *how* a child learns is neglected. Learning cannot be as optimized in such a situation, particularly if we wish all children to achieve new and higher levels of educational performance. (3) The third element is the formation of an *organizational structure* that best permits the achievement of the mission. (4) The fourth element is the implementation of a *program design* that will enhance the accomplishment of the mission. (5) The fifth element is provision for a *resource allocation rationale* which can fund the programs necessary to achieve the school's missions.

At present, no such integrating conceptual framework currently exists in education. Although Bruner (1966) described a theory of instruction as allowing for evaluation of teaching or learning, he did not extend his theory to include the purposes, organization, or administration of education. To find the conceptual support for such an endeavor, it is necessary to go outside the profession of education. Ludwig von Bertalanffy, the father of systems theory, speaks to this very issue in his authoritative work on systems theory (1968). Bertalanffy describes how, in the past, science tried to reduce observable phenomena to a level of the most elementary units. Although this process still exists, a more contemporary theory concerns problems of organization that are not understandable by investigation of the parts in isolation. Bertalanffy concludes that interest in problems of this nature signal a general change in conceptualizing problems, whether they are of inanimate things, living organisms, or social phenomena.

Education reform has typically followed the earlier method, by attacking single elements rather than the whole. Certain entities do not lend themselves to such dissection because the parts are totally dependent upon each other. Education is such an entity.

Bertalanffy suggests that there are general "system" laws that apply to any system of a certain type and asserts that general systems theory is a general science of "wholeness," a logico-mathematical discipline applicable to various empirical sciences. Bertalanffy perceived of systems theory as providing an integrative function for knowledge within a discipline as well as between and among disciplines. From Bertalanffy's perception, such integration provides a more realistic and valid conception of the world. He spoke directly of systems theory's contributions to integrative education.

Bertalanffy quotes from a number of distinguished scientists from the fields of engineering, sociology, mathematics, and biology, each of whom has spoken to the need for scientific generalists. A *scientist generalist* is one who practices science, not a particular science. It is the scientific generalist who is concerned with system problems so the parts are made into a unified whole. Bertalanffy discussed the 1951 paper given by Mather at a Symposium for Integrated Education, titled "Integrative Studies for General Education." Mather observed that, while senior college students may have a head full of facts, often the meaning of such facts had not been taught by their professors. Mather concluded that the search for basic concepts and principles was a more important effort of education and an essential element for understanding reality.

Travers (1967) made a similar observation, that knowledgeable teachers have long argued that it is far better to teach principles than facts. Understanding principles allows students to apply such understandings to a wider range of problems than knowledge of the facts themselves would allow. Bertalanffy concluded that conventional education treated each discipline as a separate domain with the general trend toward increasingly

241

smaller sub-domains unconnected with each other. Bertalanffy offered general systems theory as a means of providing interdisciplinary synthesis and integrated education.

Bertalanffy was concerned with integration of knowledge of scientific disciplines. It is with the same order of purpose and thinking that we seek educational integration so that a conceptual framework and knowledge base of education can be developed. Without a unifying conceptual framework, it will not be possible to develop a knowledge base, and, without integration of such with the purposes and structure of education and the preparation programs of professional educators, educational reform efforts will continue as a series of never-ending failures. Unless these three elements are considered within an interactive system mode, critical aspects for understanding and improving the educational enterprise will be lacking. Such a lack will lead to an imperfect understanding of the educational effort and doom subsequent reform efforts to failure.

Additional support for this approach in education also comes from the field of cognitive-developmental theory, contributors to which have included Piaget, Bruner, and Gagne. According to Hunt and Sullivan (1974), classification as a cognitive-developmental theorist involves meeting four assumptions. It is the first of these four assumptions that is most relevant to the current discussion. This assumption asserts that development involves basic transformations of cognitive structure that cannot be understood in terms of associative bonds but must be explained in terms of organizational wholes or systems of internal relations. Education's emphasis on associative bonds has been the fundamental weakness of behavioral psychology's efforts to assist learning. This emphasis on developing associative bonds has dominated education's classroom operations in recent decades. Miller (1977) speaks to the developmental nature of system development from the cell level through the complex social organizations of international relations. Bereiter (1985) also speaks to this issue, but from the perspective of the learner. He discusses the educational implications of the idea of mentally constructed settings. He cautions that all current approaches to human learning may be taking too narrow a view of what learning should be like to the learner. Regardless of how school learning may be compartmentalized into subjects, units, and the like, it seems clear that from the standpoint of the learner, all or most knowledge construction ought to be taking place within a single mental setting dedicated to producing a coherent body of world knowledge. The fragmentation of current approaches to learning and most curriculum development has been frequently criticized, but remedies such as cross-disciplinary or integrated studies miss the point. Integration must take place in the mind of the learner, with effort on the part of the learner. Bereiter

242

concludes that ways to support such an all-embracing integrative effort on the part of the learner have scarcely been touched by cognitive or instructional theory. Bereiter is probably correct in his conclusion. Nevertheless, seeking integrating and unifying theories for examining public education, and developing a conceptual framework that would encompass education's organization and purposes as they interact with children's learning processes, would be a valid and fruitful approach.

The educational mission

The mission of education has changed over the years. From the earliest days of American education, each cycle of reform has added new emphases, new objectives, and new responsibilities to the role of the schools. These increasing responsibilities and roles have been the result of social, political, and economic forces and changes in the cultural environment of schools (Dalin, 1978). This cycle of change is characterized by early enthusiasm on the part of educators for the new emphases, widespread dissemination, subsequent disappointment, and eventual decline (Slavin, 1989). What is the effect of this cyclic flurry of change and disappointment? Chaos. The schools are in a constant state of chaos as they continually and repeatedly attempt to develop and implement programs that address the fad of the year. What can be done to change this process? The first step is to identify and prioritize what the schools should be accomplishing. Because, clearly the schools can not be all things to all people, the schools should concentrate on achieving well those few goals which are derived from the reasons for why schools exist and are maintained.

What are the reasons' schools exist? There are numerous roles that have been advanced for the schools to play. These include improvement of economic productivity, social reform and development, providing equal opportunity for all, improving citizenship, and others (Elmore and McLaughlin, 1988). Arthur Bestor, author of *Educational Wastelands: The Retreat from Learning in Our Public Schools* (1953), is quoted by Boyer (1983) in *High School: A Report on Secondary Education in America*. Bestor's words are as true today as they were in 1953. He said, "The idea that the school must undertake to meet every need that some other agency is failing to meet, regardless of the suitability of the schoolroom to the task, is a preposterous delusion that in the end can wreck the educational system" (p. 56). However, defining the roles that the schools are expected and/or required to play is not the same as answering the question of why schools exist.

243

Traditionally, "Education is a systematic effort to transmit, evoke or acquire knowledge, skills, attitudes or values to achieve the aims of individuals and/or groups" (Cremin, 1978). Historically, education has possessed the quality to transmit the cultural heritage of groups to each oncoming generation. Because the aim of education in traditional societies was to transmit the cultural heritage, it was in general in harmony with the values, practices, human groupings and other parts of the society (Kimble, 1974). Educational aims have expanded in modern technological societies. Lewis and Meil (1972) have described the aims of education assigned to the common school in America as serving five functions: cohesive, civic, ethic-moral, economic, and personal development.

Sarason (1982) suggests that the schools have two major purposes. The first purpose of the schools is to develop the cognitive-academic capabilities of students. The second is to prepare them to live in a democratic society. These purposes are supposed to spring from equal values and be accorded equal status in schools. In practice, however, it is obvious that the cognitive-academic purpose is of primary concern. The development of skills for living in a democratic society are barely touched in most classrooms. As Sarason has noted, no criticism of the schools is as near as frequent as that of its failures to educate students in academic areas. Further, as Sarason has also noted, any proposal for school functions has to be justified by its contributions to the academic development of students. It is quite clear, that from society's viewpoint, schools are expected and will probably be required, to give top priority to the academic-cognitive development of students. The priority value in the culture of the schools has been on intellectual and academic achievement. It is hard to underestimate the extent of this value. The school culture rests on production-achievement as the major criterion for judging people. This is in order for them to be able to compete successfully in our society, with its stress on material accomplishments. What is missing from this equation is that the quality of a person's life is determined more by his/her personal-social competence, and being able to live effectively within a democratic society, including contributing to the society positively than by the accumulation of academic credits and IQ points.

Sarason indicates that the answer to these issues is generally answered by how schools are, not how they might be. Sarason states that people tend to be locked into *A* way of doing things; they do not to consider the range of alternatives available for doing things differently.

He puts the question in terms of the composition of the classroom. Homogeneous classrooms versus heterogeneous introduces the question of values we place on achievement versus more socially oriented goals for education. Yet, even within a homogenous classroom, there is a vast range of differences of motivation, interests, abilities, etc. Sarason concludes the very concept of the homogeneous classroom is at variance with reality.

Sarason concludes these arguments by suggesting that the "factory" model of education should be abandoned. Sarason indicates that his and his colleagues' research suggest that the character of a school's output depends largely on a single input factor, the characteristics of the entering children. Everything else — the school budget, its policies, the characteristics of its teachers — is either secondary or completely irrelevant.

Fullan (1982) supports Sarason's position. Fullan asserts that there are cognitive/academic goals and personal/social-development goals of education. The cognitive/academic goals concern the acquisition of knowledge and development of intellectual skills to obtain and understand information. The goals of personal and social development include the values and abilities that permit people to live and work independently, creatively, and with empathy and interpersonal skill. According to Fullan, not only do schools overtly neglect the development of personal-social goals, it covertly shapes development in certain directions. Fullan cites the work of Bowles and Gintis (1976) in support of this contention. These authors suggested that schools reward conformity, subordination to authority, discipline, intellectually oriented behavior (as opposed to socially and emotionally oriented behavior), and hard work independent of intrinsic task motivation. The authoritarian, undemocratic structure of the school replicates the hierarchical order of the work place.

The emphasis in schools is obviously on the development of academic and cognitive capacities of students. An equal emphasis on the development of personal-social capacities is absent. The neglect of these latter attributes probably has more to do with the behavior and management problems that schools and society experience from students than any other single cause. It is interesting to note that in some countries, for example, The Republic of Cyprus, where the mission statement of the schools speaks only to the development of personal-social responsibilities and appropriate citizenship and parental behaviors, but does not speak to the role of schools in fostering the development of academic skills, both the academic and behavior of students are at a high level.

The assumption of this book is that the primary reason schools exist is (1) to teach students how to learn and (2) to develop the personal-social skills necessary for living cooperatively within a democratic society. Second, schools exist to act as a transmitter of the cultural heritage and to provide students a forum for examining and discussing the social, political and other environmental forces and changes surrounding them. Any other role the schools may be asked to play, e.g., economic production, must be measured against the effect it will have on the schools' capacity to deliver

245

quality programs affiliated with achieving the prime mission. All educators, parents, or others may not agree either with these reasons or this priority order. However, until there is a priority of mission roles for schools, there can be little realistic expectation that educators will be able to focus their energies and talents on achieving the one mission judged to be the most relevant for education. Also, there can be little real debate that the primary mission of the schools is to teach students to learn. Other roles that the schools are asked, expected, or required to fulfill (questions of social value emphasis and/or political economic need) must be relegated to a position of secondary importance to be implemented only as additional resources and educator competence permit.

Without doubt, the primary priority of the schools should be to concentrate on the academic/intellectual and personal/social life and development of students. No other formal agency in our society has this responsibility. To do this appropriately takes a significant portion of the gross national product. Other agencies have responsibility for delivering social and mental health services, again at a significant cost. It does not make good sense for the schools to take on these additional responsibilities with significant costs attached to doing so when other community agencies were developed and are funded to deliver these programs. There is, to be sure, a great need for better coordination among the agencies involved to assure that needed services are being provided to those who need them, but the schools should not be asked to assume the responsibilities of these other agencies simply because they are the most convenient agency for doing so. These considerations lead us to the first second-order change for education.

Second-Order Change #1. The prime mission for education includes the following three elements: (1) to teach students how to learn most effectively and to generalize the process of effective learning, and (2) to develop each student's personal-social competence. (3) The outcome of education should be measured as a process of effective thinking and behaving, not as the product of a standardized test.

Four important consequences result from such a priority of the educational mission. (1) The first order of the schools is process-oriented, not product- or outcome-oriented. This means that students must be seen as the prime actors in the teaching-learning process, not the mere receptors of information. This will require a significant paradigm shift for most teachers, who tend to view students as recipients, not active participants, in the learning process. Learning to learn is a complex developmental process that requires a knowledge base of learning as it relates to different developmental stages of students as well as subject area content. (2) There are important organizational derivatives from a singular primary educational mission that are process-oriented. (3) There are significant

246

implications for the types of educational programs the schools must implement to achieve the mission and the allocation of resources necessary to provide such programs. (4) The identification of priority mission elements provides a foundation, rationale and criteria for measuring school effectiveness. As Madaus and his colleagues (1980) have noted, criteria for measuring school effectiveness should be based on goals and objectives of schooling. As he also notes, since there has not been any consensus on what these goals should be in our society, there is no basis for determining whether a school is effective or not.

The knowledge base for cognitive development

The search for an acknowledged and validated knowledge base for education has been a persistent goal of educators for several decades. The American Association of Colleges for Teacher Education (AACTE) has been paying attention to this issue in recent years. In 1983 the annual convention of this Association was devoted to the theme of "Essential Knowledge for Beginning Educators." The AACTE President of that year, Dr. Jack Gant, stated in the introduction to that convention's program, "Ideas on improving teacher education are varied and the approaches complex, but one point seems clear: That if teaching is ever to reach recognized professional status, it must be founded on a valid base of professional knowledge" (p. 1). Educators such as Schulman (1987), Valli and Tom (1988), and Henderson (1988) have made such a search a consuming goal of their professional lives. Still no agreed-upon consensus of the primary focus for such a knowledge base exists. The research attempting to develop such a knowledge base has been largely restricted to specific aspects of teacher behavior, student behavior, and classroom organization as these variables affect the teaching of specific subject areas. Despite the current zeal, however, educators have yet to accept a knowledge base that serves as the heart of the educational enterprise. The reason for this is that, until there is an acknowledged and accepted primary mission for the schools, a core knowledge base cannot be developed. If the prime mission of the schools is considered to be teaching students to learn, then the search for a core knowledge base is narrowed considerably. Although there are different ways that students learn (e.g., emotional, connotative), the common denominator to all learning is the cognitive component (Reilly, 1989).

There can only be one focus for such a knowledge base — understanding how children learn and how this learning can be enhanced. Claire Weinstein (1985) of the University of Texas at Austin, writing with more than tongue-in-cheek, reports that educational psychologists have once again found students. Weinstein asserts that for years the focus of research by these psychologists has been almost entirely on the teacher, teaching processes, teaching materials, and teaching outcomes. According to Weinstein student variables were the dependent measures in these studies. Currently, Weinstein perceives a shift in the research focus to understanding how incoming information is selected, processed, structured in memory, and recalled for later use. She attributes this shift to the cognitive revolution in psychology. Research efforts in the 1950's and 60's focused around the structure of knowledge and resulted in the re-structuring of some academic programs, notably math, science, and later language studies (Barnes, 1986). One of the most important results of this more recent revolution, according to Weinstein, has been a shift in how learners are viewed. Instead of viewing learners as passively receiving information presented by the teacher, learning is viewed as an active process that occurs within the learner and which can be influenced by the learner.

This "field" of cognitive science does not yet exist as a coherent, fully developed, and integrated body of knowledge, although it moves towards this goal daily. According to Gardner (1985), cognitive science was officially recognized around 1956. According to Gardner, George Miller, an American psychologist, has even fixed the date, September 11, 1956, the date of the Symposium on Information Theory held at the Massachusetts Institute of Technology.

Clearly, the combined fields of neurological research and cognitive psychology are developing significant new findings about brain function and learning that are of great significance to educators efforts to assist children to learn more effectively. For example, Roger Sperry (1985), in an article presented at the 26th UCLA Forum in Medical Sciences and published in *The Dual Brain*, said, "One important outcome is the increased insight and appreciation, in education and elsewhere, for the importance of nonverbal forms and components of learning, intellect, and communication" (p. 18). Sperry also makes the observation that public schools in America, from the standpoint of brain research, discriminate against the non-verbal half of the brain and that the amount of formal training given to right-hemisphere functions in American schools has been almost non-existent. Sperry also states in the same article, "The need for educational tests and policy measures to selectively identify, accommodate, and serve the differentially specialized forms of intellectual potential becomes increasingly evident" (p. 19). It is becoming increasingly obvious that the recent advances from the fields of brain research and cognitive studies have significant potential for educators, from policy-makers to individual classroom teachers.

248

The field of cognitive sciences is proposed as the knowledge and content base of education because it provides an integration of various fields of knowledge, each of that is concerned with understanding how learning occurs, under what conditions, with what groups, and at different developmental levels. It is important, therefore, from this perspective, to include within cognitive science those disciplines which contribute to this knowledge and understanding. In this consideration I begin with the premise that what is most important is the task of defining what is necessary for educators to know about how learning occurs.

In my estimation, disciplines should be included within the framework of cognitive science based on their contributions to improving the knowledge base of education and increasing our knowledge of how children learn. This approach, at variance with the usually accepted practice of defining a discipline on the basis of scientific evidence and/or scholarly study, results in a logical set of rules and parameters defining the discipline, but it is not primarily concerned with practice and application. The perspective I am suggesting is more pragmatic. It begins with the "what" of the question which in this instance asks, "What data, information, or knowledge contributes to our understanding of how children learn and how may such learning be maximized?" This perspective is not concerned with the artificial barriers of knowledge established as "disciplines of knowledge" or university departments. In my view, from the perspective of a public school classroom, the critical element is the integration of knowledge from the various fields contributing to cognitive science so that better and improved academic programs and curricula can be designed so children can learn better. As Bruner (1966) has pointed out, research on the instructional process has not been carried out in connection with the building of curricula. Research has proceeded along its own lines, rarely connected to the research needs of the schools or their efforts to build better curricula (Starr and Reilly, 1985). This is another instance where the notion of "integrative education" proposed by Bertalanffy could prove exceedingly beneficial. The primary concern and focus, however, are improving children's learning, not the intellectual discussions of what "discipline" contributes or belongs within the field defined as cognitive science.

Gardner (1985) restricts the definition of human cognitive activities to mental representations and excludes the biological and neurological sciences, on the one hand, and the social or cultural, on the other. I would include those findings and understandings of how learning occurs which are developed from the fields of biology and neurology. In the same manner that Gardner perceives the computer as indispensable for understanding the human mind, I perceive these fields as indispensable for understanding how learning occurs. Without the contributions from such fields, our

249

understanding of how learning occurs will be unnecessarily restricted, and such matters as curriculum development, teaching strategies, program design and development, and appropriate administrative and organizational practices cannot be effectively implemented. Over twenty years ago Robert Travers (1967) stated that the teacher-education curriculum usually ignored what a child could or could not learn. This observation is still valid today. The basis for what a child can learn is based on his/her neurological and biological status and the development of these potentials within each child, as moderated by richness of the social and cultural environment of each child.

I do agree with Gardner on his emphasis on mental representation and its importance in the field of human cognitive activity, but perhaps for a different reason. I would emphasize it for its importance in assisting the learning process. Mental representation, or the ability to visualize both the problem and the process being utilized for problem solution or resolution, is vital for improving and sharpening the learning process. Sternberg (1977, 1984) has provided a framework for such representations. Although Sternberg's work is more focused on intellectual development, its applications to improving learning are direct and obvious. Of particular significance for the current discussion are two elements of Sternberg's theory. First is the notion of the *component,* which is defined as an elementary information process that operates upon internal representations of objects or symbols. Second is the *metacomponent,* which is defined as executive processes used in planning and decision-making in task performance (Sternberg, 1977, 1984). Although Sternberg's theory should be read for a fuller, more comprehensive assessment of its potential for contributing to improvement of learning, these two aspects of his theory bear directly on the importance of mental representation and its importance for learning improvement. By being aware of and visualizing the object or symbol being considered, the information processes that are acting upon it, and the planning and decision-making processes one is using in the problem-solving effort, a student will be better able to remedy mistakes, improve upon such efforts in the future, and thereby improve learning. It is visualizing the processes that are being used that is critical, and teaching children how to develop, refine, and use these processes are vital for learning to learn and the improvement of learning effectiveness.

A recent report issued by The National Assessment of Educational Progress (1987) describes this mental representation in terms of "process instruction," that is, focusing on the processes that people use over time in such subject areas as reading and writing. Over fifty years ago, Woodrow (1927) demonstrated that students could improve learning efficiency by being taught learning techniques. Gruson and Zigarmi (1985) proposed guidelines for the development of a curriculum of visual thinking for early childhood education. These guidelines were derived from Piaget's theory as related to learning theory and the results of split brain research. These guidelines are helpful in developing children's mental imagery skills in the school setting. Among other findings, Piagetian and learning theory approaches to the study of mental imagery development have demonstrated that: (1) children begin to use imaginal and verbal symbolic processes with increasing frequency and effectiveness at about 6-8 years of age, (2) imaginal and verbal processes operate in separate but complementary ways, representing the concrete and abstract aspects of the child's physical and social environment, and (3) the development of imaginal and verbal processes are closely related to a child's ability to imitate actively the actions, events, and objects perceived in his environment.

Guidelines for developing a visual thinking curriculum logically consistent with the findings of Piaget, learning theory, and split brain research are: (1) Educators must become acquainted with the literature that discusses the function of imagery in learning. (2) Educators must acknowledge the disadvantages inherent in solely emphasizing verbal and written responses needed to succeed in today's schools. (3) Classroom teachers must encourage students to generate images themselves instead of constantly imposing preconceived images on their students. (4) Educators must begin to understand the differences and possibilities inherent in separate and complementary functions of the brain. Gruson and Zigarmi (1985) conclude that imagery has a role in the process of problem-solving that is not language-bound, and they offer some suggestions for classroom activities to enhance strong image generation.

Travers (1967) observed that the learning of processes represents learning mediating processes that facilitate related learning. Mediating processes include such cognitive skills as generalization, pattern recognition, classification/grouping, self-analysis, error recognition and correction, and inference. Cognitive science and mental representation are concerned with how these meditating processes are learned, how students to become aware of them, and how to facilitate the process itself. By being aware of and visualizing these processes, a student is able to study his/her own cognitive and problem-solving skills. It is from this awareness and study that the goals of generalization and transfer of learning can be achieved. These twin goals of generalization and transfer of learning have long been sought by educators, but to date have eluded all efforts at capture.

These goals first found expression in the notion of formal discipline. *Formal discipline* was founded on the belief that certain mental exercises, if learned appropriately, could train the mind so that most subject areas would be learned more easily and readily. The most difficult subjects were deemed most appropriate for producing the maximum learning benefit. Mathematics and Latin were the most popular subjects for these exercises, for clearly if the most difficult subjects could be mastered, other subjects would be relatively easy to master (Travers, 1967). As Travers points out, the notion of formal discipline is attractive on the surface, but it might also be pointed out, so are many other fads and notions about education that do not take into account the many-faceted and interdependent elements of education. Formal discipline never achieved the results its adherents had desired. For one thing, it was based on a generalization from physical training, that exercise of muscles in one situation would generalize to improvement of skill in several areas of sport activity (Travers, 1967). The result was that the notion of formal discipline did not show the generalization effect in educational practice it offered on the surface, and many children suffered untold hours of drill because it appeared plausible.

These visualization processes of cognition and problem-solving efforts are based upon biological and neurological processes. As Eisner (1982) has pointed out, concept formation is biologically rooted in the sensory systems that humans possess. To exclude these foundations upon which mental representations are built from a definition of cognitive science would be to ignore vital areas of knowledge which teachers must understand and utilize if they are to assist their students to improve their learning processes. Weinberger, McGaugh, and Lynch, (1985) in their book, *Memory Systems of the Brain*, which reviews animal and human cognitive processes, state, "Learning is a behavioral phenomenon that ultimately must be explained by cell physiology" (p. 23). Greenough (1985), writing in the same book, states, "Perfect knowledge of the mechanisms of learning would allow us to state what is necessary and sufficient for its occurrence" (p. 77).

Although a complete review of the research cited in this book is not appropriate for this book, the studies provide ample evidence that advances in understanding the physiology of the brain and its functions have important implications for education and curriculum development. For example, it appears that different forms of learning may involve different neural systems and that the systems underlying preparatory learning may differ from those involving imaging. Multiple forms of memory and learning, dependent upon the type of task involved, raise important questions related to curriculum development and instructional procedures. This issue raises serious and disturbing questions about curricula which currently appear to be developed on the basis of the presumed structure of a discipline. Is this procedure the most effective means for learning the discipline, or should the curriculum be organized on the basis of how learning occurs and information is stored, retrieved and generalized? Similarly, on what basis should information, facts and/or principles, be presented to children so that they have the best chance of learning, understanding, generalizing, and applying it? What would happen if the way a discipline is currently structured and the most effective means by which a student could assimilate this knowledge are at variance? What is the "what" of such a situation? Unfortunately, in most of today's schools, the needs of children rarely come first. For too long the artificial structures of most disciplines have dictated the formation of curriculum and the means by which children are taught. With the advances that are taking place in understanding how learning occurs, it will soon be possible to restructure curricula on the basis of this knowledge.

These are critical and fundamental questions for education that have the potential for restructuring completely the means by which education takes place. As Travers (1967) observed over two decades ago, students of education can no longer ignore the results of research in neurology if they are to acquire some understanding of the learning process. Advancements in the understanding of the neurological bases of learning since that time have greatly increased our knowledge and understanding of the factors and variables that play significant roles in learning. We ignore these findings at our children's peril.

M. C. Wittrock, an educational researcher and teacher, writing in *The Dual Brain* (1985), provides an excellent overview of the status of recent cognitive science research in his article, "Education and Recent Neuropsychological and Cognitive Research." Wittrock traces the history of the relation between education and cognitive processes from the time of Aristotle, who provided a model of the cognitive processes of memory and recollection with imagery as the basis for storing or remembering information. According to Wittrock, most of American pedagogy, until the last decade or so, has been dominated by the behavioristic model of learning that began with Thorndike's theory of stimulus-response connections. Much of American classroom instruction still emphasizes this approach, which was greatly elaborated upon by B. F. Skinner. In this model neural connections were perceived as strengthened by repeated, reinforced drill and practice. In Thorndike's model the associations were between environmental stimuli and behavioral responses, not among serially ordered images as they were with Aristotle's model. Also missing from the behavioristic model were the concepts of memory, attention, and knowledge acquisition (Wittrock, 1985). Within the last one or two decades, according to Wittrock, recent neuropsychological research on the brain, cognitive activities, and thought processes have greatly expanded our knowledge in these areas and an renewed interest in their relation to education. Wittrock concludes,

From recent research on the cognitive processes in knowledge acquisition, it seems likely that people have characteristic analytic and synthetic mechanisms that they use to make sense out of information, to relate it to what they know, and to remember and to understand it. These findings and models have led to recent studies in classroom learning that have taught children to use learning strategies and mectacognitive techniques to enhance their memory and their comprehension, often with sizable gains (p. 336).

Wittrock has also developed a model of learning as a generative process, which sees the brain as a model builder with a prime focus to generate understanding. In Wittrock's model, effective teaching depends on understanding the student's cognitive processes as well as the subject matter. From his research, Wittrock has developed a list of critical research questions that are of profound importance for teachers. He also provides a review of research on such topics as attention, knowledge acquisition, and the relationships between education and neural and cognitive sciences. One of Wittrock's most important observations is the recognition that the brain constantly seeks to impose order on incoming stimuli and to generate models that lead to adaptive behavior and useful predictions. This is a critical element for understanding how education, and particularly classroom operations, must be re-designed. Classroom operations, including teacher behavior, instructional strategies, and the curriculum, must be re-designed from the perspective of maximizing the learners' opportunities and ability to organize and impose cognitive order on information and knowledge. This means understanding how the brain functions to impose such order so that learning activities are instituted with the learner as determiner of how a particular activity will be presented. It seems warranted to assume that curricula that are built around this effort of the brain to impose order and which are supported by instructional strategies which complement this effort will lead to more effective and improved learning outcomes than are currently the case.

Jerre Levy (1982), in a review of myth and reality associated with popular notions of how children think, provides an update of what has been validated by neuropsychologists in this most important area. Levy recognizes that the whole brain is actively engaged in perception, encoding of information, organization of representations, memory, arousal, planning, thinking, understanding, and most other mental operations. Levy also recognizes that there are important hemispheric differences concerning various mental functions and provides a review of differences in such areas as language, art and music, and logic and mathematics. Levy also asserts that both hemispheres play critical roles in organizing the perceptual and cognitive processes that are prerequisite to understanding. After citing research for inter-hemispheric integration, Levy turns to the implications of this research for learning styles and educational practice. Several of these implications are of particular note. One is that whole brain learning may be better accomplished for different people with different methods. The implications of this finding for teachers and the improvement of children's learning are obvious. Levy also makes clear in this regard that the gateway into whole-brain learning may differ for different children. This suggests that a variety of instructional procedures and curriculum approaches may be necessary for each classro m, depending on a particular child's specific learning needs and styles.

Levy draws several conclusions from this review of research. First, the 1960's notion of "non-threatening" education should probably be discarded. The research indicated that challenges are what appear to excite the whole-brain, to generate interest and attention, and to provide the essential base for optimal learning. Although there has not been, to this author's knowledge, research that relates children's learning efficiency to his/her neural arousal level, it is known (Reilly, 1965; Travers, 1967) that arousal level is directly related to learning efficiency. (The *arousal level* may be defined as that state in which a student is ready, excited, and actively "turned on" to learn.) When Levy speaks of the substrate for optimal learning, it may be that this substrate is directly related to the arousal level of the individual. The implications of this avenue of research are potentially very significant. If the neurological arousal level of the individual is not at an optimal threshold level for learning, learning outcomes will be less than optimal. It is also known that emotional state, diet, drugs, lack of sleep, and sensory richness can affect this arousal level. Other factors that probably influence this arousal level are class schedules, the duration of class periods, and the intensity of information inherent in different subject areas. Teachers and administrators will probably have to learn an entirely new perceptual framework for assessing students' readiness and capacity for learning and organizing school schedules.

A second inference of Levy's review of research is that all subject matters engage the specialties of both sides of the brain, and that the aim of education is to guide the child toward a synthesis of these differing perspectives. In this regard, Levy raises the question of how this synthesis is to be achieved. It is towards this synthesis that the contributions of cognitive science are suggested as an avenue of hope. This effort towards synthesis is obviously related to assisting the brain in organizing and imposing order on knowledge. Again, classroom operations should be focused on achieving this goal and teaching children quickly the processes for achieving this order.

Support for the mediation role of the brain — i.e., reviewing and analyzing thoughts, feelings, and memories — comes from an unlikely source. Laurence Miller (1986) cites the results of an experiment conducted by Benjamin Libet and his associates at the University of California School of Medicine. In this research, carried out with neurosurgery patients, it was found that a weak electrical pulse delivered either to the hand or to the exposed sensory cortex requires about half a second processing time in the brain to reach consciousness. When the pulse was delivered to the hand, the patient became conscious of the stimulus at the same time it was delivered, not a half second later. Libet and his colleagues concluded that some brain mechanism must be "correcting" for the half second processing delay in the case of natural sensory stimulation, so that subjectively, we regard our perception of an experience as occurring at the same time as the experience itself, not half a second later. Although Miller was interested in this research for its implications for Freud's theory of repression, it has obvious implications for educational theory and practice, particularly the visualization processes discussed earlier. This research provides empirical support for the contention that there is a time when the brain is reviewing the stimulus and decoding it against previous information, memories, experience, etc. It is this period of review that teachers must be concerned with helping students to learn and formulate more effective and efficient cognitive operations.

There has been some research that has focused on the activities that can enhance the learner's active role in more effectively processing information. Weinstein (1985), in the report cited earlier, describes these activities as *learning strategies*. These strategies, each of which affects *learning outcomes*, are cognitive functions which depend partly on (1) what a learner knows about a particular topic, (2) the cognitive processes and strategic planning operations a learner uses before, during and after a learning activity, and (3) the learner's motivational state.

Although each of these factors is an important contributor to learning outcomes, it is the cognitive processes that are of most interest in the present discussion. Teaching a student to develop and refine these cognitive processes is a challenging proposition for a teacher, made more so by the lack of preparation of teachers to undertake these efforts and their lack of specific knowledge and techniques for doing so.

The importance of this task is pointed out in *Research in Brief* (January, 1987), published by the Office of Educational Research and Improvement of the U. S. Department of Education. This article, titled "Eight Pointers on Teaching Children to Think," summarized some pointers on teaching thinking skills offered in a report, "Thinking Skills," by the Mid-Continent Regional Educational Laboratory. Each of the pointers presented can assist teachers to develop and enhance students' cognitive processes in solving problems, but it is the eighth one that is of significance in this discussion. This pointer suggests that students should learn to examine their attitudes about learning and evaluate their progress. They should learn to identify what is working for them and what isn't. This task requires the mental representation of the problem and the processes used for solution that Gardner discusses (1985) and which are so important for learners to develop.

Perkins (1985) has also written on ways to foster the effective teaching of thinking skills. Although Perkins' suggestions have to do with broad, general guidelines for such efforts, they do tend to counter some of the approaches that have been used for such purposes in the past.

Numerous studies deal with recent findings in cognitive functions and as applied to various subject areas, e.g. math, science, and to a host of other educational practices and concerns. A few are worthy of mention. Quellmalz (1985), for example, has considered the basis for defining a core of fundamental cognitive skills and for designing exercises that require using such skills. Quellmalz found that philosophers, psychologists, and curriculum theorists have all analyzed and defined reasoning skills, with each discipline developing somewhat different frameworks and terminologies, but with substantial overlap. Quellmalz concludes that the cognitive processes of analysis, comparison, inference, and evaluation appear in the major conceptualizations of problem-solving, critical thinking, and intellectual performance, and he suggests that these are the fundamental skills to include in a framework that merges psychological and philosophical views of essential reasoning strategies in curriculum areas.

Winne (1985) proposes three assumptions to define a view of instruction: (1) cognitive activity is inherent and patterned; (2) school learning is goal-oriented cognitive activity;, and (3) instruction is an intentional activity in which teachers intend to influence students' learning. From these assumptions he has developed models of instruction from which he derived suggestions for enhancing cognitive achievement.

Sadler and Whimbey (1985) suggest a holistic approach to improving thinking skills and liken teaching people to think to learning to swing a golf club: it is the whole action that counts. A review of psychological research plus 10 years of trial-and-error experience led to the formulation of six principles that they recommend for a holistic approach to the teaching of cognitive skills.

These are (1) teaching active learning, (2) articulating thinking, (3) promoting intuitive understanding, (4) structuring courses developmentally, (5) motivating learning, and (6) establishing a positive social climate for learning.

Cole (1977), in an ethnographic study of the psychology of cognition, concluded that familiarity with the materials about which one is asked to reason is necessary in applying cognitive skills. Cole also concluded that cultural differences in cognition have more to do with the situations to which cognitive processes are applied than the presence or absence of a particular process. These findings have important applications for the development of appropriate curricula for disadvantaged children and the increasing numbers of children in our schools who come from different cultures.

Frederickson (1984) reviewed cognitive theories of problem-solving and suggestions made by cognitive psychologists regarding how-to-teach problem-solving. He summarizes the results of these studies with a description of how high levels of proficiency in problem-solving are acquired and how problem-solving skills might be best taught, keeping in mind a distinction between well-and ill-structured problems.

The importance of developing these critical thinking and cognitive function skills in students is demonstrated by the formation of a "Collaborative on Thinking," which includes more than 20 national educational organizations — including leading academic societies, administrative groups, and the two major teachers' unions (Olsen, 1985). The two main goals of this collaborative effort are to promote the teaching of academic content in ways that develop and encourage student thinking and to ensure that students are explicitly taught cognitive skills. Several reasons are cited for this new emphasis. Among these are that students will need critical-thinking skills more than ever if they are to be prepared for the future labor market. There has been a decline in such skills among students in the 1970's and early 1980's as reported by the National Assessment of Educational Progress (Applebee, A., Langer, J., and Mullis, I., 1987). Although the causes for this decline are not fully understood, NAEP officials have suggested that not enough emphasis is being placed on teaching students higher-order learning skills. This report also asserts that a number of education researchers have found evidence supporting such a conclusion.

Although this emerging field of cognitive science has been primarily tested and researched in education in fragmented manner, where evidence of a more comprehensive nature is available, it is most encouraging. Cognitive science provides few ready-made packages of curriculums that can be taken off the shelf and applied directly in the classroom. It does offer subject specific approaches that can be utilized, but, as an integrated body of knowledge and practice, it offers only a few. Leslie Hart offers one of these. Hart has published a number of articles and books (e.g., 1975, 1978a, 1978b, 1981, 1983a, 1983b) describing a theory of education and educational programs based generally on how the brain works and specifically on Proster Theory. Proster Theory was developed by Hart as a generic means of offering educational programs based on brain function. Although Hart's works should be read for a comprehensive description of Proster Theory and its application to education, a very brief and simplified review is provided here. Basically, *Proster Theory* is a theory of human learning. It is a not a theory of learning formed from laboratory experiments, but rather from a wide range of sources and then formed into a coherent approach or system that was applied to the learning activities of the classroom. In this sense it is avoids the criticisms that were made earlier in this book about scientists who developed their theories in settings remote from the real world of learning and which have to often proved to be of little value in the classroom setting.

Hart's goal in developing this theory was to design brain-compatible programs and curriculums of learning. The theory is an effort to develop educational means of assisting the brain to extract meaningful patterns from the array of information continuously assaulting it. It is based on the finding that the brain attempts to constantly make sense of the complex world in which it finds itself. This effort by the brain to impose order on the world seems well documented. (See the previous discussion of the works of Wittrock and Sadler and Whimbey.) It has important considerations for the development of a curriculum that is based on how the brain functions, rather than forming a curriculum on a presumed structure of a particular discipline. This function of the brain forms the backbone of Proster Theory and involves the realization that humans behave, especially with purposeful behavior, largely by programs. This means simply that a fixed sequence of behavior is used to achieve a desired outcome or objective. These "programs of behavior" are a result of the brain's efforts to impose order, to remember experiences of successful behavior in similar situations, and to detect differences in current circumstances that call for program modification. Obviously, the richer the store of previous experiences, the greater the probability of selecting the "best fit" program. It is not just a matter of environmental richness, however. It is the richness of the environment combined with the appropriate programs and the capacity to modify these programs appropriately on the basis of new information and experiences. As Hart describes the process, one must constantly select and implement the appropriate program from those stored in the brain. The process of learning involves the development of experiences, the formation of programs, the selection of the most appropriate program, and the development of the capacity to modify programs as appropriate. According to Hart, the highly subtle pattern-detection capabilities are in the neocortex section of the brain. These are capabilities that are often associated with

259

emotion in humans. Of particular interest in this regard is the emotion aroused when threat is detected. This is the emotion of fear. When threat to the organism is detected, the higher-order, newer cerebral brain functions are suspended, and the older, more reflex-oriented brain functions take over. The importance of this is that, since virtually all academic and intellectual activities and learning involve the neocortex, any perceived threat in the classroom will render inoperable those cognitive skills most necessary for optimal learning.

The alert reader will remember that one of the conclusions of Levy (1982), mentioned earlier, was that the "non-threatening" education notion of the 1960's should be discarded. At first glance this conclusion by Levy and the conclusion by Hart seem to be at variance. Levy, however, was describing what appeared to challenge the brain in order to elicit interest and excite whole-brain learning, whereas Hart was concerned with the emotion of threat.

The research that has been done to date suggests that application of Hart's theories to educational settings provides increased academic gains for weak and strong students alike. Nene (1985) reported the results of an application of Hart's Proster Theory in an elementary school with 120 students in grades K-2. This application was based on three principles of Proster Theory: (1) freedom from threat, since neocortex function is enhanced by students being relaxed, happy, and busy, (2) communication emphasis, with talking and mutual help encouraged and facilitated, and (3) reality emphasis. The activities of this program recognized the child's need to feel increasing control of his/her world by providing for manipulation, making, designing, and doing as opposed to mostly sitting and listening. A survey of parents indicated strong satisfaction with their child's progress and attitudes. The unit teachers also indicated strong approval, and the other teachers at the school expressed interest in becoming involved in brain-based programming. Iowa Test scores consistently ranged in the mid-90th percentile, and criterion-referenced tests in math indicated a high degree of 100 % mastery and vocabulary tests demonstrated growth of two to three years for both weak and strong students.

The research literature concludes that cognitive science, as derived from cognitive psychologists and educators and the results of brain research, offers a powerful potential means for: (1) serving as a generic knowledge base for education and all professional educators, (2) improving children's learning skills, (3) providing the basis for the learning process knowledge students need to master as a foundation for continued learning and the basis for re-designing how specific subject matter will be taught, and (4) raising serious questions about the adequacy of current curriculum development assumptions and procedures.

As Resnick (1984) has stated, "In offering a powerful reconceptualization of the nature of the learning process and new methods of the investigation of learning, [cognitive science] can be invaluable to education" (p. 36). Resnick also points out, "The general shape of an educationally relevant cognitive science has become apparent. It can be expected to pay off handsomely in a reasonable period of time because it confronts directly questions to which educators need answers" (p. 37).

The Educational Testing Service announced in late 1985 that it would allocate $30 million during the next 15 years to develop technologically advanced tests that instruct as well as assess after it predicted that advances in technology and the cognitive sciences would reshape the field of education in the next 20 years. Analyzing why students make the errors they do will be a distinct advantage of this next generation of tests. One of results of cognitive research has been the discovery that student errors are often the result from misunderstandings about the task at hand, rather than from careless errors.

Further, Glaser, then President of the National Academy of Education, in an address on *Research and Education* to the Royal Swedish Academy of Sciences in 1984, cited the advances in behavioral and cognitive sciences that have yielded new understandings of human mental functioning. He concluded that these advances are providing powerful reconceptualizations of the nature of the learning process and new insights into human cognition in educational processes (Glaser, 1984).

Theory of multiple intelligences

One of these insights comes from the theory of multiple intelligences, first postulated by Gardner in 1983 and expounded on more recently in the writings and research of other authors (Gardner, 1993; Gray and Viens, 1994; Salomon, 1993). The Theory of Multiple Intelligences (MI) suggests that there are at least seven intelligences; linguistic, logical-mathematical, spatial, bodily-kinesthic, musical, interpersonal, and intrapersonal. These various intelligences are the result of both individual and cultural factors, and the resulting intellectual profile of any individual is the outcome of local, cultural, and personal contexts in which they develop (Gray and Viens, 1994).

MI theory questions several traditional concepts concerning intelligence. For example, MI theory leads to the question "In what ways is this person intelligent?" as opposed to the common question, "How intelligent is this person?" The diversity of intelligences among children supports the Principle of Equifinality in that different approaches must be used to bring students with different intellectual profiles to similar goals. In addition, MI theory reinforces the primacy of the learner as the determinant of how classroom material must be structured on the basis of how each student learns and his/her particular intellectual profile. Further, MI theory has significant implications for curricular design and instructional strategies. Students with different intellectual profiles and associated learning strengths will profit most from curricula and teachers who are sensitive to these differences and strengths. Thus, teachers will need to be trained in vastly different ways than they are currently and be able to operate from a greatly expanded knowledge base about how children learn.

An active and involved role on the part of the learner in all learning activities must be the cornerstone of a re-designed curriculum. Instead of perceiving learning outcomes as depending on what the teacher presents, learning outcomes should be perceived as an interactive result of what information is presented and how students process that information. It is in providing an understanding of how students learn to process and integrate information that the field of cognitive science potentially offers its most significant contributions to the profession of education. Further, it seems logical to assume that today's teachers have not been made aware of these findings, nor are they prepared to apply them in the classroom without considerable faculty development. These considerations provide the basis for second-order change #2.

Second-Order Change #2. The core knowledge base for all educators should be a thorough understanding of cognitive science.

This change would have significant implications for all facets of educational activity. Most of today's teachers understand little of how students learn. They would need to improve their understanding considerably. Faculty development programs would have to developed which could provide this knowledge and training. School and classroom organization and practices would have to be modified significantly. Teacher preparation programs would need substantial changes to ensure that their graduates were competent practitioners of the cognitive sciences. These recommendations call for significant changes, but they are necessitated by the need to improve learning outcomes of students by focusing on the mission of the schools and providing a knowledge base that supports the mission.

Knowledge base for personal-social development

Sarason (1982) suggests that the evidence of our senses should inform us that non-cognitive processes contribute far more than cognitive skills to the quality of human life and the extent of human happiness. Unfortunately, there is little research supporting the schools' mission for developing the personal-social skills of students. In his book, *Inequality: a Reassessment of the Effect of Family and Schooling in America*, which was based on a literature review, Jencks (1972) was able to devote only four pages to non-cognitive skills. Jencks also suggested that the "factory" model of education should be abandoned.

The question must be raised, "Why is there this disparity of emphasis between two supposedly equal purposes of the schools?" One reason is certainly the lack of research supporting the teaching process for developing these skills. But this is the symptom, not the cause. The cause of the problem is that there are no fundamental values that the schools are permitted to encourage and reinforce. This is probably a reflection of society's ambivalent posture towards the question of values. Whose values should they be taught in the schools? And under what conditions? These questions may be the most important and critical questions that educators and societies have to address in the future.

Individuals develop values that tell them what in their experience is important. Values are learned and are usually long enduring. Knowledge may be replaced, skills may become outmoded, and attitudes may change as a result of life experiences; but individual values, once adopted, shift slowly, if at all. The identification of appropriate educational programs in the future will be a value-laden activity. Value judgments influence decisions regarding what aspects of the cultural heritage will be transmitted, particularly moral and ethical values. The appropriate role of education in developing individuals is a value judgment. The manner in which learning opportunities will be presented and made available to individuals as well as methods and materials in teaching will increasingly involve value judgments.

Clearly, the interaction of various values is critical. For example, the merging patterns of political, economic, ethical-moral and social, and self values and their interactions are critical in determining the types of educational programs and opportunities that are developed for the future.

If values serve a self-correcting function in society as some argue, (e.g., Salk, 1978), then education should do more than simply mirror society's values, particularly when the society appears to be losing its sense of value structure. Values cannot serve a self-correcting role for an uniformed and uncommitted public. An important function of education, therefore, is to produce an informed social consciousness, as well as an emotional and intellectual commitment to an improved society. In the future, appropriate educational programs will need to familiarize students with dilemmas facing their society and the world's people. Education will be most effective when it can assist learners to develop their beliefs and values that ultimately could lead to the solution of these dilemmas.

It will, however, require an attitude shift on the part of the American public to develop the teaching of values and appropriate behaviors as a priority for the schools' mission. The question of what values and whose values are certainly a critical one, and one fraught with heated discussion. Yet, the question must be addressed and resolved. Currently, there are too many students who are growing up without a sense of values to guide their interpersonal behavior. The signs of this valueless student and adult generation abound in society. Something must be done to ensure that future generations will not grow, develop, interact and raise children without a guiding sense of an appropriate value system.

Although there are serious questions about the place of value instruction in the schools, there can be little real debate that the schools are an appropriate place for teaching the following principles:

- Cooperative behavior.
- Honesty.
- Fairness with others.
- Wait your turn.
- Understanding and accepting individuals from different cultures.
- Why not to lie, steal, harm others.
- How to work with and within a group without losing a sense of personal identity.

There are obviously other, more profound issues revolving around the question of values instruction, clarification, and appropriate behaviors. However, if the schools were responsible for teaching the above, and were successful at doing so, our society would be a better place to live, and our children's lives would be improved immeasurably.

There is one further observation about the teaching of values that must be noted. The teaching of values in the classroom will not do much to improve our children's lives if school personnel do not practice what they preach. School personnel must model the values they seek to teach in the classroom. Any disparity between the instruction and the behavior of school personnel would be the most compelling instructional technique of all.

The criteria for success

Currently, the criterion for a school's success is measured by its relative standing of grade point averages at, above, or below state and national

264

norms. In addition, the number of graduates going on to college (not their success in college, but the number accepted), the number passing competency tests, and other such product-oriented measures are used to judge school effectiveness.

These measures have a number of misleading features about them. Take testing, for example. Achievement testing is big business in America. In 1983, approximately $500 million was spent on commercial standardized achievement tests. This amount does not include what was spent on group IQ, diagnostic or minimum competency tests (George, 1985). CTB/McGraw-Hill alone sold more than 6,000,000 achievement tests in 1987 at a cost of $2.00 per test (Gay, 1990). The unrestrained use of tests in American education has caused them to become the unquestioned criteria of school success, teacher competence, and program evaluation. Their use is so critical for determining classroom performance and effectiveness that violation of test procedure abound. Gay's (1990) results indicated that 35 % of the teachers in her sample were aware of or had participated in one or more irregularities in the administration of required achievement tests. Sixty percent of this sample also indicated that the primary reason for the violations was to improve the image of the teacher. Consider also that, on the California Achievement Test (CAT) Reading Comprehension Test, Level 13 Form E, a difference of two correct answers will result in a percentile gain of 14. For example, the percentile score for 29 correct answers is 32; for 31 correct answers the percentile is 46.

These are not the most misleading aspects of these evaluation measures. The most serious misconception of these measures is that they focus attention on the wrong aspects of school success. A successful school is one that can develop within all its students a cognitive process that allows them to reason effectively on their own about a myriad of problem areas. A successful school is also one that can inoculate within them knowledge of their own value system, a sense of values appropriate and necessary to improve their society, and a behavioral code that reflects these values. These are process variables that are not measured by current evaluation procedures used in schools.

At least four advantages of "process" variables in measuring school effectiveness exist: (1) they are more directly concerned with and related to the missions of the schools, (2) they are more accurate reflectors of school functions, emphases, and competencies, (3) they provide a means for assessing difficulties students may be having in either academic or personal-social areas and providing assistance to the student by improving the process, and (4) they are far more important to the development of an individual and society than are the product oriented measures currently in use.

Tyler (1966) indicated that since test measures exert such influence on teaching, school policy should require that a testing program be directly related to the objectives of the schools. If the schools mission is process-oriented, then the evaluation process should be directed towards assessment of this process.

Summary

The first two elements of a conceptual framework for education are the primary mission of the schools and the knowledge base necessary to accomplish the mission. Whatever other responsibilities the schools may be asked to assume, the first priority is to teach all students to learn effectively and to enhance their personal-social development. This mission includes teaching students how to generalize learning and problem-solving procedures effectively. It also involves teaching them appropriate values and behavior for living in a democratic society. It follows from this mission that the knowledge base for educators must support the accomplishment of this mission. The discipline base that best provides this support for intellectual and academic development is cognitive science. There is not yet a comparably developed knowledge base for teaching personal-social values and behaviors. The development of this knowledge base must be preceded by an attitude shift on the part of the American public that teaching values and appropriate behaviors is a responsibility of the schools. The criteria for determining school success and teacher competence must shift from a "product" orientation to one that emphasizes the development of "process" skills on the part of students.

12 A conceptual framework for education, part two: organization, program design, and resource allocation

An educational mission that asserts the primacy of learning processes and the implications of cognitive science as the core knowledge base for instructional practices, and that gives equal importance to the personal-social development of students, has important implications for school system and individual school organization. Currently, educational organization at the system and school levels are not structured in such a way as to maximize the learning potential and personal-social development of students. As Boyer (1983) has written, "the basic pattern of public schools may make bureaucratic sense — but does it make educational sense?" (p. 230). This is a basic question; what makes educational sense? To make educational sense, a school must define the best option for organizing educational systems and individual schools and classrooms, develop an appropriate program design for delivery of learning experiences, and provide an adequate resource base for program development.

Educational decision-making operates through the interdependence of policy, administration, and practice (Elmore and McLaughlin, 1988). Conflicts among these factors result from the overlapping, but undefined, decision-making authority and influence on educational policy and practices exerted by federal agencies, state legislatures, and educational agencies, local boards of education, and school superintendents and principals. Because of conflicts arising among these parties, the administration of policies often adversely affects practice, usually resulting in little reform or change of classroom practice (Elmore and McLaughlin, 1988).

Several observers and researchers of the educational scene (e.g., Dalin, 1978; Elmore and McLaughlin, 1988; and Shanker, 1987) have commented that changes have to be made at the individual school and within the classroom if educational outcomes are to be improved. Dalin (1978) has observed that, whatever goals of educational change or reform are developed, they should affect the academic life of students and the professional life of teachers. According to Dalin, the school, as an organization, becomes the focal point for change.

The professional literature supports these observations. Unfortunately, it does not propose that the system organization must also be changed to permit and support the changes desired at the individual school and classroom level. The need to assure consistency and coordination of change among policy development, the organization of schools, and classroom practices has not been sufficiently addressed. Changes in one of these, without ensuring that appropriate alterations in the other two are made, will result in achievements less than desired. Chapter 7 addressed the issue of coordination between public and teacher education at the state level. Similarly, at the school system level, there is need to coordinate changes in policy, organization, and practice at the individual school level. It must be with the system level that change begins if the freedom for sustained improvement of learning outcomes at the school and classroom levels are to be obtained.

System-level changes

The basic organizational structure at the system level requires and permits the local school board to set policies in areas not already assumed by a state agency. The school superintendent, hired by the local school board, along with assistant and associate superintendents, program directors, program coordinators, and principals, have the responsibility for administration of the policies. The profusion of policy-makers and administrators seriously handicaps efforts to achieve fundamental changes in the ways schools are organized. As Dalin (1978) has observed, it is very difficult to achieve change in bureaucratic organizations like educational systems. As he also notes, this is particularly so because of the number of special interest groups that are protective of the powers they hold.

The group that is conspicuously missing from the organizational decision-making processes are the system teachers. These are the personnel upon whom the burden of any change falls, and who have the responsibility for determining the success of any innovation or change in policy. Only recently has minor recognition been given to this serious omission. Of the many national reports calling for educational reform, not including those issued by teacher organizations, only *A Nation Prepared: Teachers for the 21st Century* (1986) recommended giving more power and autonomy in decision-making to teachers. This report recommended that groups of teachers in each school be afforded this responsibility. This report did not go far enough. It did not consider the implications of this recommendation for relationship between teachers and local school boards or administrators. It did not base this recommendation on the total concept of education and all its elements, and it did not consider the implications for teacher preparation programs and faculty if such recommendations were to be implemented. In short, the report was flawed because it did not consider the entire gestalt of the situation and the mutually dependent and causal relations that exist among the various components of the education network. Similar reports in various states suffer similar flaws. The potential for conflict between teachers and administrators because of these omissions is great. Also, the goals desired will not likely be achieved because the inter-dependent nature of the educational enterprise has not been taken into account by these recommendations.

However, this particular recommendation of this report was headed in the right direction. If education is to realize its potential for educating the youth of America, then the profession must be allowed to exercise both the responsibility and authority to determine the objectives and means for educating our youth. And they must accept accountability for the outcomes. Just as the medical profession has the responsibility of promoting and maintaining the health of citizens without outside forces determining how this shall be accomplished, so also must education be allowed to educate our youth without interference from lay people. The education profession should be held accountable for the results, but not unless it can control the objectives and means for achieving these objectives. The American public cannot have it both ways. If they want to hold educators accountable for learning outcomes, they must give responsibility and authority to the teachers. If the public wants to maintain the responsibility and authority for educational objectives, the public must also assume the responsibility for the outcomes.

Shanker (1987) has addressed this issue. He concludes that the present means of organizing curriculum, grades, and classes are outmoded. He recommends restructuring the schools so that teachers are empowered to perform educational tasks as other professionals are authorized to practice their specialty. He notes that to accomplish this goal, a professional environment must be created within the schools, and new processes, institutions, and procedures must be developed.

Elmore and McLaughlin (1988) have also addressed this issue from the perspective of their analysis of current reform efforts. They state, "to be effective educational reform efforts must (1) close the gap between policy and practice, in part, by charging practitioners with the development of solutions, rather than mandating requirements that have little or no basis in practice. . . and (4) create organizations that foster and encourage reforms of education" (p. vii).

269

If the prime mission of the schools is to promote student learning, and the achievement of this mission is determined by what happens in the classroom, then it stands to reason that those charged with such responsibility should have a significant voice in determining those policies and decisions that affect both the educational mission and practice. This will require significant alterations in the current organizational structure of schools at the system level. The following second-order changes address this issue.

Second-Order Change #3. Local boards of education should be composed of equal representation from the public and teachers elected from the system.

To re-design school systems to allow teachers the authority and freedom to develop and implement learning programs for children, current impediments to exercising such responsibilities must be removed. The first such impediment is the local board of education, and the question that must be asked is, "Do such boards currently serve well the purposes for which they were originally instituted?" If not, is there another purpose, equally important, which they could serve? The answer to both questions is no! Local boards of education no longer serve as significant decision-making bodies in the three most critical areas of school operations: curriculum, personnel, and finance. The control of these three elements has shifted significantly to the state level. Increasingly, local boards of education serve to disrupt and impede educational development and improvement. They are an anachronism that once served a very useful purpose. Today, however, they merely serve to perpetuate the myth of local control of education and provide a forum for discussion of local politics that often have little to do with sound educational decision-making. Whether elected or appointed, members of such boards often have little formal knowledge of education and its needs. These board members usually represent a political constituency that they must satisfy if they are to stay in power, and the views they often express are parochial in nature, designed to achieve political goals, not educational objectives. Because they cannot be expected to become experts in how to educate children, or to understand the educational soundness of implementing a new program of drop-out prevention, they spend time on the political implications of various issues, such as determining bus routes, rather than tackling issues of educational merit.

At the same time, for generations the American public has believed in local control of education. It is not a belief they are likely to give up easily. If local boards of education no longer provide the local control for which they were originally established and if they cannot develop the expertise to become more educationally-oriented, and less politically-oriented, is there another model that would serve both the purpose of local involvement and an educational focus? Yes. It is one of shared responsibility and authority between the public and the professional educators.

This new type of local board of education would be vested with the same responsibilities as are current boards of education. They would be responsible to the public for achieving the educational goals of the schools. They would be responsible for the hiring of school superintendents, and if need be, the firing of a superintendent. They would be responsible for developing the educational objectives of the system, the programs to achieve these objectives, and procuring the funds necessary to implement the programs. They would also be accountable for the learning outcomes of the system; accountable to the public and to the professionals who must implement the programs in the schools.

The responsibility for educational outcomes is not the sole domain of parents, other public groups, state legislators, or teachers. It is a shared responsibility among all of these groups. Second-Order Change #3 provides a means for developing this shared responsibility at the system level similar to that proposed for the state level.

This proposal is not likely to win much support from school board members, school board associations, or educational administrators. It may win support from teachers and teachers' organizations; although it may not. Although there is some feeling that teachers do not wish to be empowered with the responsibility for decision-making outside their classroom, Katz and Kahn (1966) found that empowered teachers tended to feel a sense of ownership in their schools' successes and failures. Chapman and Lowther (1982) found that teachers who operated in a leadership role were more satisfied with their careers. Hall (1976) noted that increasing job complexity results in higher challenge that leads to higher job involvement.

However, despite the evidence that empowering teachers tends to be associated with increased feelings of ownership and job involvement, as well as more career satisfaction, teachers are generally not being afforded these opportunities for increased decision-making. Super and Hall (1978) indicated that job challenge for a teacher can be quite constrained by the structure of the schools. Lortie (1986) observed that teachers, particularly in large urban districts, no longer feel that they have a voice in many decisions that affect their students. Shannon (1989) suggests that, regardless of the emphasis being placed on teachers as professionals, many are being treated as scripted technicians. Brophy (1982) describes teacher education programs as preparing their graduates to assume responsibility for developing appropriate educational objectives for their students, developing curriculum, and conducting and evaluating the results of instruction. As Brophy notes, teachers may have done all of these in the past, but currently

271

these functions are performed by school boards, school administrators, and commercial publishers.

The lack of involvement on the part of teachers in decision-making at all levels seriously detracts from teachers' freedom and authority to adapt instructional activities to the needs of their students. As Boyer (1988) has noted, state control may provide accountability, but it may deny excellence if schools are required to meet mandated educational objectives through specified curriculum that ignores individual differences of students and disallows teacher creativity in addressing these differences. By the same logic, local school systems that deny teachers a significant voice in the development of policies that affect learning activities will stifle the freedom and resourcefulness of teachers to meet their students' needs.

Gutherie (1986) has addressed some of these issues. He stated, "fundamental components of the reform strategy seem to be painfully at odds with the dynamics of organizational revitalization" (p. 306). Guthrie called for policies that would encourage local initiatives and that would reduce the tensions currently existing between state-level policy-makers and local school personnel. He proposed school-based management (SBM) as a means for developing such initiatives on the assumption that the individual school is the fundamental decision-making unit within the educational system. Other authors (Clune and White, 1988; Keene, 1986) have also discussed SBM. Although SBM can take many forms, the common denominator is increased decision-making at the local school level. A July 2, 1990, issue of *Time* magazine (Tifft, 1990) indicated that 27 states had experimented to some degree with SBM. The same report indicated that there had been varying degrees of success with it. Supporters were reported as indicating that SBM improved teacher morale and made schools more flexible, factors that increased learning. Detractors contended that many teachers found group decision-making threatening and difficult. Others argued that self-governance lowers political and turf battles from the state house to the school house. SBM is on the right track, but it does not go far enough. (See Dalin, 1978 and Elmore and McLaughlin, 1988.) SBM does not extend to the level of the local school board or to the state level, where teachers must also have a significant voice in decision-making.

In addition, the principle of equifinality (Chapter 2) indicates that the final state of the system may be reached from different starting points and conditions as well as by different routes. If the final state of the system is construed as the achievement of certain learning goals, teachers need the freedom to assess their students' needs and implement those learning activities most appropriate for achieving the objectives. This cannot be done if either a state-mandated curriculum is in effect, or if teachers are denied an effective voice in determining the local policies that will allow this freedom of determination.

272

Second-Order Change #3 may or may not be supported by the American public. Obviously, the implications of such a change are vast, far-reaching. They would change the operation of school systems and schools in substantial ways. First, policies and practices of the schools would be established with representation from those charged with the responsibility for implementing them. Election of teachers to the board could be according to criteria established at the state level and would include years of successful experience, maturity, and recognition of competence by peers. This board would include representatives from both elementary and secondary teachers. Thus, the professional educators on the board would be among the best the system had to offer.

Second, such a change would provide for accountability to both the public and those professionals working within the system. This dual accountability adds a significant dimension to the current system of school board accountability. These boards are accountable only to the public, and usually to only some segment of the public. Under current conditions, teachers are not directly accountable to the school board. Under the proposed change, they would be. What is lacking in the current structure is any accountability to the professional teachers of the system. Second-Order Change #3 addresses this lack directly and thereby adds a significant, positive element to the accountability equation.

Third, because they would have the authority, teachers would have to accept responsibility for the soundness of the educational programs they designed to achieve improved learning outcomes on the part of students.

This would place a charge of accountability on them that is currently lacking in educational systems.

Fourth, the balance of power between administrators and teachers would be reversed. Many may not perceive this as an advantage over the current system. Consider the current system and its implications for education programs, change, and improvements. A school superintendent is hired by a local board of education primarily concerned with local politics and only public reaction to its decisions. A school superintendent, if he/she expects to survive, must be responsive to the political implications and nuances of board decisions and his/her response to such decisions (Elmore and McLaughlin, 1988). Often the superintendent's plea for attending to the educational implications of board decisions falls on deaf ears or is not uttered at all because it would run counter to board thinking. Central office staff and school principals are responsible to the school superintendent and are obviously influenced heavily by the current politics of school board behavior. Educational administrators, like current school boards, are not responsible to the teaching force for the decisions they make and impose on the teachers. This system of governance does not allow the teachers a voice in the decision or a means of dissent over the soundness of the decision.

The change proposed would reverse this balance of power. Local boards of teachers would be responsible for hiring the superintendent on the basis of his/her presumed competence for administrative skill. The superintendent would be responsible for administering the system on the basis of the educational programs developed by in concert by teachers and the public. Making the superintendent and other educational administrators responsible to the shared responsibility of the public and teachers reinforces again the responsibility, authority, and accountability of teachers for professional decision-making for development of sound educational programs.

Second-Order Change #4. The center for development of academic and learning programs within the system should be a high school and its feeder schools.

The current focus for developing educational policy and programs is the central office. This is three levels removed from those whom such policies and programs are designed to affect, the students. It would be far more beneficial to students to bring the development of such policies and programs as close as possible to the students, so that policies and programs would be developed on the basis of students' needs at the level closest to them. It is also desirable educationally to provide coordination of planning and implementation of learning programs at the lowest possible level. This would be a high school and its feeder schools. These program units also would be governed by a unit board of teachers, composed of teacher representatives from each of the unit schools and from each academic subject area. These unit boards would be responsible for receiving school-based developed academic improvement plans, considering whether such would meet unit objectives, and assuring these academic plans mesh and are coordinated with unit plans and programs. Such unit boards would also be charged with ensuring implementation of research findings, development of innovative programs to meet unique needs or improve learning outcomes, and presenting the case for the unit educational plan to the local board of teachers.

Such planning at the level closest to the students involved would better assure that educational programs were designed to meet the needs of these students. Unique needs of students within each unit could be attended to more adequately because of increased planning flexibility. Curricula could be adjusted to meet unique or changing needs more readily and the nature of the schools' community could be better accommodated than at the system level. In effect, local involvement in school plans and activities should be enhanced.

In such a situation as described above, the current purpose and organizational need of a school system's central office would be severely

274

diminished. There would be a need for fewer personnel. The role of the central office would be reduced to that of a business office, operating to support the educational efforts of the academic program units. There would be need only for a business manager, a coordinator of maintenance and physical plant development, and a secretary or two for processing correspondence, personnel records, and so on. The major focus of the central office would be to relieve the academic program units and individual schools of as much paperwork as possible.

The task of personnel selection would become a responsibility of the individual schools. Thus, there would be no need for a personnel director or associate superintendent of personnel. Curriculum supervisors would be assigned and would be responsible for academic program units and/or based in individual schools. Support personnel would also be based within academic program units or schools. Transportation concerns and routes would be the responsibility of each local school.

Obviously, the responsibilities of the academic program units would be greater than could be handled by a team of teachers. Each academic planning unit would need some support staff to handle the bureaucratic functions. There is no reason, however, why several units could not use the services of the same support staff on a part-time basis to handle bus routes, etc. This decentralization of educational planning and programming may not make bureaucratic sense but it makes planning and educational sense, for it gives to those responsible for delivering the programs the authority, freedom, and flexibility to develop and implement such programs.

Second-Order Change #5. A peer review system (quality assurance) for each teacher's learning objectives and activities should be operative in each school.

This peer review system could operate at the school level, the program unit level, or both. Such a system would be designed to achieve two objectives. First, it would operate as a quality control measure to assure that the individual teacher's learning objectives and programs were based on appropriate data and that the plans used the most appropriate techniques and research findings to achieve the specified objectives. Second, such a system would act to assure parents and others outside the system that appropriate measures were being undertaken to ensure the soundness of educational decision-making concerning their children. Each parent should receive a copy of the learning objectives and strategies developed for each child and the peer review panel's comments about the appropriateness of the plan. Each parent must have the right to consult with the teacher about the plan for his/her child.

Second-Order Change #6. A committee of teachers within each school should have the responsibility and authority to hire all school personnel, including principals.

This is a vital change. Those who are responsible for seeing that the objectives of the school are achieved must have the responsibility and authority for selecting the personnel necessary to achieve such objectives. Without such authority, there is no control of the learning environment, the personnel to ensure that the objectives of the school will be achieved, or accountability control if the objectives are not achieved. Also consistent with this theme is Second-Order Change #7:

Second-Order Change #7. A committee of teachers should have the responsibility and authority for determining merit salary increases for all teachers within the school.

If teachers are responsible for selecting personnel to achieve the objectives of the school, then they must also have the responsibility and authority for rewarding those who contribute most to such achievement. They must also accept the responsibility for not rewarding those who do not contribute to the achievement of the school's objectives. If a teacher does not contribute sufficiently to the achievement of the school's objectives, then his/her peers do have the responsibility and should have the authority to remove him/her from the teaching force of that school. This leads to Second-Order Change #8:

Second-Order Change #8. Tenure for professional educators should be abolished.

Tenure was developed as a protection for academic freedom and unwarranted removal from one's position as a teacher. This is a valid concern — if professional educators are not in control of the curriculum, the learning environment, and educational objectives. If, however, educators are responsible and have the authority suggested in the Second-Order Changes #1-7, then #8 is a logical and necessary consequence. If a team of colleagues, after extensive review and analysis, determines that a teacher's efforts are not contributing to achieving the objectives of the school and are, in fact, harmful to children's learning, then they have the responsibility, and must have the authority, to remove that teacher from his/her teaching position. The criteria is what is in the best interest of the students. It is not the protection of the teacher's job but the protection of the students' rights for effective and competent teaching that must serve to determine who will be allowed to enter and stay in the profession of education. If educators are to achieve the status and respect of a true profession, they must exercise this responsibility.

Re-design of elementary schools

As indicated previously, elementary schools are a child's introduction to the world of hope. These schools should be organized and administered to

276

maximize the fulfillment of this hope. The content taught in these schools should also maximize achieving this goal. This section will consider the organization and administration of these schools.

Second-Order Change #9. The system of annual grade levels should be abolished in elementary schools and replaced by two cycles of four and three years.

Second-Order Change #10. An elementary school teacher should be assigned to a class cycle and not change classes on an annual basis.

As indicated in previous discussions, the graded school system at the elementary level provides a disjointed, discontinuous series of planning efforts that are not in the best interests of children's learning. The current system requires that each year the students have a new teacher, who must learn her students' needs in order to adequately plan for them. By the time the teacher has learned their needs, strengths, and weaknesses, there are only 7-8 months left in the school year. It is only at the end of this "getting to know" time that the teacher is able to set specific learning objectives for her students. These have to be accomplished in about five months, since the end-of-year testing usually takes place during March. Then the teacher fades out and the students are passed on to another teacher who repeats the same process.

This disjointed planning process could be avoided and a more functional unit of planning and program be implemented with the changes proposed. The four-year cycle would begin with kindergarten and end with third grade. The second cycle would begin with fourth grade and run through sixth grade. By instituting these two cycles of four and three years, several distinct and definite advantages would be gained over the current system.

First, teachers would be assigned to the same class of students for either a four-or three-year period. This would allow the teacher to develop and implement learning strategies and programs based on a time period that not only allowed, but demanded, development of long-term planning and programming for learning outcomes on a more rational developmental schedule for children in this age range. The teacher would be able to plan on the basis of a four-or three-year period in which to realize his/her learning objectives. Slower-learning children would have more time in which to learn without the fear or stigma of annual failing. Faster-learning children's needs could be better accommodated with a longer time period in which to plan for them.

Second, teachers in most states are currently certified to teach ranges of grades (e.g., K-3, 4-6) at the elementary level. Thus, they have been prepared to teach the necessary knowledge, skills, and content within each of these two cycles. By being assigned to one class of students for three or four years, the teacher's professional development activities would be

277

focused on increasing knowledge and skills necessary for achieving his/her learning objectives for that class.

Third, the teacher would assume full responsibility for determining the learning objectives for his/her class for either the four-or three-year period. He/she would also be given the authority to implement the programs necessary to achieve these objectives, and be held accountable for their achievement.

Administration of elementary schools

The concept of Head Teacher, Headmaster, or Principal of a school has long been a tradition in American education. The idea of a head teacher or master teacher was appropriate when schools were small and the number of teachers in each was few. As schools grew in size and the number of teachers increased, it seemed logical to appoint one teacher as the principal teacher to coordinate the functions of the school. Although the name remained, over time the distinction of being named principal for outstanding teaching became less and less common, until today there is no connection at all. Although the principal of elementary schools, according to some theorists (e.g., Lipham and Hoeh, 1974) is supposed to be the instructional leader of the school, this notion has little real meaning. The principal is defined as the leader of the school and has the responsibility for ensuring the effective functioning of the school. However, this responsibility does not extend to the authority for decision-making in the three most critical areas of school function: personnel, curriculum, and finance. In the previous section it was proposed that a core of teachers be responsible for determining the learning programs for the students. This leaves only personnel selection and finance.

Previous second-order changes have proposed that teachers be given the responsibility, control, and authority to make many of the most critical decisions of education. If the changes here proposed were implemented, what would the role of the principal in the elementary school be?

There are many necessary and critical functions that go into making an effective elementary school. Certainly, the most important of these is what is done by teachers for developing student learning. This factor includes (1) personnel selection, (2) learning strategies and programs, and (3) the resources necessary to implement these strategies and programs. Of these, the first two must be the responsibility of teachers. However, if teachers were also responsible for procuring the resources necessary for implementing the first two of these functions, such effort would detract substantially from effectively carrying out these two functions. Therefore,

278

the prime responsibilities of an elementary principal, or a secondary principal for that matter, would be maintaining a safe environment, processing paperwork, and procuring the resources necessary to allow teachers to carry out their prime responsibilities effectively. This role definition of teachers and principals changes the character and balance of the current power status of teachers and principals in elementary schools. In the change proposed here, the teachers become the pivotal group for determining effective school programs. The principal in this framework becomes a support person to help ensure that the resources and conditions of the school are available to carry out the programs of the school. The principal should be concerned with record keeping, plant maintenance, transportation, raising funds, cafeteria oversight, and other such responsibilities. He or she should assume as many non-instructional duties as possible to let the teachers free to concentrate on their prime responsibility, improving student learning.

Re-design of secondary schools

Secondary schools are an entirely different environment than are elementary schools. Their objectives are different and their student groups have different developmental needs. Thus, their organization and administration must be different from elementary schools and matched to the needs of the students and objectives for secondary schools. However, their efforts must be coordinated effectively and efficiently with those of elementary schools. Secondary schools must expect and achieve a different result from elementary schools, yet their efforts must be a continuation of the process begun in elementary schools. They also must be distinctly different, more flexible, and must provide for a wider range of options than do elementary schools. The combination of this need to provide continuation and consistency of the educational process and, at the same time, to serve a vastly different student group and provide more flexibility, demands a significantly different organizational structure and set of administrative practices in secondary schools than is now apparent in most of these schools.

The differences between middle schools/junior high schools and senior secondary schools should also be mentioned at this point. These differences are not easy to specify, especially those between middle schools and junior high schools and junior high schools and senior high schools. The differences between these levels blur as one attempts to examine differences among them. Organizational patterns and administrative practices tend to be the same at all three levels. Although there is an increasing literature on practices appropriate for middle schools, these schools tend to replicate those of junior high schools but at a grade or two below the typical junior high school. Junior high schools tend to be miniature versions of high schools. If one walks into most middle schools, except for the size of the students, it is difficult to tell whether it is a middle school, a junior high school, or a senior high school. To be sure, this is not true of all schools at these levels, but it is more the rule than the exception.

The grade-level patterns of these schools also add to the confusion. Some middle schools include grades 5 and 6, some 5, 6, and 7, some 6 and 7, some 6, 7, and 8, some 7, 8, and 9. Some junior high schools include grades 6 and 7, some 7 and 8, some 7, 8, and 9. Senior secondary schools include any grade combination from 8 through 12.

What does this similarity of organization and administrative practice and confused grading pattern tell us? It tells us very clearly that the mission, purposes, and objectives of these schools are very diffuse, unclear, non-systematic, and non-functional. Boyer (1983) said it very clearly, "what is needed. . . is a clear and coherent vision of what the nation's high schools should be seeking to accomplish" (p. 67).

The confused and confusing grade pattern of middle, junior high, and senior high schools also tells us that there is not a program of education that is consistent with and which follows logically from the objectives and learning programs of elementary schools. If there were, there would not be the confusing array of grade levels for middle or junior high schools, reflecting which ever happens to be in vogue in a particular community. It was proposed in the preceding section on elementary schools that they be divided into two successive cycles of four and three years, with administrative practices supporting achievement of learning objectives at the end of each of these cycles. This basic pattern is also proposed for secondary schools and is based on a recognition of the developmental needs of students in the secondary school age range, the purposes and objectives such schools should serve, and an organization pattern that would enhance achieving those objectives.

Second-Order Change #11. Secondary schools should consist of two successive three-year cycles.

Second-Order Change #12. The first cycle of secondary schools should provide for all students a generic introduction to the basic disciplines of knowledge and the development of effective communication skills.

Second-Order Change #13. The second cycle of secondary schools should encourage students to concentrate in one of four areas of knowledge or vocational development. These four areas are (1) mathematics, (2) natural and physical sciences, (3) arts and humanities, and (4) vocational skill areas.

280

Few would probably argue with Boyer (1983) who contended that a core curriculum at the secondary level should include the following:

- Mastery of Communication Skills
- Literature
- The Arts
- Foreign Language
- History, including American History, Western Civilization, and non-Western Studies
- Social Memberships and Institutions
- Civics
- Science
- Mathemathics
- The Use of Technology
- Health
- Vocational Development

It is not the specific courses that are of debate. Rather, it is the *means* by which the various knowledge areas of the curriculum are organized for effective instruction and related to the learning experiences of previous school years.

The logic of these second-order changes is obvious. The six years remaining after elementary school, could be divided into two cycles of three years each. Each of these two parts would have a different mission, with each being based on (1) a continuum of educational development, (2) the developmental patterns of these age ranges, and (3) a knowledge of the desired result at the completion of senior high school.

Second-Order Change #11 would allow the development of critical thinking skills begun in elementary school to be continued at the high school level. These skills should have been initially developed at the elementary school level. During the first three years of high school, in what could be termed *general high school*, the focus should be on introducing all students to the various disciplines of knowledge, learning the interdependence of these disciplines, and learning how to integrate and synthesize knowledge from the various disciplines. All students would also be expected to master the skills of effective communication. These skills would include written communication, verbal communication, and a functional level of skill in at least one foreign language.

It should be possible to accomplish these objectives within the time and framework suggested. The mission of these general high schools would be more focused than are today's various combinations of middle, junior, and senior high schools. With a more clearly defined mission, resources can be more effectively and efficiently directed towards accomplishing this mission. The intent of these general high schools is to prepare the student for entering a senior high school where specialization is encouraged. To make effective use of such specialization, students must have been exposed to the basic disciplines and have learned how to communicate effectively. Regardless of what area of knowledge specialization a student elects at the senior high level, he/she must have as good a grasp of the world around him/her as is possible to master. The areas of specialization at the senior high level are visualized as areas of knowledge and skill, each one serving a different purpose for different students' needs. The first two, mathematics and the natural and physical sciences, are intended for those who intend to find employment in areas of technology, either following a university education or upon completion of high school pursuing further technical training. The arts and humanities area is intended for those who are primarily interested in the human heritage and the expression and improvement of the ways that persons must learn to work and live with each other. The vocational skill area is intended for those students who plan to enter the world of employment upon completion of high school.

It is not intended that students should concentrate exclusively upon the area of specialization they elect. All students should be exposed to all areas, but they should concentrate in their area of specialization. A proposed distribution of this senior high school curriculum is:

- General core curriculum   20-30%
- Area of specialization   30-40%
- Each of the other three areas 10% (30% total)
- Electives   10%

The general core curriculum would continue a student's development and mastery of communication skills and knowledge of the world about him. Elective courses should be interest-based.

Second-Order Change #14. Secondary schools should operate on the basis of positive sanctions, expecting and treating students as mature and capable of responsible behavior.

This proposal may appear to be obvious and not needed, but it is. There are too few secondary schools that operate on this basis. It is, in fact, the basis on which the entire system and organization of secondary schools must be operated. The developmental patterns and needs of adolescents must be recognized, understood, and used as the basis for framing secondary school expectations. Adolescents are moving towards adulthood — many at an astonishing speed. Their development is towards independence, towards maturity, towards assuming total responsibility for their behavior and their lives. They will test and resist rules in their efforts to break away from dependence and demonstrate their independence. It is often by breaking the rules that adolescents demonstrate their independence to their peers and at the same time measure their own developmental status by testing themselves against established standards. The more rules and regulations there are, the more strongly the message is conveyed to adolescents that they are expected to break them. The more rules, the more confined and restricted they feel when their need is for guidance and support in accepting responsibility for their own behavior.

The question is how can these students best be assisted to achieve this sense of personal responsibility? By imposing more rules and regulations? Definitely not! They can best be helped in this critical developmental period by expecting the type of behavior we expect them to demonstrate as adults, exhibiting a sense of self-worth and responsibility for their decisions and behavior. How can secondary schools foster the achievement of this important objective? First, throw out the current student handbooks that list the countless rules, regulations, and negative sanctions. Substitute a new one that provides a framework of expected positive, adult, mature behavior. On the whole, secondary students know right from wrong; they know the rules of good conduct. Secondary schools must demonstrate in words and action that students are trusted and that they are capable of independent, worthwhile, and responsible behavior.

Second, and closely related to the first notion is the issue of the attitude of the teachers, the administrators, and parents. If the attitude of these critical role models is one of positive expectations, adolescents will be far more likely to respond in kind. But, if adolescents live in a world where these role models exhibit an attitude of distrust, adolescents are likely to also respond in kind.

Secondary schools play an important and critical role in shaping the type of adult into which the adolescent will develop. By exhibiting trust, by encouraging and expecting mature, responsible behavior with academic study, with peers, and with authority figures, the chances are far more likely that these are the qualities these adolescents will exhibit as adults.

Academic program design

The fourth consideration for a conceptual framework for the schools deals with those programs the schools should be responsible for implementing and the goals of these programs. There are essentially two types of academic programs that need to be considered for both elementary and secondary schools. First, there are those which are concerned with permanent and enduring processes, emphases, or content areas. These might include such elements as learning processes in elementary schools, reading comprehension development, and the traditional academic emphases, such as math, science, English, etc. The programs that encompass these activities might be termed "core" to signify that are needed to achieve the primary learning and academic mission of the schools. *Core programs* may be defined as those which have enduring status as the means of achieving prime and fundamental objectives of the schools' mission and which override consideration of other programmatic concerns and priorities.

Currently, programs that could be described as primary serve to achieve the two fundamental objectives that have been used to achieve the two primary purposes of the schools: fostering good citizenship and education for industrial development and competence. The relative emphasis on either of these has shifted over the years, but they have been maintained as the principal purposes of the schools.

As noted earlier, during the decades of the late 1950's, 1960's, and 1970's, social reform became a priority purpose of the schools and overshadowed both of the two primary objectives noted above. Without a clear statement of mission and a conceptual framework within which the social reform objectives could be analyzed for concordance with the mission of the schools, social reform programs were grafted to the schools' programs and were eventually rejected. Such objectives and programs of social reform, if conceived of as ancillary programs in the manner defined here, would have allowed both the schools and the public to have implemented and evaluated such programs and then made a decision whether they should be accorded the status of a primary program. As the situation is now, the merits of these programs, and there were many, have largely been dismissed or negated in the resurgence of the demand for education for industrial development.

The second type of program would be characterized by a short-term, time-limited purpose. It would not detract from the resources necessary to carry out the prime mission of the schools. To implement the program, the educational personnel would need additional specialized training. These programs might be characterized as "ancillary" to indicate that they are not critical to accomplishing the schools' prime mission. *Ancillary programs* may be defined as those which are not inconsistent with the objectives of the primary programs and which do not detract from the achievement or resources of primary programs. They have a specific, usually short-term purpose and are primarily derived from changing or developing demographic and social characteristics of intellectual, educational, or economic value.

284

The shorter-term purposes of ancillary programs are generally appropriate first-order responses to changing environmental conditions. It is possible that they could develop into primary programs over time if their purposes were demonstrated to be of such predominate and overriding importance to the nation that its absence would have a serious, debilitating effect on the national interest.

Ancillary programs can be important contributors to the quality of educational and social life not only of schools, but also of the entire school community. They can enrich the intellectual, social, and emotional lives of both the students of the schools and the parents and other community members of the schools. All such programs that the schools could possibly deliver are neither the prime responsibility of the schools nor appropriate for the schools to deliver. Therefore, there is the need to review and analyze such programs to determine whether their objectives are consistent with the mission of the primary programs. Without such a framework for analysis, the schools will be continually subject to the fads and whims of passing public attention, resulting in dilution of the quality of the primary programs and poorly researched and analyzed ancillary programs.

There are many ancillary programs that are appropriate for the schools to consider implementing. For example, drop-out prevention, child-rearing practices for pregnant teenagers, and programs for abused children are totally appropriate for school implementation. Some programs would be most appropriate for cities but not for rural areas. Some sections of a state will need certain types of programs, while other sections of the state will not. In those areas that face a significant rise of unemployment, it would be appropriate for the schools to implement programs which help students understand and cope with the changing life style of their parents and the emotional and financial stress that accompanies such difficult circumstances. The potential for such programs is endless, but each must be considered within the context of the schools' mission and the criteria for such programs. These issues lead to Second-Order Change #15.

Second-Order Change #15. All programs offered by the schools should be defined as either core or ancillary. Core programs should receive priority resource allocation.

There is one other point concerning ancillary programs that needs to be considered. Some of these programs will be promoted by persons with strong convictions, and the emphasis and fervor these adherents often bring with them to support such programs can make it difficult to reject their pleas and demands to institute such programs immediately. It is not in the best interests of children to institute such programs until they have been subjected to careful and extensive review and analysis and a determination that such program is appropriate for an evaluative trial.

The implementation of AIDS educational programs in the schools is an example of such a shorter-term, first-order educational purpose. Other examples of such programs are ensuring all children have their shots, the development of drop-out prevention programs, various programs funded by the federal government, and so forth. It is interesting to note that most of the attention, rhetoric, political harangues, and resource allocations (other than the percentage of funds that go to teacher salaries) are devoted to these shorter-lived, first-order purposes of education.

Each type of program must be consistent with the long- and short-term purposes of the education system, logically related to the mission and conceptual framework of the schools, and within the capabilities, responsibility and authority of the teachers to achieve.

It is interesting to examine which programs and purposes become assigned or attached to the schools. Although such will not be discussed here, such a review reveals what can happen to an educational system when there is not a clearly defined and limited set of purposes for the schools, supported by a conceptual framework and logically related program design. Although many of these ancillary programs can be implemented through the schools and be easily incorporated into the conceptual framework presented below, when these ancillary programs have no logical relationship to the prime mission of the schools or when, by their very nature, they establish additional purposes for the schools, unnecessary time, energy, and resources are siphoned away from the primary purposes of the schools.

The basic decision that has to be made about most of these ancillary programs is whether the schools are to be solely concerned with intellectual and academic matters or whether the schools are also to serve as a social reform and human service delivery system. If the latter is to be the case, then an entirely new set of purposes, program structure, and operations has to be established for the schools. New types of personnel, and many more personnel, will have to be prepared. Program priorities and costs will have to be developed and then integrated with the priorities and costs for delivering the traditional academic and intellectual programs of the schools.

This discussion is not to belittle those ancillary programs that have been demonstrated to make valuable contributions in improving the quality of life for children. Clearly, the social conditions many children live in have a serious, delimiting effect on their chances of maximizing their educational and intellectual potential. Should the schools provide the social programs to help alleviate these conditions, or should they restrict themselves to the intellectual and academic programs they can best deliver, while trying to ensure the coordination of service delivery by other agencies to these children?

Before American public schools can deliver educational programs effectively to certain children, their social conditions need to be remedied. For example, drop-outs and potential drop-outs. What is the school's role with these students? The number of these students is increasing daily. They represent a lost national resource, and, more importantly, a tragic loss of human spirit. Should these students be allowed to drop out? Should they be required to stay in school and disrupt the learning of other students? Should their parents be required to provide for their continuing education? The conditions that force these students to leave school are primarily social in nature, not intellectual or academic, except as a secondary factor. The question is whether it is within the mission and capabilities of the schools to attack these social ills directly in an effort to change them or leave the social programs to those who are trained and have the resources to deal with them. The cost to the schools in providing for these ancillary programs is very great. Is the school the most appropriate agency then to deliver these programs? School personnel are not trained to plan or implement these socially oriented programs, and they detract from the primary mission of the schools.

If the American public wishes the schools to fulfill its primary mission, and serve these other purposes as well, then the schools need to be re-conceptualized as an educational and human service agency. This would require significant changes in the preparation of personnel, the addition of significant new types and numbers of personnel, the re-training of existing personnel, new physical facilities, and the addition of a new bureaucratic system. Since the cost of these additions would be significant and would detract from the need to significantly improve students' learning, and since other existing agencies could meet these social needs, such a plan does not seem worth the additional expense.

Allocation of resources

Currently, most schools are funded on the basis of enrollment. Although, this seems an equitable means for ensuring that all children are provided the same basic amount of tax funds for their education, there are three fundamental flaws associated with this method. First, it is a concept built around the notion of raw material. That is, children are so many units of equivalent raw material that can be processed uniformly. However, this method of allocating funds denies certain realities. First, *all children do not have equal needs*. It costs more to deliver adequate programs to some children than it does to other children, and the current method of allocating funds contradicts our professed belief in the concept of individual differences.

287

Second, it ignores the fact that some educational programs are more expensive to deliver than others, yet the current, most common procedure for allocating funds does not consider individual program costs, nor does it allow such programs to be developed at the level closest to that at which they are to be implemented. The current means of allocating funds occurs at the central office of each school system, with funds allocated, with some small differential, on the basis of school level and the number of students enrolled. This method does not allow for those closest to the students (the teachers) to determine the program needs and resources best suited for enhancing the learning capabilities of their students.

Third, the current method does not allow those most knowledgeable and closely associated with the needs of students to develop the program priorities necessary to meet the needs. Those who are the most knowledgeable and who have the responsibility for delivering instruction should have the majority involvement for determining the program design to meet identified needs. Allocation of resources should then be based on the costs of the prioritized programs, not the number of students served.

A recent study by the Public School Forum of North Carolina (Pechman, 1987) made clear the consequences of current allocation procedures. The design of this study included three goals: time use analysis, working conditions survey, and an applications transfer study. The findings will not surprise many teachers. It was found that decision-making does not sufficiently involve teachers and other key staff; the school budget is not controlled by the site manager; building-level staff are rarely included in schoolwide planning and decision-making; and there is a disparity in the basic quality of school facilities and availability of resources.

To develop the most appropriate and adequate program based on student need, the nature and type of educational program to be offered must be generated at the level of the teacher. Program development must begin at the level closest to the point where it will be delivered, and this means developing the program on the basis of the teacher's knowledge of the students and their needs and capabilities.

This concept for generating program development is related directly to the proposals for allowing teachers to be associated with and responsible for student learning for more than one year. This would allow teachers to plan programs over an extended period, to present the costs necessary to implement the program plan and, when allocated funds, be assured that such would be available for the duration of the planned period. It would also permit teachers to modify the program plan and priorities on the basis of the funds allocated. This discussion leads directly to the presentation of Second-Order Change #16 and 17.

Second-Order Change #16. The allocation of resources to schools should be on the basis of the costs associated with a particular program.

Second-Order Change #17. Educational programs must be developed by teachers at the school level, forwarded through the Academic Planning Unit for coordination, and delivered to the local board of education (public and teacher representatives) for review, action, and allocation of funds.

These two changes would accomplish several important goals. First, program planning would be the responsibility of teachers. Second, they would allow program priorities and allocation of funding to be determined by teachers. Third, they do not require additional funds for program implementation. They simply allow the programs and their priorities to be established and directed by teachers.

It should be noted here that the total school system budget should be allocated to the local board of education. This includes funds from all sources — federal, state, local, and private. It would be this board's responsibility to determine allocations of resources according to the program priorities as determined by each school and academic program planning unit. It would, however, be the responsibility of each school's teachers to determine salary allocations and increases within whatever broad guidelines were established by either the local board and/or the state.

Summary

This chapter has discussed three of the critical elements that are necessary components of a conceptual framework for the schools. These are the organization of schools, school program design, and a change of method for allocating resources to schools. The changes recommended are consistent with the prime mission focus and knowledge base proposed for the schools. The changes recommended must be seen in an integrated fashion. One change by itself will not be sufficient to cause the coordinated improvement in student learning outcomes, which is the fundamental objective of educational change or reform. The organization of the schools must be altered to allow learning experiences to be implemented in a manner that will optimize their learning impact. The schools' programs must differentiate between those which are critical for achieving the prime mission of the schools and those which are not. And the allocation of resources to schools must be sufficient to adequately fund the primary programs, and it must be based on program cost, not school attendance figures.

13 Teacher preparation programs: second-order changes

The three previous chapters have outlined the third-order changes required to coordinate educational improvement efforts in public and teacher education, and they proposed a series of second-order changes for public education. Obviously, such changes in public education could not occur unless the personnel responsible for delivering educational services in the public schools were prepared to do so. This means that the format, content, and instructional processes of teacher education programs would have to change dramatically to do so effectively.

As was discussed in Chapters 4 and 10, the mission of the public schools should provide the orientation for continuing improvement of teacher preparation programs. To provide the context for this process to be implemented, changes in the structure, faculty composition, and curricula of universities and teacher preparation programs would be necessary. These include generic changes at both the university and teacher preparation program levels and specific changes in elementary, secondary, and K-12 teacher preparation programs. This chapter presents and discusses 16 second-order changes related to these generic and specific problem areas.

Recommendations concerning teacher education faculty

As was indicated in Chapter 4, the main problems in teacher preparation programs stem from the faculty of the schools, colleges, and departments of education. It is only logical, therefore, to begin with changes in the faculty to cause the other changes that are necessary in structure, purpose, objectives, and curriculum. Therefore, the initial second-order change deals with the faculty of these educational units.

Second-Order Change #18. Tenure for faculty should be removed in favor of time-limited contracts.

There are a number of caveats to this proposed change. First, there would have to be assured procedures to guard against capricious and unwarranted dismissals of faculty. This means that there would have to be specific objectives of the preparation program against which the contributions of the faculty member could be measured.

Second, the weighting of research and scholarship, teaching effectiveness, and service contributions would have to be modified and specified for salary increases and continued employment so that each faculty member could determine how to allocate his/her time within the responsibilities assigned to him/her. University administrators would have to accept the fact that, if they expect faculty to play a leadership role in improving teacher education programs and public schools, the reward structure for such effort will have to be comparable to efforts expended in research activities.

Third, and finally, there would have to be vastly improved and more valid measures of assessing each of the three areas mentioned above. Currently, our measures for assessing these dimensions of faculty activity are poor.

No doubt this proposed change will receive little support, especially from higher education faculty. Cries of anguish and assertions of the author's naïveté will certainly be raised, and strong, eloquent and learned arguments demonstrating the need and value of tenure will be brought forth. The need for tenure to defend the citadel of academic freedom will be cited. But what about the other side of the argument, i.e., academic responsibility? How responsible have higher education faculty members been in ensuring that education for our schools' teachers has been afforded the resources needed to accomplish this mission? How responsible have higher education faculty members been in understanding the complexities of preparing teachers to work and teach in today's technologically and sociologically complex world? How responsible have higher education faculty members been in coming out of their discipline's ivory tower and assisting schools of education to better prepare teachers? How many have taught in a public school to better understand the range and depth of problems encountered by public school teachers?

This proposal for change is not just an angry response to the failings of higher education faculty with these issues. It is an effort to jolt these faculty members into thinking about their responsibilities in a more comprehensive manner than they have in the past. The need for inter-disciplinary thinking, the need for integration of learning, the need for assumption of responsibility for concepts and events outside one's own little discipline enclave, and the need for revitalizing faculty all demand a new and changed perception on the part of higher education faculty. However, unless the protective mantle of tenure is removed, it is unlikely that faculty will assume these responsibilities and engage in these behaviors. Second-order change must be imposed from forces outside the system, so it is highly unlikely that faculty would propose such a change themselves. Removing tenure from higher education faculty would do more to revitalize faculty than any other action possible, and it could be done without jeopardizing academic freedom. It would remove job security from those who probably abuse the protections of tenure the most, and, for those who do not abuse tenure, job security should not be a problem.

Second-Order Change #19. Boards of trustees should establish and implement a reward system and plan of resource allocation, that recognize equally those programs which emphasize research and scholarship (development of knowledge) and those professional programs that emphasize the development of practitioner competence (demonstration of knowledge).

The rationale for this recommended change is obvious. Faculty members and university administrators have not generated the conditions or rules for rewarding faculty efforts to improve practitioner competence. Until education faculty are provided the same resources and rewards for working to improve the knowledge base and skills of education personnel, we cannot expect to see significant improvement and change in teacher education programs. It is not likely that faculty and/or university administrators will generate these rules or conditions if left to their efforts. As stated by Wilson Elkins, retired president of the University of Maryland (1954-1978), "It is very difficult for an institution to improve itself from within. There are too many vested interests," (Callcott, 1981, P. 172). Elkins also stated, "The departments determine what happens in a university" (P. 94). Since this observation is consistent with the proposition of second-order change, that the rules for such change cannot be generated from within the organization, it must become the responsibility of an agent outside the organization, in this case, the boundary personnel of trustees, to generate both the conditions and rules for such change.

Second-Order Change #20. The orientation of faculty within schools of education must be dramatically changed.

The meaning of this proposed change is that faculty in schools of education must change their perception of what it is they are about. Their current prevailing attitude of acceptance of the status quo must change. They must begin to accept and act upon the conviction that the world of public education needs and demands teachers who are prepared to assume more and different responsibilities, that children need to learn more, and to learn differently, and that the success of such efforts is dependent upon a revitalized education faculty.

293

It is improbable that all, or even most, of today's education faculty will be able to make such changes, particularly those who are in the older age brackets. It is vital that new faculty members, hired to replace those older faculty who resign or retire, or hired to swell the ranks as enrollments in schools of education increase, have a commitment to the new mission for the public schools. It will not be sufficient to hire new faculty members in the same image of those older faculty members who retire. These new faculty members must be able to contribute to the development of a new conceptual base for education, and this conceptual base must revolve around the mission of public schools. This mission is addressed in the following two proposals for second-order change.

Mission of teacher education programs

Second-Order Change #21. The prime objective of teacher education programs should be to teach how learning occurs and is maximized in children and how to develop and increase their personal-social competence.

Second-Order Change #22. The second prime objective of teacher preparation programs is to provide teacher candidates the knowledge base and skills necessary to effectively use a variety of techniques to foster maximum learning and personal-social development in children.

If these two second-order changes in the objectives of teacher preparation programs are accepted, then a number of other changes in the structure, organization, and curriculum of these programs must be made. However, before continuing to a discussion of these issues, it is necessary to describe some of the implications of these two second-order changes.

These second-order changes provide a focus for teacher education programs that is consistent with Second-Order Changes 1 & 2 presented in Chapter 10. Such a coordination of purpose does not currently exist. There is, in fact, little agreement among the variety of purposes existing in public schools and those espoused by teacher preparation programs. A number of reasons are responsible for this diversity of purpose. Certainly, the decentralized structure of the educational system in America explains a great deal of the diversity. Without a systematic process for examining the goals and objectives of the thousands of school systems and the hundreds of teacher preparation programs, there is currently no means for ensuring a common prime purpose.

Program structure

If the faculty conditions and the mission of schools of education change, the next logical element of teacher education programs that must be examined is the structure of these programs. The current structure of teacher education generally follows a model of two years of liberal studies, and, for elementary education students, a year of education courses followed by a semester of student teaching with a semester for electives somewhere along the line. For secondary education students, the general pattern is two years of liberal studies followed by a year of acquiring enough courses in a discipline to qualify for a major. In some disciplines it requires more than a year to acquire sufficient courses for a major. This academic specialization is followed by a semester of methods of teaching, two-to-four courses in professional education, and a semester of student teaching (Huling and Hall, 1982). There are exceptions to this structure, but, in general, it is the one followed. Second-Order Change #23 addresses this issue.

Second-Order Change #23. The structure and sequence of education for teacher education students must be totally revised.

The objective set for teacher education students is to enable them to become as competent as possible. To achieve this goal, they need to know as much as possible about how learning takes place in children. The "what" of the question is, what structure and sequence of education will best achieve this goal? The following proposed changes for more adequately preparing teacher education students are generic in nature. Specific proposals for preparing elementary and secondary teachers are offered in following sections. The following proposals are not premised on the assumption that an adequate teacher education program can be accomplished within four years. Despite arguments to the contrary (e.g., Hawley, 1985), it is difficult to imagine how an adequate teacher preparation program could be accomplished in less than five years. It is not, however, the time that should determine the nature of the program. Rather, the components and requirements necessary to develop the most adequate program must determine the length of the program. The length of the program is a secondary consideration and a by-product of the necessary program components.

To become an excellent teacher, a prospective teacher must know how children learn, and she/he must have the knowledge, skills, and methods to foster such learning most effectively, and a content to impart to students. It is also vital that teachers know the developmental aspects of the age level she/he will teach and the means for fostering the personal-social competence of this age group. It is not essential that a teacher have a background in the liberal arts. It is useful and desirable, but not vital. A liberal arts background is most useful for becoming a well-educated person, but the most useful part of a liberal arts curriculum, that of learning how to integrate such knowledge, is lacking from most liberal arts curriculums.

The structure and sequence of program components proposed below are designed to emphasize the most vital elements necessary for becoming an excellent teacher. Although the liberal arts are not neglected, this component is proposed in a significantly modified fashion than has been the case previously.

Most university students do not have to declare their intention to major in education until the end of their second year of study. This is too late for a student planning a career in education. Such declaration should be made before the end of the freshman year of study. The freshman year should be spent in sampling from each of the major areas of the liberal arts with an emphasis on developing communication skills.

In the second year of study, the prospective teacher should begin work in education, with an emphasis on cognitive science and its applications and child development, with some additional work in the liberal arts. The third year should include more advanced work in cognitive science, and the beginning of directed child study and observation with various age ranges. Additionally, a third-year student in teacher education should begin to concentrate in an academic discipline. This holds true regardless of whether the prospective teacher expects to teach at the elementary or secondary level. During the fourth year, a prospective teacher should spend more time in the public schools, again with different age groups, and have responsibility for teaching small groups at different age levels. Fourth-year students should also complete requirements for a dual major, one in cognitive science or child/adolescent development, and the second in an academic discipline. Work in professional education with an emphasis on instructional technology, small group instruction, the ethics of education, and educational decision-making should be included during this year.

The fifth and sixth years should be spend completing any necessary course work and in an extended internship under a minimum of two supervisors (each at a different time). This experience should be combined with a series of weekly seminars focused on integrating the knowledge and skills attained during the first four years of study. Time also should be allowed for electing courses or experiences that would allow a student to improve areas of weakness.

The intent of the above structure and sequence is designed to achieve four goals. The first goal is to avoid a lockstep progression from a series of liberal arts courses, through an academic discipline, through professional education courses, through student teaching to graduation. Rather, it is proposed that an integrated series of courses from the major areas of study throughout the student's program be implemented, with the courses from the liberal arts chosen to enhance and compliment those components most critical for a teacher. The focus is on integration of knowledge, for as Yeats

296

pointed out, specialization without integration is dangerous (Keller, 1983). Almost 50 years ago, James (1940) made a similar observation. He wrote, "The intellectual life of man consists almost wholly in his substitution of a conceptual order for the perceptual order in which his experiences originally came" (p. 51). Further, Bell (1966) noted that the rationale for general education has severely eroded and its intellectual structure has lost coherence. These observations reinforce the comments made in Chapter 10 concerning the need for integration of knowledge on the part of the learner, and that the liberal studies have failed in this critical assignment.

Second, the sequence of courses proposed is designed to foster an early identification with the profession of education, rather than with an academic discipline. This is considered vital for all professional educators.

Third, the earliest introduction to the world of education is made in those areas most vital for a prospective teacher, i.e., cognitive science and child development. It is proposed that early and extended work in these areas be taken so that when the student gets to the point of choosing an academic discipline, it will be with a background of cognitive science and its applications to the school setting. This should force the student to begin considering the ways that his/her discipline emphasis could best be taught to public school students. This is in contrast to learning the discipline first and then having scant attention paid to the implications of learning at some future date.

Fourth, there is provision for an extended and graduated series of clinical and field experiences timed to run concurrently with the theory being learned in classroom courses. The key to success of this intent is the timing and the amount, frequency, and immediacy of the supervision provided. To be most effective, such supervision and feedback on performance should be immediate and frequent.

The curriculum for prospective teachers must also be changed significantly, but these changes are specified separately under the sections dealing with elementary and secondary education later in this chapter.

There is another aspect to the structure of teacher education programs that must be changed. This is the control that they have over those students who wish to become teachers. In most institutions of higher education that have teacher preparation programs, the only students that are actually education majors are those preparing to teach in elementary schools. Secondary school teachers are generally majors in an academic department (Huling and Hall, 1982). Also, in most institutions, students who wish to teach music, physical education, etc., major in that department or particular school. At the graduate level much the same pattern prevails. Schools of education generally control the programs of educational administration and school counseling. Programs in school psychology are to be found in departments of psychology and schools of education. Programs in school social work are generally found in units outside the school of education. It is this mixed control that creates the different orientations and non-education based professional identification of many professional educators discussed in Chapter 10. In order to provide a professional identification with the profession of education and to ensure that there is provided a common base of knowledge for all professional educators, Second-Order Change #24 is proposed.

Second-Order Change #24. All students who intend to work in the public schools as professional educators, at either the undergraduate or graduate level, should have their primary major in the education unit and have their curriculum determined by the education unit.

Administrators and faculty in schools of education may support this proposal privately for various reasons. Publicly, they may not be as supportive, for fear of antagonizing their campus colleagues. Administrators and faculty outside the school of education will probably not support this proposal. Two reasons will account for most of this opposition, but only one will be openly discussed. The public reason for not supporting this proposal will revolve around the argument that the quality of education students will receive under this proposal will decline unless the discipline faculty are in control of determining the students' curriculum. This is a serious concern and one that must be carefully considered. If it is a valid concern, that the academic quality of students would decline under this proposed change, then it should not be implemented. However, if we accept as valid the impressions that most people currently hold of the quality of our teaching force and education programs, it is obvious that something must be changed. It is also clear that the most serious concern is directed at the secondary schools, the teachers of which have the least amount of contact and work in professional education courses. Further, under the changes proposed in this chapter, the amount of work in an academic discipline would not decrease significantly. *When* students took their work in an academic discipline would change, and there would be more work taken in professional education, but this would be a significantly different type and sequence of professional education work than has previously been the case.

The private reason that administrators and faculty outside the school of education would not support this proposal for change is that they would fear the loss of student credit hours. Since unit funding is based on the number of student credit hours generated, this might result in the loss of unit funding (Freeman, 1980). Administrators want to avoid a loss of funding at all costs, even if the change proposed would result in improved learning on the part of the prospective teachers, for it is the level of funding that drives an academic unit.

There is one final generic change that needs to be made in teacher education; indeed, throughout all of higher education. This has to do with the manner in which educational programs are financed. As briefly mentioned earlier, educational units are supported on the basis of their student productivity. The data from the Peseau studies (1980, 1982) reveal this quite clearly. But the amount of funding is not the only serious problem. Even more serious is the basis on which such funding is provided. The current basis of funding is student credit hours, generated as these hours are translated into equivalent full-time students. This is, by far, the most common means of determining resource allocations to higher education units. What this process ignores is the differences in cost of delivering different types of programs to students.

For example, a department of history is concerned with teaching a variety of classes to students. However, the professors of history do not have to be concerned with the applied aspects of what they teach. They do not have responsibilities for supervising their students as do education faculty members. Second-Order Change #25 is designed to change this situation.

Second-Order Change #25. Resource allocations to academic units should be based on the costs of program delivery, not student credit hours *generated.*

This proposal is consistent with one made in 1985 by the Commission for Educational Quality to the Southern Region Educational Board (Commission for Educational Quality, 1985). This proposal would require significant changes in the operations of most academic units. Those that are applied would have to develop accurate cost figures for delivering their programs. These costs may result in a need to limit enrollments to the number that could be taught in a quality fashion with the resources available. On the other hand, non-applied programs may have to accept more students since the costs of delivering those programs are not as expensive as applied ones. Consideration would also have to be given to the differences in delivering applied and non-applied programs at the undergraduate and graduate levels.

Elementary education

The preceding discussion has focused on those generic changes in teacher education programs that must be considered if significant change and improvement are to be achieved. This section deals specifically with those related to elementary education. The following section deals with specific changes in secondary education.

There are two types of changes recommended for elementary education. The first set concerns those changes necessary to provide consistency with those changes proposed previously for elementary schools. The second set is concerned with changes necessary in schools of education even if those changes proposed earlier were not to be accepted or implemented. These are changes necessary in schools of education that, under any circumstances, must be made if public education is to be expected to increase learning and improve the personal-social development of children.

Second-Order Change #26. Elementary school teachers should not be recommended for certification unless they have completed two academic majors, one in either cognitive science or child development and the other in a content area such as reading, special education, mathematics, etc.

There are two reasons for this proposed change. First, each elementary school teacher should have a major in one of the two most critical areas for an elementary school teacher, cognitive science or child development. In addition, each teacher must be expert in a content area. The structure and organization of an elementary school, where a teacher is responsible for teaching all subjects to one particular group of children, should prohibit all elementary teachers from majoring in the same content area. That would not allow the necessary expertise in all content areas to be available within each elementary school. The objective is to develop a cadre of teachers in each elementary school who collectively possess expertise in each of the subject areas of the school's curriculum. Through appropriate hiring procedures, it would be possible to ensure that the teaching force of each school represented all necessary academic backgrounds. This change would provide for each elementary school to have an expert in each curriculum subject available as an in-school consultant. The achievement of this objective must begin with the change proposed in the curriculum of the elementary school teacher education program.

Second-Order Change #27. Students in elementary school teacher education programs must be prepared to assume responsibility for the same class of students for a three- or four-year period.

Teachers in today's elementary schools are conditioned by experience and training to expect a different class of students every year. If this cycle were changed to being responsible for the same class of students for a three-year cycle, it would require the development of a different attitude towards teaching, a different set of expectations and skills for assessing child development and learning rates, and a different set of skills for planning the curriculum and monitoring student progress. Again, the achievement of this change is dependent on change in the teacher preparation program.

300

Second-Order Change #28. Elementary school teacher education students must decide during their second year of study to concentrate at either the K-3 level or the 4-6 level.

The reason for this change follows from the changes proposed for modifying the organization and curriculum emphases of elementary schools. During the K-3 periods, the emphasis is on learning processes. This means those education students concentrating at this level must understand more of the developmental stages of children within this age range, and the means of initiating and enhancing learning processes with children of these ages. Prospective teachers for grades 4-6 must emphasize more the initial content of various subjects and so must receive a different curriculum and develop a different set of skills while in training.

Second-Order Change #29. Prospective elementary school teachers must be prepared to assume new dimensions of responsibility, including K-12 curriculum coordination, hiring and firing personnel, colleague evaluation, and determining colleagues' salary increases.

The development of the knowledge and skills necessary to assume these responsibilities is absolutely essential if the profession of education is ever to slip its bounds of captivity and become a true profession. As was discussed in Chapters 10 and 11, the education of children will best be accomplished by having the practitioners of education assume the responsibilities for the learning of children. In order to achieve this objective, these personnel must be prepared to assume these responsibilities by receiving appropriate training in the attitudes, concepts, and techniques that will allow them to successfully carry out such responsibilities.

Second-Order Change #30. Ideally, the curriculum for prospective elementary school teachers will reflect the following components and time allocations.

Component	Credit Hours	Time Allocation
1. Liberal Studies	45	3 Semesters
2. Cognitive Science & Child Development	30	2 Semesters
3. Academic Content Area	30	2 Semesters
4. Professional Education	24	1.5 Semesters
5. Clinical Experiences/Internship	33	2 Semesters
6. Electives	15	1 Semester
Totals	177	11.5 Semesters

This will appear an inordinately long preparation program to most readers knowledgeable about the length of teacher education programs. It

301

will especially appear long to those who are still resisting changing the typical four-year teacher preparation program to five years. The program proposed above will require essentially six years to complete, excluding any summer work. A brief description of the rationale for each of the components and the suggested amount of work in each follows.

Liberal Studies

The hours for this component of the recommended program is lower than in most teacher education programs for several reasons. First, liberal studies programs have not generally achieved one of the major purposes they use to justify their programs' own existence at practically all college and university programs — that is the goal of teaching students to develop their rational abilities, their cognitive skills, and the qualities of their mind (Carbone, 1980) This goal has not been achieved to the extent that liberal arts faculty suggest or desire. Fischer (Bowen, 1987), suggests these U.S. college students too often fall short in the ability to think critically and reason their way to a sound conclusion. Fischer believes these students are trained to giving the "answer, as opposed to learning how to make a good argument" (p. 61). Some experts lay the blame for this at the doorstep of America's colleges, saying that they fail in their vaunted claim to teach students to think critically. If this assertion is valid, there may be a number of reasons. Kitchener and King (Bowen, 1987) have advanced the argument that college students are not yet mature enough to learn the judgmental processes that must precede critical thinking. They assert that such critical thinking is a developmental process that does not appear until the middle 20's. The work of Jean Piaget (Hunt and Sullivan, 1974) suggests that logical thought begins with concrete operational thought, about the age of seven, and develops, beginning around age 11, into formal operational thought, which is the capacity to utilize abstract thought (Hunt and Sullivan, 1974). Kitchener and King (Bowen, 1974) point out that Piaget was dealing with the development of logical thought, as opposed to their concern with judgmental decision-making, which involves more than the ability to think logically. Thus, one possible reason liberal studies may not be able to teach students to think critically is that students lack the maturity to render the judgments that such thinking requires. They may be able to think logically, as would be expected in fields such as mathematics, but they may not be reflect that skill in the social sciences.

Another possible reason that liberal arts studies have not been able to teach students to think critically is that the professors of this component have never been taught how to teach such skills. Most professors of the courses in the liberal arts are well versed in their subject matter but have

302

had no work in pedagogy and, therefore, have not been trained to teach critical thinking skills.

A third reason for the lack of success in teaching critical thinking skills in the liberal arts is that each of the program areas within this component is concerned primarily with teaching only its subject matter and not the integration or integrative skills necessary to synthesize knowledge from a variety of content areas. This is a particularly difficult task to accomplish when teacher education students, as well as those planning careers as social workers, nurses, mental health workers, receive only a passing introduction to the liberal arts. These students often take a variety of unrelated courses from separate disciplines with no effort made by the faculty at integration (Ducharme, 1980). The traditional indifference and hostility by liberal arts faculty displayed towards teacher education students exacerbates this situation (Ducharme, 1980). Since integration of knowledge must take place in the mind of the learner, it is understandable how the above factors negate the potential of a liberal arts curriculum.

Freeman (1980) suggested that the current management systems of universities shape the form and content of liberal education, not that conceptions of liberal education shape the management procedures.

A fourth reason for the failure of liberal arts to be able to teach critical thinking is that this is a skill dependent on being learned at an early age, and success with it at a later age depends upon the effectiveness of this earlier learning. This was a major consideration in the recommendation for emphasizing cognitive science and learning processes in the early elementary years.

Whatever the reason, liberal arts programs have not been successful in teaching critical thinking to students. Since they have not been successful, one major reason for requiring extensive work in this component is removed. Instead, a lesser amount of work in this component is suggested, with the work taken under the direction and control of education faculty. This work should be specifically chosen to complement the goals of the teacher education program. It is recommended that such work be focused on communication skills, psychology and sociology, history and the development of civilization, and international relations. A lesser amount of work in the sciences is suggested unless a student majors in one of these disciplines.

To accomplish this goal, another second-order change is required, since currently, the structure of most university requirements for liberal studies mandates that all students should be exposed to the basic sets of knowledge. Second-order change #32, which is specified in the following change section, addresses this issue.

Cognitive Science and Child Development

As emphasized throughout this book, this component of teacher education and public education is considered the most critical for improving learning outcomes in children. These elements must be thoroughly understood by teachers, and, as such, they require significantly more study than is currently required in teacher education programs. Actually, they should require the equivalent of a university major if these elements are to become the knowledge base of the profession of education. It is not only learning and understanding each of these emphases that is critical, but also learning how each of these emphases is interdependent with each other and how the schools' curriculum must be developed from a knowledge of this integration. The development of this knowledge will require at least one year of study.

Academic Content Areas

As indicated earlier, each elementary school teacher should have two academic majors, one in cognitive science or child development and one in a subject matter field. The reason for this is to ensure that each elementary school has at least one expert in each of the subjects to be taught in the elementary school. It is not just a matter of allowing teacher education students to choose a subject matter field, and a collection of courses within it. The courses selected should be more than a random selection; they should be chosen on the basis of a logical rationale to achieve such purposes as understanding the structure and framework of the discipline and the sequence of courses that will most readily achieve this goal.

Professional Education Courses

Currently, most teacher education programs require a small number of courses dealing with child development and learning theory. These would no longer be necessary if the recommendation for requiring cognitive science or child development as major concentrations for all elementary teacher education students was implemented. Instead, a new set of professional education courses revolving around the following will be necessary: ethics of education, K-12 curriculum coordination, consultation theory and methods, methods of teacher assessment, education of the handicapped, child assessment, small group organization and dynamics, and the use of technology in enhancing learning. Of particular relevance and need would be courses in curriculum planning, development, and organization on the basis of learning styles and rates, and a series of courses designed to integrate the four major components of study, i.e., liberal arts, the academic content area major, the cognitive science and child development major, and the professional education coursework.

Clinical Experiences

Logically sequencing and integrating clinical experiences for teachers is as vital as logically sequencing and integrating all other learning experiences. Clinical experiences should be planned to coincide with and complement the didactic courses of the students. Thus, students should gradually be exposed to real school conditions and be expected to assume increasing responsibility for all aspects of being a professional educator. The final year of preparation should be a full-year internship in which students begin the school year with all other teachers and end it when all other teachers do.

Besides the critical nature of integrating such clinical experiences with didactic course work, the key to successful clinical experiences is the nature and type of supervision provided. All clinical experiences must be closely observed, critiqued according to the objectives for the experience, and provided immediate feedback to the student concerning his/her performance. Appropriate and effective supervision depends on sufficient contact with the student to be able to provide the supervision as needed. It cannot be dependent on university supervisors coming to the school once every two weeks to supervise a student. Thus, education faculty should not be responsible for providing supervision to their students. This responsibility should be turned over to the public school faculty who should have sole responsibility for determining if a student has successfully completed a particular clinical experience.

However, not all school systems have the inclination, resources, or sufficient and appropriately trained faculty to undertake this responsibility. School systems that are interested in serving as a host for clinical experiences for teacher education students should meet criteria established for such a purpose. This could be done on a state, regional, or national basis, although this author's preference would be for a currently approved national accrediting body, such as NCATE, to assume this responsibility. Such school systems should be required to provide more than a cooperating teacher to supervise the work of the student. Providing seminars by experienced teachers, exposure to a variety of grade levels, types of schools, and a host of other professionally enriching experiences should be expected of such systems.

Second-Order Change #31. The National Council for the Accreditation of Teacher Education should develop criteria for approving school systems that wish to provide student teaching and internship experiences for educational personnel. States should require such approval for teacher education programs before placing their students for such experiences.

Electives

As described previously, elective courses should be used to strengthen demonstrated areas of weakness in a student. This objective means that a system of assessment, monitoring, evaluation, and consultation must be in place to ensure that students are constantly kept aware of their progress and needs.

Required structural changes in elementary education programs

The changes in elementary education programs recommended above are necessary to prepare elementary teachers to assume those new responsibilities caused by those second-order changes specified previously for elementary schools. Two other second-order changes are necessary to ensure that these changes can be achieved in elementary education programs. These have to do with changes in the structure of these programs within the campus education unit, but they will also require changes in university governance mechanisms.

Second-Order Change #32. Responsibility for determining all teacher education curriculum components should be under the direction of faculty in the education unit.

This means that those faculty members who understand the requirements for becoming an excellent teacher and who have the responsibility for ensuring that prospective teachers are prepared excellently have the authority for determining the program and experiences necessary to produce a teacher at a defensible level of excellence. Currently, faculty in campus education units are responsible for the quality of their teacher education graduates, but they have only limited authority for determining the nature of the curriculum for these students. The often heard argument that teacher education is an all-campus responsibility is a spurious one. There may be, and usually is, an all-campus coordination and control of teacher education programs. This coordination and control are usually exercised diffusely , but when blame is assigned for a lack of quality in teacher education programs or students, it is only the faculty of the education unit that are specified. It is time to quit kidding ourselves. If we want high quality teachers, we must provide the teacher education faculty with both the responsibility and authority for determining the quality of these programs. If they fail in this assignment, they should be dismissed from their positions.

306

Second-Order Change #33. All programs preparing personnel to work in public schools, at both the undergraduate and graduate levels, should be under the control of faculty in the education unit.

This proposal for change is similar to Second-Order Change #32. It suggests that any programs preparing teachers that are currently responsible to an academic unit other than the education unit should be administratively responsible to the education unit. To improve the quality of teacher education programs and learning outcomes in our public schools, it is just not the schools and teacher education programs that must change. Significant alterations in the attitudes of all university faculty and the structure of university governance will have to take place to ensure improved quality of our public schools. An interdependent, complex set of factors determines the quality and quantity of children's learning. It is not possible to tinker with one aspect and expect significant change or improvement. The entire fabric and process of the educational network must be changed and improved in a coordinated fashion if significant improvements in children's learning outcomes are to be achieved.

Required changes in secondary education programs

There have been few changes in secondary schools or the preparation of secondary school teachers in decades. Lasley and Applegate (1982) state that current beliefs and assumptions about the nature and content of secondary teacher preparation must be reexamined. These authors concluded that critical questions needed to be asked and some fundamental assumptions about secondary teacher preparation challenged.

Huling and Hall (1982) have suggested that the high school is among the best known and least understood institutions in America. These authors concluded, from a review of recent literature on secondary education, that there was very little written concerning the interrelations that must exist within a high school. Also, according to these authors, while catalog descriptions of secondary teacher preparation programs may appear inadequate, the picture becomes worse under close examination. These authors concluded that many of the reasons for these inadequate programs were beyond the control of teacher education faculty and the result of institutional forces that resist change in teacher education.

Both high schools and secondary education programs have remained resistant to change (Boyer, 1983; Confrey, 1982; Ducharme, 1982; Goodall and Bunke, 1980). What changes need to be made to bring about the necessary modifications and improvements in preparation programs necessary to implement the type of second-order changes proposed for

307

secondary education? These changes are presented in the following discussions.

Second-Order Changes 22-27, 29, 30, 32 and 33 also apply to secondary education programs. These changes are particularly important if significant improvements in secondary school students' learning are to be obtained.

The current format for preparation of secondary school teachers does not encourage identification of these teachers within the education profession. However, it does foster education students' identifying with a discipline that then shapes the perception and orientation of the teacher towards the profession of education. The problem is that education is responsible for the teaching of students of many disciplines in the secondary schools.

The integration of these disciplines is critical for the development of rational thinking skills and sound and mature decision-making in secondary school students. These goals could be achieved with better results if the teachers of each discipline identified first with the profession of education and secondly with their particular discipline. Then these teachers would appreciate and view the framework and purposes of the profession of education from a broader perspective. Such an identification with the profession would also enable these teachers to learn, appreciate, and assist the integration of discipline study within these schools. The achievement of this objective is necessary if the changes in format, structure, and curriculum proposed in Chapter 11 for secondary schools are to be realized. The key lies with the implementation of Second-Order Changes 32 and 33.

Besides these two changes, a number of specific changes in current secondary programs must be achieved if significant improvements in the quality of these schools and the learning of secondary school students are to be achieved.

The format of the curriculum for preparing secondary teachers must be radically redesigned. Neither state requirements for accreditation or certification nor university requirements provide assurance that current program structures or curriculums meet the standards suggested in this book. Weible and Dumas (1982) concluded from their survey of secondary teacher certification standards that, with the exception of student teaching and educational psychology, state minimum requirements for professional education often fail to meet the standards of the National Council for the Accreditation of Teacher Education (NCATE) and the National Association of State Directors of Teacher Education and Certification (NASDTEC).

In many respects the curriculum changes proposed here for secondary teacher education programs parallel those suggested for elementary education students, for similar reasons. The differences in the two curriculums do not differ with respect to the basic rationale supporting the proposed changes, nor do they differ in the purposes which they are designed to accomplish. The basic difference in the two curriculums is that elementary education students focus on learning and development principles of younger children, and secondary school teachers focus on learning and development principles of adolescence. The liberal studies component, the academic content component, the professional education component, the clinical experiences, and the electives component would be similar. There would be differences in how different subjects are taught. For example, how a teacher teaches history would be different from how a teacher teaches chemistry. These differences and their implications for curriculum design and classroom organization would have to be addressed in the professional education component. For example, history might better be taught in two-hour periods three times a week, while chemistry would better be taught in two two-hour periods plus two three-hour lab periods. The implications of these decisions on class scheduling and organization are obvious. These decisions are best left to the professionals responsible for the teaching — the teachers. These implications were also a major determinant of the proposal to have teachers responsible for coordinating the curriculum and the scheduling of classes as proposed earlier.

A second major change that must occur in the preparation of secondary school teachers concerns their attitude toward adolescents. In many respects this attitude reflects a larger societal notion towards adolescents that revolves around a notion that adolescents must be strictly governed by tightly controlled negative sanctions. This becomes a self-fulfilling prophecy. We must develop a much more positive attitude towards adolescents and their potential; and we must provide them the opportunities to develop and display this potential. Perhaps, if the schools developed and displayed a more positive attitude and approach towards the capabilities of adolescents, the number of drop-outs and rate of academic and social failures in our schools would not be as great as it is currently.

Required changes in other teacher education programs

Besides elementary and secondary education programs, there are a number of other teacher education programs that should be addressed. These include such preparation programs as music education, art education, physical education, and a few others. In most respects these programs currently reflect problems similar to those described in secondary preparation programs. Three problem areas in particular need to be changed. First, these programs must also come under the control of faculty in the campus educational unit. Therefore, Second-Order Changes 32 and 33 must also apply to these programs, for the same reasons discussed under change of secondary preparation programs.

Second, the curriculum format for these programs must be modified according to that proposed for elementary education students and for reasons similar to those supporting the change of secondary preparation programs. One major difference between the curriculum format proposed for secondary programs and these other teacher education programs might be the extent of work required in the academic content area. Such disciplines as music and art may require more than 30 semester credit hours to adequately prepare these students in their content area. If so, this additional work should be required but with no less amount of work required in other components.

Third, these program areas tend to prepare their students to assume positions in grades K-12. This is not an appropriate expectation. The differences in development between a six-year-old and an 18-year-old are so vast that it is not logical to assume that a teacher can be familiar with all the nuances of these differences without extensive preparation at all levels of development represented in this age range. The same argument also extends to the differences in learning within this age range. If anything, if a student is being prepared to teach the full K-12 grade range, it would be expected that such student would have much more extensive preparation in child and adolescent development and principles and techniques of learning. This is not the case. These students take no more academic work in these areas than do other teacher education students. Neither do these students usually have clinical experiences or student teaching in different school levels or with the age range represented in grades K-12. Therefore, it is important that students in these programs also concentrate at either the elementary or secondary level, and it should not be expected that they can be prepared to adequately teach across the K-spectrum.

Summary

This chapter presented the second-order changes necessary to provide (1) the university conditions to allow teacher education preparation programs the opportunity to institute needed improvements and (2) the specific changes necessary to coordinate teacher preparation program improvements with the changes and improvements proposed for public education. It is not expected that these proposals will be implemented quickly. In fact, they should not be. They represent an desired set of changes that would allow the improvement process to develop. They would need careful review and consideration and a planned process and sequence of implementation. The initiative for their review and action should be undertaken by faculty members of education units, with due regard for the significance and

310

importance of such changes. Additional initiatives for review should be undertaken by boards of trustees and university presidents. The combination of faculty members, university administrators, and trustees would provide a powerful impetus for change.

14 Preparation of educational administrators: second-order changes

Administrators of America's public schools have an almost impossible job. They have tremendous responsibility, but little real authority or capacity to affect those dimensions of their position that matter most to student learning. They are held accountable for achieving results in a context where the mission and objectives for the schools are ill-defined, constantly shifting, and under the control of concerned but uninformed lay people.

Although the role of educational administrators was not mentioned prominently in most of the national reform reports (Hoyle, 1989), previous attention had been given to this category of professional educator. This attention has not been flattering.

The problems of educational administration

During the 1970's and early 80's a number of authors (Bates, 1982; Hodgkinson, 1978; Foster, 1980, 1984) protested the prevailing assumptions of educational administration. Miklos (1987) raised the fundamental question of the content of educational administration preparation programs. Miklos questioned the conceptual base of these programs and concluded that curriculum change will occur as a function of concepts derived from the social sciences. Miklos raised the correct question but, unfortunately, did not address the correct solution — the nature and purpose of the schools.

The 1986 publication of the Southern Region Educational board, *Effective School Principals*, indicated that, as a result of the educational reform movement, improved educational performance and outcomes would be expected, but that principals might be the weak link in improvement efforts. This report also indicated that higher education must play a key role in changing how principals are prepared to work in the schools. This report obviously recognizes that changes are necessary in educational administration at both the public school and higher education levels. However, it fails to take into account (1) the difficulties of achieving structural change at either level, or (2) an organizational structure for the schools other than the current one.

At the annual meeting of the Education Commission of the States (Mooney, 1987), former Governor Bill Clinton of Arkansas told the Commission that a new breed of leader was necessary for the public schools. According to then Governor Clinton, principals and superintendents fall into one of three categories: Those waiting for retirement, those who have the initiative and talent to carry out major improvements, and those who want to be strong leaders but face too many obstacles. According to the then Governor , most school administrators fell into this latter category. He identified the following problems of leadership that must be resolved: too much bureaucracy, a lack of innovation at all levels, inadequate training of school administrators, and too little firsthand knowledge of classroom activities among administrators. The Governor urged that new academic and managerial programs be supported.

Although former Governor Clinton correctly identified some of the problems of school leadership, he did not identify the correct solution. What he proposed, apart from support for new academic and managerial programs which were not defined, was essentially more of the same. The solution to the problem of school leadership lies in understanding the context and mission of the schools as a set of mutually interdependent variables as they interact with students and teachers, and boundary groups of the schools, such as parents, textbook publishers, bureaucracies and special interest groups. The school leadership problem cannot be solved without achieving change and improvement concurrently in these other sectors of school functioning.

The Report of the National Policy Board for Educational Administration (1989) concluded that the field was frozen through years of accommodation. The Board noted that changes proportional to the problems were needed, and since the problems were systemic, the reform efforts must be exhaustive. Among other findings, this report noted that educational administration faculty spend relatively little of their time in either research or teaching, that student course-taking was haphazard, and that some programs provided students no opportunity to practice their skills through clinical experiences. Other equally severe criticisms of standards of performance and quality control were noted in this report. Although the report concludes that its recommendations for reform should keep the needs of public school students foremost, only one of the nine recommendations offered mentioned the teaching-learning process, and then as only one of seven curriculum elements.

Pitner (1988) suggested that the match between activities and behaviors of administrators and the preparation they receive is not a good one. Achilles (1984), Griffiths (1988) and Schibles (1988), among others, have described the sorry state of educational administrator preparation.

In its *Leaders for America's Schools* (1988), the National Commission on Excellence in Educational Administration freely admits and describes the problems of educational administration at both the public school and higher education levels. A considerable number of recommendations for change are offered by this report. These recommendations focus on changes that assume the continuation of the current organizational format of the schools. They also recommend changes within the program structure and course content sequence of educational administration preparation programs. However, these recommendations consider neither a changed organizational format in public schools, nor the necessary inter-relationship that must be developed between teacher preparation and educational administration preparation programs. This report seems to operate on the assumption that educational administrators are, and will continue to be, the only leaders of the schools.

Most school administrators come from the ranks of teachers. The motivations for leaving the classroom to become a school administrator are many and varied. Certainly, one of the key factors is that school administration offers a significantly higher rate of pay than does teaching. As long as this condition continues, the field of educational administration will continue to lure many of the most effective teachers from the classroom to the administrative offices.

Unfortunately, the field of administration also attracts many ineffective, dissatisfied, and disgruntled teachers. If appropriate identification, selection, and preparation of educational administrators were the only, or the major problem, of school administration, it would be relatively easy to develop procedures to rectify these problems. Unfortunately, these are not the major problems.

Hoyle (1989) concludes that the many attempts of reform have been done with little if any empirical research or systematic evaluation of administrator effectiveness. Cunningham (1989) correctly identifies the problem when he states, ". . . the failure of the educational administration professoriate, rests with building program reconstruction on obsolete assumptions" (p.1). Cunningham goes on to note that, if faculties of educational administration are going to be successful with reform efforts, they must begin with a clean conceptual slate.

Cunningham makes a valid point. The reform of educational administration will require a different conceptual base for educational administrators than has been developed to date. The major problems of educational administration are insidious and endemic to the control and structure of public education and to the type and character of educational administration preparation programs. The problems associated with the control and nature of public education were discussed previously and the second-order changes necessary to remedy these conditions were proposed in Chapters 11-13. A critical element of these proposed changes was a significant alteration of the mission, organizational framework, and authority hierarchy of the schools. This revised authority hierarchy included reversing the nature of the current relationship that exists between teachers and educational administrators at all levels.

The changes proposed provide teachers with the autonomy and power to coordinate and direct the learning activities of children. It was proposed to give teachers much of the authority and accountability responsibility that are currently vested in school administrators. These changes would alter significantly the nature of public school administration and the type of preparation programs that exist for these personnel. Even if the changes that are proposed for the reversal of teacher and administrator roles are not accepted, the preparation programs for school administrators, in most cases, need to be substantially modified. These types of changes will not be discussed here. [See Reilly (1984).] The changes that are proposed in this Chapter are consistent with those proposed for school administrators in Chapters 11-13.

The rationale for not proposing changes for educational administration preparation programs beyond those consistent with the changes proposed in previous chapters are two interdependent ones. First, any changes proposed for educational administration preparation programs must be consistent with a conceptual base derived from a set of objectives and role expectations and limits based on the requirements and description of educational administrators' responsibilities. This is not currently the case. As has been noted previously, programs preparing personnel for the public schools are often based on principles and concerns far removed from the realities of working in public schools.

There are two major reasons for this incongruity. The first reason for this discrepancy between the reality of the public schools and the forces shaping the concepts, curriculum, and methods taught in education personnel preparation programs is the ego-spawned reluctance of universities to accept the proposition that their programs should consider and be based equally on the needs of the public schools and the results of their research and need for independence. This discrepancy was revealed in research conducted by the author and a colleague (Starr and Reilly, 1985). In this research the needs of educational administrators and the past, current, and anticipated research efforts of university faculty were shown to have no congruence.

One basic flaw in the development of appropriate preparation programs is the lack of a mechanism between the public schools and preparation programs for developing a coordinated and true partnership for determining what should constitute the most appropriate program. This problem was discussed previously, but two elements of it need to be repeated here for emphasis. These elements are (1) the general refusal by universities to accept the idea that a perfectly acceptable and appropriate reason and basis for structuring and/or changing a preparation program are the needs of the practitioners of a particular discipline, and (2) faculty rewards for assisting public schools in improving their effectiveness should be equal to those rewards for research and scholarship (Reilly, 1987).

The second reason for this discrepancy between the reality of the public schools and the nature of most educational administration preparation programs is the lack of a viable conceptual base on which to structure such a program. The literature dealing with the roles of educational administration makes it clear that *no one is quite sure what an educational administrator, particularly school principals, should be doing.* The history of educational administration is revealing in how it demonstrates the accidental manner in which the principalship developed into its current position of non-academic leadership in the schools (Cubberly, 1916; Reeder, 1931). In the earliest days of schools in America, school principals were called Head Teachers, and then Head Masters. They were selected for these positions on the basis of their effectiveness as a teacher. (Incidentally, they are still called this in some regions of the world, usually in those countries that previously were subject to British colonization.)

During these early times, these Head Teachers were primarily teachers expected to attend to the logistical and minor administrative matters of the school, as time from teaching permitted (Lipham and Hoeh, 1974). It was clear that the prime expectation was teaching. This is still the model in some regions of the world, for example, the Republic of Cyprus and the Soviet Union. In Cyprus all principals (or Head Masters as they are called) are required to teach, regardless of the size of the school. Although the size of schools in Cyprus is, on the average, not nearly as large as in the United States, the principle behind this requirement is a worthy one to consider. As one of these principals told the author, which was later reinforced during a conference with a Ministry of Education official, "How can we have credibility with teachers if we ourselves don't teach?" In terms of the educational administration theory that proposes the principal as the instructional leader of the school, this is a concept well worth consideration. There are, however, very few principals in America today that have a daily, required teaching assignment.

It was the growth of American cities, leading to the increased size of schools, which led to the demise of the head teacher as a teacher. With the

317

increased size of schools, more and more attention and time had to be devoted to administrative concerns. Soon, the tasks involved in running the school consumed the entire day, or at least, that is what was said. The notion of the principal as a teacher, first and foremost, became lost. It was not long before the business of running a school and maintaining the bureaucratic processes that supported education demanded more and more administrative personnel.

Additional administrative positions were developed and the operational tasks involved in running the schools became a business in themselves, connected remotely and tangentially to the prime objective of the schools, i.e., enhancing the learning of children. It should be noted here that many of the bureaucratic positions and processes generated by schools were mandated by the countless rules and regulations spawned by state and the federal governments. These rules and regulations go on and on, and one has to wonder if their publication has measurably improved the learning capabilities of children.

The current organizational framework of education and the administrative positions necessary to support it may be required to implement the bureaucratic procedures required, but this approach carries with it two serious and fundamental flaws. First, the development of an administrative hierarchy that derives its purpose for existence primarily from a need to support itself constantly needs to find additional reasons for continuing its existence. Thus, it continues to grow, but not with the purpose of supporting or improving the achievement of the prime purpose of the schools, i.e., children's learning. Educational administration has grown, and continues to grow in size and numbers to maintain itself, not because improving children's learning demands increased numbers of administrators.

The second consideration in the growth of educational administration is that it has done so without a conceptual base related to the achievement of the prime objectives of America's schools. This is obviously related to the first consideration. It is true that, during the 1960's and 70's, an increased number of educational administrators was necessary to carry out the mandates and demands of social reform as they impacted the public schools. Increased numbers were also necessary to keep track of and respond to the swelling number of rules and regulations emanating from the federal, state, and local levels. This time appears to be past, and, even if it is not, social reform is not the prime objective of the schools.

If the prime objective of education had been kept clearly in focus during recent decades by both policy-makers and educational personnel, perhaps the schools would not have been as severely criticized as they have in the past few years. However, educational administration grew as a field of study without a conceptual base derived to keep the prime objective of education foremost and clearly in perspective. Consequently, programs of educational administration have been developed around and from theories of administration. They were not generated from a conceptual framework for the schools, or from a knowledge base of learning and how administration of schools can and should enhance learning objectives.

Currently, there are a number of theories of educational administration. Some of these theories are quite elaborate and make much sense, if their basic assumptions of the purposes of educational administration are accepted. It is these assumptions about the purposes of educational administration that must be examined before an examination of the validity of the theory itself. It is at that level that these theories fail the test of supporting the prime objective of education. If the basic assumptions about the purposes of education are accepted, most of these theories are logical and internally consistent. Some authors (Cotton and Savard, 1983) assert that the principal is the instructional leader of the school. Goodlad (1983) asserts, however, that principals' detachment from curriculum and instruction is because few of them have been prepared as instructional leaders.

Other authors (Edmonds, 1979; Lipham and Hoeh, 1974) assert that principals should be the managers of the school environment. This suggestion seems consistent with those authors who provide their description of the characteristics and activities of principals of effective schools. Still others suggest that the principal should be the change-agent for the schools (Stiegelbauer, 1984). This author (Reilly, 1985) suggests that the principal should be the educational, versus instructional, leader of the school.

Besides failing the test of purpose, each of these assertions and suggestions suffers from a similar and more fatal flaw. None of these recommendations for the role of educational administrators or school principals envisaged the possibility of an educational structure that did not have educational administrators as supraordinate to all other personnel within the school system. Thus, these recommended roles for school principals all continue with the assumption that the principal was, and should be, the pivotal person for school leadership and school operations. Once this assumption is discarded, or at least put aside to consider other alternatives, a number of other possible approaches to public school and system operations and developments quickly emerge. Discarding the current state of educational administration for the moment allows an examination of the conceptual base of public school administration and enables second-order change alternatives to be considered.

As indicated previously, the conceptual basis underlying each of the recommendations for school principals mentioned above proceeds from the same assumption of the importance of the principal as the main player in school leadership. None of these propositions includes suggestions for levels of educational administration above that of the school principal, apparently under the assumption that these levels of school system administration are inviolate. Therefore, theories of school administration and, particularly, those for school principals, were developed from, and were embedded within, a set of assumptions and a conceptual bias about the structure and nature of schools. These have prevented the formation and evaluation of alternative structures of school system organization and the governance hierarchy. Once these previous assumptions have been laid aside and consideration is given to alternative organizational structures, it is possible to develop more appropriate frameworks for improving learning outcomes for children.

It is with this conceptual freedom that consideration of new and/or alternative methods of school organization, within a context of school objectives that emphasize the primacy of enhancing children's learning capabilities, and second-order changes elevating teachers to the pivotal role of school and instructional leader were made in Chapters 8 and 9. As indicated in those chapters, the recommendations were made on the basis of giving prime responsibility, authority, and accountability to those who must achieve the prime objectives of education. Obviously, if these responsibilities are given to teachers, then the responsibilities and authority of principals and other educational administrators must decrease accordingly.

What then of the educational administrator? Is there still a role for such a person, and, if so, what? The answer to the first of these questions is yes. The answer to the second was provided in Chapters 11-13. It is expanded upon below with those second-order changes necessary to provide the training appropriate for developing the knowledge and skills for persons to assume such positions in public schools.

One of the basic tenets of this book is that teachers should have the responsibility and authority for determining the professional decisions necessary for improving learning outcomes in children. Similarly, teachers should be free from all the mundane administrative affairs necessary to maintain an optimum environment for improving learning outcomes. This means that teachers should be free from having to collect lunch money, doing bus duty, doing cafeteria duty, and so forth. Instead, they should have the final say in such decisions as what the priorities for new audio visual equipment are, what reading series should be used in grades one through three, etc.

The responsibilities for school principals would be implementing the policies of the teachers as determined by the Coordinating Council of the

320

Academic Planning Unit (Second-Order Changes 1, 4, & 17). In this context the school principal is more analogous to a hospital administrator than to the chief executive officer of a business.

In a similar fashion, the roles of associate/assistant superintendent and superintendent would also change. They would change from their current functions of coordinating and implementing system policies as determined by state law and the local school board to those of director of purchasing, director of maintenance, director of business affairs, etc. These personnel would no longer have a role to play in determining or interpreting policy. These activities would be the responsibility of teachers as coordinated through teachers' councils and/or committees.

It is with the school principals that the most visible changes to educational administration would be apparent. These are the school personnel, except for the superintendent and a particular child's teacher, that are the most visible to the general public. With the recommendations for change made in this book, the visibility of the principal would disappear, and the visibility and importance of the teachers as meaningful shapers and determiners of school policy, programs, and operations would emerge.

Proposed changes

With the responsibilities of the principal as herein defined, the nature of the preparation program for such personnel would also change dramatically. It will be necessary to develop a significant paradigm shift concerning the role and authority of teachers and educational administrators. This shift would have significant impact not only on the practice of educational administration, but on the type of preparation programs required for these personnel. It would no longer be necessary to prepare such personnel at the graduate level. They would not need teaching experience, and they would not have to be the highest paid personnel in the system. The following proposals for second-order change address these issues.

Second-Order Change #34. Educational administration preparation programs should be established to prepare such personnel at the undergraduate level for entry level positions in the public schools.

It would not be necessary to prepare educational administrators at the graduate level to assume the position as a public school administrator with the responsibilities recommended for them in this book. Of course, this proposal is not likely to be met with great favor from educational administrators, and many arguments will be raised against this recommendation. Some of these arguments will even be valid, but only within the context of school system structure and organization as it exists today. Again, if today's structure and organization of school systems are put aside, and consideration given to alternative structures, then other plans can emerge which provide the opportunity to design a school system structure and organization that is formed specifically to achieve the objectives of the system.

The second-order changes proposed in this book do this by recommending the teachers as the prime persons responsible for achieving the objectives of the schools. If this notion is accepted, then the responsibilities of educational administrators must assume a lower priority and set of role assumptions than is currently the case. These responsibilities, as described in Chapters 8 and 9, demand no more than an undergraduate degree to accomplish.

Second-Order Change #35. A recommended curriculum for preparing educational administrators at the undergraduate level is as follows:

Component	Credit Hours
1. Liberal Studies	45-60
2. Academic Major (Business, Public, Administration)	30-45
3. Education — Required	27-30
A. History of Education	
B. Organization of Education	
C. Objectives of Education	
D. Child and Adolescent Development	
E. School Law, Rules, and Regulations	
F. Ethics of Education	
G. Internship	
4. Education — Desirable	12-15
A. Public Relations	
B. Educational Program Planning	
C. Consultation Methods	
D. Family and Child Relations	
5. Electives	12-20
Total	126-170 Semester Hours

Second-Order Change #36. There should not be certification for personnel hired in positions of administration in the public schools. Tenure should not be granted to individuals in these positions.

The intent of this proposal for change is three-fold. First, these personnel would not be working with or responsible for students' learning in the schools. Therefore, no certification would be necessary. Second, these personnel would be responsible to the teachers of the school. Consequently, teachers would need the authority to hire and fire for cause. Third, the major task of these personnel is business operations and maintenance of the school facility. This does not require a major in education, but, since principals would be working in the educational enterprise, they would need to be familiar with those areas of education identified under the required education component outlined above. As long as a person had this knowledge, there would be no reason not to hire him/her for the position, regardless of where it was learned.

Obviously, if these recommendations for change were put into effect, there would need to be significant modifications in the faculty of educational administration preparation programs. The most obvious of these would be a reduction in number of faculty. There would not be the need for the same student-faculty ratio for an undergraduate program as exists for a graduate program. In addition, there would be a reduction in the number of courses that would have to be taught by educational administration faculty. Only six of the required and elective courses, including internship, recommended in Second-Order Change 35, need to be taught by educational administration faculty. It would be very surprising if this number was not a substantial reduction in the number of courses listed and taught by most programs of educational administration. It would be quite possible to staff a program of the sort recommended here of some 24-30 students with no more than two faculty members.

Despite the anguished cries of outrage, two considerations must be kept in mind. First, the context for recommending these proposals for change is from a perspective that ignores the current structure and organizational framework of public education. In this context, with a goal of designing a framework and profession of education that provides the responsibility and authority to those who do the real work of education, it is the teachers who must have the control of the educational enterprise. Second, many educational administrators will argue against these proposals because, if enacted, these administrators would face a loss of power and control. But what system and organizational structure of education will provide the best learning opportunities for our children? It is the answer to this question that must guide and determine the structure and organization of education, not the displacement or loss of face that might be encountered by some educational administrators.

15 Support-service practices and preparation programs: second order changes

Nothing yet has been mentioned about the type and use of student support services at either the elementary or secondary school levels. These services are critical for continued improvement of the instructional program of the schools. The personnel providing these services include curriculum supervisors, school media personnel and librarians, guidance personnel, school psychologists, and school social workers, among others. The majority of services are generally delivered from three of these professional types, guidance counselors, school psychologists, and school social workers.

The number of these professionals in the schools varies, depending on the particular state and section of the country. Some of these professionals work in the schools but are called by various names. For example, school social workers may be called home-school coordinators; school psychologists may be called psychometricians or something similar. There are great numbers of these personnel, particularly guidance counselors. Of these numbers, some have received certification in one of these fields but without completing an academic program in that field. Thus, there are guidance counselors who have received certification in school psychology simply by completing a number of additional courses, usually intelligence testing, beyond their masters degree in guidance counseling. Similarly, there are individuals who have completed an academic program with a major in sociology, or a related field, and received certification as a school social worker. In many instances, this limits the contributions these individuals can make to the children they are serving. They often have not completed a professional program in the area in which they received certification. Whatever their training, the services provided by these personnel often suffer from lack of coordination, poor organization, and professional identity and affiliation problems that prevent maximum gain being achieved from these services.

How each of these professionals serves the schools, teachers, and students differs from the others. For example, media personnel, librarians, and guidance personnel tend to be school-based. The other personnel tend to be system-or district-based, they are responsible for a number of schools, and/or they may have restrictions placed upon them by their professional orientation or the persons to whom they are administratively responsible.

Such problems may prevent these personnel from delivering maximally effective services. The first section of this chapter describes some of the problems encountered in practice by guidance, school psychological, and school social worker personnel at the school system and individual school levels. It also presents a number of second-order change proposals for improving both the practice and preparation program levels. The remaining portions of the chapter describe the problems of medial and curriculum supervisor personnel and discusses how the services of these personnel might be improved.

Problems of practice: guidance personnel, school psychologists, and school social workers

Each of these fields has a long and honored tradition of assisting persons to cope more adequately with their lives, particularly if they were experiencing difficulties in such efforts. It was only natural, therefore, that this would continue as these professionals entered the schools to assist children. Although the services of these professionals are available to all children, in practice, those experiencing problems receive the majority of their attention. However, guidance personnel, because of their training and because they are school-based, probably spend the least time with students not experiencing learning or adjustment problems. Instead, their time is usually spent in assisting with course schedules, helping students choose a vocation or a college, and similar activities.

In general, the practitioners of these three professional specialties tend to perceive their role as a helping one, with their prime focus on those students expressing learning or adjustment problems. Guidance personnel focus on truancy and discipline problems, and, when time permits, they offer counseling assistance to students. School psychologists spend a majority of their time testing students to determine their eligibility for special services and programs. School social workers work with students who are experiencing learning and adjustment problems and their families. These are all vital and necessary services. Often all three specialties are involved in working with the same child and/or family, sometimes without knowledge of each other's efforts.

Although a number of organizational patterns attempt to provide a structure and coordination for delivery of these support services, the coordination of such service delivery is often poor because of the manner in which such services are organized. Most guidance personnel are school-based and thus report to the school principal. There is usually a coordinator or director of guidance and counseling services at the system level. In some school systems, this coordinator of guidance services is also the coordinator or director of support services, sometimes called special services, student services, or pupil personnel services. In such situations, school psychological services and school social work services also report to this coordinator. In other school systems there may be a director of psychological services and a director of social services. In such situations there will also be a director of guidance services. All three may provide services in such situations, then report administratively to a pupil personnel director or director of student services who may also have responsibility for special education programs and services, special reading programs, and other such services. In any of these organizational patterns, the support services are administered, and usually conceived of, as separate from the mainstream instructional programs and activities of the school, thereby reinforcing the notion that these services are primarily for "special" children.

These organizational patterns make it extremely difficult for these professionals to coordinate and effectively deliver their services to students. The coordination and delivery of services are hindered by the various financing sources, by the professional orientation received in training, by questions of "turf," and by the question of who is the client.

No doubt problems in these areas can seriously impede learning and place children in deplorable and untenable situations. However, to what extent should schools go in attempting to resolve these problems? Not very far. Other agencies in the community are better equipped with more resources and with more and better trained personnel to work with these problems. Educational support personnel should restrict their efforts to working with those problem areas that offer the potential for speedy resolution. With situations that are chronic and severe, these school personnel should operate as case managers. This means that they would coordinate and ensure that necessary services are being delivered by appropriate community agencies to these situations. Because of their daily access to these children, these personnel are in the best position to ensure such coordination, but they should not deliver such mental health and social services themselves.

The final difficulty in attempting to coordinate effective delivery of these services is one of control. Which of these professional specialties is in charge of coordinating services to students? The answer is none. These professionals are taught to make independent, professional judgments regarding those they serve. Each is unwilling to subordinate this professional decision-making to others or to accept that their specialty area should allow one of the other specialties to assume coordinating responsibility. Fortunately, the professionalism of the practitioners of these specialties prevents these professional "turf" battles from interfering with providing the services children need. This is more a result, however, of personalities than of the structure or processes of the system.

The lack of coordination of services results in three problems. First, these three specialty areas tend to focus on serving "special" or "problem" students. Second, these services are not as effectively coordinated as they might be. Third, there is an overlapping of service delivery from these three specialties. The question is whether there is a more appropriate model for provision of these services?

The different levels of certification these individuals can receive also handicap effective service delivery. For example, in some states, certification of guidance counselors, school psychologists, and school social workers vary greatly. Each level of certification corresponds to an academic degree level, or a specified number of academic courses beyond a degree level if one has majored in one area and wishes to be certified in one of the other two areas. In some states, school social workers can be certified at the bachelors, masters, and doctoral levels. Guidance counselors and school psychologists can be certified at the masters, sixth year, and doctoral levels. This confusing certification probably leads to less efficient support services being delivered to children than needs to be the case; however, they are not the major problems afflicting the delivery of these services by these professionals.

There are four major obstacles to improving the delivery of these services. These are (1) the professional orientation of each of these areas, (2) confusion over who controls and coordinates the delivery of services by these professionals, (3) the organization and administration of these services, and (4) identification of the client of these professionals. Each of these will be considered in turn.

The first problem is the professional identity and affiliation of the three professional areas. As will also be seen in the chapter that discusses secondary schools, this is a major problem that is preventing the profession of education from delivering the most effective services to children. None of these professional areas — guidance counselors, school psychologists, and school social workers — identify primarily with the profession of education. Their primary professional identification is with their respective professions, i.e., counseling, psychology, or social work.

328

Even though they are school employees, graduates of programs in these three areas, if asked what his profession is, will rarely answer "an educator." Does this make a difference in the quality and effectiveness of services delivered to children? Many professionals will say no. They have been brought up professionally to identify with their respective professions and have been indoctrinated since their professional preparation days to believe that is true.

It certainly is true that these three groups represent the most highly trained of all those who work in the schools. It is also certainly true that they have made a positive, significant difference in the lives of countless children. Yet, their affiliation with a profession other than education prevents the most coordinated and effective system of support services to be delivered to all children. However, the education profession does not yet determine the nature of the training programs that produce these professionals. Each of the respective professions do. Thus, the nature of the preparation program is developed by persons outside education. Each of these specialties has its agenda of issues, politics, and objectives with which to contend. Unfortunately, education and the schools are rarely among them.

These professionals view their roles in the schools as largely determined by each profession's view of what its client group is and what particular knowledge and skills its graduates can offer to children in the schools.

Thus, the objectives of each of these professional areas in the schools are not determined by educators, but rather by counselors, psychologists, and social workers. Education does not currently have a conceptual framework or administrative structure that would allow the efforts of these professionals to be effectively coordinated and delivered to all children. Without such a framework and administrative structure, the efforts of these professionals are often fragmented and diluted.

Another problem generated by the failure to identify with the education profession is that the services of these professional support areas are not directly related to the process of education or to all children. Each of these areas has a history and tradition of helping those who are having problems coping and/or adjusting to life. This tradition has been largely maintained in the schools. The children with which these professionals work in the schools tend to be troubled ones, either by learning or social/emotional problems. No doubt these services are needed and such services must be maintained. It is improving the effectiveness of these services and extending them to all children that is the desired goal. This requires coordination and identification with the profession of education, rather than with a profession outside education. To achieve this goal, significant alterations in training and in the structure and administration of these services would have to be instituted.

329

The second problem is determining who controls and coordinates the efforts of these professional areas. There is no single answer to this question. It varies considerably from state to state and school system to school system. In most school systems, guidance counselors are school-based, especially at the senior high and junior high/middle school level. Many systems have guidance counselors at the elementary school level as well. In many school systems, guidance counselors report to a Director of Guidance Services. In such situations, the guidance personnel are responsible to both the school principal and the guidance director. In some systems, these guidance personnel report to a Director of Student Services, or Support Services, or Child Services, or someone with a similar title. This person may or may not be a counselor. It may even be someone with an administrative background only.

School social workers usually work out of a central or district office and are usually assigned to a specific number of schools. Their clients are usually referred to them by a teacher, principal or guidance counselor. They generally work on a case-by-case basis, attempting to coordinate efforts of the home, school, and community agencies. They generally report to a central office or district office administrator, who more likely has a background in special education or counseling than in social work. The social workers and guidance personnel may reports to entirely different people.

The structure for delivery of school psychological services is similar to that of the social worker. School psychologists generally work out of a central or district office and are responsible for a certain set of schools and/or program areas. They report administratively to a person who may or may not be the same person to whom the social workers and guidance personnel report. Like the social workers, school psychologists work on a referral basis from school personnel. School psychologists are often restricted to working only with a certain type of student. In many systems, because their salaries are paid from special education funds, their efforts must be restricted to these children of school psychologists. Although they can offer so much more to teachers and students, school psychologists are often restricted to only testing children to determine their eligibility for special education programs.

Thus, a combination of teacher, principal, state rules and regulations, and the administrative arrangement that exists determines which students can receive their services. The quality of services depends on the referral system in a given system, the perceptiveness and willingness of a given teacher to refer a student for assistance, the willingness of a principal to refer a student, the various programs available within a given system, the number of each of these professionals within a system, and the particular combination of schools to which the available professionals are assigned.

330

As indicated above, the organization and administration of these support services are random in nature. They are structured on the beliefs and attitudes of the administrators of a given system and are generally not coordinated across areas. It is unusual to find all three services coordinated under one administrative structure, and it is rarer yet to find these three services combined with special education under one administrative structure. The basic difficulty is that school administrators seem unsure how to make the fullest and best use of these professionals. Certainly, special education must be maintained. Special education teachers need school psychologists to evaluate the children to make sure they meet the eligibility requirements for these programs. Many school administrators are not sure what social workers are supposed to be doing, but they are nice to have around to handle difficult parents, coordinate activities with other community agencies, make sure sick children have a ride home, or get to a welfare appointment, or coordinate some other home-school activity, such as attendance problems or truancy. The general perception seems to be that special education personnel, school psychologists, and school social workers work with problem children but have little to offer the non-problem child. Guidance personnel are school-based and come under the principal, who assigns them a variety of tasks and responsibilities. When social workers are not available, guidance counselors tend to offer some of the same services, although they generally consider themselves to be developmentally oriented and work more often with the "normal" child.

The fourth (and perhaps the most critical) problem is determining the client for these professionals. The most frequent answer is the student. This is understandable, although it is inaccurate. These professionals have been trained professionally to deliver services to individuals, and in the schools, with its referral system, the natural client appears to the individual student referred. The structure of the organization and the rules and regulations that determine the financing for special programs are based on the students that must be served. Since the schools exist to meet the needs of the students, it is only logical to assume that the student be the client of these professionals.

However, this assumption creates a number of problems. First, the school psychologists and school social workers are assigned students on the basis of a referral system that is often two or three steps removed from the classroom. The guidance counselors, being school-based, are in a much better position to deal directly with either the student or the teacher who initiated the referral. If, as often happens, the problem of the student is beyond the capability of the guidance counselor, he/she must refer the student to one of the other two support service personnel. The school psychologist does not often become involved in direct-service treatment.

331

He/she often works through a consultation model with the teacher(s), guidance personnel, parents, or others who are involved with the student. The school psychologist's efforts are usually restricted to those referred for special education program consideration, and the demand for testing services usually precludes time for many other activities. Certainly, the range of knowledge concerning learning and development of the average school psychologist is vastly under-utilized for all students in a school system.

Second, it is generally the classroom teacher who is experiencing a problem with a student. When he refers the student for special services, he may assume that the student's problem(s) are beyond his/her capability to deal with in the classroom. Unfortunately, this results in absolving the teacher from further responsibility for the student's learning. The special education system in the schools allows this to occur all to frequently.

The complex system of referral, assessment, and placement for special education services further reinforces the notion that, once a child is in the referral process, he/she is no longer the regular classroom teacher's responsibility. It is this attitude of non-responsibility that is so damaging to developing the best learning program for the student. Although unknowingly, the school psychologist abets this attitude by testing the child to determine if he/she is eligible for special services outside the regular classroom. So also does the school social worker, who attempts to convince the parents that such placement is in the best interests of the child. It is the structure, organization, and administration of the system that leads to this attitude. If the structure of the system was such that each student remained the responsibility of the regular classroom teacher, then the support personnel would be consultants available to assist each teacher in working more effectively with each child in the regular classroom. Therefore, the regular classroom teacher, not the student, would be the client for all support personnel.

The problem is that these professions often have higher degrees and they identify with professions other than education. They primarily work with students experiencing problems, or with tasks outside the mainstream of classroom activity. Therefore, many teachers and parents assume that their knowledge and skills exceed their own. Therefore, their recommendations are considered to have greater validity than the perceptions of the teacher. In addition, because these support personnel are generally concerned with individual students experiencing problems or with students who are presenting problems to the regular classroom teacher, they do not focus their efforts on assisting regular classroom teachers with their prime responsibility — the improvement of learning for all children.

To a significant extent, this results from attitudes and perceptions developed during the preparation program. The regular classroom teacher, faced with too many children for effective teaching, is often only too happy to have someone else assume prime responsibility for the students experiencing problems and causing disruptions in the classroom. If a support person, who usually has higher professional credentials than the teacher, asserts that the student has a learning disability or other problem that interferes with learning, the teacher is often relieved of responsibility for the student's learning. In many cases, the student is removed from the classroom for "special education." This can mean anything from total removal from the regular classroom, partial removal from the class for special resource assistance and/or tutoring, to a variety of pull-out programs that serve mostly to disrupt the regular class activity and the particular student's involvement in the regular class.

The major point regarding special education programs, and the variety of support personnel that are involved with these programs, is that they are too poorly coordinated to deliver the most effective and efficient educational services to children. The reasons for this are complex and interdependent. As indicated previously, a major reason is the organizational structure of schools for delivery of these services. A second major reason is the categorical program funding that is provided for students with different types of problems. To attract funding for these programs, students must be identified as meeting the criteria for one of these programs. Thus, a great deal of time, perhaps most of the time of school psychologists, is spent in testing these students to determine whether they meet the criteria for these special education programs.

Many educators deplore the notion of these categorical programs. These educators believe that these children could be better served if they were not categorized and stigmatized by labels such as mentally handicapped. If special funding for these children is to be continued, it should be on a non-categorical basis, so that more effective use of the funds could be determined by local school needs, conditions, assessments, and priorities. Unfortunately, however, to date these funds are still provided on a categorical basis.

The third (and perhaps most critical) reason for this lack of coordination of support services is the means by which these support personnel are trained. The support personnel being considered are school counselors, school psychologists, school social workers, and, in a different sense, special education teachers. As discussed earlier, these personnel are responsible to different elements of the school organization hierarchy. School counselors and special education teachers are school-based. School psychologists and school social workers are generally assigned from the central or district office to a number of schools, or they are responsible only to a particular type of student, e.g., special education students. This lack of coordination is greatly exacerbated by the model of training each of these types of personnel receives.

Rarely are these four types of personnel trained in one academic department. The general model of training is school counselors and special education teachers are prepared within a school, college, or department of education. In some educational units, both of these program areas are within the same department, but this is not universally true. For the most part, school psychologists are trained within the educational unit, but they may also be trained within the department of psychology, which is found predominantly within the college of arts and sciences, or its equivalent. When the school psychology program is located within the educational unit, it may be found within the departments of educational psychology, counselor education, special education, as a free standing unit, or within some other organizational unit. School social work programs are found predominantly within a college of arts and sciences, even though it is an applied, practitioner-oriented program. The same observation holds true for those school psychology programs located within colleges of arts and sciences.

What is the impact of this diversity of administrative housing for these preparation programs? There are two major ones. First, there is rarely a coordinated, common core program that students within these programs share, even though the great majority of these personnel will spend most of their professional time in the public schools, working with the same problem, and/or with the same students. If these professionals in training will be serving essentially the same population in the schools, it would seem important that they receive a coordinated common curriculum, or at least a curriculum that prepared them to coordinate their services to their common clients. This is decidedly not the case. In many cases, coordination of a sort does occur, although far too many children needing coordinated services slip through the cracks, receiving only the services of the individual professional who received the original referral. As indicated previously, this is partially the result of the organizational and administrative structure of the school system. It is also the result of the uncoordinated means by which these support personnel are trained. Restricting for the moment the consideration of services of these support personnel only to those students experiencing behavioral or emotional problems and/or difficulties in learning, it would appear to be far more beneficial to these students, and probably far more cost effective also, if a coordinated delivery of services was available and implemented. This would mean a second-order change of the structure and coordination of these services at the public school level. It just does not make sense to have three or four different professionals involved with the same child,

334

attempting to achieve the same objectives within the framework of the school's policies and resources, and each dealing with a different aspect of the child's life, when one professional could be prepared to deliver each of these services or to manage and coordinate the delivery of these services by outside community agencies.

A typical case of such a student often follows. A regular classroom teacher observes that a child is not learning as quickly as his/her peers, and, after attempting numerous techniques with no noticeable improvement, the teacher refers the student to the school psychologist for testing. After a wait of several weeks or months, depending on when the school psychologist can schedule the testing, the student is administered a battery of tests.

If the student is at the elementary level, a guidance counselor is probably not involved. If the student is at the middle/junior high/senior high school level, a counselor will probably be involved since the student's problem is more likely to involve emotional or behavioral problems. The counselor's role would be to discuss the situation with the student, his/her teachers, and/or the parents, and to gain the cooperation of all in a remedial program.

The elementary student who is referred to the school psychologist receives a battery of tests, generally not with the major intent of diagnosing the problem and developing a treatment plan as would be the case outside the school, but with the intent of determining whether the student is eligible to receive services. If eligibility is affirmed, a placement committees will determine in which program to place the child. Once the child is placed in the program, he generally never again emerges full time in a regular classroom, and he always to carries a label, and stigma, of whatever program in which he was enrolled. The parents' role in this process is to give permission for the testing to take place and hopefully to agree with the decision to place the child in whatever program is considered appropriate.

As might be expected, parental reactions to these decisions vary. Usually, a school social worker or home school coordinator is available will explain the situation and attempt to gain the cooperation of the parents. Sometimes, however, this task falls to the resource teacher, a guidance counselor, the school psychologist, the principal, or the regular classroom teacher. When such a variety of personnel may be involved, both the opportunities for miscommunication and the need for coordination are greatly increased. And since some of these personnel are not trained in consultation theories and techniques, or in principles of handicapped children, the possibilities for error are greatly increased.

This lack of coordination of services in the public schools results from university training programs not focusing on the development of practitioner competence. Each type of professional is trained according to the dictates of his profession, rather than according to the needs of the

335

education profession as perceived by the classroom teacher. Because the majority of these support preparation programs are at the graduate level, the role of research versus practitioner competence is also a factor in determining the nature of the preparation program. Being a graduate program also seems to dilute the emphasis on developing a coordinated and comprehensive preparation program among these support areas.

Many of these support personnel, particularly school psychologists, spend most of their time assessing students for special programs. They rarely have the time to spend working with either special or regular classroom teachers. Their knowledge and skills could be of immense value in assisting teachers in these classes. More and more, school counselors are developing a knowledge base in principles of human development. School psychologists are particularly well versed in learning theory and principles of cognition, and school social workers are well trained in consultation methods and working with small groups and individuals. All of these specialties are important for the schools. They could play a much more vital role if their services were consolidated and delivered in a coordinated fashion. Yet, each of these professionals is trained apart from the others, learning to view the world of education from the perspective of his particular discipline, never really becoming a part of the world of mainstream education. Thus, the blame for the unsatisfactory situation in the schools must be shared by the various professional training programs and the public schools. The various disciplines have narrow views of education and their professional pride and affiliation and resulting need to defend their autonomy causes their professionals to identify more with the specialty than with education. The school systems themselves lack a structure that would provide effective coordination and consolidation of services.

Proposed changes

Two major difficulties inhibit effective utilization of these professionals' knowledge and skill to improve the instructional program and learning outcomes. The first of these is the organization and coordination of these support services. The second is the focus of their efforts, their role, and the client group they should be serving. Second-Order Change # 37 and 38 address these two issues.

Second-Order Change #37. A sufficient number of support personnel should be assigned to each academic planning unit (as defined in Second-Order Change #4) so that its teachers have immediate access to any of these support services.

This proposal means that each academic planning unit will have assigned to it enough curriculum specialists, psychologists, media personnel, etc., to enable teachers within the unit to have access to the support person they need with no more than a two-day delay. Thus, the number of support personnel assigned to an academic planning unit will vary according to the number of teachers within the unit.

Some of these support personnel should be school-based. It would be desirable to have media personnel, guidance personnel, school psychologists, and school social workers assigned on a school basis, with at least one such person assigned to no more than two schools, depending on the size of the school. It would be preferable if each were assigned to only one school. Curriculum specialists may work out of a school but they should be available for consultation to a specified number of teachers, by cycle in the case of elementary schools, or by subject area in the case of secondary schools.

The purpose of this reorganization is to bring sufficient numbers of these support personnel as close as possible to their client group. Services can then be provided more quickly, more efficiently and effectively, and with greater results in terms of improving student learning than is now the case.

Who is the client group for these support personnel? This question has been argued for years in practically all of these professional specialties, except for curriculum specialists. School psychologists, guidance personnel, and school social workers seem to believe their client is the student, and they usually deliver services directly to the student, often without informing the teacher of the nature and reason for the service.

In the case of school media personnel and school librarians, the picture is somewhat less clear. Their client group includes both teachers and students, with services delivered to both. The question of client group has not been as seriously debated among these professionals as it has with those three professional specialties noted above.

The client group for curriculum specialists has always been the teacher, and other possible groups have not been debated.

Second-Order Change #38. The client group for all support personnel as here defined is the teacher.

One of the basic principles of this book is that teachers should be the instructional leaders of the school and responsible for decision-making concerning the instructional program delivered to students.

This is in keeping with the belief that the primary mission of the schools is to promote learning. To improve the instructional program being delivered to each student, the knowledge and skills of these support personnel must be at the disposal of the teachers. Each of these professionals has a unique talent to offer teachers in this regard. This does

337

not mean that these support personnel will or should not have direct contact with or deliver services directly to students. Such could not be the case. It does mean that the primary mission of these personnel is to support the instructional program teachers deliver to students.

Educational support personnel

Educational Support Personnel is a term for the new type of professional support person who would perform the duties of school guidance personnel, school psychologists, *and* school social workers. As indicated earlier, these personnel must be trained with a professional orientation developed from the framework and objectives of education and the mission of the schools. The term emphasizes the central focus of these personnel, on how child and adolescent development influences learning needs and expectations.

It would be preferable for one or more of these personnel to be assigned to each school within the academic planning unit. The emphasis at each level of school and within each school would differ. At the elementary level, one of these personnel should be assigned to each cycle of children and remain assigned to that cycle as it progressed through the school. This would allow a continuity of service provided to teachers, based on a knowledge of the history of the children. These personnel would also be responsible for any necessary testing of these children, establishing contact with the parents of the children, and reporting this information to the teacher for instructional background and decision-making.

At the secondary level, these personnel should be assigned by cycle. During the first three-year cycle, these personnel would continue to work closely with the home. There would probably be less need for individual testing but more need for group testing, such as achievement, aptitude, interest and vocational tests. This information would be needed by the teacher for instructional strategy development and by the student for educational and vocational decision-making.

In the second three-year cycle of the secondary school, these personnel should be assigned to one of the four major academic groupings. They would continue to work closely with teachers on matters of instructional strategy and with students on educational and vocational decision-making. Contact with the homes would be maintained as necessary.

At both school levels these personnel would concentrate on the interaction among learning needs, patterns, and expectations and the appropriate level of development of the student. The emphasis of these personnel would not be on the subject matter being taught, but on the learning principles involved in teaching children. They would be the

338

experts on child development for the level of school they serve, on classroom organization and learning, and on other matters affecting helping children learn more effectively at different developmental stages.

Preparation program changes: guidance, school psychological, and school social worker personnel

Second-Order Changes #37-38 addressed the problems met by service delivery by these personnel at the school system level. The following proposed Second-Order Changes present those changes and improvements necessary at the training program level to coordinate training emphases with changes recommended for the public school level.

Second-Order Change #39. School guidance personnel, school psychologists, and school social workers should receive a common training program.

The implications of this proposal are profound. It is also not a new proposal. Arbuckle (1966), in his classic book on pupil personnel services, made much the same proposal. Although his suggestion was concerned primarily with providing a common core curriculum for school counselors and school psychologists, the principle is the same as suggested here. The objectives of these professionals are essentially the same, and there is a common body of knowledge and skills that provide the basis for their professional activities in the school setting. As indicated previously, there is significant overlap in the services provided to students by these professional specialties. Although each has a specific area of emphasis, the significant amount of overlap in their responsibilities and orientation and the organizational patterns under which they labor tend to dilute the total effect these efforts could have for all students. The combined effect of the changes proposed in Second-Order Changes 17 and 18 would change dramatically the nature of support services available to teachers to help all students.

These changes include the advantages and benefits that are discussed below. At least one school system, the Charlotte-Mecklenburg School System (NC) has instituted such a plan whereby they required all guidance personnel and school social workers to obtain certification as a school psychologist. These personnel, along with previous school psychologists, were each assigned to an elementary school. Although, to this author's knowledge, there has not been a published report of this effort, observation indicates that it is working well. It is also interesting that Magary (1972) notes that the City of Los Angeles requires its elementary counselors to have the school psychologist certificate. A suggested curriculum for a common training program for school guidance personnel, school psychologists, and school social workers is outlined in the second section of this chapter.

By making these support service personnel responsible to the academic planning unit, with the teacher as the client, the role of each of these support service professionals becomes much more focused. This proposal clearly identifies the instructional program as the top priority of a school's mission, with the teacher in change of instruction. This clarifies the question of who is in charge of the services delivered to students. It is the teacher.

These proposals also change the nature of the client group of these specialties in two ways. First, the direct client group becomes the teacher, not the student. Second, the children to be served by this change become the class of all children, not just those with special learning needs.

The nature of the organizational pattern for providing support services is also clarified by these proposals. By making the teacher the focal point for coordinating support services, it is necessary to bring these services closer to the teacher so that access to and provision of these services is direct and immediate. This is accomplished by assigning enough of these personnel to each academic planning unit to carry out its programs effectively.

Second-Order Change #40. Universities offering more than one program in the support service areas should consolidate such programs in one department within the school of education and develop and require a common core curriculum for this new area.

Second-Order Change #41. Universities offering such a program should use the title of Department of Educational Support Services for these programs.

Second-Order Change #42. State departments of public instruction (education) should dispense with separate certification for school counselors, school psychologists, and school social workers in favor of one new certificate for Education Support Service Professionals.

Second-Order Change #43. A common core curriculum for Educational Support Service Professionals should be reflected by the following components and elements. This program would exist only at the graduate level.

Component	Elements	Credit Hours
1. Learning and development	A. Advanced cognitive science B. Advanced child development C. Advanced adolescent development	9
2. Individual & group assessment	A. Individual assessment– intelligence & academic B. Group assessment – intelligence & academic	12
3. Individual & group interventions	A. Individual – theory & methods B. Group – theory and methods	12
4. Program planning, implementation & evaluation	A. Theory and methods of implementation, evaluation & program planning B. Theory and methods of program implementation & intervention C. Theory and methods of program evaluation	9
5. Special populations	A. The handicapped B. Potential drop-outs, drug problems, etc.	9
6. Human relations & small group dynamics	A. Theories and methods	9
7. Case coordination & management	A. In-school coordination B. School-community coordination	9
8. Clinical experiences and internship-professional ethics		15
Total Program Hours		84

The program recommended is an extensive one, borrowing freely from a number of program areas to develop one that is built coherently around a concept of the knowledge base and skills these personnel will need in order to deliver more effective services to the schools. Once the assumption is made that the training of these personnel should result in only one type of professional, not several, it is logical to develop a curriculum for such a program based on how these personnel should function in the schools. The length of the program would require approximately two and a half years to complete, excluding summer school attendance. This is to bring these personnel to an entry level of knowledge and skill for delivering the services recommended. The length of the program is not significantly greater than the entry level required for most school psychologists (60 semester credit hours plus a year of internship) (National Association of School Psychologists, 1981), or to obtain a Masters of Social Work (MSW) (a minimum of 60 semester credit hours), the preferred entry level to the profession of social work. Even counselor education programs are requiring a minimum of 42 semester credit hours for entry level to the profession, and many such programs are requiring more. Thus, the program recommended is not much greater than those currently in existence for most of these professional areas.

This curriculum provides a core of knowledge and skills that would allow a new type of professional to emerge, a professional who is prepared to consult with teachers and parents about children's learning and development, to assist regular and special classroom teachers with planning, implementing, and evaluating academic programs, to conduct individual and group assessment programs, and to provide case management for those students who need case coordination services. Thus, the essential core services provided by school counselors, school psychologists, and school social workers are incorporated into one training program. Specialization in any component of this program could and should be done at the doctoral level.

It is not expected that these recommendations will be warmly received by the members of these three specialties. The changes proposed threaten their authority, their autonomy, and their livelihood. However, to change and improve the situation, the profession of education, at both the public school and higher education levels, must control the preparation programs of those personnel who will work within the schools. These support personnel currently provide a vital and needed service to teachers and students. Yet, the services they could provide would be enhanced significantly by coordinating their efforts and establishing a common core curriculum and preparation program for entry level work in the schools. If any individuals wanted to specialize in one of these three areas, they could easily do so at the doctoral level. The critical point is that the profession of education — not psychology, not counseling, and not social work — must determine the kind of preparation these personnel need to work in the schools.

Media personnel

The concept of media personnel grew out of school librarians. In many ways, the nature of this professional specialty remains the same — to organize information and knowledge in a logical manner and make it available to patrons. Whereas such information and knowledge were

342

formerly stored primarily in books, advances in technology have now made it possible to store vast amounts of information on computer discs. Presumably, future advances in technology will further increase the amount of information available and ease the means by which it can be accessed. Thus, media personnel will not only have to select books and periodicals and contend with the vast new amounts of knowledge immediately accessible through technology, they will also have to understand the technology well enough to teach it to students and teachers. The emphasis in media centers must include not only making information and knowledge available, but integrating this knowledge in new and previously impossible ways. This adds an entirely new dimension to the role of media personnel as they seek to assist teachers in teaching children to synthesize knowledge from various discipline areas.

In elementary schools, media personnel will also have an important new responsibility. Since the objective of elementary schools would be on teaching children how to learn, teachers will need additional assistance in learning how to use computers in developing students' cognitive skills and in gaining access to new curriculum materials and procedures for teaching learning. There will be less emphasis on discipline-based knowledge than at the secondary level.

At the secondary level, media personnel must concentrate more on providing access to discipline- and subject-knowledge. In addition, there must be added emphasis on resources and methods for knowledge integration. Again, technology will make much more knowledge available, so teachers should expect more from students.

At both the elementary and secondary levels, but particularly at the secondary level, media centers (libraries) should be open from before school opens until late at night. Since the objective of the schools is to foster learning, it does not make sense to keep these centers open only during school hours. Opening these centers for longer hours, and encouraging and expecting students to use these facilities, sends an important message to students, teachers, and parents alike.

These media centers could also act as professional resource centers for teachers. Research findings on learning, new curriculum materials, etc., can all be made available to teachers by using these centers in more appropriate ways.

Curriculum specialist advisors

The current title for most of these personnel is curriculum-instructional specialist or something similar. As pointed out previously, they actually spend very little time in direct supervision and they should not be supervising curriculum or instruction. That is the role of teachers. However, there is a very important role for these personnel to play in advising on curriculum development and instructional matters. They should certainly be available at the academic planning unit level to provide assistance and recommendations concerning the overall coordination of the curriculum within the unit. They should be responsible also for staying abreast of new developments in curriculum theory and instructional practices and for bringing these developments to the attention of the appropriate teachers and media personnel.

At the elementary level, these personnel should concentrate on assisting teachers with developing instructional strategies for improving learning. They should also be generalists in curriculum areas of elementary schools, reading, math, etc.

At the secondary level, these personnel currently concentrate mainly on subject matter fields. However, to assist teachers in knowledge integration and instructional strategies, they should concentrate on one of the four major emphasis areas indicated previously, instead of being a curriculum specialist in a specific subject area such as biology or history.

Curriculum advisors at both school levels have a very important role to play in assisting new teachers in adjusting to the profession. It is these teachers who will need the most support and assistance. Curriculum advisors could play a very significant role in assisting these new teachers by providing them the necessary feedback and advice they need to be effective in helping children learn.

Summary

Support service personnel provide vitally needed support services to teachers, children, parents, and others in need of such services in our schools. Their efforts could be enhanced by improving the organization and coordination of their services and by consolidating the role of guidance, school psychological, and school social worker personnel. The professional life of these support personnel could go on as it does currently, and many children and adults would continue to benefit from their efforts and services. The question is whether these benefits could be increased and improved by a different approach to the delivery of these services. The answer to this question is a qualified "yes." Many of these increased benefits could be realized by implementing the second-order changes proposed. As helpful and productive as these changes might prove to be, lasting change and improvements in the delivery of these services will not

344

occur until changes at the public school level and in the preparation programs for these personnel are implemented. Changes at both levels must occur; change and improvement in only one will be negated if changes at the other level do not also occur.

16 Prospects and processes for achieving second- and third-order changes

The first chapters of this book described critical problems of education and the failures of educational reform to address these difficulties. Additional chapters addressed principles and characteristics of education as a system and the educational change process. Later chapters presented a series of second- and third-order changes designed to resolve these problems. This chapter describes the prospects for achieving the changes proposed, and finally, the processes and issues that must be attended to if these changes are be achieved.

The prospects for achieving second-order changes

The processes for achieving the changes proposed in this book are complex and interdependent. They will probably be strongly resisted. The changes proposed would not be easy to achieve under the best of conditions — a receptive environment willing to consider implementing changes of the nature and magnitude recommended. This type of reception cannot be assumed, because the changes proposed would significantly alter the basic power hierarchy of the educational enterprise, re-configure the means whereby instructional services are delivered to students, and re-define the mission, organization, and functions of public and teacher education. These are not changes that will be accepted gratefully by many educational and political leaders. The changes proposed represent areas of human attitudes, values, and behaviors that are among the most resistance to change. Yet, the changes suggested are those necessary if education is to significantly increase student learning and improve other student outcomes.

Education is a political process, and change of its basic structures will require a significant understanding of the political system and its operations. Sarason (1982) asserts that a school system, like any other major social institution, is political in both the narrow and the general sense of that word. That is, the behavior of people (students, teachers, administrators, parents) and the stability and changes in classroom, school, and system structures have to be seen in terms of seeking, allocating, and using power. Introducing, sustaining, and assessing an educational change are political processes because they inevitably alter or threaten to alter existing power relationships, especially if the process implies, as it usually does, a reallocation of resources. Sarason argues that few myths have been as resistant to change as the one that assumes the culture of the school is a non-political one, and few myths have contributed as much to failure of the change effort. He goes on to state, "Schools are political institutions in that their organization reflects conceptions of power: How it can be attained, who should have it, what can be done with it, and what one should do when the possession of power is challenged" (p. 292). Thus, the power of various constituencies must be recognized and enlisted in the change effort.

Berman and McLaughlin (1978) indicate in their report that, in the small number of instances where change seemed to have been successful, teachers had become a constituency for change. Therefore, *enlisting teachers as advocates of the change effort is imperative.* They can block any change effort by simply doing nothing. However, teachers alone cannot achieve significant change. Harvey (1990) suggests that it is critical for successful change to define what is desired, not what is desired to discard.

Even though most reform efforts have called for these changes, that they have not been achieved indicates the resistance to alteration. Morrish (1976) notes that anthropologists believe that resistance to change is proportional to the amount of change required in the receiving system and that individuals tend to resist most strongly at the point where the pressures of change exert their greatest pressure. Certainly, the resistance to the changes here proposed can be expected to be great.

The changes proposed would require a significant alteration of the current power structure controlling education, and it is precisely for this reason that the changes proposed have not been previously adopted and that educational reform efforts have not been successful. The dilemma faced by educational reformers is this: In order to achieve significant change and improvement of education, the schools must be re-structured. Their missions must be limited, their organization and administrative practices altered, and the responsibility for their control shared between those who must make the changes (the teachers) and those affected by the changes (parents/students). This requires second- and third-order changes of the nature proposed in this book. However, to achieve these changes, the policy-makers must renounce their authority over education. Thus, there is a direct and positive relationship between the implementation of second-

and third-order change and the redistribution of power, authority and control of education. Unless this relationship is clearly understood and used for implementing educational reforms, the goals of reform will not be accomplished.

Sarason (1982) believes that those who are or may be affected by the change should have some part in the change process, because only through such involvement can they become committed to the change. He summarizes:

- The more committed more groups are to a proposed change, the more likely the goals of change will be achieved. This provides no guarantee of success. It is a necessary but not sufficient element of effective change procedures.
- The recognition that parents and other community groups should be involved in the change process is tantamount to redefining them as resources capable of contributing to the change process.
- The more differentiated the constituencies to the change, the greater the likelihood that the adverse consequences of limited resources will be diluted. (p. 295)

When constituencies are viewed in this way, it is easy to see that those groups who are or may be significantly affected by any proposed change must be responsible for implementing the changes.

Sarason adds that educational personnel made a great mistake when they accepted responsibility for the schools. Their mistake was in not ensuring control of the resources necessary to achieve the goals. Elmore and McLaughlin (1988) have a different perspective. They report that both policy-makers and the general public tend to substitute external authority for the authority and expertise of educational practitioners. Federal policy has communicated a fundamental hostility and indifference to the authority and expertise of educational practice. Kirst (1988) and Zimpher (1977) agree with Elmore and McLaughlin. Kirst's review indicates that control of public education has been shifting from the local level during the past 30 years to a combination of state-level control and special interest groups at the federal, state, and local levels. Zimpher reports that control of teacher education been almost entirely in the hands of state-level officials since 1965. There are two critical points in these comments. First, who determines the policies, practices and appropriate outcomes of public and teacher education? Clearly educators do not. They have the responsibility, but not the authority. They do not share equally in policy-making and decision-making authority. The second and more critical issue is that educators made a critical strategic error when they accepted, or had

349

imposed upon them, responsibility for educational accountability and learning outcomes without insisting on equity in policy development for educational goals, procedures, and outcomes at the federal, state and local levels.

Another element of the change process that must be considered is the availability of resources — human and financial. Sarason (1982) has identified several key facets that relate to this issue. First, achieving educational goals is integrally related to the quantity and quality of resources that can be mustered, both financial and human. Second, the fewer resources that can be mustered, relative to those required by the formulation of the goals, the less chance there is to realize any goals, and the more reason one has to reformulate goals. Finally, in order to have an impact, the quantity and quality of resources have to be perceived by others as having strength or power. Sarason also suggests that how one formulates goals implicitly or explicitly determines the quantity and quality of resources needed. Further, there is always a universe of alternative goals that can be considered, and, if we do not consider that universe, it is largely because we are committed to a "Single" way of doing something. The commitment to a "Single" way is based on a set of values and beliefs that are barriers to seeing and accepting alternatives.

Sarason raises another question related to the resource problem: Who has formulated the goals of change? He suggests that, in many efforts at educational change, the formulator has been an individual or small group of people.

The proposals for change addressed in this book also assault generally accepted beliefs that some dimensions and/or types of change are immune to substantial or significant modification. These factors are discussed next.

A report by the Rand Corporation (Greenwood, Mann, and McLaughlin, 1975) described five critical dimensions of change and the relationship of each to the prospects of achieving change desired. These dimensions are (1) the centrality of change, (2) the complexity of the change, (3) the nature and amount of the change, (4) the consonance of the change with accepted values, and (5) the visibility of the change. Dalin (1978) described four types of change and the prospects for achieving each. These are (1) technological change, (2) behavioral change, (3) organizational change, and (4) social change. Each of these is considered below and its relation to the type of changes presented in this book discussed.

Dimensions of change

The centrality of the change

Centrality refers to the extent a particular change would alter the goals, norms, or patterns of behavior that are perceived to be central to the institutional setting. The more the change would alter these factors, the more resistance may be expected to the change.

Clearly, the second-order changes recommended would alter significantly these factors in public and teacher education. For example, the degree of educational leadership that would be required by teachers would not only change their behavior dramatically, it would also alter the norms and behaviors of local school board members, principals, and other administrators.

This type of change, where the behavioral norms of two groups would be altered significantly, with one gaining power and the other losing power, is extremely difficult to achieve. There are two major obstacles to this type of alteration. The first is that the group(s) losing power can be expected to resist strongly any such change. The second obstacle, and a far more challenging one to counter effectively, is that the group gaining power may either not desire an increase in decision-making authority or may not be able to exercise it appropriately. The assumption in this situation is that teachers would welcome an increase in decision-making authority. This may not be a valid assumption. Leiberman (1988) observes that teachers are mainly invested in matters affecting curriculum and instruction, since that is the material about which they care and with which they feel most comfortable and most prepared. Teachers have not been prepared to deal with the specifics of running a school, and, therefore, they may not be keen about assuming such responsibilities. A study by Metropolitan Life (1986) found that, although 97% of classroom teachers thought they should have the primary decision-making authority for selecting textbooks, only 31% thought they should have the primary role in peer review, 42% in the selection of new principals or decisions about school-level budget decisions.

This type of response to change from teachers would have a dooming effect on the success of the change effort. Therefore, any attempt to achieve change that would significantly affect the central norms of the institution must ensure that those who would gain in decision-making authority are both ready and willing to assume such responsibility and have the capacity to do so.

The complexity of the change

The complexity of the change refers to the degree of interdependence of the modifications and the extent of change required in the attitudes and behaviors of groups within the system. This is perhaps the primary reason the type of second- and third-order changes proposed have not been recommended or attempted previously. The changes proposed are extremely complicated and would require significant alteration of attitude and behavior on the part of many, frequently quite powerful, groups.

There is little doubt that the changes proposed are complicated. They would require change on the part of many groups, from governing agencies to classroom teachers. The success of the changes proposed are also mutually dependent. That is, their success depends not on one or two of them being implemented, but on all of them being implemented. For example, providing teachers the level and extent of decision-making authority recommended would not achieve the desired outcomes if appropriate changes in teacher education programs were not also made to prepare teachers to assume these additional responsibilities.

When changes recommended are as complicated as those proposed here, the degree of coordination required for successful outcomes of the changes must be equally intricate. The degree of coordination required is directly proportional to the complexity of the changes proposed. Such coordination requires careful planning and sequencing of the phases of change so that development and implementation of the changes proceed in an orderly and systematic fashion. The more complex the change effort, the more time will be required for the change process to be accomplished.

The nature and amount of the change

This factor refers to the amount of change required from an individual, as contrasted with the two previous factors that required change on the part of groups. The critical aspect of this factor is the level of difficulty the change represents for an individual. The more difficult the change required, the more an individual member of the system can be expected to resist the change.

The changes recommended would require significant change on the part of some members and much less on the part of others. Teachers in public schools and faculty members of teacher education programs would probably have the most difficult degrees of change to achieve. They would need to alter their teaching methods, learn new processes of instruction, and develop new content capacities. The development of these new capacities would have to be aided by significant inducements and incentives.

The consonance of the change

This factor refers to the extent to which the goals, values, and practices of the recommended changes are consistent with those of the system considering implementing the change.

The goals of the second-order changes proposed may be perceived by public school and teacher education personnel as relatively consistent with those currently operative. The most probable disagreement would be with the values and practices recommended.

The current goals of education clearly include the improvement of student learning outcomes. This goal is supported and accentuated by the changes proposed.

It is the value system represented by the proposed changes — cognitive science as the knowledge base of education, control of teacher education programs to education faculty — that will probably be most resisted by many educators and some segments of the public. In addition, the practices recommended — doing away with tenure, teachers serving on local school boards — will probably also be strongly resisted by various groups, with specific groups resisting particular changes proposed. The cumulative effect of these resistances may be quite powerful.

The visibility of the change

This change factor refers to the extent to which the change process is observable and monitored by groups inside and outside the system. The process, pace of implementation, and degree of success or failure of the change effort must be public. This factor should be responded to by those responsible for the change effort in a systematic fashion, according to a published schedule. Since it is primarily concerned with an accountability process for monitoring the change process implemented, this change factor will be considered more extensively later in this chapter

Types of change

Technological change

Technological change can be a major variable that affects the life of an organization (Aldrich, 1972). Dalin (1978), however, reports that educational changes in technology have had little effect in education since they have tended to maintain the status quo in society. Technological change is not a primary focus of the changes recommended in this book and will not be considered further.

Behavioral change

Most change efforts require a degree of behavior change in individuals, ranging from minimal to significant. Certainly, the changes proposed would require extensive behavioral change on the part of individuals, from classroom teachers to those on governing bodies. The number of individuals who would have to change and the extent of the behavioral change required by the proposals are formidable. The extent of behavioral change required would not be easy to achieve, and significant resistance to the amount necessary can be anticipated.

Organizational change

Organizational change can include a number of elements. Such elements as group norms, organizational structure, authority hierarchy, leadership behavior, and the climate of the organization can all be embraced under this factor. The second-order changes suggested would impact each of these, as well as virtually all critical elements of school system organization and many organizational aspects of teacher education preparation units.

These changes would not be easy to achieve. Any one of them by itself would not be easy to achieve, but, when combined, they present an intimidating array of obstacles.

Social change

Social change refers to the redistribution of power, resources, and opportunities within a society or social sub-system. This type of change has not been successfully achieved at the society level through educational change efforts alone (Dalin, 1978). At a social sub-system level, i.e., an educational system, there is little history of such changes being attempted.

The changes proposed in this book call for significant redistribution of the power, as well as for new concepts and mechanisms for allocating resources within the educational system. The redistribution of power would result in a reversal of the power hierarchy within the system (teachers and administrators) and in a new shared authority of power at the system governing level (teachers and representatives of the public). The redistribution of resources would be handled by new mechanisms for allocating resources, e.g., program-dependent cost analyses, teacher determination of merit allocations.

The combined effect of these redistributions would be significant and probably resisted strongly. Although the public might be prepared to share policy decision-making power with teachers, it is unlikely that educational administrators would willingly forgo their power status and authority within the system. They would, probably, have to be compelled from higher authority sources to do so. The resistance to redistribution of resources within the system would probably rest on two factors. The first factor is the amount of resources required to implement the changes. If additional resources were not required, then less resistance could be anticipated. The second factor is whether the change outcomes would warrant a change in resource allocation methods.

Summary of dimensions and types of change

It seems unlikely that the changes proposed in this book have a high probability of implementation. The dimensions of change they target focus on educational system elements largely immune to significant alteration. The challenges to existing central educational norms, the complexity of the changes, and the nature and amount of change required on the part of individuals all support a low probability that the changes proposed would be considered for implementation. Although the objectives of the recommended changes appear to be consistent with existing educational goals, the extent of the changes called for will probably be challenged.

The one dimension of change that might support the proposed changes is visibility. The scale of the changes proposed would make them highly visible. Therefore, the change process would be open review and analysis by those concerned with improving student outcomes. However, this dimension would not come into play until the process of change had been initiated.

The types of change necessary to implement the second- and third-order changes proposed are those described by Dalin (1978) as the most difficult to achieve. These include changes in individual behavior, organizational functions, and the bases and mechanisms for resource allocation. Reasons for considering the changes include the probability that these changes would not necessarily result in additional resource requests. They would provide more focused priorities for schools' resource expenditures, and, they would offer a higher probability of stricter accountability and outcome measurement.

A framework for change expectation

Achieving the changes proposed is possible. The following section presents a framework for this case. It is followed by the processes and mechanisms necessary to allow the changes to be implemented.

Many educational reform efforts have failed because those responsible for designing and managing them lacked knowledge of the educational change process. Therefore, a complete understanding of the educational change process should result in better designing and managing of the change plan and in a higher probability of achieving the desired goals of change.

Several aspects of the change process must be understood as fundamental aspects of the change process if the change effort is to succeed. These include three key perspectives and four factors critical for the process, the barriers to change, and basic mechanisms by which change policy goals can be translated into specific implementation strategies.

Perspectives of the change process

Dalin (1978) has identified three critical aspects of the change process as fundamental for developing effective change programs. The contributions of each of these must be understood in its own right, and in combination with each of the other two.

Change as process

Change is a process that takes place over time. It is not a product that can be produced overnight. The time required for the change process to produce the desired results depends on the complexity of the change, its centrality, the change required by the system members, and its agreement with accepted institutional norms. The time required will also vary according to the type of change to be implemented — technological, behavioral, organizational, or social. The more types that must be included, the longer the time required. Social and organizational change normally require more time to achieve than technological or behavioral change.

Educational change must also be expected to develop in a non-linear manner. It is highly probable that change will occur by stages and involve a continuing series of interactions involving complex interchanges among individuals, institutions, and system sub-units. These interactions must also involve interchanges between system members and groups outside the system.

A critical factor in determining the probable success of complex educational change is the time allotted for the process to be designed, implemented, and evaluated. More time will be required to achieve complicated changes than for relatively less complex changes. In this regard, the coordination and management of complex change efforts from the concerned agents, both internal and external to the system, will be critical factors in determining the success of the change.

356

Change as a systemic process

Change in educational systems must be perceived as a systemic process, whereby introducing change at one point will produce changes, often unintended, at other points of the system. These systemic processes affect and are affected by the formal and informal networks existing among individuals, system sub-units, and special interest groups both within and external to the system. The probable success of an educational change effort will depend on the strength of these relationships on any particular aspect of the change, and the change manager's ability to anticipate and cope with these relationships. It is critical for the decision-maker to understand the dynamics at play in the interactions among the various networks.

Change as a multi-dmensional process

Change is a process that must involve the use of different perspectives if it is to be effectively designed and managed. It is possible to view change as a political process, a technical process, an organizational process, and an individual process. Each of these plays a role at different times and to varying degrees. Each must be considered vital to the success of the change process. Therefore, the designers and managers of the change process must be sensitive to these different perspectives and to the influence each may have at a particular time in the change process.

Factors involved in change

Dalin (1978) has identified four factors that are especially critical for understanding the educational change process at a general and abstract level. They are (1) the educational setting, (2) the environment, (3) the innovation (change), and (4) the change strategy. These factors were distilled from some 150 case studies from a large number of different political, cultural, organizational and educational settings.

The educational setting

The educational setting includes such elements as financing, decision-making, support structure, size, and school level. According to Dalin, cost level is not necessarily an important variable in predicting the outcome of change. More important are the means by which resources are allocated and the incentive structures provided for change.

357

The decision-making structure of a system does exert an influence on the change process. Less clear is the exact means by which this influence is exerted. Dalin does note that there is some evidence to suggest that the closer the decisions about implementation are to actual practice, the higher the probability of change.

The support structure of the educational system, school, or organizational unit under consideration consists of the larger system that surrounds the system (the environment of systems). The manner in which the components of this system environment interact is a significant factor in determining the rate and direction of change. Although little is known of precisely how these interactions affect system and sub-system functions, clearly the influence they can wield is great.

The size of the system is clearly a factor to consider in developing change strategies. The larger the system, the more complex the change process. The size of a system provides both benefits and hindrances with certain types of changes. These effects must be considered in developing change strategies.

The level of the system that is targeted for change is also a major factor to consider in arriving at a change strategy. It is obviously easier to achieve change at a classroom level than for an entire school, and so on. The changes proposed in this book will require careful consideration of a change strategy because they would affect a large, interdependent system.

The environment

Dalin lists seven areas of the educational environment that must be considered in arriving at a prediction of the probability of achieving educational change. These areas include the economy, political stability, social expectations, the labor market, teacher unions, technological change, and the relationship of education to other social sectors involved in educational activities.

Each of these areas must be considered in its own right as exerting an influence on the process and acceptability of any particular change. In addition, interactions among these areas must be considered. For example, social expectations may be conducive for achieving change, but the economy may not be sufficiently stable or able to provide the resources necessary to achieve the change desired.

Long-term political stability appears critical for allowing the implementation of change to have a sufficient duration for assessing change outcomes. This is valid for all levels of educational operation, but particularly so for changes at a state or national level. As Dalin notes, educational reforms usually take many years from initiation to institutionalization.

The nature of the change refers to the significance and extent to which the proposed change(s) will affect individuals. That is, will the change require an individual or group to learn a new skill, to stop a traditional practice and learn another, or will it require a new attitude towards one's behavior or that of another group? This element tends to vary with the centrality and complexity of the proposed change but differs in that it focuses on the individual. Strategies must be developed which permit individual capacity-building.

The extent to which the goals of the change are consistent with the values of the individual is an important variable. The more distant these are, the more difficult it will be to achieve the support of the individual. However, if individuals agree with the goals of the change effort, she/he will tend to support it.

The goals of the change must remain fairly constant over time. This factor tends to vary with the political stability of the system. Another factor to be considered is that either the change process or the outcomes may result in alteration of the change efforts.

The change strategy

The strategy developed for implementing change must be a careful consideration of the factors related to the change goals and the groups that have to approve the change, that will have to change, and that will be affected by the change. Each of these groups possesses different needs, attitudes, and desires for change. The change strategy developed must consider each of these groups and the strategies and tactics that will most appeal to them. It is quite possible that different strategies will have to be developed for each group, and possibly sub-groups as well.

Consideration must also be given to which groups will be involved in initiating the change effort and the relationship that group has with the educational agencies and public groups that would be affected by the change. Questions concerning the decision-making authority and structure for considering and implementing the change effort should be attended to and resolved before instituting any change effort.

The types of change

Dalin (1978) describes three types of change required by the recommendations in this book. These are (1) behavioral change, (2) organizational change, and (3) social change. A fourth type of change not discussed by Dalin is attitude change. For purposes of this discussion, attitude and social change will be presented together.

Behavior change

Changes in behavior will be required by practically all participants in the educational enterprise. Administrators and teachers will have to change significantly as previously discussed. The public will have to change their behavior by learning to share authority for decision-making with teachers. State legislatures will have to change their behavior by learning not to use education for political advantages unrelated to the change efforts undertaken. Others also will have to change behavior.

These changes will not be easy. They will require significant effort on the part of those involved, particularly those who will lose power as a result of the changes. The behavioral changes required will have to be carefully considered by the state coordinating body, including who will be affected, and in what manner and to what extent they will be affected. Planning to achieve behavioral change will be difficult, but it is a necessary aspect of achieving second-order change.

Organizational change

Organizational change of education should be relatively easy to achieve compared to the difficulty of achieving behavioral and attitudinal change. Once the decision to implement specified mission priorities has been made, the decision regarding the appropriate knowledge base necessary for achieving the mission goals should be evident. The organization structure best suited for implementing the programs required for achieving the mission should also be apparent. Thus, organizational change of education is a function of the schools' mission and the knowledge base supporting the achievement of the mission. Again, this should be a decision determined locally, since there may be local factors that affect the specific form of the organizational format.

Attitudinal and social change

These may be the most difficult types of change to achieve. They are also the most critical. To implement the types and levels of change recommended, the attitudes of the public, professional educators, and policy-makers towards education will have to change dramatically. The public's current distrust of educators' competence to improve student learning outcomes and achieve other goals will have to be moderated at the least. The changes proposed require a period of educational stability wherein the necessary capacity-building, programmatic changes, planning and coordination can be undertaken without constant and haphazard change and disturbances. This period of stability for program development and change requires an attitude of trust and patience on the part of legislatures and the public. This is a difficult change to accomplish because neither the public nor the legislatures are used to either trust or patience with education. However, if significant change and improvement of educational outcomes are to be achieved, these variables must be a prerequisite of the process.

If the attitudes of these groups are moderated and sufficient time allowed for development of the change process described, social change will have been achieved. Although the record of achieving social change through education is not an optimistic one (Dalin, 1978), it is possible. The factor that must be kept in mind is that social change is not a product, it is a process. It is a process that can be affected either by a specific outcome, or by interacting with another change process. In this situation, instituting a process of educational change could result in a social change process, prompted by the desire to improve student learning and yielding the attitudinal changes necessary.

Summary of change as a process

The process of change is a complex affair, affected by forces, groups, and interests internal and external to the system. Only by understanding these interactive elements of the process, engaging in a process analysis, and taking into account the interaction of the type of change as it interacts with the system characteristics, will designers and managers of educational change have a reasonable chance of success.

Barriers to change

Dalin (1978) has identified four types of barriers to achieving effective change. These include value, power, practical, and psychological barriers. Each of these must be understood, and where possible, anticipated so that effective strategies can be developed for overcoming them.

Value Barriers

These are barriers to change erected as a result of individuals and/or groups having different value systems from those they perceive as the causes and possible effects of change.

Power barriers

These are barriers which result from a redistribution of power and/or control of resources within a system. The more significant and far reaching the effects of a change, the more likely it is that this type of barrier will be encountered.

Practical barriers

Practical barriers can arise from a number of aspects of the change process. They can include appropriate resistance to the change because it is badly conceived or managed, a lack of sufficient resources to achieve the change, or because the change process failed to consider critical aspects of the effects of the change.

Psychological barriers

At times individuals seem to have a built-in resistance to change. Resistance to change can be anticipated even with no logical reason for opposition evident and no threat to the power, values, or status of individuals or groups apparent.

Summary of barriers to change

Any significant educational change will meet these types of resistance to the change effort (Dalin, 1978). A number of them can be operating at the same time, making it difficult to isolate and respond to them. In order for the change process to be effective, possible resistance must be anticipated, and strategies developed to confront and counter them before they can do irreparable damage to the change process. Managers of the change process should also be alert to the possibility that resistance to the change may signal difficulties in the implementation process that must be adjusted (Dalin, 1978).

Policy goals, implementation strategies, and the change process

McDonnell and Elmore (1987) have identified four mechanisms that can be used to translate policy goals through implementating specific actions for achieving desired educational outcomes. These mechanisms are:

- Mandates: rules governing the action of individuals and agencies, intended to produce compliance.

- Inducements: the transfer of money to individuals or agencies in return for certain actions.
- Capacity-building: the transfer of money for investing in material, intellectual, or human resources.
- System-changing: the transfer of official authority among individuals and agencies to alter the system by which public goods and services are delivered. (p. v)

Mandates

Most educational reform efforts have used mandates to achieve their goals. Mandates tend to be extensively utilized because they appear to be the most practical way to solve problems. They are relatively inexpensive, send a clear message concerning the desired goals, and can be quickly implemented. The expected consequence of mandates is compliance, and, although they generally require few resources to initiate, they can require considerable resources to monitor and enforce (McDonnell and Elmore, 1987).

Mandates also have two other costs. First, there is the human cost of compliance. Individuals and organizations are required to behave in uniform ways to the mandates. Deviations from the mandates are not encouraged and so risk-taking and experimentation on the part of the individuals and organizations affected may decline. The result is uniformity and stagnation. The second type of cost is avoidance. Under conditions of enforced compliance, avoidance of the mandate is almost bound to develop. There are many methods of avoidance — feet-dragging, bartering with the enforcement agency — but the intent of all is to escape the mandate (McDonnell and Elmore, 1987).

The primary beneficiaries of mandates tend to be specific groups. For example, PL 94-142 benefited handicapped children.

There are two assumptions underlying the use of mandates. The first is that the mandate is necessary and good in its own right, and that action is required on the part of those affected by the mandate without regard of their capacity to carry out the mandate's directives. Second, there is the assumption that the action required by the mandate could not be accomplished without it (McDonnell and Elmore, 1987).

Inducements

Inducements are most often used when there is little agreement about the type of change necessary to resolve a particular problem (Ingram, 1977). Inducements provide authority to an organization to transfer resources or authority to an individual or institution in return for production of some service or product of value. Inducements are generally accompanied by rules and regulations to ensure that the funds expended or transferred are used according to the intent of the transferring agency or policy-makers.

There are benefits of inducements for both the agency and the recipients of the inducements. However, there are hidden costs to inducements such as administrative expenses to monitor the expenditure of the funds.

There are three primary differences between mandates and inducements. First, mandates use rules to affect performance; inducements use money. Second, mandates expect compliance, and inducements expect the demonstration of a service or product of value. Third, mandates require all agencies and institutions affected to comply with the required action, regardless of their capacity to do so. Inducements assume that individuals and institutions vary in their capacity to deliver particular performance levels and that additional money is one way to increase performance (McDonnell and Elmore, 1987).

Two assumptions about inducements are being made: (1) that the service or product would not be delivered at the desired level of skill without additional funds and (2) that individuals and institutions vary in their capacity to achieve certain levels of performance and that money induces improved performance (McDonnell and Elmore, 1987).

Capacity-building

Capacity-building is the attempt to improve the capabilities of individuals or institutions to deliver a product or service for which the return may not be immediate. Capacity-building is a form of insurance and investment for the future. As such, it can often be difficult to convince policy-makers that it is a worthwhile investment to make in the present. This is particularly evident in tight money times when the competition for scarce funds is greatest.

The main difference between the benefits of capacity-building and mandates/inducements is the time of their pay-off. Capacity-building results in future, often vaguely perceived, benefits. Mandates and inducements produce relatively immediate pay-offs (McDonnell and Elmore, 1987).

There are two assumptions about capacity-building: (1) that investing in the present in the development of knowledge, skill or competence improvement will pay dividends in the future, and (2) that capacity development is good in its own right or will provide dividends in other areas (McDonnell and Elmore, 1987).

System-changing requires the transfer of authority to govern the system with the expectation that such a change will improve the effectiveness and/or the efficiency of the system or alter the political network operating the system. System-changing may result in the creation of new agencies or in the dissolution of existing agencies or classes of institutions (McDonnell and Elmore, 1987).

Two assumptions must be made about system-changing: (1) that the existing institution, under current conditions, cannot achieve the results desired or necessary, and (2) that changing the authority hierarchy will produce the results desired or considered necessary (McDonnell and Elmore, 1987).

These four methods of achieving particular policy goals provide policy-makers a range of possible actions. Each of these methods can be used to achieve particular goals, providing the policy-makers recognize the relationship between the goal desired and the method best suited for achieving the goal. Policy-makers must also be aware of the assumptions and consequences of choosing a particular method to achieve the goal.

Summary

The framework for achieving the second- and third-order changes recommended rests on the assumption that once policy-makers understand more completely the nature and content of the educational change process, they will make more informed decisions concerning educational change and improvement efforts. The process of educational change must also be perceived within the context of education as a system. The factors discussed in this section provide a framework for identifying and understanding the critical elements an educational change effort must address, the types of barriers that can be anticipated in any change effort, and the four implementation strategies that policy-makers can use in seeking educational change. These elements of educational change can serve as a framework for conceptualizing the processes for achieving second- and third-order change.

A process for achieving second- and third-order changes

A process for achieving the types of change suggested for improving student learning and other outcomes is not a process to be undertaken lightly. It is a complex, difficult, and inter-dependent process, requiring intensive and cooperative actions by many individuals, agencies, and institutions. It requires a new and trusting belief in the competence of schools, a new role for state-level agencies and individual schools, and a coordination of programs and services not commonly seen among agencies and institutions. In short, it requires a re-framing of the process of educational change.

To begin the process, five principles of system operation and educational change have to be understood and endorsed by policy-makers who have the authority to initiate the process. These are (1) the Principle of Equifinality, (2) the Principle of Entropy, (3) the Principle of Regulation, (4) the Time Perspective, and (5) the Visibility of the Change Process. Each of these is discussed before a discussion of four phases of the process necessary for achieving third-order change. Following this discussion, the final section of the chapter provides a presentation of three aspects of the change process necessary for achieving second-order change.

Principles of system operation and educational change

The principle of equifinality

The first principle of the educational change process that must be addressed by policy-makers is the principle of equifinality. This principle of system operation asserts that it is possible to arrive at the same end point (goal) by different routes and from different starting (baseline) points. The implications for education are clear. Local school systems, individual schools, and students within each school vary significantly in their levels of educational attainment. Thus, it is not probable that they will be able to attain the same levels of learning outcomes under conditions that require adherence to standardized curricula or to other mandates requiring conformity to state or school system procedures. Teachers at the classroom level, the school level, and the school system level must be free to develop the learning procedures and activities that best suit the needs of their students in relation to the learning goals desired.

This principle must be addressed by policy-makers early in their deliberations concerning educational reform efforts. They must decide whether it will be a cornerstone on which to base additional changes of educational improvement. If this principle is agreed to by policy-makers, then other aspects of the educational change process can be developed within the context of promoting local determination of educational procedures for achieving learning outcomes.

Agreement to this principle includes also the responsibility for accountability of the decision-making at the local level and of the learning outcomes achieved. If the authority for decision-making at the local level is granted, the responsibility for the adequacy and appropriateness of such decisions must also be assumed by the local level.

The Principle of Entropy

The principle of entropy states that in open social systems the tendency over time is towards increased centralization of policy development, decision-making, and the use of mandates to achieve policy goals. This tendency must be resisted if the principle of equifinality is established and followed as an operating procedure. It is very easy for policy-makers to move into a posture of assuming centralized control when conditions and/or outcomes desired do not appear to be attaining the established goals.

The Principle of Control

The principle of control as derived from systems theory is concerned with the processes of feedback and regulation. Feedback is concerned with detecting disturbances between the desired and actual state of affairs. Regulation is concerned with control of the feedback mechanisms.

It is with feedback that teachers will be able to detect whether their decision-making is moving their students towards the learning goals established for them. It is also by feedback at higher levels of system operation that the differences between the desired and actual state of affairs can be measured. Feedback can be used, therefore, to determine whether the educational reform efforts are moving in the desired direction at an acceptable pace. This ability requires, however, that the goals of education be clearly specified so that exact measures of the difference between the desired and actual state of affairs can be obtained.

The specification of such goals must be directly related to the mission priorities established for education. Clearly, if mission priorities are established, then more concern and resources can be directed towards those with higher priority. Measures of accountability can then weigh progress as measured against the priority of the mission elements.

Regulation of feedback mechanisms is primarily concerned with the variety of information transmitted through a system's communication channels. If feedback is to be effective, it must deal with information that provides the necessary data for decision-making. The type of data needed for such decision-making must be determined before the need to make the decision. The sources from which the feedback data will be obtained must also be informed of the kind of data needed.

367

When policy-makers contemplate instituting educational reform efforts, it is on the basis of feedback that has indicated an unacceptable difference between the desired and actual state of affairs. If an educational change effort is to be kept on track, the goals of the change must be clear and unambiguous. There must be no confusion about what are the desired outcomes. Feedback mechanisms can then be developed from appropriate sources, which will serve two purposes. First, the actual process of the change effort can be measured against the projected direction and pace of change. Second, the benchmarks of goal accomplishment can be evaluated against those desired.

A final word on educational feedback. Most measures of educational attainment are measured by some form of test, usually commercially developed. These tests are probably not suited for obtaining the type of data needed for measuring the process and products of educational change. New methods would have to be developed to provide more accurate measures of the process.

The time perspective

The time perspective of the change process is a critical variable in determining educational change outcomes. Most educational reformers, as well as the general public, expect the changes instituted to demonstrate results in a relatively short time. This is a self-defeating expectation. Effective educational change takes time, often a considerable time. The time perspective for achieving significant educational change will take years, overlapping several election year cycles.

There must be an understanding of this time perspective, and there must be a commitment on the part of policy-makers to the time necessary to develop, implement, and evaluate the effects of educational change. This commitment must outweigh political advantages to be gained by criticizing educational change efforts and attempting to constantly re-design educational progress during election campaigns.

It will take years to achieve significant educational change. Consider the appropriate steps that must be take place before the demonstration of educational change outcomes, particularly those proposed in this book. First, there must be recognition that the only appropriate and authority invested group to promote the type of long-term change proposed is a state legislature. A state legislature is the only body that has the authority to convey the responsibility and control of educational change and improvement to another body.

Second, there must be an understanding among the policy-makers, the public, and professional educators that, in the past, development of educational policy goals has been a political process. This political process has generally resulted in a choice of policy and implementation pattern based on which key constituents would win or lose with different alternatives (McDonnell and Elmore, 1987). This process has to be discarded in favor of one that believes that improving student learning is more important than achieving short-lived political gain by keeping education in a constant state of random and non-systematic reform.

Third, policy-makers (the state legislators) must identify the mission priorities for the schools. The development of educational mission priorities is an appropriate responsibility for a legislative body. However, once these priorities are established, the legislative body must stay out of the discussion of the means by which these goals will be attained. It is appropriate for a legislative body to expect and demand progress reports once the process of change has been initiated.

Fourth, there must be a realization and acceptance of the fact that significant educational change will take years to produce demonstrable results. This recognition must be honored by succeeding legislative bodies for as long as progress is being made towards the goals desired.

Fifth, the body assigned the responsibility for coordinating educational change efforts must be appointed and elected. It will need time to work out a plan of educational change and the proper timing and phasing of systematic development of educational improvement efforts. This plan will need to consider the changes needed in both public and teacher education, the coordination and sequence of change phases for each, and the benchmarks and time table for implementing changes in each.

Sixth, it must be recognized that both education and change are developmental processes. Sufficient time must be allowed for teacher preparation programs to modify their programs to emphasize the mission priorities established for the public schools. It may take as long as 10 years for enough teachers trained in the new format to make a difference in the schools. It may take another six years before the teachers have made a demonstrable difference in learning outcome measures for sufficient numbers of students. Harvey (1990) points out that educational reformers often blunder by attempting too great a change early in the process. The change process must be developmental.

Seventh, there must be must be an assessment of the readiness and capacity of the public and the profession to adopt the type and levels of change under consideration. If the changes considered are worthy of implementation, the readiness and capacity of these groups to accept them must be assessed, or the changes, regardless of their merit, may not be adopted. Thus, a plan for readiness and capacity-development must be constructed. This effort could take considerable time and must be a recognized factor in developing a time perspective for change implementation.

In summary, the time perspective for achieving significant educational change is much greater than political leaders seem to have been willing to accept. The initiation of a successful educational change process will require state legislatures to adopt educational policies that recognize this fact. Once these policies are in place, progress can be made to implement phases of educational change, and educators can be relatively free of concern that next year will bring a change in policy, or new mandates that erase progress of current efforts.

The visibility of the change process

The visibility of the change process is a critical ingredient for ensuring that continued progress is maintained towards the desired goals. This visibility should begin with the first efforts of a coordinated and systematic change plan. The public, as well as professional educators, deserve to know the process that will be used in attempting to achieve improved student outcomes. The public and elected professional educators should be involved in dialogue concerning the mission priorities that educators can and should strive to achieve. Once these have been established, the change process agreed to and its time table should be published. Regular and frequent reports of progress and problems should be published. The reasons for the problems and the means used to remedy them should be published also. The problems should not be minimized, but emphasis should be placed on solution efforts.

Summary

There are several critical elements of the processes described above. They include political leadership, change, commitment to the principles of equifinality, an understanding of the principles of entropy, regulation, the time perspective, establishing new processes for achieving change, and efining mission priorities for the schools.

The mission priorities

The identification and definition of the primary mission for the schools, and any additional prioritized mission elements, is an essential aspect of the educational change process. Unless the mission elements are clearly specified and defined there can be no effective educational change. The consequence of a vague, ambiguous, and non-prioritized set of mission elements for the schools is a continuation of the status quo. That is, students and professional educators will continue to be at the mercy of a continuing series of random changes of educational reform because the reformers do not understand the necessity for planned change to accomplish the objectives of education.

A clearly specified mission statement is necessary to identify the additional changes that must be a function of mission identification. These include the knowledge base necessary to support the mission goals, and the organization, administrative practices, and prioritized resource allocations changes that must be consistent with the mission objectives.

The mission identification for the schools must involve a process that involves input from the public and the profession of education. Input from the public is necessary because (1) it is the public's right, and (2) the public must agree with the desired priorities of the mission. Professional educators must be involved because they can inform the public whether the profession can accomplish the mission goals, and if not, what resources or capacity-building would be required to achieve the goals.

As discussed in a previous section, it is the state legislature that must initiate the process of such discussions. A state legislature is the only body with the necessary authority to implement such a process of educational change. However, once the mission elements have been identified and prioritized, the legislature should remove itself from the process of change, except to receive periodic progress reports. The next steps in the change process require constant attention if it is to be successful. The legislature does not have the time or knowledge to involve itself in the remaining steps of change. The next step is to establish a body responsible for coordinating the change processes necessary for mission goals to be accomplished.

The need for and role of coordination

The need for coordination of the change process effort is a result of the complex and inter-dependent nature of the task. Fundamental changes such as those suggested in this book can only be accomplished under conditions of a planned and systematic approach to the issues and problems identified. There must be a commitment to a systematic effort, or the risk of the process becoming arbitrary and haphazard becomes a very real danger. This would result in the goals of the change effort not being realized.

The need for coordination is great because of the multitude of institutions, agencies, and individuals that must be involved in the process.

371

There is the need for coordination within and among the public school sector, local school boards, state education agencies, and teacher preparation institutions. There is also a need to coordinate changes within each of these bodies. The task of coordinating change efforts among and within these groups is a formidable task. It will require patience, determination, and objectivity. The role is not an easy one.

Chapter 10 discussed the nature of the agency needed to coordinate the change process. The role of this body is coordination, rather than determination, of the substance of the change effort. This body should concern itself with planning the change process phases, i.e., identifying the logical progression of steps that must be followed to ensure the process is implemented correctly. Table A.1 identifies the phases and order of changes that must be considered.

Third-order changes

Third-order changes are those required (1) to put in place a mechanism for developing the conditions that allow second-order changes, and (2) to maintain the process and effect of second-order changes. Third-order changes must come first to provide the necessary planning, coordinating and deliberate body to systematically implement and review progress of second-order changes. Without attention to these factors, the risk of unintended results and the negation of desired results is high. Although the task of the third-order change body would be complex and difficult, by itself its efforts would not lead to the changes or educational outcomes desired. These accomplishments must be the result of the second-order changes implemented.

Mechanisms for implementing second-order change

There are three primary implementation mechanisms for instituting second-order changes that must be considered. These are (1) system-changing, (2) capacity-building, and (3) inducements. These are taken from the discussion presented earlier of McDonnell and Elmore's (1987) work.

System-changing

System-changing is the transfer of authority from one group to another in the expectation that such a transfer will result in the achievement of outcomes not realized under conditions of current authority. This book has

372

proposed such a transfer of control from the public and educational administrators to a shared authority and responsibility for educational outcomes between the public and teachers.

Such a change of authority cannot be accomplished over night. It must be carefully planned and sequenced if it is to be effective. Consideration must be given to the legal, political, and programmatic concerns and issues that would be sure to erupt from such a change. Especially, consideration would have to be given to the capacity of the teachers to undertake the new responsibilities that they would have to assume.

Capacity-building

The current capacity of teachers to undertake the responsibilities that such a system change would entail is suspect. Certainly, at the very least, there would have to be assurances that the competence of teachers to assume the responsibilities proposed would have to be examined. It is unlikely that teachers currently have the capacities required. First, they have not been prepared to assume such responsibilities. Second, they have been conditioned in the schools that they are not to undertake such responsibilities. Third, many may not wish to assume such responsibilities.

However, if education is to achieve significant changes of the types recommended, teachers must assume these new responsibilities. In order for teachers to take on these additional responsibilities, two types of capacity-building will have to be implemented. First, pre-service programs will have to prepare prospective teachers in both the attitudes and behaviors necessary for accepting these responsibilities. This means that teacher education faculty must teach these new attitudes and behaviors. This might be a difficult task for current faculty to implement.

Second, and probably far more difficult, the current teaching force will have to develop these new attitudes and behaviors. Such an effort will be difficult because these teachers will have to develop a set of attitudes and behaviors that are counter to those most teachers currently possess. Faculty development programs concerning these issues will have to be carefully developed and implemented. The role of the coordinating agency with both the pre-service and the in-service programs would be critical. The time involved for this type of capacity-building would be significant.

Capacity-building of current and pre-service teachers must be the first priority of any plan to achieve significant educational change. It is teachers' competence in the classroom and with policy decisions that will ultimately determine whether the educational changes proposed will achieve their objectives. Changes in educational practice cannot be instituted or expected before the capacities of teachers have been developed to the point where

373

they can competently implement the actions necessary to achieve the change goals. Thus, the coordination of plans and actions to develop the capacities of teachers must be a prime consideration for change implementation.

Inducements

Inducements are a fundamental means for achieving change. The transfer of resources to promote the changes desired are a critical part of any change effort. In today's educational world, the availability of resources is less important than the basis on which they are distributed. It is the rationale on which the resources are allocated that must be changed. Two factors are important in this regard. First, according to the principle of equifinality, different resource amounts will be required for the different approaches instituted to bring disparate groups by different routes to equivalent end points. It must be recognized that meeting different groups of students' learning needs will require different amounts and type of resources. The flexibility for transferring resources to meet these needs must be determined locally. Second, funding for resource allocation should be based on program need, not on the number of students involved. Allocating funds should be a local decision, in which programs are measured against the mission priority and the probability of the programs' contributions to the mission.

The use of inducements can be a valuable aid for achieving educational change goals. However, in order to be maximally effective, the flexibility and authority for using inducements must be a local decision. It is only at the local level that the understanding of the specific relationship between the probable benefits of the transfer and the programs contributions can be adequately assessed. Therefore, the local level must have full authority for allocating resources among and within programs.

Overcoming barriers

There will obviously be resistance to the changes proposed here. Each of the types defined by Dalin (1978) can be expected. Attempts at significant change carry with them a built-in resistance to their success. Expected barriers are, however, not reasons to desist from the attempt. By careful planning and coordination, by making the change process highly visible, by specifying goals and procedures, by reporting progress and problems, and by dealing realistically with the uncertainties that change promotes in individuals, the potential damage of the barriers to the change effort can be substantially reduced.

It is unlikely, however, that all barriers can be reduced or eliminated. The legislature and coordinating body can expect to be intensely lobbied by special interest groups and some professional organizations. Local groups can be expected to exert pressure at both the local and state levels for specific purposes. However, by understanding these types of barriers, policy-makers will be able to understand the motivation and nature of the resistance and be better able to deal with the barriers they meet.

The phases of change

Careful attention must be paid to the coordination and timing of the change effort. Certain types of change have to precede others, and some groups and institutions will have to implement changes at different times during the change process. Table A.1 indicates the type of change required, and the order of the change phase for each second-order change proposed. Three change phases are used. Changes in the first phase must precede those in the second phase, and those in the second phase those in the third phase. Table A.2 identifies the group, agency, or institution that must implement each second-order change.

Chapter summary

This chapter has discussed the prospects for achieving second- and third-order change. According to conventional wisdom, the prospects of success are not high. The processes for achieving the changes proposed would be difficult and complex, and they would require the development of significant improvements in the attitudes and behavior of a large number of individuals, groups, and institutions. The issues and procedures that would have to be addressed and resolved for second- and third-order changes to occur were presented and discussed.

Appendix

Table A.1
Type of change and phase order of change for each
second-order change

Public education

Second-Order Change #	Type of Change	Phase Order
1	Governance, Attitude	First
2	Attitude	Second
3	Attitude, Policy	Second
4	Attitude, Policy	Second
5	Attitude, Policy	Second
6	Attitude, Policy, Behavior	Third
7	Attitude, Legislative, Behavior	Second
8	Legislative, Governance, Attitude	Second
9	Attitude, Policy	Second
10	Attitude, Policy	First
11	Attitude, Policy	First
12	Attitude, Policy	First
13	Attitude, Policy	Second
14	Attitude	First
15	Policy	First
16	Legislative	First
17	Attitude, Policy	Second

Teacher education

Second-Order Change #	Type of Change	Phase Order
18	Legislative, Governance	First
19	Legislative, Governance, Attitude	Second
20	Attitude, Behavior	First
21	Attitude	First
22	Attitude	Second
23	Attitude, Policy, Behavior	First
24	Attitude, Policy, Behavior	Second
25	Governance, Attitude	First
26	Legislative, Governance, Policy	First
27	Legislative, Attitude	Second
28	Attitude	Second
29	Attitude	Second
30	Attitude, Policy, Governance	First
31	Attitude, Governance	Third
32	Governance	First
33	Legislative, Governance, Attitude	First

Educational administration

Second-Order Change #	Type of Change	Phase Order
34	Attitude, Governance, Behavior	First
35	Governance, Attitude	First
36	Legislative, Governance, Attitude	First

Support personnel

Second-Order Change #	Type of Change	Phase Order
37	Policy, Governance	Second
38	Attitude	First
39	Attitude, Policy	First
40	Attitude, Governance	First
41	Attitude	Third
42	Policy, Governance	First
43	Policy, Governance	Second

Table A.2
Agent responsible for implementing each second-order change

Public education

Soc.#		STATE			UNIVERSITY			LOCAL
	Legis.	Board of Educ.	Educ. Agen.	Trustees	Admins.	Faculty	Educ. Fac.	Board of Educ.
1	x	x						x
2		x						
3	x							x
4			x					x
5								x
6	x	x						x
7								x
8	x							
9		x						x
10		x						x
11		x						x
12		x						x
13		x						x
14								x
15		x						x
16	x	x						
17		x						x

Teacher education

Soc.#		STATE			UNIVERSITY			LOCAL
	Legis.	Board of Educ.	Educ. Agen.	Trustees	Admins.	Faculty	Educ. Fac.	Board of Educ.
18	x			x	x	x	x	
19				x	x			
20					x		x	
21							x	
22							x	
23							x	
24						x	x	
25	x			x	x	x	x	
26			x				x	
27		x					x	
28							x	
29	x	x						x
30					x	x	x	
31		x				x	x	
32				x	x	x	x	
33					x	x	x	

379

Table A.3
Summary list of second and third order changes by topic area

Educational administration

		STATE		UNIVERSITY				LOCAL
Soc.#	Legis.	Board of Educ.	Educ. Agen.	Trustees	Admins.	Faculty	Educ. Fac.	Board of Educ.
34		x			x	x	x	
35					x	x	x	
36		x						

Support personnel

		STATE		UNIVERSITY				LOCAL
Soc.#	Legis.	Board of Educ.	Educ. Agen.	Trustees	Admins.	Faculty	Educ. Fac.	Board of Educ.
37								x
38								x
39					x	x	x	x
40					x	x	x	
41					x	x		
42		x	x					
43					x	x	x	

Third order changes-state level

Third-Order Change #1. Each state should, by action of the state legislature, establish a state level Educational Policy and Coordination Committee (EPCC). The responsibilities and authority of this Committee are described below.

Third-Order Change #2. The composition of the EPCC should be as follows. One-third of the membership (total membership no more than 15) should be elected by local boards of teachers; one-third should be elected by university faculty teaching full-time in teacher education units from public and private institutions of higher education; and one-third of the membership should consist of two legislators appointed by the legislature or governor, and three should be parents appointed by the state parents' association.

Third-Order Change #3. Educational units on each college and university campus should be re-configured as free-standing professional schools, responsible for the preparation of all personnel who seek professional employment in the public schools, or as a teacher educator.

380

These units should be headed by an individual who reports directly to the president or chancellor of the campus, as a Vice-President for Educational Affairs, with authority equivalent to a Vice-President for Academic or Health Affairs.

Third-Order Change #4. State legislatures that are interested in reforming the structure of education should establish a Study Commission, chaired by a state legislator knowledgeable about education, and composed of members representing parents, teachers, and business leaders. No member of this Commission should be a member of a group, board, or association which represents a vested interest in the current decision making chain of education. Represenatives of current education boards and associations should be invited to attend Commission meetings as observers only.

Public school education

Second-Order Change #1. The single prime mission for education is teaching students how to learn most effectively and to generalize the process of effective learning.

Second-Order Change #2. The core knowledge base for all educators should be a through understanding of cognitive science.

Second-Order Change #3. Local boards of education should be composed of equal representation from the public and teachers elected from the system.

Second-Order Change #4. The center for development of academic and learning programs within the system should be a high school and its feeder schools.

Second-Order Change #5. A peer review system (quality assurance) for each teacher's learning objectives and activities should be operative in each school.

Second-Order Change #6. A committee of teachers within each school should have the responsibility and authority to hire all school personnel, including principals.

Second-Order Change #7. A committee of teachers should have the responsibility and authority for determining merit salary increases for all teachers within the school.

Second-Order Change #8. Tenure for professional educators should be abolished.

Second-Order Change # 9. The system of annual grade levels should be abolished in elementary schools and replaced by two cycles of four and three years.

Second-Order Change #10. An elementary school teacher should be assigned to a class cycle and not change classes on an annual basis.

Second-Order Change #11. Secondary schools should consist of two successive three year cycles.

Second-Order Change #12. The first cycle of secondary schools should provide for all students a generic introduction to the basic disciplines of knowledge and the development of effective communication skills.

Second-Order Change #13. The second cycle of secondary schools should encourage students to concentrate in one of four areas of knowledge or vocational development. These four areas are (1) mathematics, (2) natural and physical sciences, (3) arts and humanities, (4) vocational skill areas.

Second-Order Change #14. Secondary schools should operate on the basis of positive sanctions, expecting and treating students as mature and capable of responsible behavior.

Second-Order Change #15. All programs offered by the schools should be defined as either dominant or ancillary. Dominant programs should receive priority resource allocation.

Second-Order Change #16. The allocation of resources to schools should be on the basis of the costs associated with a particular program.

Second-Order Change #17. Educational programs must be developed by teachers at the school level, forwarded through the Academic Planning Unit for coordination, and delivered to the local board of education (public and teacher representives) for review, action, and allocation of funds.

Teacher and Higher Education

Second-Order Change #18. Tenure for faculty should be removed in favor of 5-7 year contracts.

Second-Order Change #19. Boards of trustrees should establish, and cause to be implemented, a reward system and plan of resource allocation, which recognize equally, programs which emphasize research and scholarship (development of knowledge), and professional programs emphasize the development of practitioner competence (demonstration of knowledge).

Second-Order Change #20. The composition of faculty within schools of education must be dramatically changed.

Second-Order Change #21. Preparation programs for teachers should have as their prime objective teaching how learning occurs and is maximized in children.

Second-Order Change #22. The second prime objective of teacher preparation programs is to provide teacher candidates the knowledge base and skills necessary to effectively utilize a variety of techniques to foster maximum learning in children.

Second-Order Change #23. The structure and sequence of education for teacher education students must be totally revised.

Second-Order Change #24. All students who intend to work in the public schools as professional educators, at either the undergraduate or graduate level, should have their primary major in the education unit and have their curriculum determined by the education unit.

Second-Order Change #25. Resource allocations to academic units should be based on the costs of program delivery, not student credit hours generated.

Second-Order Change #26. Elementary school teachers should not be recommended for certification unless they have completed two academic majors, one in either cognitive science or child development and the other in a content area such as reading, special education, or a specific discipline area such as mathematics.

Second-Order Change #2. Students in elementary school teacher education programs must be prepared to assume responsibility fopr the same class of students for a three or four year period.

Second-Order Change #28. Elementary school teacher education students must decide during their second year of study to concentrate at either the K-3 level or the 4-6 level.

Second-Order Change #29. Prospective elementary school teachers must be prepared to assume new dimensions of responsibility, including K-12 curriculum coordination, hiring and firing personnel, colleague evaluation, and determining colleagues' salary increases.

Second-Order Change #30. Ideally, the curriculum for prospective elementary school teachers will reflect the following components and time allocations.

Component	Credit Hours	Time Allocation
1. Liberal Studies	45	3 Semesters
2. Cognitive Science & Child Development	30	2 Semesters
3. Academic Content Area	30	2 Semesters
4. Professional Education	24	1.5 Semesters
5. Clinical Experiences/Internship	33	2 Semesters
6. Electives	15	1 Semester
Totals	177	11.5 Semesters

Second-Order Change #31. The National Council for the Accreditation of Teacher Education should develop criteria for approving school systems which wish to provide student teaching and internship experiences for educational personnel. States should require such approval for teacher education programs prior to placing their students for such experiences.

Second-Order Change #32. Responsibility for determining all teacher education curriculum components should be under the direction of faculty in the education unit.

Second-Order Change #33. All programs preparing personnel to work in public schools, at both the undergraduate and graduate levels, should be under the control of faculty in the education unit.

Educational Administration

Second-Order Change #34. Educational administration preparation programs should be established to prepare such personnel at the undergraduate level for entry level positions in the public schools.

Second-Order Change #35. A recommended curriculum for preparing educational administrators at the undergraduate level follows.

Component	Credit Hours
1. Liberal Studies	45-60
2. Academic Major (Business, Public, Administration)	30-45
3. Education — Required	27-30
A. History of Education	
B. Organization of Education	
C. Objectives of Education	
D. Child and Adolescent Development	
E. School Law, Rules, and Regulations	
F. Ethics of Education	
G. Internship	
4. Education — Desirable	12-15
A. Public Relations	
B. Educational Program Planning	
C. Consultation Methods	
D. Family and Child Relations	
5. Electives	12-20
Total	126-170 Semester Hours

Second-Order Change #36. There should not be certification for personnel hired in positions of administration in the public schools. Tenure should not be granted to individuals in these positions.

Support Personnel

Second-Order Change #37. Each academic planning unit (as defined in Second-Order Change No. 4), should have assigned to it a sufficient number of support personnel to enable the teachers of that unit to have immediate access to any of these types of support personnel.

Second-Order Change #38. The client group for all support personnel as here defined is the teacher.

Second-Order Change #39. School guidance personnel, school psychologists, and school social workers should receive a common training program.

Second-Order Change #40. Universities offering more than one program in the support service areas should consolidate such programs in the campus educational unit within one academic department and develop and require a common core curriculum for this new area.

Second-Order Change #41. Universities offering such a program should use the title of Department of Educational Support Services for these programs.

Second-Order Change #42. State departments of public instruction (education) should dispense with separate certification for school counselors, school psychologists, and school social workers in favor of one new certificate for Education Support Service Professionals.

Second-Order Change #43. A common, core curriculum for Educational Support Service Professionals should be reflected by the following components and elements. This program would exist only at the graduate level.

Component	Elements	Credit Hours
1. Learning and development	A. Advanced cognitive science B. Advanced child development C. Advanced adolescent development	9
2. Individual & group assessment	A. Individual, intelligence & academic B. Group, intelligence & academic	12
3. Individual & group interventions	A. Individual, theory & methods B. Group, theory and methods	12
4. Program planning, implementation & evaluation	A. Theory and methods of program planning B. Theory and methods of program intervention C. Theory and methods of program evaluation	9
5. Special populations	A. The handicapped B. Potential drop-outs, drug problems, etc.	9
6. Human relations & small group dynamics	A. Theories and methods	9
7. Case coordination & management	A. In-school coordination B. School-community coordination	9
8. Clinical experiences and internship-professional ethics		15
Total Program Hours		84

Bibliography

Achilles, C. (1984). 'Forecast: Stormy weather ahead in educational administration.' *Issues in Education*, 2(2), 127-135.

Albrecht, J. (1984). 'A nation at risk: Another view.' *Phi Delta Kappan*, 65 (10), 684-685.

Aldrich, H. (1972). 'Technology and organizational structure: A re-examination of the findings of the Aston group.' *Administrative Science Quarterly*, 17 (1), 26-43.

Altbach, P. (1985). 'The great education 'crisis'.' In Altbach, P., Kelly, G., & Weis, L. (Eds.). *Excellence in education: Perspectives on policy and practice*. Buffalo, NY: Prometheus Books.

American Psychological Association. (1980). *Accreditation handbook.* Washington.

Applebee, A., Langer, J, & Mullis, I. (1987). *Learning to be literate in America.* Princeton, NJ: Educational Testing Service.

Arbuckle, D. (1966). *Pupil personnel services in the modern school.* Boston: Allyn and Bacon, Inc.

Ashby, W.R. (1968). Regulation and control. In W. Buckley (Ed.), *Modern systems research for the behavioral scientist.* Chicago: Aldine Publishing Co.

Astin, A. (1985). *Achieving academic excellence.* San Francisco: Jossey-Bass.

Astroth, K. (1994). 'Beyond ephebiphobia: Problem adults or problem youths?' *Phi Delta Kappan*, 75(5), 411-413.

Atwood, M. (1964). 'Small-scale administrative change: Resistance to the introduction of a high school guidance program.' In Miles, M. (Ed.) *Innovation in education.* New York: Teachers College Press.

Bacharach, S. (1990). *Education reform: Making sense of it all.* Boston: Allyn and Bacon.

Barnes, D. (1986). 'Recent trends in education.' *The Teacher Educator*, 21(4), 16-29.

Barnett, H. (1953). *Innovation: The basis of cultural change*. New York: McGraw Hill.

Bates, R. (1982). 'Towards a critical practice of educational administration.' *Studies in educational administration No. 27*. Armidale, NSW, Canada: Commonwealth Council for Educational Administration.

Beeby, C. (1966). *The quality of education in developing countries*. Cambridge, Mass.: Harvard University Press.

Bell, D. (1966). *The reforming of general education*. New York: Columbia University Press.

Bennett, W. (1986). *First lessons: A report on elementary education in America*. Washington: U.S. Department of Education.

Bereiter, C. (1985). 'Toward a solution of the learning paradox.' *Review of Educational Research*, 55(2), 201-226.

Berman, P. & McLaughlin, M. (1976). 'Implementation of Educational Innovation.' *Educational Forum*, 60, 345-370.

Berman, P. & McLaughlin, M. (1978). *Federal programs supporting educational change, Vol. VIII: Implementing and sustaining innovations*. Santa Monica, CA: The Rand Corporation.

Berrien, F.K. (1968). *General and social systems*. New Brunswick, NJ: Rutgers University Press.

Bertalanffy, L. von. (1968). *General system theory*. New York: George Braziller, Inc.

Bestor, A. (1953). *Educational wastelands: The retreat from learning in our public schools*. Urbana, IL: University of Illinois Press.

Bloom, A. (1987). *The closing of the American mind*. New York: Simon and Schuster.

Blumberg, A. & Greenfield, W. (1980). *The effective principal: Perspectives on school leadership*. Boston: Allyn and Bacon.

Borrowman, M. (1956). *The liberal and the technical in teacher education*. New York: Teachers College Press.

Bowen, E. (1987). 'Can colleges teach thinking?' *Time*, February 16. 16.

Bowen, H. & Schuster, J. (1986). *American professors: A national resource imperiled*. New York: Oxford University Press, Inc.

Bowles, S. & Gintis, H. (1976). *Schooling in capitalist America*. New York: Basic Books.

Boyer, E. (1983) *High school*. New York: Harper and Row.

Boyer, E. (1985). 'America's schools: The mission.' In Johnston, W. (Ed.) *Education on Trial: Strategies for the Future*. San Francisco: Institute for Contemporary Studies.

Boyer, E. (1988). *School control: Striking the balance.* Princeton: Carnegie Foundation for the Advancement of Teaching.

Brandt, R. (1989, May). 'On teacher empowerment: A conversation with Ann Libermann.' *Educational Leadership,* 46(8), 23-26.

Brickell, H. (1964). 'State organizations for educational change: A case study and a proposal.' In Miles, M. (Ed.). *Innovation in education.* New York: Teachers College Press.

Brophy, J. (1982). 'How teachers influence what is taught and learned in classrooms.' *Elementary School Journal,* 83, 1-13.

Broudy, H. (1975). 'Why the schools are unresponsive.' In F. Ianni (Ed.), *Conflict and change in education.* (pp. 378-383.) Glenview, IL: Scott, Foresman and Co.

Brown vs. Board of Education of Topeka, KS. 345 U.S. 972

Bruner, J. (1966). *Toward a theory of instruction.* Cambridge, MA: The Belknap Press of Harvard University Press.

Bruner, J. (1983). 'Thoughts on school reform.' In Bossone, R. & Polishook, I. (Eds.) *School reform and related issues.* New York: The Graduate School and University Center of the City University of New York.

Buckley, W. (1967). *Sociology and modern systems theory.* Englewood Cliffs, NJ: Prentice-Hall.

Buckley, W. (1968). 'Society as a complex adaptive system.' In W. Buckley (Ed.), *Modern systems research for the behavioral scientist .* Chicago: Aldine Publishing Co.

Burns, T., & Stalker, G. (1961). *The Management of innovation.* London: Tavistock Institute.

Burns, T. & Stalker, G. (1966). *The Management of innovation.* London: Social Science Paperbacks.

Cadwallader, M. (1968). 'The cybernetic analysis of change in complex social organization.' In W. Buckley, (Ed.), *Modern systems research for the behavioral scientist.* Chicago: Aldine Publishing Co.

Callahan, R. (1962). *Education and the cult of efficiency.* Chicago: University of Chicago Press.

Callcott, G. (Ed.) (1981) *Forty years as a college president: Memoirs of Wilson Elkins.* College Park, MD: University of Maryland Press.

Carbone, P. (1980) 'Liberal education and teacher preparation.' *Journal of Teacher Education,* 31(3), 13-17.

Carnegie Foundation for the Advancement of Teaching. (1985). *Carnegie survey of teaching.* New York. Author.

Champion, R. (1984). 'Faculty reported use of research in teacher preparation courses: Six instructional scenarios.' *Journal of Teacher Education,* 35(5), 9-12.

389

Chapman, D. & Lowther, M. (1982). 'Teachers satisfaction with teaching.' *Journal of Educational Research,* 75(4), 242-247.

Chin, R. & Benne, K. (1961). 'General strategies for effecting change in human systems.' In: Bennis, W., Benne, K. & Chin, R. (Eds.). *The planning of change.* New York: Holt, Rinehart and Winston.

Chubb, J. & Moe, T. (1990). *Politics, markets, and America's schools.* Washington: Brookings Institution.

Clark, D. (1978). *Research and development productivity in educational organizations.* Occasional Paper No. 14. National Center for Research in Vocational Education: The Ohio State University.

Clifford, G. & Guthrie, J. (1988). *Ed school: A brief for professional education.* Chicago: University of Chicago Press.

Clinchy, E. (1991). 'America 2000: Reform, revolution, or just more smoke and mirrors.' *Phi Delta Kappan,* 73(3), 210-18.

Clune, W. & White, P. (1988). *School based management: Institutional variation, implementation, and issues for further research.* Rutgers, NJ: Center for Policy Research in Education.

Coalition of Essential Schools. (1988). *Prospectus.* Providence, RI: Education Department, Brown University.

Cohen, D. (1982). 'Policy and organization: The impact of state and federal educational policy in school governance.' *Harvard Educational Review,* 52(4), 74-99.

Cole, M. (1977). 'An ethnographic psychology of cognition.' In Johnson-Laird, P., & Wason, P. (Eds.), *Thinking: Readings in cognitive science.* Cambridge: Cambridge University Press.

College Board News. (1984, Summer). *Excellence forum: Task forces to make recommendations.* 12 (4), 2. Author.

Commission for Educational Quality. (1985) *Improving teacher education: An agenda for higher education and the schools.* Atlanta: Southern Regional Education Board.

Commission for Educational Quality. (1986). *Effective school principals.* Atlanta: Southern Regional Education Board.

Conant, J. (1964). *Shaping educational policy.* New York: McGraw Hill.

Confrey, J. (1982). 'Content and pedagogy in secondary schools.' *Journal of Teacher Education,* 33(1), 13-16.

Coombs, P. (1968). *The world educational crisis: A systems analysis.* New York: Oxford University Press.

Coombs, P. (1985). *The world crisis in education.* New York: Oxford University Press.

Cooper, B. & Boyd, W. (1987). 'The evolution and training for school administrators.' In Murphy, J. and Hallinger, P. (Eds.) *Approaches to administrative training in education.* New York: SUNY Press.

390

Cornbleth, C. (1986). 'Ritual and rationality in teacher education reform.' *Educational Researcher,* 15(4), 5-14.

Corrigan, D. (1985). 'Politics and teacher education reform.' *Journal of Teacher Education,* 36(1), 8-11.

Corrigan, D. (1986). *Agenda for educational reform.* Prepared for the College of Education Fall Faculty Meeting, Texas A & M University.

Corwin, R., & Edelfelt, R. (1978). 'The limits of local control over education, Section 1.' In Andrews, T. and Bryant, B. (Eds.) *Perspectives on organizations: Schools in the larger social order.* Washington, DC: American Association of Colleges for Teacher Education.

Cotton, K. & Savard, W. (1980). 'The principal as instructional leader.' Portland, OR: Northwest Regional Lab. Cited in Rutherford, L., Hord, S., Huling, L., & Hall, G. (Eds.) (1983). *Change facilitators: In search of understanding their roles.* Austin, TX: Research and Development Center for Teacher Education, University of Texas.

Council of New Jersey State College Locals. (1984). 'Educational reform: The New Jersey experience.' *The New Jersey voice of higher education.* Union, NJ: Council of New Jersey State College Locals.

Cremin, L. (1978). *The education of the educating professions.* (19th Charles W. Hunt Lecture.) Washington, DC: American Association of Colleges for Teacher Education.

Cremin, L. (1990). *Popular education and its discontents.* New York: Harper and Row.

Cuban, L. (1984). 'Transforming the frog into the prince: Effective schools research, policy, and practice at the district level.' *Harvard Educational Review,* 54(2), 129-151.

Cuban, L. (1988a). 'You're on the right track, David.' *Phi Delta Kappan,* 69(8), 571-572.

Cuban, L. (1988b). 'A fundamental puzzle of school reform.' *Phi Delta Kappan,* 69(5), 340-344.

Cuban, L. (1990). 'Four stories about national goals for American education.' *Phi Delta Kappan,* 72(4), 265-271.

Cubberly, E. (1916). *Public school administration.* Boston: Houghton Mifflin.

Cubberly, E. (1934). *Public education in the United States.* Boston: Houghton Mifflin.

Cunningham, L. (1989). *Commentary and observations.* Columbus, OH: The Ohio State University.

Dalin, P. (1973). *Case studies of educational innovation: Strategies for innovation in education.* Vol. IV. Paris: Center for Educational Research and Innovation, Organization for Economic Cooperation and Development.

391

Dalin, P. (1978). *Limits to educational change?* New York: St. Martin's Press.

Darling-Hammond, L. (1984). *Beyond the commission reports: The coming crisis in teaching.* Santa Monica, CA: The Rand Corporation.

Darling-Hammond, L. (1991). 'National goals and America 2000: Of carrots, sticks, and false assumptions.' *The Education Digest,* 57(4), 25-27.

Darling-Hammond, L., & Berry, B. (1988, March). *The evolution of teacher policy* (JRE-01). Santa Monica, CA: RAND.

De La Luz Reyes, M., & McCollum, P. (1992). 'Language literacy, and educational reform.' *Education and Urban Society,* 24(2), 171-77.

Dembo, M., & Gibson, S. (1985). 'Teachers sense of efficacy: An important factor in school improvment.' *Elementary School Journal,* 86(2), 173-84.

Department of Education, (1991). *America 2000: An Education Strategy. Sourcebook.* Washington, DC. Author.

Department of Education, (1991). *America 2000: An Education Strategy.* Washington, DC. Author.

Dodd, A. (1984). 'A new design for public education.' *Phi Delta Kappan.* 65(10), 690-693.

Douglass, H., & Grieder, C. (1948). *American public education.* New York: The Ronald Press Co.

Downs, G. & Mohr, L. (1976). 'Conceptual issues in the study of innovation.' *Administrative Science Quarterly,* 21, 700-714.

Downs, G. & Mohr, L. (1979). 'Toward a theory of innovation.' *Administration and Society,* 10, 377-408.

Ducharme, E. (1980). 'Liberal arts in education: The perennial challenge.' *Journal of Teacher Education,* 31(3), 7-12.

Ducharme, E. (1982). 'When dogs sing: The prospect for change in American high schools.' *Journal of Teacher Education,* 33(1), 25-29.

Ducharme, E. (1985). 'Establishing the place of teacher education in the university.' *Journal of Teacher Education,* 36(4), 8-11.

Dunham, A. (1969). *The college of the forgotten Americans: A profile of state colleges and regional universities.* New York: MacGraw-Hill.

Dyer, E. & O'Connor, D. (1983). 'Crisis in library education.' *Wilson Library Bulletin.* June, 860-863.

Edmonds, R. (1979). *A discussion of the literature and issues related to effective schooling.* CEMREL, Inc. Vol. 6. St. Louis.

Eicholz, G. & Rogers, E. (1964). 'Resistance to the adoption of audio-visual aids by elementary school teachers.' In Miles, M. (Ed.). *Innovation in education.* New York: Teachers College Press.

Eisner, E. (1992). 'The federal reform of schools: Looking for the silver bullet.' *Phi Delta Kappan*, 73(9), 722-723.

Eisner, E. (1993). 'Why standards may not improve schools.' *Educational Leadership*, 50(5), 22-23.

Elmore, R. & Mclaughlin, M. (1988). *Steady work: Policy, practice, and the reform of American education*. Santa Monica, CA: The Rand Corporation.

Elmore, R. (1991). 'Foreword.' In Hess, J. *School restructuring, Chicago style*. Newbury Park, CA: Corwin Press, Inc.

Evangelauf, J. (1987). 'National board to certify schoolteachers to be chartered this summer.' *Chronicle of Higher Education*, February 25. 1,6.

Evangelauf, J. (1987). 'Reform of teacher education said to require professional status and cooperative efforts.' *The Chronicle of Higher Education*, February 11. 1, 20.

Faidley, R. & Musser, S. (1989). 'Vision of school leaders must focus on excellence, dispel popular myths.' *NASSP Bulletin*, 73(414), 9-13.

Fantini, M. (1975). 'Educational agenda for the seventies and beyond.' In F. Ianni (Ed.), *Conflict and change in education* (pp. 383-395). Glenview, IL: Scott, Foresman and Co.

Feistritzer, C. (1983) *The condition of teaching*. Princeton: The Carnegie Foundation for the Advancement of Teaching.

Finn, C. (1992). 'Up from mediocrity: What next in school reform?' *Policy Review*, 61, 80-83.

Firestone, W.A. (1989). 'Educational policy as an ecology of games.' *Educational Researcher*, 18(7), 18-24.

Fiske, E. (1991). *Smart schools, smart kids: Why do some schools work?* New York: Simon & Schuster.

Florio, D. (1983). 'Curing America's quick-fix mentality: A role for federally supported educational research.' *Phi Delta Kappan*, 64(6), 411-415.

Fogarty, B. (Ed.). (1983). 'Educational administration 1959-1981: A profession in evolution.' *Special issue of Educational Administration Quarterly*, 19(3),141-152.

Foreman, M. (1985). *The subject is excellence*. Raleigh, NC: North Carolina Association of Educators.

Foreman, M. (1986). *Minority educators: Are they an endangered species?* Raleigh, NC: North Carolina Association of Educators. XXXIII, (24), p.1.

Fossey, R. (1992). *School choice legislation: A survey of states*. (CPRE Occasional Paper). New Brunswick, NJ: Consortium for Policy Research in Education.

Foster, W. (1980). 'The changing administrator: Developing managerial praxis.' *Educational Theory,* 30(1), 11-23.

Foster, W. (1984). 'Toward a critical theory of educational administration.' In Sergiovanni, T. & Corbally, J. (Eds.), *Leadership and organizational culture.* Urbana, IL: University of Illinois Press.

Fowler, F., Boyd, W., & Plank, D. (1993). 'International school reform: Political Considerations.' In Jacobson, S. & Berne, R. (Eds.), *Reforming education.* Thousand Oaks, CA: Corwin Press, Inc.

Frederickson, N. (1984). 'Implications of cognitive theory for instruction in problem-solving.' *Review of Educational Research,* 54(3), 363-407.

Freeman, L. (1980). 'The management of liberal education.' *Journal of Teacher Education,* 31(3), 31-33.

Fuhrman, S., & Elmore, R. (1990). 'Understanding local control in the wake of state education reform.' *Education Evaluation and Policy Analysis,* 12(1), 82-96.

Fuhrman, S., Clune, W., & Elmore, R. (1988). 'Research on education reform: Lessons in the implementation of policy.' *Teachers College Record,* 90(2), 237-257.

Fuhrman, S., Elmore, R. & Massell, D. (1993). 'School reform in the United Statres: Putting it into context.' In Jacobson, S. & Berne, R. (Eds.), *Reforming education.* Thousand Oaks, CA: Corwin Press, Inc.

Fullan, M. (1982). *The Meaning of educational change.* New York: Teachers College Press.

Fullan, M., & Miles, M. (1992). 'Getting reform right: What works and what doesn't.' *Phi Delta Kappan,* 73(10), 744-52.

Futrell, M. (1989). 'Mission not accomplished: Educational reform in retrospect.' *Phi Delta Kappan,* 71(1), 8-14.

Gant, J. (1983). *President's message. Essential knowledge for beginning teachers.* Annual Meeting Program, American Association of Colleges for Teacher Education. Detroit, MI.

Gardner, H. (1983). *Frames of mind: The theory of multiple intelligences.* New York: Basic Books.

Gardner, H. (1985). *The mind's new science.* New York: Basic Books, Inc.

Gardner, H. (1990). 'National goals and the academic community.' *The Education Digest,* 55(6), 41-43.

Gardner, H. (1993). *Multiple intelligences: The theory in practice.* New York: Basic Books.

Gay, G. (1990). 'Standardized tests: Irregularities in the administration of tests affect test results.' *Journal of Instructional Psychology,* 17(2), 93-103.

George, P. (1985, September/October). 'Coaching for tests: A critical look at the issues.' *Curriculum Review,* 25, 23-26.

394

Gideonse, H. & Joseph, E. (Eds.) (1984). *Increasing research capacity in schools of education: A policy inquiry and dialogue.* Cincinnati, Ohio: Fleuron Press.

Ginsburg, R., & Wimpelberg, R. (1987). 'Educational change by commission: Attempting trickle down reform.' *Educational Evaluation and Policy Analysis,* 9(4), 355-358.

Glaser, R. (1984). *Research and education.* An Address to the Royal Swedish Academy of Sciences on the Occasion of the Spring 1984 Meeting of the National Academy of Education.

Goertz, M. (1986). *State educational standards.* Princeton, NJ: Educational Testing Service.

Goodall, R., & Bunke, D. (1980). 'Planning the future of teacher education: Reflections and   projections.' *Action in Teacher Education,* 2, 25-30.

Goodlad, J. (1979). *What schools are for.* Bloomington, IN: Phi Delpa Kappa Educational Foundation.

Goodlad, J. (1983). 'The problem of getting markedly better schools.' In Frymier, J. (Ed.). *Bad times, good schools.* West Lafayette, IN: Kappa Delta Pi.

Goodlad, J. (1984). *A place called school.* New York: McGraw Hill.

Goodlad, J. (1992). 'On taking school reform seriously.' *Phi Delta Kappan,* 74(3), 232-38.

Graham, P. (1984). 'Schools: Cacophony about practice, silence about purpose.' *Daedalus,* 113(4), 29- 57.

Gray, J. & Viens, J. (1994), 'The theory of multiple intelligences.' *National Forum,* LXXIV(1), 22-25.

Greenwood, P., Mann, D. & McLaughlin, M. (1975). *Federal programs supporting educational change. Vol. III. The process of change, R-1589/3.* Santa Monica, CA: The Rand Corporation.

Greeson, L. & Zigarmi, D. (1985). 'Piaget, learning theory, and mental imagery: Toward a curriculum of visual thinking.' *Journal of Humanistic Education and Development,* 24(1), 40-48.

Griffiths, D. (1964). 'Administrative theory and change in organizations.' In Miles, M. (Ed.). *Innovation in education.* New York: Teachers College Press.

Griffiths, D. (1988, April). *Educational administration: Reform PDQ or RIP.* Paper presented at the Annual Meeting of the American Education Research Association, New Orleans.

Griffiths, D., Stout, R. & Forsyth, P. (1988). *Leaders for America's schools: The report and papers of the NCEEA.* Berkeley, CA: McCutchan Publishing Co.

Guba, E., & Clark, O. (1967). 'An examination of potential change roles in education.' In *Rational planning in curriculum and instruction.* Washington, DC: National Educational Association.

395

Guskin, A. (1980). 'Knowledge utilization and power in university decision making.' *New Directions for Program Evaluation,* 5, 45-55.

Guthrie, J. (1986). 'School-based management: The next needed educational reform.' *Phi Delta Kappan,* 68(4), 305-309.

Hacker, A. (1984). 'The schools flunk out.' *The New York Review of Books,* 31(6), 35-40.

Halberstam, D. (1986). *The reckoning.* (1986). New York: William Morrow and Co.

Hall, A.D. & Fagen, R.E. (1968). 'Definition of system.' In W. Buckley (Ed.), *Modern research for the behavioral scientist.* Chicago: Aldine Publishing Co.

Hall, D. (1976). *Careers in organization.* Pacific Palisades, CA: Goodyear.

Harris, L. & Associates, Inc. (1986). *The American teacher-1986.* New York: Metropolitan Life Insurance Co.

Harris, L. & Associates, Inc. (1988). *The American teacher-1988.* New York: Louis Harris and Associates.

Hart, L. (1975). *How the brain works.* New York: Basic Books, Inc.

Hart, L. (1978a). 'The new brain concept of learning.' *Phi Delta Kappan,* 59(6), 393-396.

Hart, L. (1978b). 'Brain compatable learning.' *Today's Education,* 67(4), 42, 45.

Hart, L. (1981). Brain, language, and new concepts of learning. *Educational Leadership,* 38(6), 443-445.

Hart, L. (1983a). 'A quick tour of the brain.' *School Administrator,* 40(1), 13-15.

Hart, L. (1983b). *Human brain and human learning.* New York: Longman Inc.

Harvey, O. (1967). 'Conceptual systems and attitude change.' In Sherif, C. & Sherif, M. (Eds.). *Attitude, ego-involvement and change.* New York: J. Wiley.

Harvey, T. (1990). *Checklist for change.* Boston: Allyn and Bacon.

Hatch, T., & Gardner, H. (1993), 'Finding cognition in the classroom: An expanded view of human intelligence.' In (Ed.) Salomon, G. *Distributed cognitions,* Cambridge, MA: Cambridge University Press.

Havelock, R. (1971). *Planning for innovation through dissemination and utilization of knowledge.* Ann Arbor, MI: University of Michigan.

Hawley, W. (1985). *Should we abolish undergraduate teacher education? A critical analysis of an ncreasingly popular idea.* Unpublished manuscript.

Henderson, J. (1988). 'A curriculum response to the knowledge base reform movement.' *Journal of Teacher Education,* 39(5), 13-17.

Herriott, R., & Gross, N. (1979). *The dynamics of planned educational change.* Berkely, CA: MuCutchan Publishing Corporation.

Hess, G. (1993). 'Decentralization and community control.' In Jacobson, S. & Berne, R. (Eds.), *Reforming Eucation.* Thousand Oaks, CA: Corwin Press, Inc.

Hilfiker, L. (1969). *Relationship of school system innovativeness to selected dimensions of interpersonal behavior in eight school systems.* Madison, WI: Center for Cognitive Learning.

Hodgkinson, C. (1978). 'The failure of organizational and administrative theory.' *McGill Journal of Education,* 13(3), 271-278.

Hodgkinson, H. (1986). 'Reform? Higher education? Don't be absurd!' *Phi Delta Kappan,* 68(4), 271-274.

Hoffman, C. (1993). 'On the road to excellence in education.' *Appalachia: Journal of the Appalachian Region,* 26(1), 4-11.

Holmstrom, E. (1985). *Recent changes in teacher education programs.* Washington, D.C.: American Council on Education.

Honig, B. (1990). 'Six target areas for reaching national goals.' *The Education Digest,* 56(2), 18-22.

House, E. (1974). *The politics of educational innovation.* Berkeley, CA: McCutchan.

Howe, H. (1986). 'The prospect for children in the United States.' *Phi Delta Kappan,* 68(4), 191-96.

Howe, H. (1991). 'America 2000: Bumpy ride on four trains.' *Phi Delta Kappan,* 73(3), 192-203.

Howe, H. (1992). 'Sins of omission in 'America 2000.' *The Education Digest,* 57(6), 29-32.

Hoy, W. (Ed.). (1982 Summer). 'Special issue on research and thought in educational administration.' *Educational Administration Quarterly,* 18.

Hoyle, J. (1989, August). *Educational administration: Knowledge and faith. The president's lecture.* Paper presented at the Annual Meeting of the National Council of Professors of Educational Administration, the University of Alabama, Tuscaloosa, AL, August 18, 1989.

Huberman, A. (1973). *Understanding change in education: An introduction.* Paris, France: United Nations Educational, Scientific and Cultural Organization.

Hudelson, D. (1992). 'Roots of reform.' *Vocational Educational Journal,* 67(7), 28-29, 69.

Huling, L. & Hall, G. (1982). 'Factors to be considered in the preparation of secondary school teachers.' *Journal of Teacher Education,* 33(1), 7-12.

Hunt, D. & Sullivan, E. (1974). *Between psychology and education.* Hinsdale, IL: The Dryden Press.

Hunt, D. (1981). 'Teachers adaptation: "Reading" and "flexing" to students.' In Joyce, B., Brown, C. & Peck, L. (Eds.) *Flexibility in teaching: An excursion into the nature of teaching and training.* New York: Longman.

Ingram, H. (1977). 'Policy implementation through bargaining: The case of federal-grants-in-aid.' *Public Policy*, 25, 499-526.

Jacobson, S. & Berne, R. (Eds.) (1993). *Reforming education.* Thousand Oaks, CA: Corwin Press, Inc.

James, W. (1940). *Some problems in philosophy.* New York: Longman.

Jencks, C. (1972). *Inequality: A reassessment of the effect of family and schooling in America.* New York: Basic Books.

Jencks, C., & Riesman, D. (1968). *The academic revolution.* New York: Doubleday.

Joyce, B., Hersh, R., & McKibbin, M. (1983). *The structure of school improvement.* New York: Longman.

Kaestle, C. (1983). *Pillars of the republic: Common schools in American society, 1780-1860.* New York: Hill and Wang.

Kantor, K. (1987). 'Teaching writing since Darmouth: Broadening the context.' *English Education*, 19(3), 171-180.

Kast, F., & Rosenzweig, J. (1985). *Organization and management: A system and contingency approach.* New York: McGraw-Hill.

Katz, D. & Kahn, R. (1966). *The social psychology of organizations.* New York: Wiley and Sons.

Katz, E. (1963). 'Diffusion of new ideas and practices.' In Schramm, W. (Ed.). *The science of human communication: New directions and new findings in communications research.* New York: Basic Books.

Katz, M. (1968). *The irony of early school reform: Educational innovation in mid-nineteenth century Massachusetts.* Cambridge, MA.: Harvard University Press.

Katz, M. (1975). 'Twentieth century school reform: Notes toward a history.' *Class, bureaucracy, and schools.* New York: Praeger.

Kearns, D. (1988). 'An educational recovery plan for America.' *Phi Delta Kappan,* 69(8), 565-570.

Keene, T. (1980). 'School-based management: Missing link in accountability?' Education, 101, 32-40.

Keller, G. (1983). *Academic strategy.* Baltimore: The Johns Hopkins University Press.

Kelly, G. (1985). 'Setting the boundaries of debate about education.' In Altbach, P., Kelly, G., & Weis, L. (Eds.) *Excellence in education: Perspectives on policy and practice.* Buffalo, New York: Prometheus Books.

Kimball, S. (1977). *Culture and the educative process: An anthropological perspective.* New York: Teachers College Press.

King, W. & Cleveland, D. (Eds.) (1980). *Strategic planning and management handbook.* New York: Van Nostrand Reinhold Company.

Kirst, M.(1988). *Who should control our schools: Reassessing current policies.* Stanford, CA: Center for Educational Research at Stanford, School of Education, Stanford University.

Kirst, M. (1991). 'View on America 2000-New American schools component of President Bush's education strategy.' *Educational Researcher,* 20(7), 27-28.

Krepel. T., Grady, M., & Paradise, L. (1992). 'National goals, local priorities.' *The American School Board Journal,* 179(7), 31-32.

Lapointe, A. (1984). 'The good news about American education.' *Phi Delta Kappan.,* 65(10), 663-667.

Lasley, T. & Applegate, J. (1982). 'The education of secondary teachers: Rhetoric or reform?' *Journal of Teacher Education,* 33(1), 3-6.

Leithwood, K. & Jantzi, D. (1990). *Transformational leadership: How principals can help reform school cultures.* ERIC ED323622.

Leithwood, K. & MacDonald, R. (1981). 'Decisions given by teachers for their curriculum decisions.' *Canadian Journal of Education,* 6, 103-116.

Levine, A. (1978). *A handbook on undergraduate curriculum.* San Francisco: Jossey-Bass.

Levine, A. (1980). *Why innovation fails.* Albany, NY: State University of New York.

Levy, J., (1982). 'Children think with whole brain: Myth and reality.' In *Student learning styles and brain behavior.* Reston, VA: National Association of Secondary School Principals.

Lewis, A. (1991). 'From Washington.' *School shop/Tech directions,* 51(2), 54-55.

Lewis, A. & Miel, A. (1972). *Supervision for improved instruction.* Belmont, CA: Wadsworth Publishing Co.

Lieberman, A. (1977). 'Political economic stress and the social reality of schools.' *Teachers College Record,* 79(2), 259-266.

Lieberman, A. (1989). *Privatizational and educational choice.* New York: St. Martin's Press.

Lighthall, F. (1973 February). 'Multiple realities and organizational nonsolutions: An essay on anatomy of educational innovation.' *School Review,* 255-87.

Lipham, J. & Hoeh, J. (1974). *The principalship: Foundations and functions.* New York: Harper and Row.

399

Lippit, R. (1967). 'The teacher as innovator, seeker and sharer of new practices.' In Miller, R. (Ed.). *Perspectives on educational change.* New York: Appleton-Century-Crofts.

Little, J. (1981). *School success and staff development: The role of staff development in urban desegregated schools.* Washington, DC: National Institute of Education.

Lloyd, S. (1991). 'National certification: A challenge to history teachers.' *The History Teacher,* 24(3), 313-319.

Lortie, D. (1986, April). 'Teacher status in Dade County: A case of structural strain.' *Phi Delta Kappan,* 67(8), 568-575.

Madaus, G., Airasian, P. & Kellaghan, T. (1980). *School effectiveness: A reassessment of the evidence.* New York: McGraw-Hill.

Magary, J. (Ed.). (1967). *School psychological services.* Englewood-Cliffs, NJ: Prentice-Hall.

Marsh, P. (1964). 'Wellsprings of strategy: Considerations affecting innovations by the PSSC.' In Miles, M.(Ed.). *Innovation in education.* New York: Teachers College Press.

Marvyama, M. (1968). 'The second cybernetics: Deviation-amplifying mutual causal processes.' In W. Buckley (Ed.), *Modern systems research for the behavioral scientist.* Chicago: Aldine Publishing Co.

McCall, J. (1988). *The provident principal.* Chapel Hill, NC: Institute of Government, University of North Carolina.

McCarthy, M. (1990). 'Teacher-testing programs.' In Murphy, J. (Ed.), *The education reform movement of the 1980s: Perspectives and cases.* Berkley, CA: McCutchan.

McDonnell, L. & Elmore, R. (1987). *Alternative policy instruments.* Santa Monica, CA: Center for Policy Research in Education, The Rand Corporation.

McDonnell, L. *Restructuring American schools: The promise and the pitfalls.* Background paper commissioned for Education and the Economy: Hard Times Ahead, a conference sponsored by the Institute and the Economy, Teachers College, Columbia University. Brewster, MA: September 5-7, 1989.

McLaughlin, M. (1990). 'The Rand change agent study revisited: Macro perspectives and micro realities.' *Educational Researcher,* 19(9), 11-16.

Miklos, E. (1987). *Reforming the educational administration curriculum.* Paper presented at the First Annual Convention of the University Council for Educational Administration. Charlottesville, VA. October 30-November 1.

Miles, M. (1964). 'Innovation in education: Some generalizations.' In Miles, M. (Ed.). *Innovation in education.* New York: Teachers College Press.

Miles, M. (1964a). 'On temporary systems.' In Miles, M. (Ed.). *Innovation in education*. New York: Teachers College Press.

Miles, M. (1964c). 'Planned change and organizational health: Figure and ground.' In *Change processes in the public schools*. Eugene, OR: University of Oregon.

Miles, M. (1967). 'Some properties of schools as social systems.' In Watson, G. (Ed.) *Change in school systems*. Washington, D.C.: Cooperative Project for Educational Development, National Training Laboratories, National Educational Association.

Miles, M., Fullan, M. & Taylor, G. (1978). *Organizational development in schools: The state of the art. Vol. III, OD consultants/OD programs in school districts*. New York: Center for Policy Research.

Miller, J. (1977). *Living systems*. New York: McGraw Hill.

Miller, L. (1986). 'In search of the unconscious.' *Psychology Today*, 20, 12, 60-64.

Milstein, M., & Golaszewski, T. (1985). 'Effects of organizationally based and individually based stress management efforts in elementary school settings.' *Urban Education*, 19(4), 389-409.

Mitchell, B. and Gallagher, K. (1987). 'The latest reform binge: Quality in school governance and administration.' *Planning and Changing*, 18(3), 131-141.

Mooney, C. (1987 July 15). 'States told they must take steps to find new breed of leaders for public schools.' *The Chronicle of Higher Education*, 19, 20.

Morita, A., Reingold, E., & Shimomura, M. (1986). *Made in Japan*. New York: Dutton.

Morrish, I. (1976). *Aspects of educational change*. New York: John Wiley and Sons, Inc.

Mort, P. (1964). 'Studies in educational innovation from the Institute of Administrative Research.' In Miles, M. (Ed.). *Innovation in education*. New York: Teachers College Press.

Nathan, J. (1990). 'Implementing the national education goals.' *Principal*, 70(2), 29-31.

Nathan, R. (1989). 'The role of the states in American federalism.' In V. Horn (Ed.), *The state of the states*. Washington: Congressional Quarterly press.

National Association of School Psychologists. (1981). *Standards*. Washington, Author.

National Commission for Excellence in Teacher Education. (1985 March 6). 'A call for change in teacher education.' *The Chronicle of Higher Education*, 13-22. Author.

National Commission of Excellence in Educational Administration. (1987). *Leaders for America's schools: The report of the NCEEA*. Tempe, AZ: University Council on Educational Administration.

National Commission on Excellence in Education (1983). *A nation at risk: The imperative for educational reform*. Washington, D.C.: Department of Education.

National Education Association. (1991). *Goals 2000: Mobilizing for Action. Achieving the National Education Goals*. Washington, DC. Author.

National Education Goals Panel, (1991). *The National Education Goals Report: Building a Nation of Learners. Executive Summary*. Washington, DC. Author.

National Policy Board for Educational Administration. (1989). *Improving the preparation of school administrators: An agenda for reform*. Charlottesville, VA: School of Education, University of Virginia.

Nene, C. (1985). 'Brain-compatible learning succeeds.' *Educational Leadership*, 43(2), 83-85.

North Carolina Department of Public Instruction. (1985). *Persons teaching in North Carolina public schools during 1984-85 who completed undergraduate teacher education programs from a North Carolina institution of higher education in the past five years*. Raleigh, NC: North Carolina Department of Public Instruction.

Nussbaum, B. (1986) 'Badgering its allies won't cure America's ills.' *Business Week*, October, 20. 29.

Nystrand, R. (1992). 'The new agenda for the nation's schools.' *Education and Urban Society*, 25(1), 18-29.

Office of Educational Research and Improvement. (January, 1987). 'Eight pointers on teaching children to think.' *Research in Brief*. Washington, D. C.: U. S. Department of Education.

Olson, L. (1985). '$30-Million project will develop tests for next century.' *Education Week*, V, 10, 1, 14.

Olson, L. (1985). 'Education groups join forces to improve students' thinking skills.' *Education Week*, V, 10, 4.

Ottinger, C. (Compiler). (1987) *1986-87 fact book on higher education*. New York: American Council on Education and Macmillan Publishing Co.

Passow, H., (1984). 'Tackling the reform reports of the 1980s.' *Phi Delta Kappan*, 65(10), 674-683.

Pechman, E. (1987). *The condition of being an educator*. Raleigh, NC: Public School Forum of North Carolina.

Pellicer, L. (1988). *High school leaders and their schools. Volume 1: A national profile*. ERIC Ed 299711. Reston, VA: National Association of Secondary School Principals.

Pellicer, L., & Stevenson, K. (1991). 'America 2000: A principal challenge for the 21st century.' *NASSP Bulletin*, 75(538), 84-93.

Penning, N. (1989). 'The silver lining in education's thunderclouds.' *The School Administrator*, 46(2), 50-51.

Penning, N. (1992). 'Don't look to congress for systemic reform plans.' *The School Administrator*, 49(6), 24.

Perkins, D. (1985). 'Teaching thinking skills.' *Innovation Abstracts*. 7 (23) Austin, TX: National Institute for Staff and Organizational Development.

Peseau, B. (1980). 'The outrageous underfunding of teacher education.' *Phi Delta Kappan*, 62(2), 100-102.

Peseau, B. (1982). 'Developing an adequate resource base for education.' *Journal of Teacher Education*, 33(4), 13-15.

Peterson, P. (1983). 'Did the education commissions say anything?' *The Brookings Review*, 2(2), 3-11.

Pitner, N. (1982, February). *Training the school administrator: The state of the art*. Eugene, OR: CEPM, University of Oregon.

Pitner, N. (1988). 'School administrator preparation: The state of the art.' In Griffiths, D., Stout, R. and Forsyth, P. (Eds.), *Leaders for America's schools: Final report and papers of the National Commission on Excellence in Educational Administration*. San Francisco: McCutchan Publishing Co.

Plank, D., & Adams, D. (1989). 'Death, Taxes, and school reform.' *Administrator's Notebook*, 33, 1-4.

Popkewitz, T., Tabachnik, B. & Wehlage, G. (1982). *The myth of educational reform*. Madison, WI: University of Wisconsin Press.

Quellmalz, E. (1985). 'Needed: Better methods for testing higher-order thinking skills.' *Educational Leadership*, 43(2), 29-35.

Raths, J. (1980). 'Suggested standards for general education.' *Journal of Teacher Education.*, 31(3), 19-22.

Ravitch, D. (1983). *The troubled crusade: American education 1945-1980*. New York: Basic Books.

Ravitch, D. (1992). 'National standards and curriculum reform: A view from the department of education.' *NASSP Bulletin*, 76(548), 24-29.

Reeder, W. (1931). *The fundamentals of public school administration*. New York: Macmillan.

Reichart, S. (1969). *Change and the teacher: The philosophy of a social phenomenon*. New York: T. Crowell

Reilly, D. (1965). *The effect of level of arousal, interpersonal connotation and quality of performance in chronic schizophrenics, alcoholics, and normals as measured by quantitative electroencephalogram and reaction time.* Unpublished Doctoral Dissertation, Rutgers, the State University, New Brunswick, NJ.

Reilly, D. (1968-69). 'Goals and roles of school psychology: A community based model.' *Journal of school psychology,* 7, 35-37.

Reilly, D. (1971). 'Auditory-visual integration, sex, and reading achievement.' *Journal of Educational Psychology,* 62, 482-486.

Reilly, D. (1972). 'Auditory-visual integration, school demographic features, and reading achievement.' *Perceptual and Motor Skills,* 35, 995-1001.

Reilly, D. (1973). 'A note on the relationship between auditory-visual integration skills and intelligence.' *Perceptual and Motor Skills,* 37, 138.

Reilly, D. (1984). 'The principalship: The need for a new approach.' *Education.* 104(3), 242-247.

Reilly, D. (1986). 'Educational leadership: The missing element.' *Education,* 106(4), 421-428.

Reilly, D. (1986). 'Educational research: Leader or non-participant in educational decision making?' *Education,* 107(2), 155-160.

Reilly, D. (1989). 'A knowledge base for education: Cognitive science.' *Journal of Teacher Education,* 40(3), 9-13.

Reilly, D. and Starr, N. (1983). 'Change of change for education.' *Education,* 103(3), 223-230.

Resnick, L. (1984). 'Cognitive science and educational research: Why we need it now.' *Improving education: Perspectives on educational research.* Pittsburgh, PA: National Academy of   Education.

Rogers, E. (1962) *Diffusion of innovations.* New York: Free Press.

Rogers, E. (1965). 'What are innovators like.' In Carlson, R. et al. (Eds.). *Change processes in the public schools.* Eugene, OR: University of Oregon.

Roemer, M. (1991). 'What we talk about when we talk about school reform.' *Harvard Educational Review,* 61(4), 434-48.

Rosenholtz, S. (1989). *Teachers workplace.* New York: Longman.

Sadler, W. & Whimbey, A. (1985). 'A holistic approach to improving thinking skills.' *Phi Delta Kappan,* 67(3), 199-203.

Salk, L. (1978). 'Anticipating tomorrow's schools.' In L. Rubin (Ed.) *Educational reform for a changing society.* Boston: Allyn and Bacon.

Sarason, S. (1982). *The culture of the school and the problem of change.* Boston: Allyn and Bacon, Inc.

Sarason, S. (1990). *The predictable failure of educational reform.* San Francisco: Jossey-Bass Publishers.

Schlecty, P. & Vance, V. (1983). 'Institutional response to the quality/quantity issue in teacher training.' *Phi Delta Kappan,* 65(2), 94-101.

Schmuck, R. & Miles, M. (1971). *Organizational development in schools*. Palo Alto, CA: National Press Books.

Schneider, J. (1992). 'Beyond politics and symbolism: America's schools in the years ahead.' *Equity and Excellence*, 25(2), 156-91.

Schoderbek, P., Schoderbek, C. & Kefalas, A. (1985). *Management systems*. Plano, TX: Business Publications, Inc.

Schon, D. (1967). *Technology and change*. New York: Dell Publishing Co.

Schulman, L. (1987). 'Knowledge and teaching: Foundations of the new reform.' *Harvard Educational Review*, 57(1), 1-22.

Schwebel, M. (1982). Research productivity of education faculty: A comparative study. *Educational Studies*, 13, 224-239.

Schwebel, M. (1985). 'The clash of cultures in academe: The university and the education faculty.' *Journal of Teacher Education*, 36(4), 2-7.

Selznick, P. (1949). *TVA and the grass roots*. Berkeley: University of California Press.

Sergiovanni, T. & Carver, F. (1980). *The new school executive: A theory of administration*. New York: Harper and Row.

Shanker, A. (1986). 'A case for restructuring public education.' *Teacher Education Quarterly*, 13(4), 65- 67.

Shannon, P. (1989). 'The struggle for control of literacy lessons.' *Language Arts*, 66(6), 625-34.

Shedd, J., & Bacharach, S. (1991). *Tangled hierarchies: Teachers as professionals and the management of schools*. San Francisco: Jossey-Bass.

Shibles, M. (1988). *School leadership preparation: A preface for action*. Paper presented at the Annual Meeting of the American Association of Colleges for Teacher Education, Washington, DC.

Sizer, T. (1984). *Horace's compromise: The dilemma of the American high school*. New York: Houghton-Mifflin.

Sizer, T. (1992). 'The substance of schooling.' *American School Board Journal*, 179(1), 27-29.

Slavin, R. (1989). 'PET and the pendulum: Faddism in education and how to stop it.' *Phi Delta Kappan*, 70(10), 752-758.

Smith, M. S., & O'Day, J. (1991). 'Systemic school reform.' In S. Fuhrman & B. Malen (Eds.), *The politics of curriculum and testing*. Bristol, PA: Falmer.

Sperry, R. (1985). 'Consciousness, personal idenity and the divided brain.' In Benson, D. and Zaidel, E. (Eds.), *The dual brain*. New York: The Guilford Press.

Spindler, G. (1963). *Education and culture: Anthropological approaches*. New York: Holt, Rinehart and Winston.

Starr, N. & Reilly, D. (1985). 'Establishing a research database in teacher education: A synergistic approach.' *The Capstone Journal of Education*, 6(1), 8-15.

Starr, N. (1987) *Reported importance of teaching in public, comprehensive colleges and universities*. In Contributed papers: Improving university teaching. June 29-July 2. Haifa, Israel.

Steiner, G. (1965). *The creative organization*. Chicago: University of Chicago Press.

Sternberg, R. (1977). 'Component processes in analogical reasoning.' *Psychological Review*, 84(4), 353-78.

Sternberg, R. (1984). *Mechanisms of cognitive development*. New York: W. H. Freeman.

Stiegelbauer, S. (1984). 'Leadership for change: Principals' actions make a difference in school improvement efforts. *The newsletter of the research & development center for teacher education*, 2(1) 1-2, 6.

Super, D. & Hall, D. (1978). 'Career development: Exploration and planning.' *Annual review of psychology*, 29, 333-372.

Sussman, L. (1971). *Innovation in education: United States*. Paris: OECD.

Task Force on Higher Education and the Schools (1981). *The need for quality*. Atlanta, GA: Southern Regional Education Board.

Task Force on Teaching as a Profession, Carnegie Forum on Education and the Economy (1986). *A nation prepared: Teachers for the 21st century*. Hyattsville, MD: Carnegie Forum on Education and the Economy.

The Metropolitan Life survey of the American teacher 1987. (1987). New York: Metropolitan Life Insurance Company.

Theis-Sprinthall, L. (1982). *Promoting the conceptual and principles thinking level of the supervising teacher - A replication*. Unpublished research report. St. Cloud, MN: St. Cloud State University.

Tifft, S. (1990). 'Power to the classroom.' *Time*, July 2, 1990.

Timan, T. & Kirp, D. (1989). 'Education reform in the 1980's: Lessons from the states.' *Phi Delta Kappan,* 70(7), 504-511.

Time. (1989). *The big shift in school finance*. October 16. 48.

Toffler, A. (1970). *Future shock*. New York: Random House.

Travers, R. (1967). *Essentials of learning*. New York: The Macmillan Company.

Travers, R. (1973). 'Educational technology and politics.' In Travers, R. *Second hand book of research on teaching*. Chicago: Rand McNally.

Trotter, A. (1991). 'Testing the mettle of national tests.' *The American School Board Journal,* 178(9), 44-45.

Tyack, D. (1984). *One best system*. Cambridge, MA: Harvard University Press.

Tyler, R. (1966). 'What testing does to teachers and students.' In A. Anastasi (Ed.). *Testing problems in perspective*. Washington: American Council on Education.

U.S. Department of Education. (1984). *The nation responds: Recent efforts to improve education*. Washington, DC: U.S. Department of Education.

U.S. Department of Labor. (1992). 'What work requires for schools: A SCANS report for *America 2000.*' *Economic Development Review*, 10(1), 16-19.

Valli, L. & Tom, A. (1988). 'How adequate are the knowledge base frameworks in teacher education?' *Journal of Teacher Education*, 39(5), 5-12.

Vickers, G. (1968). 'Is adaptability enough?' In W. Buckley (Ed.), *Modern systems research for the behavioral scientist*. Chicago: Aldine Publishing Co.

Wassermann, S. (1984). 'What can schools become?' *Phi Delta Kappan*, 65(10), 690-693.

Watson, G. (1967). 'Toward a conceptual architecture of a self-renewing school system.' In Watson, G. (Ed.). *Change in school systems*. Washington, DC: National Training Laboratories, NEA.

Watzlawick, P., Weakland, J., & Fisch, R. (1974). *Change*. New York: W.W. Norton and Co., Inc.

Weible, J. & Dumas, W. (1982). 'Secondary teacher certification in fifty states.' *Journal of Teacher Education*, 33(4), 22-28.

Weick, K. (1976). 'Educational systems as loosely coupled systems.' *Administrative Science Quarterly*, 21, 1-19.

Weinstein, C. (March, 1985). 'Learning strategies: The flip side of teaching strategies.' *Innovation Abstracts*. 7, 19. Austin, TX: National Institute for Staff Development and Organizational Development.

Welch, W. (1979). 'Twenty years of science education curriculum development: A look back.' In Berliner, D. (Ed.) *Review of research in education*. Vol. 7, 282-306.

Williams, R., Wall, C., Marin, W., & Berchin, A. (1974). *Effecting organizational renewal in schools: A social systems perspective*. New York: McGraw Hill Book Co.

Winne, P. (1985). 'Steps toward improving cognitive achievements.' *The Elementary School Journal*, 85(5), 673-693.

Wise, A. (1977). 'Why educational policies often fail: The hyperrationalization process.' *Curriculum Studies*, 9(1), 43-57.

Wise, A. (1979). *Legislated learning*. Berkeley, CA: University of California Press.

Wise, A. & Leibbrand, J. (1993). 'Accreditation and the creation of a profession of teaching.' *Phi Delta Kappan*, 75(2), 133.

Wittrock, M. (1985). 'Education and recent neuropsychological and cognitive research.' In Benson, D. and Zaidel, E. (Eds.), *The dual brain*. New York: The Guilford Press.

Zimpher, N. *Teacher education governance of the state level: A comparative analysis*. Paper presented at the Annual Meeting of the American Educational Research Association, New York: April 4-8, 1977.